"*Topgrading* combines a tautly developed conceptual framework with dozens of examples of how and where the concepts were successfully supplied. . . a priceless guide for leaders of organizations of any size, in any field."

LARRY BAYTOS, SR. V.P. HUMAN RESOURCES (RETIRED)
THE QUAKER OATS CO.
AUTHOR OF DANTE'S DILEMMA: MBAS FROM HELL

"Topgrading is a philosophy and practice that clearly distinguishes organizations that desire to reach and maintain world-class status. Brad Smart's selection process is built on technically correct assessment techniques and validated through years of successful experiences with a wide variety of positions and organizations. It works!"

MEL MCCALL, SR. V.P. HUMAN RESOURCES
COMPUSA

"The notion of topgrading is unarguable and compelling. Of course we are entitled to a team made up of all 'A' players—we are already paying for them, and talent wins. Why then is the practice of topgrading so elusive? In this highly readable text, Brad Smart offers a thoughtful and practical exploration of topgrading—how to identify 'A' players, how to nurture and develop people with potential to become 'A's, and how to create a sustaining 'A' culture. Now that Smart has put a name to it, topgrading will be widely recognized as one of the essential and defining leadership skills."

STEPHEN RABINOWITZ, CHAIRMAN, PRESIDENT & CEO
GENERAL CABLE CORPORATION

"Topgrading is not just desirable but essential for organizational success in this competitive world. Brad has helped me grow and has helped DSC evolve from a warehousing company to a growth-oriented, leading-edge supply chain management company."

ANN DRAKE, CEO
DSC LOGISTICS

"Have you ever hired someone for whom you had high expectations, only to suffer bitter disappointment in that individual's performance? Have you ever paid the heavy price of search, hire, and relocate, only to witness internal disruption as the person failed in his job? Have you ever chosen the wrong man or woman to advance to more responsibility? Dr. Brad Smart's groundbreaking research shows 53% of such decisions are mis-hires. Winning companies have learned to topgrade—they succeed at getting and promoting the best. You can too. Dr. Smart tells how. Don't miss this one."

CURT CLAWSON, SR. VICE PRESIDENT
AMERICAN NATIONAL CAN

"I have used Brad for over 10 years in my ongoing efforts to build and enhance our own A team. Topgrading represents the kind of breakthrough I would expect from Dr. Smart. I will use it as a standard practice here at DCM. American industry, I believe, will adopt topgrading as a necessary human resource optimization process in order to be competitive on a global basis, and survive."

DAVID GOTTSTEIN, PRESIDENT
DYNAMIC CAPITAL MANAGEMENT, INC.

"Brad narrows the target and then tells you how to hit it. For anyone who believes good people make a difference, this is excellent reading."

LESLIE G. RUDD, PRESIDENT
STANDARD BEVERAGE CORPORATION

"Once again Dr.'s Brad and Geoff Smart have made the next quantum leap finding the keys to success in personnel selection . . . manpower planning; right person, right place, right tools for selection and placement, use the knowledge in this book and you will succeed."

JOHN M. EIDEN, PRESIDENT & CEO
CONTINENTAL WOODWORKING CO.

"The author's lucid and crisp delineation of talent and its cultivation as the sine qua non of prosperous organizations and fulfilled individuals is cradled persuasively and absorbingly astride a savory introduction and an epilogue spiced with an attainable, dazzling, and competitive future for men, women, and the organizations and institutions they serve."

ROBERT PERLOFF
DISTINGUISHED SERVICE PROFESSOR EMERITUS
OF BUSINESS ADMINISTRATION AND PSYCHOLOGY
KATZ GRADUATE SCHOOL OF BUSINESS,
UNIVERSITY OF PITTSBURGH

Topgrading

HOW LEADING COMPANIES WIN
BY HIRING, COACHING AND KEEPING
THE BEST PEOPLE

BRADFORD D. SMART, Ph.D.

PRENTICE HALL PRESS

Library of Congress Cataloging-in-Publication Data

Smart, Bradford D.
   Topgrading : how leading companies win / [Bradford D. Smart].
      p.   cm.
   Includes index.
   ISBN 0-7352-0049-1 (case)
   1. Industrial management.   2. Leadership.   3. Employees—
Recruiting.   4. Teams in the workplace—Training of.   I. Title.
HD31.S5776 1999
658.4—dc21   98-41351
                                                          CIP

Printed in the United States of America

This publication is designed to provide accurate and authoritative information in regard to the subject matter covered. It is sold with the understanding that the publisher is not engaged in rendering legal, accounting, or other professional service. If legal advice or other expert assistance is required, the services of a competent professional person should be sought.
   . . . *From the Declaration of Principles jointly adopted by a Committee of the American Bar Association and a Committee of Publishers and Associations*

10 9 8 7 6 5 4 3 2 1

ISBN 0-7352-0049-1

ATTENTION: CORPORATIONS AND SCHOOLS

Prentice Hall books are available at quantity discounts with bulk purchase for educational, business, or sales promotional use. For information, please write to: Prentice Hall Special Sales, 240 Frisch Court, Paramus, New Jersey 07652. Please supply: title of book, ISBN, quantity, how the book will be used, date needed.

 PRENTICE HALL PRESS
Paramus, NJ 07652

A Simon & Schuster Company

On the World Wide Web at http://www.phdirect.com

Prentice Hall International (UK) Limited, *London*
Prentice Hall of Australia Pty. Limited, *Sydney*
Prentice Hall Canada, Inc., *Toronto*
Prentice Hall Hispanoamericana, S.A., *Mexico*
Prentice Hall of India Private Limited, *New Delhi*
Prentice Hall of Japan, Inc., *Tokyo*
Simon & Schuster Asia Pte. Ltd., *Singapore*
Editora Prentice Hall do Brasil, Ltda., *Rio de Janeiro*

To Mary,
My Super A Player

Acknowledgments

I owe a tremendous debt of gratitude to so many:

- To Dr. Geoff Smart, a true intellectual partner, for his many contributions to topgrading theory and valuable edits. Had Geoff not been expanding his own firm, G.H. Smart & Company, Inc., when this manuscript was written, he would have been a co-author. Nonetheless, he authored many paragraphs in this book, and he will deservedly own the trademark for "Topgrading."

- CEOs and presidents who provided opportunities for me to practice topgrading in their companies—Jack Welch, Larry Bossidy, Bob Bohannon, Mike Lockhart, Steve Robinowitz, Ted Waitt, Charles Butt, Jim DiMatteo, Dan Josephs, Ann Drake, Joe Lawler, Curt Clawson, Charles Corsentino, Christos Cotsakas.

- Contributors to Chapter 13, Don Weiss and Brad Levin.

- Shirl Hamm, for her incredible patience and professionalism in creating this entire manuscript from my hand scratchings, and for revising each chapter seven or eight times.

- Many others with whom I have worked, including CEOs, presidents, and senior functional executives, who have been partners in projects over the years, who served as survey respondents in studies for this book, edited chapters, and contributed in other ways—in alphabetical order—Mark Abbott, Paul Anderson, Ed Baker, Larry Baytos, Bob Beck, Harry Beckner, Donald Boyce, Welton Bragg, Fred Breidenback, Tom Brock, Greg Brown, Roger Burns, Greg Capito, Ram Charan, Mike Cheshire, Bill Conaty, Liz Conklyn, Bob Cornog, Christos Cotsakas, Terry Curtis, Joe Davidson, Carol Devine, Jeff Dill, Clieve Dumas, John Eiden, Dick Emmert, John Eyler, Halley Faust, Dick Foster, Philip Francis, Peter Friedes, Jim Gannon, Susan Gauen, Dick Goodwin, Barney Gottstein, Dave Gottstein, Robert Gottstein, Dan Grabos, Raf Haddock, Phil Henderson, Jim Herb, Krystal Holland, Larry Hollaran, Ed Kaplan, Greg Kaufman, Richard Kent, Shirley Kerfoot, Rich Kinsley, Joe Lawler, Clyde Lowstutter, Bruce Margolis, Bob Mariano, Mel McCall, David McConkey, Jac Meacham, Pete Mercer, Phil Milne, Gay Mitchell, Craig Morrison, Paul Mullen, David Murphy, Dane Neller, Rick Nevel, Bob Perloff, Dave Ransburg, Don Redlinger, Steve Rhinesmith, Dave Robino, Paul Rostron, John Rubino, Leslie Rudd, Sam Salkin, Marc Saperstein, Frank Schmidt, Ron Schut, Lew Sears, Bill Seltzer, Kate Smart, Alice Smedstad, Bill Smithburg, Mike Snell, Roger Stangeland, Rick Stewart, Tom Sumrall, Eric Tollefsen, John Trani, Mitch Vernick, Ron Villani, Gil Vuolo, Fred Wackerle, Dick Washburn, Larry Washow, Gary Wendt, Bill White, Jill Wine-Banks, Doug Woods, Mel Zahn, and LaNette Zimmerman.

Contents

PART THREE
CIDS Interviewing
223

APPENDICES
317

THE ABILITY TO MAKE GOOD DECISIONS
REGARDING PEOPLE REPRESENTS ONE OF THE
LAST RELIABLE SOURCES OF COMPETITIVE
ADVANTAGE, SINCE VERY FEW ORGANIZATIONS
ARE VERY GOOD AT IT.

PETER DRUCKER

Introduction: Talent Wins

In the face of increasing international and domestic competition, two senior managers vie to outperform each other. Both strive to improve their team's performance. Both have read about the latest management trends. Both have attempted some version of quality and process improvement. Both have discovered, rediscovered, and re-rediscovered the customer. One senior manager has a team of a couple of A players, many B players, and a few C players. The other senior manager has all A players; she has been uncompromising in replacing C and B players with As. Hers is a *dream team*. Which manager would you bet on to win?

After studying literally thousands of successful and failed careers, and over one hundred successful and failed companies,[1] one overriding factor emerges: talent. Human capital. The single most important driver of organizational performance and individual managerial success is talent. The ability to actually do what every company and every manager professes to do— hire the best—is what distinguishes premier companies from mediocre firms, successful versus ordinary careers. The vast majority of organizations and managers simply can't figure out how to overcome the many obstacles to packing their team with A players. *Topgrading* shows how companies and individuals gain and hold that talent edge.

---

[1] In 27 years I have consulted with 125 companies. Roughly one-third have more than 20,000 employees, one-third have 1,000–20,000, and one-third have fewer than 1,000 employees. Half are manufacturing/construction, 43 percent are service (consulting, finance, government, not for profit, and so forth), and 7 percent are retail.

1

Topgrading is the best-practices manual on how to maximize talent. Simply put, topgrading is the practice of packing the team with A players and clearing out the C players. *A player* is defined as the top 10 percent of talent available at all salary levels—best of class. With this radical definition, you are not a topgrader until your team consists of *all A players*. Period.

Topgrading shows you how premier companies such as General Electric gain a talent advantage, how every manager can benefit from learning leading-edge techniques. Jack Welch, Chairman and CEO of GE, said, "The reality is, we simply cannot afford to field anything but teams of A players." *Topgrading* offers you:

- The enabler of all corporate initiatives to improve performance
- The ultimate personal career-development manual
- A "silver-bullet" technique for near-perfect assessment of talent
- A guide to effectively coaching your people
- Insight and advice based on more than 4,000 career case studies
- An easy read

Why is *Topgrading* "the enabler of all corporate initiatives"? The Information Age has put a premium on *talent*, more than any corporate resource. *Topgrading* will help you become very good at building this competitive advantage. Topgrading is the one catalyst that enables other initiatives to work. Process reengineering, TQM, globalization, and capital expenditures on technology all work best in topgraded organizations. Why? Because A players figure out how to make valuable management initiatives work and C players kill good ideas.

Topgrading has turbocharged the talent advantage not only for mega corporations such as General Electric and AlliedSignal, but also for fast-growth high-tech companies and even small family-owned businesses. From the executive suite to the shop floor, when your company has dream teams of A players and your competitors have fewer As and a lot more C players who suck energy out of everyone, you'll win. Companies with too many C players lose market share, lose profitability—lose, lose, lose! If the playing field is at all level except for talent, your superior talent will assure that you win.

***Topgrading* is the ultimate personal career-development manual**. Having assessed and/or coached over 4,000 managers in all industries and in more than 40 countries, I'll help you become an A player and surround yourself with A players. You will acquire insights into how the world's best talent assessors, both within premier companies and consultants to those companies, assess people to determine if they are A players across 50 managerial competencies. You will also learn the quickest ways to improve each competency. You will learn what makes A players "tick," what helps them develop their strengths and overcome those stubbornly resistant shortcomings, and how some C players become A players. These techniques, plus nuggets of personal career advice, are interspersed throughout the book.

Five percent of managers in my experience seem to be topgraders; they are almost always A players. Five percent of companies are topgraders; they pack their teams with A players. The rest "make do" with a few A players, a bunch of B players, and enough C players to cause problems for everyone. With all the talk about the importance of human capital, why do companies have so few As and so many Cs? Poor assessment of talent is one reason.

Topgrading **delivers a silver-bullet assessment technique**, the Chronological In-Depth Structured (CIDS) interview. CIDS can boost your hiring success rate from 50 percent to 90 percent or better. It's not perfect, but close enough that it permitted entire companies to topgrade in one year, replacing C players with almost all A players and a few Bs. If you attempt to topgrade and your batting average in replacing C players is only .500, you will fail. CIDS is not just desirable, but necessary in assuring that you replace Cs with As.

The talent world today reminds me of a super-modern medical facility that, unfortunately, is lax on cleanliness. There are too many bugs, so few patients get well. In the mid 1800s Dr. Joseph Lister invented and perfected antiseptic surgical procedures. Lister (that's right, Listerine® is named after him) killed bugs with antiseptic and more than 90 percent of his patients survived. Surgeons not using antiseptics had patient survival rates of about 50 percent.

Similarly, topgraders assess talent with a 90 percent (plus) success rate, while the rest of the world stumbles along with 50 percent, or less.[2] Remarkably, the rest intuitively know they should assess talent better, but fail. Stuck in old ways, most managers are not overcoming obstacles to topgrading; they are like surgeons who fail to use antiseptics.

Even *Fortune* 50 companies with strong CEO commitment to topgrading fail when they use common, dull, invalid assessment-interview approaches. Managers may decide to replace C players with A players, but with only a 50 percent success rating in hiring, the average company never achieves dream teams of A players. To write a book on surgical procedures but not disclose the importance of antiseptics, or to write one on topgrading theory, merely mentioning that a highly accurate assessment tool exists, would cheat you, the reader.

The CIDS interview is thoroughly explained in *Topgrading*, and you can use it tomorrow for the most revealing interview of your career. Premier companies such as General Electric and AlliedSignal have embraced it as their best practice. So can you, and your company. CIDS is the *world-class standard* for achieving close to error-free hiring.

---

[2] Chapter 5 presents sources of these statistics.

A guide to effectively coaching your people. The chapters on coaching can help managers who neither like, nor are good at, coaching their people. Armed with unprecedented insight into people provided by the CIDS interview, you can immediately tap and develop that newly hired talent better with high-impact coaching techniques. Smart & Associates surveys[3] over the years have shown that only about half of employees at all levels consider their manager a good coach. That leaves about half of all managers deficient in coaching. *Topgrading* offers proven techniques for coaching A players to be even more effective, and for "fixing" weaker points that prevent B players from becoming A players.

Insights and advice based on more than 4,000 career case studies. This book is based not on 50 case studies, but on thousands of first-hand, exhaustive interviews of successful managers' entire careers. The insights, conclusions, and advice in *Topgrading* came from 27 years of working with dozens of organizations, many premier in their industries.

As a management psychologist, my job is to "pick 'em and fix 'em." That is, I interview prescreened, cream-of-the-crop managers as finalist candidates for selection and promotion. I've audited entire management teams, using the CIDS interview. I coach managers to become or remain A players, starting with that same CIDS interview to learn how they stack up on all 50 management competencies.

With those 4,000 managers I have studied, my CIDS interview approach did not casually touch on two or three jobs held. There was an average of 10 jobs for 4,000 managers. Do the math—that's 40,000 job case studies in which I asked the interviewee:

- What were your expectations for the job?
- A few weeks after starting the job, what did you find? What was in good shape? Bad shape?
- So, what did you do? What were your most important decisions? How did you handle politics, problem people, scarce resources?
- What were your successes, and failures? Likes and dislikes? And regrets? (You can learn a *lot* from hearing what smart, ambitious managers regret.)
- How were successes achieved?
- What were your bosses like? What did they feel were your strengths and weaker points?

---

[3] Tens of thousands of respondents to employee opinion surveys plus several more thousand participants in 360-degree surveys. (They are called 360-degree surveys because usually respondents are bosses, peers, and subordinates, providing feedback from all directions.)

- Why did you leave the job? Were you promoted, nudged out, pursued a better opportunity?

The answers, spread across entire careers, reveal how managers changed, what helped them grow, what set them back, how they beat the odds. The insights can help you succeed.

Topgrading **is an easy read.** I don't know about you, but I skim books and articles for useful nuggets and appreciate authors who help me find the good stuff. But the good stuff for one reader wanting to learn specific details is different from the conceptual good stuff of interest to another reader. Generous use of headings and summaries will help you spot the major conclusions.

Part One shows how premier companies topgrade. Chapter 1 introduces topgrading, followed by a chapter identifying major obstacles to topgrading and how companies overcome them. Chapter 3 summarizes the most extensive and shocking statistics published on the costs of mis-hires. This original research shows that the average cost of mis-hiring someone under a $100,000 base salary is $840,000, and the average cost of mis-hiring someone in the $100,000–$250,000 base-salary range is $4.7 million. These numbers give a hint of how valuable it can be for you to improve your hiring success rate from a typical 50 percent to an achievable 90 percent. This is *essential* to the creation of a dream team of A players.

Chapter 4 addresses the moral dilemma of firing people. It concludes that a *failure* to redeploy hopeless, chronic underperformers is immoral. Chapter 5 describes the present sorry state of recruitment and then offers a best-practices blueprint. Original research among very senior executives points the finger at external recruiters, blaming them for poor hiring results. I point the finger right back at you, the hiring manager, and show you and your Human Resources people how to get the best results from search firms. Part One concludes with case studies, showing how small and large companies topgrade and how an individual midmanager earned a promotion through topgrading.

Part Two is for individuals—how to become an A player and to coach others effectively. Chapter 7 holds out an ideal for career success that includes that elusive balance everyone wants, but few enjoy. Chapter 8 helps you fix your weaknesses, which is more important than spending additional time developing your strengths. Chapter 9 will help you understand how the CIDS interview can make you a lot better coach NOW, and Chapter 10 presents three case studies to help you apply the coaching principles with finesse and ease.

Part Three presents the most important technique in topgrading—the Chronological In-Depth Structured (CIDS) interview. It's the equivalent of Dr. Lister's antiseptics. Chapter 11 spells out the mechanics of CIDS interviewing, and Chapter 12 teaches you how to master advanced interviewing tactics.

Chapter 13 is on legalities, coauthored with the world's most successful author on the subject, Donald Weiss.

Follow the advice in Parts One to Three and you will easily retain your top talent. When you hire A players, coach them well—by creating dream teams that annihilate the competition, you earn loyalty.

Finally, the Epilogue looks to future applications of topgrading. In many respects the future is here and the world is crying out for topgrading applications—in government, finance, education, community-service organizations, and in your personal life.

Before I am accused of bias, let me admit it: *all* organizations, *all* businesses, live or die mostly on their talent, and any manager who fails to topgrade is nuts, or a C player. OK, I said it. The ability to survive barriers to entry, natural disasters, currency fluctuations, new competition, and economic downturns all flow from human capital. Nothing else matters nearly so much. If financial folks view the world through numeric prisms, I happen to view the world through talent prisms.

Now for some housekeeping chores, beginning with definitions. To "mis-hire" is to mis-select, mis-promote, mis-transfer, or mis-place a person. "Executive" is a level in an organization, not a title. "Manager" is both a level between executive and supervisor and a generic term meaning "boss." "My manager" is the person I report to whether that person has the title of CEO, Vice President, Director, Manager, or Supervisor. A "leader" is someone who is followed, whether the followers are inspired, threatened, or motivated in other ways. "Subordinate" refers to the people reporting to a manager. It carries with it the unfortunate connotation of "inferior," but it is the least bad alternative in the English language, since "associate," "staff," or "team member" all have at least one other definition.

Real names of people and organizations are used with their permission. In other cases client anonymity is maintained by my using examples in which the cosmetics (geographic region, type of company, and so on) have been changed, while retaining the substance.

I hope *Topgrading* will be a pain reliever for your company. It may not be Dr. Lister's cure-all, but it's the closest thing I've seen to one for corporate well being. This book will also, I hope, be a career booster for you personally. It is chock full of insights into how you can become, and remain, an A player, which is key to not only career success but happiness in life. Your career should be brighter when you hire better people, promote better people, and frankly, when you more smoothly and comfortably nudge nonperformers out. Any manager—any reader—can immediately ratchet up talent in his or her team using CIDS-based interviewing and coaching. With supremely accurate insights provided by the CIDS interview, you can replace C players with A players, enjoy having a "dream team," and qualify as a "topgrader." Use CIDS-based coaching to help A players remain A players, and to salvage C and B players, as well. Every C or B player you can coach to become an A player doesn't just make you feel good, but saves replacement costs and disruption in the workplace.

Topgrading **is not for the faint-hearted.** Those predisposed to protect "dead wood" will take issue with the basic underlying philosophy of this book. Those who, way down deep, would sooner see an organization die than nudge a hopelessly incompetent person out of a job, should not read this book. That person is probably not an A player, will not become an A player, will not want to hire A players, will not want to coach people to become A players, has difficulty retaining A players, and does not belong in a premier, topgraded organization. *Topgrading* is for A players and all those aspiring to be A players.

Everyone wants to know the key to individual and corporate success. I think I know. Forty-thousand case studies devoted to scrutinizing 50 competencies provide some clues. Jack Welch of General Electric asked me which, of all those competencies, was *the single most important* for helping someone become an A player. Larry Bossidy of AlliedSignal asked the same question. So did Ted Waitt, CEO and largest shareholder of Gateway. After the CIDS interview, managers frequently say, "Wow, Doc, since you've been studying careers in such detail for so many years, can you give me the secret to success?"

Yup. Topgrading. Selecting A players and removing C players. Because talent wins.

PART ONE

Topgrading
for
Companies

NOTHING OUR COMPANY DOES IS MORE IMPOR-
TANT THAN HIRING AND DEVELOPING SUPERIOR
TALENT.

LARRY BOSSIDY, CHAIRMAN AND CEO
ALLIEDSIGNAL

1. Topgrading: Every Manager's #1 Priority

Topgrading is a best-practices manual for gaining a competitive edge in talent. This chapter defines topgrading in simple terms and then presents short examples of companies that topgrade. A new but useful definition of "A player" is offered, a definition allowing for A players at *all* levels in a company. Some complexities in understanding topgrading concepts are explored, including when to hire under- and overqualified A players, why it is necessary to redeploy C players, and how topgrading relates to diversity. Finally, this chapter concludes with a broader, all-encompassing definition of topgrading.

WHAT IS TOPGRADING?

Top•grade (tŏp"grād) *v.* -graded, -grading, -grades, -tr. 1. To fill every position in the organization with an A player, at the appropriate compensation level.

This is an original definition. Dr. Geoff Smart and I came up with it[1] because we were unhappy with less potent terms like "upgrade." Suppose a manager with a team of ten C players is happy when one retires, opening up a spot. Perhaps a B player is hired. The team is still lame, but the manager

---

[1] Bradford D. Smart and Geoffrey H. Smart, *Topgrading the Organization* (Directors & Boards, 1997).

11

has "upgraded." Pretty weak. Upgraders lose to topgraders. Topgrading requires upgrading and upgrading and upgrading until the entire team of ten consists of ten A players. When you are topgrading, you by definition are not accepting a mixture of A, B, and C players. You are proactively doing whatever it takes to pack your team with *all* A players.

Topgrading turns the traditional selection world on its head. Typically, when there is a perceived talent shortfall, Human Resources will be asked to recruit "above the midpoint." That is, following a job analysis and preparation of a job description, a salary range is established, and rather than aim for the midpoint in the range, the company aims higher, to attract the higher level of talent needed. So, it might target candidates at the seventy-fifth percentile of the range. "You get what you pay for" is the rationale.

Trouble is, most companies *don't* get what they pay for. With a 50 percent mis-hire rate (see Chapters 3 and 5), companies are paying for A players and too often getting C players. Topgrading offers a totally new perspective:

> ▶ Instead of paying top dollar for talent, get top talent for the dollars you pay.

Topgraders are not cheap; indeed, circumstances described in this chapter might justify paying above the *entire* accepted salary range. But the topgrader is more rigorous than the upgrader, more thorough in assessment, and more certain to "get what you pay for."

In the 1992 and 1996 Olympic Games, the American basketball Dream Team had no problem crushing its competitors. What was the primary source of its competitive advantage? Better strategic thinking? Better business processes? Was the team a learning organization? Was it the team's commitment to embrace change and innovation?

No. The Dream Team's fundamental competitive advantage was clearly the talent. All other advantages flowed from this primary driver of performance. The team was comprised of high performers, or A players. There were almost no B players and certainly no C players to drag the organization's talent level down.

Proactively seeking out and employing the most talented people can have a multiplier effect on the creation of other competitive advantages. High performers, the A players, contribute more, innovate more, work smarter, earn more trust, display more resourcefulness, take more initiative, develop better business strategies, articulate their vision more passionately, implement change more effectively, deliver higher quality work, demonstrate greater teamwork, and find ways to get the job done in less time with less cost. Across my sample of thousands of senior managers, only 25 percent of their direct reports were A players, 55 percent were B players, and 20 percent were C players.

WHO IS TOPGRADING?

McKinsey & Co., a premier global consultancy, is known for its commitment to seeking out and employing the best people available at every level. This philosophy comprises one of the points in its mission statement. AlliedSignal, General Electric, Microsoft, Procter & Gamble, and 3M attract and retain A players and quickly redeploy C players. These giants of business and industry topgrade as a way of life.

There are, however, plenty of smaller companies that also topgrade. You may recognize them as the grocery store with uncommonly friendly employees, the dry cleaner that goes out of its way to serve you, or the restaurant where every member of the staff seems competent, responsive, and enthusiastic. The most successful organizations in my experience have at least 75 percent of their people in the A-player range and have almost no C players.

From 1991 to 1994, Nielsen International's CEO Christos Cotsakos reorganized the non-U.S. businesses of the world's largest marketing firm. Cotsakos (now CEO of E-Trade) found that too many C players were comfortable with slow growth; he initiated a program that required every senior manager to reapply for his or her job. All but two of the top 50 managers changed jobs; some were promoted or reassigned, and many left voluntarily or were terminated. Chronological In-Depth Structured (CIDS) interviews were so accurate (see Chapters 11 and 12) no mis-hires were experienced in the 48 internal and external recruitments. Cotsakos's topgraded organization achieved record financial performance in 1992–1995. He was then promoted to President of AC Nielsen Worldwide. He said, "We topgraded at a frenetic pace—hiring, assessing, coaching, firing, reorganizing."

Beginning in the mid-1980s, Chairman and CEO James DiMatteo of Dominick's Supermarkets, a $2.5 billion grocery retailer, initiated the topgrading process. The CEO and his officers were evaluated using the Chronological In-Depth Structured (CIDS) interview and received executive coaching every two years. No senior executives were removed, though several A players were added to the team. However, almost one-fourth of the store managers were deemed C players and were redeployed (most became department managers) after extensive feedback and job coaching. The topgrading process helped to identify and develop an internal executive, Robert Mariano, who was subsequently promoted to president. From 1985 to 1995, the firm's value grew by 15 times under DiMatteo and since then the firm has experienced a very successful IPO.

General Electric benefits from its unusually thorough and effective systems to assure that its businesses are "packed" with A players. The firm accomplishes this by hiring A players, by developing its B players into A players, and by removing the very few C players who do not improve and do not fit other positions. Chairman and CEO Jack Welch frequently says that his job is to get the right players on the field and to occasionally call the big plays.

He calls himself the "top personnel guy around here," affirming his personal commitment to hire and promote the best people. In the latest GE Annual Report,[2] Welch says in his Letter to the Shareholders, "As we go forward, there will be nothing but As in every leadership position in this company. They will be the best in the world, and they will act to field teams of nothing but A players."

Officers at GE are periodically put through an extremely comprehensive tandem (two interviewers) assessment and development process. For each officer and prospective officer, Human Resources professionals or external management psychologists conduct a CIDS interview and confidential coworker interviews and then provide hard-hitting feedback to the individual in a 15–20-page report containing specific developmental action plans. Chapter 6 elaborates on this topgrading best practice.

The list of topgrading successes goes on. Ann Drake became CEO of her father's $100 million warehousing company and built it into a $200 million technology-driven logistics company, DSC Logistics, in only three years. Despite executive coaching of the team she inherited, only 2 of her top 20 managers proved to be forward-looking A players, capable of adapting to Drake's new strategic direction. CIDS interviews produced a better than 90 percent success rate in hiring her new management team. Drake personally drives topgrading concepts throughout all 38 DSC Logistics locations.

Steve Rabinowitz became CEO of General Cable in 1994 when the company lost $20 million on $800 million in sales. CIDS-based management assessment and coaching resulted in replacement of half the top team. The new managers were screened with CIDS interviews. The superior talent of the topgraded team helped a 1997 IPO succeed: General Cable stock rose 72% in the first year and sales topped $1.2 billion. The one mis-hired manager quietly found another job and left within months. Rabinowitz said, "On our road show, the analysts said our management team was much stronger than teams of much larger companies. That's what topgrading is all about."

WHAT IS AN A PLAYER?

Again, Geoff Smart and I developed a unique, but very practical definition:

A player (ā plā...r) *n.* 1. One who qualifies among the top 10% of those available for a position.

An A player, then, is best of class. "Available" means willing to accept a job offer:

---

[2] 1997 GE Annual Report, released in 1998.

- At the given compensation level
- With whatever bonus and/or stock comes with it
- In that specific company with a certain organization culture (family friendly? dirty politics? fast paced? topgraded and growing?)
- In that particular industry
- In that location
- With those accountabilities
- With those resources
- Reporting to a specific person

Figure 1.1 provides an *abbreviated* set of competencies to give you a feel for how A players differ from Bs and Cs. This particular example includes competencies for division president; very different competencies would be appropriate for different jobs. Keep in mind that to qualify overall as an A player one need *not* meet all of the A-player competencies. (Appendix E provides a very complete list of 50 competencies.)

Defining an A player as "top 10 percent of talent available" sounds simple. It isn't, but I'll use Hollywood to try to simplify it. Remember the movie *Groundhog Day*? Bill Murray was a weatherman who woke up every day to the same Groundhog Day, where he would be in the same little Pennsylvania town to see if the groundhog would cast a shadow. Every day he arose at 6:00 A.M. to relive that same day. His behavior could change, he could even commit suicide, and yet he'd wake up the next day to the same tune on the radio, the same breakfast, and so forth.

Suppose you had an opening for, say, systems manager, paying $75,000. Suppose you did a massive recruitment and 100 candidates, all in the ballpark from a credentials point of view, lined up outside your door next Monday morning wanting to apply for the job. Suppose further that you hired all 100, one at a time for a year—a 100-year experiment. At the end of each year, the clock would be wound back and you would relive that same year, but with a different systems manager—just as in the movie *Groundhog Day*.

At the end of the 100-year experiment, you would rank all 100 of the systems engineers from #1 to #100. The top 10 percent talent, the top ten in proven value of contribution, were by definition the A players. The next 25 (25 percent) were B players, and the rest were C players. Get it?

Some companies rate people on promotability, and they should. But that is different. In topgrading A, B, C players are designations corresponding to the current job. Where do B and C players fit in? The percentages are arbitrary and might vary by industry. Goldman Sachs, the premier investment banking firm, may consider an A player the top one tenth of 1 percent; with hundreds and hundreds of the best and brightest applying, they can afford such a selective definition. (Premier companies *earn* a fabulous selection ratio of hiring the single best of 400 or 500 applicants.) Over the years most companies I have worked with have used these definitions:

Figure 1.1

Summary of Critical Hiring Competencies

Position: President (base compensation level of $250,000)

	A PLAYER	B PLAYER	C PLAYER
Overall Talent Level	Top 10% of those at this salary level	65th–89th percentile at this salary level	Below the 65th percentile at this salary level
Vision	Facilitates the creation and communication of a compelling and strategically sound vision	Vision lacks credibility; is somewhat unrealistic or strategically flawed	Embraces tradition over forward thinking
Intelligence	130 or higher IQ; a "quick study"; able to rapidly perform complex analyses	120–129 IQ; smart, but not as insightful as an A player	110–119 IQ; has difficulty coping with new, complex situations
Leadership	Initiates needed change; highly adaptive and able to "sell" the organization on change	Favors modest, incremental change, so there is lukewarm "followership"	Prefers the status quo; lacks credibility, so people are hesitant to follow
Drive	Passionate; extremely high energy level; fast paced; 55 (+)-hour work weeks	Motivated; energetic at times; 50–54-hour work weeks	Dedicated; inconsistent pace; 40–49-hour work weeks

Resource-fulness	Impressive ability to find ways over, under, around, and through barriers; invents new paradigms	Open-minded and will occasionally find a new solution	Requires specific direction
Customer Focus	Extremely sensitive and adaptive to both stated and unstated customer needs	Knows that "customer is king" but does not act on it as often as A players	Too inwardly focused; misjudges the inelasticity of demand for the firm's products and services
Topgrading	Hires A players and employees with A potential; has the "edge" to make the tough calls and remove chronic C players	Hires mostly Bs and an occasional costly C player; accepts less than top performance	Hires mostly C players; crises occur due to low talent level; tolerates mediocrity
Coaching	Successfully counsels, mentors, and teaches each team member to turboboost performance and personal/career growth	Performs annual performance reviews and some additional feedback; is "spotty," inconsistent in coaching	Inaccessible, hypercritical, stingy with praise, and late/shallow with feedback; avoids career discussions
Team Building	Creates focused, collaborative, results-driven teams; energizes others	May want teamwork but does not make it happen	Drains energy from others; actions prevent synergy
Track Record	Exceeds expectations of employees, customers, and shareholders	Meets key constituency expectations	Sporadically meets expectations
Integrity	"Ironclad"	Generally honest	"Bends the rules"
Communication	Excellent oral/written skills	Average oral/written skills	Mediocre skills

A Player: top 10 percent of talent available
B Player: next 25 percent
C Player: below the top 35 percent

Companies in a fast-growth mode are naturally interested in screening talent not just for the present but for future jobs. They hire promotable people. So there might be designations of 1-2-3 assigned for promotability. For example:

1: promotable to executive-committee level (EVP, COO, CEO)
2: promotable one or two levels above present job
3: not promotable

Combining the two systems, a topgraded organization expecting rapid growth has all A players, including a lot more A1s and A2s than A3s. However, even fast-growth companies need some A3s—A players who are not promotable. Exactly how many 1s, 2s, 3s a company needs goes beyond the scope of this book. Corporate strategy produces structures with boxes on organization charts to be filled. Succession plans include super charts with pictures of the A1s, A2s, A3s for three and five years out. Line managers must look at the charts and say, "Great, we have all the talent, all the depth we need to achieve our strategic goals." Or, "Damn, it will be impossible to achieve our strategic goals because we lack the bench strength!" *Topgrading* does not spell out the details of how succession plans are done, but rather focuses on an ideal—a very practical ideal—of filling every box with an A player.

An added value in defining an A player as top 10 percent of talent available at all salary levels is *not* demeaning lower-level people just because they are not promotable. A terrific store manager may not be promotable, but why say, "She's only a C player." You don't see a Wal-Mart greeter named "Employee of the Month" wearing a pin saying, "I'm just a C player." A players are *not* just the future superstars—future presidents or #1 salespeople. Everyone in the company should be an A player, and proud of it. CEOs should treat all those A players the way Sam Walton did, as A players.

Fast-growing companies must hire promotable people, must do succession planning, must build talent "benches," and *Topgrading* recognizes all that. But hiring and firing take place *now*, with respect to current (and near-term) jobs, so its definitions start with A, B, C. That's where the real action, the heat, takes place. Companies failing to topgrade for this year waste their time talking about hiring all A players in five years. It starts *now*, or "it" ain't topgrading.

COMPENSATION AND TOPGRADING

Compensation is by far the most important of the "availability" factors. In daily organizational life, A players are referred to as the "top 10 percent talent available *for the bucks*." But how many "bucks"? Human Resources people get paid to determine the "market" for various jobs; it's not very difficult.[3] Assigning the *right* compensation is more complicated and extremely important; too often that judgment is screwed up by bureaucrats more concerned with "organizational equity" ("If a new hire gets close to Pat's salary, she'll quit") than beating the competition. You, as a hiring manager, must assert yourself to be sure compensation policy bolsters, not hinders, topgrading.

The amount of compensation necessary to attract a certain level of talent of course varies as talent supply and demand factors change. Just prior to the Gulf War aircraft engineers were hot, but after the war they were "a dime a dozen." Few entry-level engineers were hired during this low period. Five years from now a war might break out, demand for engineers will skyrocket, and entry-level engineers will be paid almost as much as the manager who hired them. You pay what you have to pay to get the human capital you need.

High tech is so hot, it seems that every high-tech person's compensation is skyrocketing. Managers who would earn $80,000 in low tech earns twice that, *plus* fabulous stock options, in some high-tech companies. It's all about supply and demand.

Topgraders must determine the level of talent needed and pay what the market demands, even if internal equity might be jarred. Superb general managers are so scarce that boards will tell headhunters, "Get the talent and we'll pay what we have to." Three clients are (as of this writing) searching for presidents and have said, "We need the absolute top talent we can find, so money will not be a deal breaker." In reality they are saying, "We'll offer top 10 percent of pay for presidents of companies this size, and we expect top 10 percent of talent at that compensation level." So many companies are struggling with their information technology problems that CIOs are in super demand; the president of a client company recently offered a CIO candidate 50 percent more than his (the president's) compensation. A Wall Street firm recently offered a $5 million signing bonus to a CIO candidate.

Paradoxically, organizations that topgrade do *not* necessarily pay more than their competitors for talent. Topgraders tend to look harder to find talent, screen harder to select the right people, and act more quickly to confront nonperformance. In relation to their competitors, these companies get disproportionately better talent for the compensation dollars they spend. A company that begins a serious topgrading effort finds it easier to recruit top talent because the company suddenly has a brighter future. Figure 1.2 graphically portrays the talent-salary ratio.

A players are the most "cost-effective" employees, since their talent, the value of their contribution to the organization's performance, exceeds the value contributed by Bs and Cs. This is true at any given compensation level.

---

[3] Note: For readers whose employers are too small to have HR departments that acquire compensation surveys, the Internet has dozens of useful sites. See www.dbm.com/job guide, www.jobsmart.org, www.careers.wsj.com, and www.bis.gov.

Figure 1.2 Talent-Salary Relationships

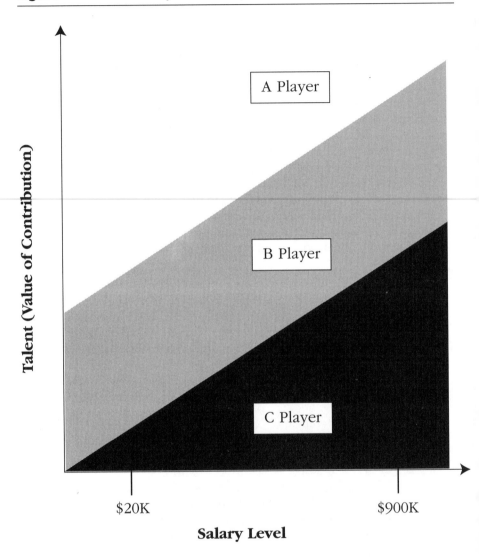

In addition, the minimum value of contribution a person must make to be considered an A player increases as the salary level increases.

Remember, A players exist at *all* salary levels, and so do C players. Why would a board of directors pay a C player CEO $900,000? They didn't intend to hire a C player, but the mis-hired CEO turned out to be below the thirty-fifth percentile of executives available at $900,000. The board blew it. And, why would an A player accept a $20,000 job? Perhaps that A player understands that her night manager job at a fast-food store is the highest paying job where she qualifies among the top 10 percent of talent available. If she somehow were hired to run an upper-end department store, a job paying a lot more than $20,000, she might be a C player. After ten years of additional growth, perhaps she will be an A player worth $100,000 per year. For now, she's smart to take a job where, as an A player, she can succeed and build her credentials for bigger, higher-paying retail management positions in the future.

A person can be enormously talented, but if those talents are not within the competencies for a job, they can be worthless. Your company might not need an A-player sculptor or marine biologist. Indeed, a very talented person could account for negative value: for example, a skillful unabomber could literally blow up your strategic plans. Too often companies fill jobs without determining exactly the competencies needed.

If a supervisor can be an A player, and a CEO of a multibillion-dollar company can be a C player, how do we apply a common standard? Simple. We simply define the league, the salary range, and talk about an A player in it. A typical way of relating our definition of an A player to a common standard is to make job titles the standard: senior executive (senior vice president and above), vice president, director, manager, supervisor. For example:

"Sally is an A-player director of marketing, at an $85,000 base."

"You think she's promotable to vice president of marketing, which has a $110,000 base?"

"No, I'm sure she's among the top 10 percent of directors of marketing available at her pay, but she definitely is not in the vice president *league* yet, not an A player at $110,000."

CAN A PLAYERS BE INCOMPETENT?

Yes. One way is to set the compensation too low. In the *Groundhog Day* example, suppose you had set the salary at $25,000 rather than $75,000 for Systems Manager. Suppose major problems were taking place in Systems. You advertised the job at only $25,000, and you got the dregs: wholly unqualified candidates, but 100 of them. Cab drivers, bag ladies. You hired all 100, one at a time for one year, and 100 years later you concluded not one was successful. Even the top 10 percent, the A players, weren't good enough. So, an A player in a B league is apt to be a B player in an A league. If you underhire, if you hire at too low a salary for the job, you can hire a grossly incompetent A player.

> ▶ You must hire A players at the right salary level—in the right league.

Another way an A player can be a poor performer is if a boss stifles him or her; or, if a product is canceled, rendering the job the A player is in unnecessary; or, if the performance bar is set so high no one, not even the #1 A player in the universe, could succeed. Require your A-player manager to run the store during the busiest hours *and* clean the tables *and* shovel the parking lot and your A player will fail to achieve your silly performance expectations, earn an "incompetent" rating, and probably quit.

WHEN TO HIRE "OVERQUALIFIED" A PLAYERS

Fast-growing companies can easily get into trouble by living for short-term rather than longer-term needs. When the company was $10 million in sales, paying $50,000 for an operations manager was sufficient to attract and hold the necessary talent. The company grew to $100 million in three years. Naturally, midmanagers' salaries rose. The operations manager job became more complex and the operations manager is paid $80,000, not because he is worth it, but because the job is worth paying that much for. But what if the company outgrew the talent? It happens all the time, so A players drop to B players, who drop to C players—not because their absolute level of talent has diminished, but because their talent has declined *in relation* to the salary they are paid. The operations manager could go back to a $50,000 job and be an A player. Perhaps he should, because with his compensation skyrocketing 60 percent in three years and his talent (skills) increasing at a lesser rate, the Peter Principle kicked in.

Forward-looking, fast-growing companies will *hire for the talent and compensation level needed three years from now.* One client grew from $2 million to $500 million in five years. There was no time to grow talent internally. They sensibly hired senior managers for the $500-million level when the company was founded.

Companies that topgrade invest in their employees. Rather than passively watching the company outgrow its talent, they provide ongoing coaching, training, and development. Rather than document ignorance in a work force, to justify terminations, they help people remain A players. Rather than battle courts in age-discrimination suits, they help aging employees maintain leading-edge skills. Topgrading is about both hiring A players *and* developing them to remain A players. Firing C players is essential to topgrading mostly when the hiring and developing steps have failed.

Another situation in which it may be wise to "overpay" for an A player at a high level of absolute talent is in a turnaround situation. The pool of candidates available for a standard compensation level may be too small and undertalented, due to the unattractiveness of the employment prospects of joining a troubled company. Therefore, the firm may decide to pay a higher level of compensation (including stock options, and the like) in order to be able to attract sufficiently talented A players. You also might have to "overpay" because of an unattractive location, a declining industry, or because you have a reputation as a less-than-desirable boss.

In these situations people are overpaid in relation to their skills and marketability in general, but are *not overpaid* in relation to what the troubled company requires. Granting "battle pay," even a 50 percent signing bonus, might be exactly what the company needs to attract A players at the high level, the league, to enable it to succeed.

Underpay and you might get too little talent, but overpay and you might give away the store. Overtalented people become bored and quit, or even worse, retire on the job. It's all about supply and demand. You need to get the salary right, and if that means paying a bonus to attract turnaround talent, you aren't "overpaying" at all.

REDEPLOYING C PLAYERS

Topgrading requires redeploying C players (and even B players). Chapter 4 thoroughly deals with redeploying chronic C players—those who remain C players even with extensive coaching and training.

Redeploying chronic C players is not downsizing, and it does not necessarily mean having to fire anyone. It is acting on the recognition that someone places below the thirty-fifth percentile of talent available at a given salary level. That's not good enough. By definition, A players are knocking at your door, available to you at not a dime more in salary than your C players. C players suck the creative energy out of your organization. They fail to prevent problems and then can't fix them. A tremendous amount of your time is wasted undoing what C players did or doing what they should have done. They screw up teamwork. Instead of hiring A players, they hire more C players. These underperformers are your stealth "Dr. Kevorkians," assisting in your career suicide and your company's. As demonstrated in Chapter 3, the costs of hiring C players—mis-hires—is a huge burden.

Redeploying initially involves progressive, documented steps to train or coach someone to become an A player. It involves careful assessment of individual talent, resulting in prying the square peg out of the round hole and inserting it in a square hole, maybe at a lower salary. And yes, it involves nudging misfits who can't be salvaged out of the organization. Done properly (see both Chapter 4 on style and Chapter 13 on legalities), C players feel they have been fairly treated but can't succeed, so they quit before being fired.

WHEN TO HIRE "UNDERQUALIFIED" A PLAYERS

Occasionally firms hire high-potential people who will be superior performers in future roles, but may seem underqualified initially. The person may be a B player in the near future with the potential to become an A player. For example, a CPA firm might hire a recent college graduate who has a limited technical background but exceptional intelligence, energy, and tenacity. The company believes that the new recruit will be a C player auditor in the first year, but become an A player in the second year. At the time the entry-level auditor is hired, should she be referred to as a C player or an A player?

Another example: When companies are dissatisfied with prospects within their industry, they sometimes recruit outside their industry, hoping to find candidates with superior talent and potential, but who will have to experience a "learning curve" as they transition into a new industry. Usually they initially appear underqualified, but later when their results shine, they prove they were A-player caliber all along.

My rule of thumb is this: If the person was a C or B player but became an A player within 18 months, he was an A player all along, merely growing into the job. If the person will be a B player for more than 18 months but demonstrates A potentials for the same job, he is a B player with A potentials.

WHEN TO HIRE SHORT-TERM OR PART-TIME A PLAYERS

Mergers and downsizing have put a lot of talent on the street. Many were B players, but after being downsized out of a job, they would be willing to work for a lot less money. In another role, they could be an A player. The corporate vice president of manufacturing at a $5 billion company earned $250,000 base and after losing his job might happily go to a $500 million company and be an A player, earning $150,000. A manager of accounting at a $10 million company might be happy to join a $1 million company as CFO, though at a lower salary. Not necessarily, but maybe.

In order to downsize and not be nailed with age-discrimination suits, some companies offer early retirement for managers. A players 55 years of age take the parachute along with C players. The A players typically do not want to fully retire and would be delighted to take an easier job, for lesser pay. Ann Drake, already cited as CEO of DSC Logistics, has a part-time senior manager who could earn a lot more money working full time for much larger companies, but has chosen a more balanced lifestyle instead.

An A player midmanager at Chrysler might be on a decline to B player and want to work only three more years. His energy and creativity are far from depleted, but are diminishing a bit. A much smaller and simpler company might be desperately in need of leading-edge manufacturing expertise. The Chrysler experience can enable him to function as an A player at the smaller firm (at an appropriately lower salary, of course), bringing the small company up to speed. However, in three years the new company will need to progress to the next level, and he won't have the "horsepower" to do it. Two years after joining the smaller firm, he should hire his replacement—a high-potential manager who can learn from him but has the drive, energy, and tenacity to eventually function as an A player in the boss's job. Choreographing the decline of the former Chrysler manager with the growth curve of his replacement is not so complex as it might seem. Occasionally a downsized manager, even one on the decline, can offer a great deal of talent for the salary, thus qualifying as an A player.

WHEN IS A B PLAYER "GOOD ENOUGH"?

After redeploying C players, frequently replacing them with A players, companies wonder, "Do we have to go all the way and remove B players?" Why not be happy with mostly As and a few Bs; after all, the team is a lot stronger than when it consisted of a few As and the rest Bs and Cs. Won't the disruption and cost of replacing Bs with As offset the advantages of having As in their place? Don't we need some "blockers and tacklers," some good, solid B players who do the work but aren't necessarily promotable? The answer is, perhaps you need blockers and tacklers, but rarely is a B player "good enough."

Please remember that A, B, C represent talent for the *current job.* Promotability is rated separately (1, 2, 3 or whatever) and if you don't need more promotable people to meet strategic goals, fine, keep your As who are not promotable. These are A-player blockers and tacklers; they don't lose their A-player designation just because they aren't promotable.

Now let's discuss your B players—your employees who are between the tenth and thirty-fifth percentiles of talent available, when A players (top 10 percent) are available right *now*, knocking on your door. Should you replace those Bs with As?

If your recruiting processes are deficient, and half the time you find yourself replacing loyal B players with mis-hired C players, an edict to "replace the Bs" could be self-destructive. Your topgrading adventure will be a nightmare, with morale plummeting. I don't worry about the morale of chronic C players, who should be be concerned about job security, but when A players' morale declines, big trouble looms. Firing C players and hiring C players as replacements will motivate your A players to quit. Chapters 11 and

12 will help you achieve an excellent hiring batting average, making redeploying B players and replacing them with As more achievable, and therefore more advisable.

Whether to replace Bs with As, or not, depends in part on the competition. If you have upgraded and obliterated the competition, perhaps you can get by with some B players. But, if your less-than-topgraded company is tops, number one in the industry, be careful—that fact alone is sufficient to invite in a new competitor. How high are the barriers to entry? What if a CEO with a topgrading mentality joined a competitor? Can you afford to bet that your B players will continue to be good enough?

The World Champion Chicago Bulls could play Dustin Hoffman at point guard and not suffer an additional defeat, if all the other NBA teams played a C player too. Could McKinsey or Goldman Sachs be as successful if their percentage of B-player professionals increased from 5 percent (that's a guess) to 25 percent? No way! In investment banking, entertainment, and general management consulting, premier firms soon die if their B players are not replaced with A players. Are you willing to bet your career and your company's future that your industry is somehow "different" from businesses that cannot afford B players?

Are there exceptions, special circumstances in which retaining a B player is truly the smartest course of action? Probably, but most are apparent, not real, exceptions. For example, suppose you plan to close the Houston plant in two years, and the plant management team there consists of all B players—people who have to be told what to do, but do it reasonably well. Other plant teams have A players who are much more creative and proactive. The Houston B players were going to be replaced until you decided to close the plant. To topgrade the plant would take six months, and it would take another six months for the team to jell and really make creative contributions. And then fire them all a year later? No. Actually, the moment you redefined their jobs as "holding the Houston fort" for two years, they became A players—the top 10 percent of talent available for a hold-the-fort job for two years. So, maybe this situation is *not* an exception.

Let's look at another example of when it might *seem* appropriate to "live with" a B player: Your A-player administrative assistant is so, so valuable that you overpay her, reducing her from top 10 percent of talent available to a B player (at that sky-high pay). Suppose you are disorganized and that $30,000-per-year administrative assistant organizes you—no, saves your butt, almost daily. You are certain she is an A player at $30,000, but at $40,000 you could hire someone better—someone who can stay later (yours has two young children), someone who has a nicer voice (yours has a harshly uneducated speech manner), and someone who can organize you. The hiatus, the transition from the B to the A, could involve a few weeks of catastrophic disorganization. Bottom line, it's not worth the risk, the time, the hassle, to replace her. Furthermore, for an additional $10,000 she provides you "insurance," because there is no way she'll leave you. You're a good boss, she likes the job, and it's very unlikely she would exceed $40,000 in pay elsewhere. So, you pay her $40,000, a salary at which she is a B player in the marketplace. Maybe you are overpaying her $10,000 per year, but maybe not. If you replace her, your disorganization for a month could cost the shareholders millions. Essentially, you have redefined her job and competencies, valuing stability so much that, well, for $40,000 maybe she is among the top 10 percent of guaranteed stable administrative assistants available to you. With that redefinition, she just became an A player at $40,000—a B player in the job market, but an A player to you. Make sense?

In a rare instance, the cost of disruption in replacing a B with an A might be excessive. Warren Buffett has been criticized for paying the division presidents of Berkshire Hathaway too much. He says they are doing such a terrific job, so why not pay them above the normal rate? My guess is that this billionaire, whose time is worth so much, figures that the dozens of hours necessary to replace a president would not be as valuable as Buffett's using that time to manage his corporate portfolio. Saving $100,000 per year on a division president could have meant Buffett's missing that brilliant move into bonds in 1997, a decision worth hundreds of millions of dollars to his shareholders.

Another example of when it is OK to hang on to B players is if your recruitment approaches are so broken, you can't find A players to replace B players. You are certain they exist, but for various reasons (explored in Chapter 5) you just can't land one.

Yes, retaining a few B players can make sense when:

- Paying less will get you both an A player but also an unacceptable level of disruption or wasted time; for example, paying $50,000 salary rather than $75,000 gets you an A player (top 10 percent of talent available at $50,000), but someone so inexperienced you will have to waste too much of your time training the person.
- The person is a B player in the job marketplace but an A player to you, because of your unique circumstances.
- Your recruitment processes are so flawed, A-player candidates who otherwise would be available simply aren't found.

Please don't think in terms of finding excuses to retain C and B players. You're not Warren Buffet, so your time isn't so precious that using some of it to replace a B with an A player is too disruptive. If your recruitment machine is broken, don't throw up your hands in defeat—fix it! The smartest, sharpest A players I know in all industries never stop raising the bar on talent. That means they have 90 percent A players, not 50 percent. And their 10 percent B players have A potentials or they can usually be thought of as "special-circumstance A players."

TOPGRADING AND DIVERSITY

The soul of topgrading embraces discrimination on the basis of talent and potential—*not* religion, gender, race, or the absence of handicaps. That soul cringes at the thought that white male C players would bypass female A players because "we are uncomfortable with female managers."

Topgrading can shake up the management ranks. If a company is underperforming, topgrading can result in changing one-third of all managers. Therein lies opportunity to bring in A players *and* achieve diversity goals.

I would prefer to use the term "inclusify," and delete "diversify." As companies globalize, they seek *not* to emphasize differences but to include more, to enrich the mix of human capital. They hire and promote more Hispanics/Latinos, because they start doing business in those neighborhoods. They include more women in management because more women are customers.

Companies guilty of discrimination sometimes toss bodies into jobs to avoid or resolve class-action suits, to make the problem go away. In their eagerness to prevent or resolve a disparate impact charge, they might lower the performance bar. The soul of topgrading cringes at tokenism.

Forward-looking topgraders inclusify *without* lowering standards. If a retail company is going to move into Asian geographic areas, they want more A-player store managers who are Asian. There aren't enough qualified Asian store managers? Then they recruit like mad, broadening the target area from 10 square miles to 20, or 200 miles. They hire early and train Asians so that when the stores open A-player Asians are prepared. They work the previously all non-Asian organization culture to make it more attractive to Asians. Talent is the key word. They don't solely staff with Asians, but it would be foolish to attempt to build a retail division to serve Asians without plenty of Asian marketing, operations, and human resources involvement.

Last year I conducted a team-building meeting for a U.S.-based international company. Not one executive was a white American male. Why, because of an EEO lawsuit? No. Because of pressure by minority politicians? No. This executive melting pot was designed by market forces and topgrading values. Sure, there are white American male marketplace constituencies to be included, but in the choice of these ten managers whiteness, maleness, and American birth were not so important as talent.

Some companies need a legal threat to inclusify. Most, in my experience, are motivated far more by market forces. A multibillion-dollar international (not yet global) company, a government supplier, passed its affirmative action audit with flying colors. The CEO said, "That is a hollow victory. The government says we have enough females, but we don't. Our marketing studies show our ads appeal to males; our management is 95 percent male, but our customers are 60 percent female, and our competitors are killing us advertising and building products to meet female customers' needs." A year later the company had a lot more female managers. Because those female managers are A players, the company is coming back in the marketplace. It's hard to topgrade without diversity, or inclusivity, today.

RETAINING A PLAYERS

Un-topgraded companies and those in the process of topgrading struggle to retain A players. Topgraded companies usually experience little difficulty holding on to their superior talent. General Electric, for example, has been a topgraded company for years, and lost only 5 percent of its senior managers in 1997 to external searches.

The same incentives used to attract top talent to begin with provide "golden handcuffs":

- a winning, high-performance organization culture
- the fun and excitement of working with dream teams of A players
- the opportunity to grow, to meet challenges, to rise in stature and title
- competitive pay and stock options

But what if "simply" being part of a topgraded company is insufficient to lock in loyalty? In the very late 1990s A-player managers are in such demand that weekly calls from search executives are the rule, not the exception. A players are not extortionists, but if equally attractive companies are offering 50-percent increases in total compensation to leave, asking "Why should I stay here?" is common. Topgraded companies have A players at the helm, executives who don't wait to hear their top talent complain that they are undercompensated, underutilized, underappreciated. Topgraded companies are seldom so desperate as to offer a secret "retention bonus" to keep an A player on board. Instead, they *anticipate* external offers and proactively increase pay to compensate A players what they are worth. I've known dozens of senior managers who, in fact, *rejected* a retention bonus, saying, essentially, "Boss, now you'll increase my pay 25 percent to match my outside offer, but forget it—if I was worth it, why didn't you pay me that amount before I'm about to leave? I'll resign and join a company that doesn't need a threat of quitting to pay people appropriately."

Topgraded companies communicate with their talent and get the major, tangible reward mechanisms—pay, stock, benefits—right. A-player managers also tend to be experts in creating the psychic gratification people want, through any means conceivable, such as:

- special projects, task forces, seminars
- job movement/enrichment
- personal coaching

~izza parties (for the younger teams)
- business travel with spouses (who otherwise feel left out)
- status (being featured in a company magazine)

Methods for retaining lower-level employees go beyond the scope of this book, and have been written about extensively. My premier clients are becoming increasingly family-friendly, offering day-care centers, sabbaticals, casual attire, and superb communications. They improve morale and earn greater loyalty through these initiatives.

Topgraded companies found it relatively easy to retain A-player managers during the incredible bull market of the 1980s and 1990s, because stock options were too valuable to walk away from. However, during economic downturns, stock options obviously diminish in value, and retaining top talent is much more difficult. Some companies then direct task forces to create retention programs—career paths requiring less frequent relocation, special projects to enhance people's skills, presentations to the CEO for visibility—whatever it takes.

Watch out! Though *topgraded* companies keep their A players, lesser companies frequently experience high turnover among the A players they hire. They can retain a few A players—the chosen few "fair-haired boys/girls" who actually like being in a mediocre company because there are so few A players with whom to compete. Even sluggish, bureaucratic companies try to hire an occasional A player with the promise "things will get better around here." But if things don't get better, the A players quit, leaving B- and C-player managers saying, "I guess we just can't hold on to super-talented people." Uh huh. Translation: "We're meekly going through the motions of topgrading."

When department managers topgrade, but the rest of the company is lame, retaining A players is challenging. The excitement of being part of a dream team is offset by the frustrations associated with working with C players in other departments. Therefore, the more pervasive the topgrading commitment in a company, the easier it is to retain the As.

When an un-topgraded company launches a major topgrading initiative, retaining A players is also challenging. Pockets of C players not yet topgraded drive A players crazy. Saying "hang in there as Cs are replaced by As" satisfies the As who have worked there for years and are thrilled that the company is finally getting its act together. However, A players recruited from terrific topgraded companies become impatient. They just can't believe the sea of incompetence around them, the wasted hours because C players mess everything up. These A players need care and feeding—encouragement, support, pep talks. The perceptive boss must pull the right levers—a vision of how the stock will skyrocket for one person, a commitment to accelerate topgrading for another, or a "Pat, you've been killing yourself for us and we appreciate it, but dammit, it's the Fourth of July weekend, so get the heck out of here for three days and turn off your cell phone!"

Take heart. Though retaining A players requires finesse, sensitivity, and bold action during the early stages of topgrading, it's not very difficult when you have arrived, when your organization qualifies as "topgraded."

In general, the best results in management retention come from bosses regularly "taking the pulse" of their A players ("Are you happy?" "Is there anything we need to do to lock you in for several more years?") and responding before an external job offer is seriously considered. If you sense a key member of your team may be "looking," talk, listen, and cut through the bureaucracy to find golden handcuffs. And, above all, topgrade your entire organization and encourage your CEO to do so company-wide, so you're A players are preoccupied with maximizing the success of a powerful team, not frustrated and "looking."

A BROADER DEFINITION OF TOPGRADING

This chapter began with a simple definition of topgrading—filling every position in the organization with an A player, at the appropriate compensation level. As we have put "meat on them-there bones," some necessary complexity has been included. Drawing these thoughts together, topgrading involves:

1. Proactively searching out, identifying, hiring, and retaining A players for every job

2. Having all A players, or at least those with potentials to be A players within 18 months

3. Using the most advanced and rigorous assessment methods to make less than 10 percent mistakes in hiring and promoting A players

4. Improving the existing human capital by providing employees coaching necessary to become and remain A players as jobs and salaries grow

5. Redeploying chronic C players, even B players, into internal positions where they can be A players, or outside the company

6. Achieving inclusivity goals without lowering performance standards

Topgrading can begin at any level. For maximum shareholder value, it must begin with the board of directors stepping up to the plate to retain an A player CEO and executive team of A players. But even if your company is not topgrading, *you* can implement most topgrading principles.

CHAPTER 1 CHECKLIST: ARE YOU A TOPGRADER?

Yes	No		
❏	❏	1.	My team consists of all A players, or those with A potentials at the appropriate salary level.
❏	❏	2.	Instead of paying top dollar for talent, I get top talent for whatever dollars (salary) I pay.
❏	❏	3.	I know it's dumb to say, "A $50,000 salary will get me only a B player, so we should pay $75,000 to attract an A player." The correct statement is, "A players exist at all salary levels, but at $50,000 even the top 10 percent of talent is not good enough. We need an A player in a bigger league, someone in the top 10 percent of talent available in the $75,000 league."
❏	❏	4.	More than 90 percent of my external hires are successful.
❏	❏	5.	I have the "bench strength" to assure a team of all A players three years from now.
❏	❏	6.	In relation to my competitors, I look harder to find talent, screen harder to select the right people, and act more quickly to confront nonperformance.
❏	❏	7.	I carefully determine competencies for any jobs I intend to fill.
❏	❏	8.	I realize I can create a C player out of an A player by overpaying, stifling a person's talents, putting a square peg into a round hole, or failing to train someone.
❏	❏	9.	I provide ongoing coaching and training, to help A players remain A players as their jobs become more complex and pay more.
❏	❏	10.	I have no chronic C players.
❏	❏	11.	My C and B players have plans to develop into A players, move into other jobs where they can be A players, or leave the company.
❏	❏	12.	I do not waste time "fixing" problems that C players should have prevented.
❏	❏	13.	I don't use "short-term results" as an excuse not to topgrade.
❏	❏	14.	I don't use "but the competition hasn't topgraded" as an excuse for me not to topgrade.

❏ ❏ 15. I retain B players only in unusual circumstances, such as when replacing them with A players would be too disruptive or when the benefits would be too short term (plant closing coming soon).

❏ ❏ 16. To retain my A players, I "take their pulse" regularly and proactively meet their needs.

❏ ❏ 17. I inclusify without lowering performance standards.

If you answered "no" to more than two or three of the preceding questions, you are not a topgrader, and you are not alone. The practice of hiring and promoting the most talented people available at a given salary level is a powerful but unusual practice. Building a talent advantage over your competitors requires a high degree of focus and energy.

Every manager, from supervisor to CEO, is charged with the awesome responsibility of increasing shareholder value; topgrading provides a powerful tool. You can ask if you have the top 10 percent of the talent available, and if not, "Why am I paying for A players and not getting them?" You can measure if your hiring success rate is around 90 percent; if not, "Why am I not using the most advanced selection methods available to screen people?" You can ask why so many C players are causing problems when, for the same salaries, A players can drive shareholder value upward.

By increasing the talent level, you can expect to see key performance indicators go up and your career prospects soar. Since so few companies, so few individual managers, topgrade, it represents a reliable source of competitive advantage. For now. But it's not easy. There are many obstacles to topgrading. Chapter 2 explores the most common and problematic obstacles and helps you over, around, and through those barriers.

MAN IS NOT THE CREATURE OF CIRCUM-
STANCES. CIRCUMSTANCES ARE THE CREATURE
OF MAN.

BENJAMIN DISRAELI, 1804–1881

2. Obstacles to Topgrading: How to Overcome Them

Many managers are committed to the idea of employing only highly talented people, but find its implementation challenging. I have asked thousands
of senior managers to describe what they have done to increase the talent levels of their teams. Their responses, gleaned for over 25 years, show most
prevalent psychological and organizational obstacles that managers face in
ratcheting up their organization's talent. This chapter briefly presents the
major obstacles to topgrading and presents the best practices to overcome
them—approaches that have succeeded in dozens of topgrading engagements
in which I have been involved.

1. "C PLAYERS DON'T HIRE A PLAYERS."

Solution: Require the C players to hire A players and oversee the selection
process yourself.

This is the single biggest deterrent to topgrading. If I'm a C player, why
in the world would I hire someone who could get my job? I may be a C player, but I'm not stupid! The most normal, predictable human action is to not
hire someone who will get me fired.

Some B players would prefer not to have A-player competition around.
Search firms all hear "I want to hire the best talent," but quickly read between
the lines and sense when a B-player manager will feel uncomfortable hiring
someone smarter, a better leader than he or she is.

B-player managers who can hire and control A players are smart to do
so, and everyone can win. The B player creates a dream team and in fact
might function close to an A player. With a successor in place, the B player

34

will have a better chance for promotion. I know a dozen B players, even a few CEOs, who function as A players *only* because they topgrade. They are mediocre on many key managerial competencies, but they are superb at topgrading—hiring A players, removing C players.

The common reality, however, is that neither B nor C players ordinarily welcome people better than they are because the boss might say, "Joe, it's great that you hired Pete, thanks a lot, but we need only one of you and, well, Pete's our choice."

In your organization, redeploy B- and C-player managers who aren't becoming As. And, in the meantime, require them to hire As. Talk to recruiters yourself to be sure they don't cull A-player candidates (because of "signals" from your B player). Interview finalists yourself. If your B player grows and becomes an A player, terrific. If you are sure the B player should be replaced, sensibly impose an A-player successor on the B player. The B player might even be a willing party to finding his replacement if there is another role where he can be an A player.

2. "WE THINK WE ARE HIRING A PLAYERS, BUT THEY TURN OUT TO BE C PLAYERS IN DISGUISE."

Solution: Perform more accurate assessments using at least one Chronological In-Depth Structured (CIDS) interview.

Mis-hiring is due to inaccurate assessments of candidates for selection or promotion. Managers accustomed to only a 50-percent success rate in hiring will understandably be hesitant to replace a C-player plodder with a possibly worse performer, following an expensive, disruptive job-change process. So, improving one's hiring success rate is the solution, not tolerating mediocrity. The most accurate way to assess a person's talent is to conduct the Chronological In-Depth Structured (CIDS) interview, which is described in Part Three. A CIDS interview typically lasts three to four hours and covers the candidate's entire career history with a fine-toothed comb.

Stop here and glance through Appendix A, the CIDS Interview Guide. Part Three teaches you how to use the Guide, but I'll be referring to CIDS interviews throughout the book, so it's worth your time to familiarize yourself with the Guide now. Recent research (see Chapter 11) strongly suggests that this sort of interview is the most accurate assessment method. In contrast, these studies also concluded that the all-too-popular informal interview is a far less accurate method for assessing talent.

People are mis-hired because the hiring manager (that is *you*, not someone in Human Resources) does not fully understand the candidate's strengths, weaker points, potentials, and needs. Most companies continue to put candidates through a series of brief "tell me about yourself" interviews, which result in a typical hiring success rate of 50 percent (half of the new hires work out).

In comparison, organizations that conduct in-depth interviews typically are successful at hiring people that meet or exceed their performance expectations 90–95 percent of the time. The CIDS interview can help you clearly identify who are the A-player candidates. In addition, a more thorough understanding of the strengths and weaker areas of your new hire can speed her cultural assimilation process and help you begin a developmental process with her, as well. Chapters 9 and 10 instruct you how to become a successful coach of your new hire, following the CIDS interview *you* conducted.

Frequent mis-hiring is a powerful deterrent to replacing B players, not just C players. With a "50–50 toss-up," it just doesn't seem worth the costs and hassles to remove an "OK" performer. The replacement may be an A player, but could too easily be a C player. With 90 percent or better accuracy, however, aggressive managers continue the ratcheting-up process, beyond replacing Cs to replacing Bs.

3. "OUR HUMAN RESOURCES PEOPLE ARE OVERWORKED AND UNDERSTAFFED, SO WE DO NOT EXACTLY HAVE A PIPELINE OF A PLAYERS GOING THROUGH THE OFFICE."

Solution: Do more yourself to recruit, and define all your management jobs to include ongoing recruitment.

Chairman and CEO of AlliedSignal Larry Bossidy says: "The responsibility to recruit superior managerial talent is a role the CEO cannot delegate. HR professionals are critical players, but the CEO must own the process if the organization is to understand that topgrading is a key priority. That means a visible, systematic, and persistent commitment of the CEO."

A-player CEOs assure a fully topgraded HR function, so that A-player HR professionals are effective recruitment "partners" with the managers they serve. Successful leaders find that they are in the "recruitment business" for life. They are constantly on the lookout for talented people—at professional gatherings, university programs, community service boards, and so forth. They keep a network file so when a position opens up they can immediately tap their network for candidates or referrals. This way, they save the cost and time of a search, and their finalist candidates have been personally pre-screened.

In one client organization, a manager makes a point of having breakfast or lunch with prospective recruits *two or three times per week*. Other managers in his organization marvel at the high level of talent in his division. A high-tech client in a growth mode calculated that its managers spend 25 percent of their time in recruitment activities. Contrast these examples with the countless companies in which managers rely exclusively on the HR department for candidates and do not get involved in the recruitment process until finalists are presented.

Chapter 5 presents best practices in recruitment.

4. "SEARCH FIRMS JUST DON'T PRODUCE ENOUGH A-PLAYER CANDIDATES."

Solution: Manage the search process, including search firms, much more thoroughly.

There is widespread dissatisfaction with search firms these days. Chapter 5 cites original research and spells out how search firms can be managed effectively and produce A-player candidates.

5. "I WANT TO RAISE THE PERFORMANCE BAR BUT ALMOST EVERY TALENTED PERSON I BRING IN FROM THE OUTSIDE IS REJECTED BY THE CURRENT CULTURE AND ENDS UP QUITTING."

Solution: Provide new A players air cover, protection from undermining by existing personnel.

This is a common problem. A manager realizes her company, unit, or department is far from world class. The low-performance culture is often characterized by low accountability, fear of change, autocracy, low innovation, and lots of excuse-making: It reinforces itself with an incestuous promote-from-within policy. C players chew up and spit out A players who, "gee, too bad, just didn't fit around here."

It is critical to seek out and employ A players who will help drive the culture-change process with some finesse, not a sledge hammer. Those A players must have the competencies, skills, and attitudes to simultaneously earn the respect of the present culture while creating the new, *desired* culture. That's a tall order; A players can be rejected by the old culture unless you provide them protection. Make it clear to the others that these new hires have your full support, monitor that support, reward active supporters, and quickly correct those who plant land mines to destroy the "outsiders."

6. "WE CAN'T AFFORD TO HIRE A PLAYERS."

Solution: Yes you can—you already pay for *all* A players.

A players are available at all compensation levels: They are people above the ninetieth percentile of overall talent of all potential candidates at *every* compensation level. You already are paying for A players, whether or not you get them. That means that a company that is paying its C-player marketing director a $90,000 base salary could hire an A player for the same salary. The definition of A player is closed, air tight; you cannot *not* pay for an A player. Is this a semantic game? No!

Perhaps you mean you can't afford to hire an A player at a higher salary level. Aha! That's different. You need an A player at $150K, not an A player at $90K. Perhaps you think you can afford to hire only a B player for an A league, but realize that you need an A player to compete in an A league. Figure out a way to afford it, or expect to suffer—100-hour work weeks yourself, burnout in the person you underhire, or failure by the person you hire. A players hire more A players, oftentimes saving search fees. This is another huge cost advantage to topgrading.

7. "I DO NOT WANT TO FIRE LOYAL C PLAYERS."

Solution: Redeploy chronic C players anyway.

C players should be given a fair chance, though sometimes brief, to become A players with extra training and coaching. If this does not work, it may be wise to narrow the person's job to include only those responsibilities that the person is competent performing, and pay accordingly. A C player can be considered one who is overpaid and/or underperforming. By reducing pay, and/or improving performance, C players can become B players, or A players. Obviously a caricature can be made of this; cutting pay across the board is more apt to cause massive departures of A players than conversion of Cs to As. Nobody is a C player all of the time. People are C players when they are mis-hired, mis-promoted, or mis-deployed within their companies. Not facing *your* mistakes or *your* inherited problems is *your* responsibility. Face it, or maybe someone will conclude that you aren't an A player.

Theoretically, everyone can be an A player. The best organizations ask the question, "In what sort of role (and for what level of pay) can this person be an A player?" Such organizations creatively align individuals' responsibilities to be consistent with their strengths and weaknesses. In the 1980s, more than 700,000 companies sought bankruptcy protection; more than 450,000 firms folded. Former Dial Corp Chairman John Teets said that at a meeting of CEOs the most common self-criticism was not moving fast enough to remove long-term, underperforming managers. Just as A players provide an uplifting force to an organization, C players can sink the ship. The best way to avoid firing loyal, beloved C players is to not hire or promote them over their heads.

Again: Leaving people in jobs in which they are chronic C players hurts the firm's chances of survival and growth and hurts your performance. Occasionally companies can demote people without harming their morale. It's worth considering creative ways to do it. Chapter 4 expands on the C-player problems, addressing the ethical, moral, and practical issues in firing C players.

8. "OUR PROBLEMS WILL SOON CLEAR UP BECAUSE WE ENGAGED A MANAGEMENT CONSULTING FIRM, AND THEIR REPORT LOOKS GREAT, SO TOPGRADING ISN'T NECESSARY."

Solution: Topgrade first.

Great management initiatives combined with a cast of A players can reasonably be expected to increase a company's performance. However, expensive consulting engagements can fall flat when the company managers lack the talent to drive successful implementation. In chess, great strategy will not prevail if one player has all pawns while the opponent enjoys a board full of royalty. Talent is a necessary ingredient to making management initiatives convert to shareholder value. Indeed, it is the grand enabler of all management initiatives (see Figure 2.1).

I cringe every time I hear about an undertalented company trying to implement process reengineering or some other initiative and push decision-making responsibility down in the organization. Underskilled or undertalented employees are given decision-making authority and end up making bad decisions. Performance inevitably suffers.

In contrast, organizations that topgrade are able to drive improvements in strategy, productivity, innovation, quality, customer service, and speed-to-market. They experience greater success in these areas because they have the most competent employees on whom to rely. Having consistently strong operational performance can be a powerful force in building shareholder value. Of course, other factors such as macroeconomic trends, currency fluctuations, industry changes, and customer preferences can all affect shareholder value as well.

> ▶ "At the end of the day, you bet on people, *not* on strategies."
>
> Larry Bossidy, CEO
> AlliedSignal

I am not saying talent is the *only* driver of shareholder value, but that it is a key one—and one of the few that managers can directly control. Ratcheting up the talent level of a company is a lot easier than trying to affect the strength of the U.S. dollar.

The idea behind topgrading is so simple, I am continually shocked that so few companies do it. Far too often, managers at all levels make the costly mistake of trying to "manage their way" to excellence with low performers on their team.

Figure 2.1

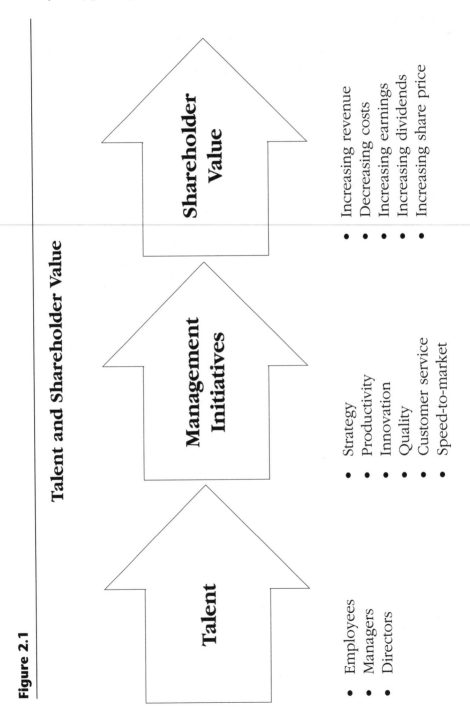

Talent and Shareholder Value

Shareholder Value

- Increasing revenue
- Decreasing costs
- Increasing earnings
- Increasing dividends
- Increasing share price

Management Initiatives

- Strategy
- Productivity
- Innovation
- Quality
- Customer service
- Speed-to-market

Talent

- Employees
- Managers
- Directors

9. "WE COULD NEVER ATTRACT A PLAYERS BECAUSE OF OUR LOCATION, INDUSTRY, CURRENT FINANCIAL PROBLEMS, AND SO ON."

Solution: Pay more in compensation to attract the level of talent necessary to beat the competition. Or if location is a terrible recruitment obstacle, consider moving.

The president of a division of AlliedSignal found that he had to pay senior managers 25 percent more to attract them to a small rural town. For a high-tech client, a 50 percent "location incentive bonus" was necessary. You pay what you need to pay in order to attract the talent necessary to achieve your goals.

Compensation is closely connected to the definitions of the A, B, and C player. No NBA franchise will pay $50 million per year for Michael Jordan, because at that level, even he is not worth it. It is extremely important to determine the right level of pay, but it is equally important to understand the relationship between pay and talent, supply and demand (see Figure 1.2). The president of the AlliedSignal division concluded that at $100,000 he could attract A players (by definition, that is true) for a job, but the overall level of talent for those A players was not high enough to achieve his company's goals. He therefore made the appropriate decision to raise the target pay to $125,000, and at that level search firms were able to generate A-player candidates with the higher level of talent necessary.

If you own a football franchise and decide to advertise a job as place kicker for a pay level of $15,000, the top 10 percent of talent available (the A players) might include no one, absolutely no one who can consistently kick a 40-yard field goal. All NFL franchise owners have concluded that they need A players available and willing to sign on at a pay level considerably above $15,000 in order to achieve the team goals.

Some managers are particularly good at attracting talent *without* paying a premium. They perform the equivalent of a full-court press. They seek to understand and address every individual need of the candidate and convey unrelentingly how enthusiastic the firm is about him, how much "we need you and like you," and so on. Passive hiring managers say, "Let's touch base next week," while the most successful managers never end the recruitment pressure until the person is physically on the job. Even then, they assume that another job offer may be lingering, so they "lock in" the new hire with attention, involvement, and respect.

The CIDS interview is especially helpful for identifying the candidate's needs as they relate to the job. What does the candidate *really* want in her boss? What types of responsibilities does the candidate love to have? What does she dislike? What are her long-term goals? What does she want to learn? Conducting a CIDS interview provides the answers to these questions. It helps companies craft "dream jobs" for A players by modifying the job description a bit and increases the likelihood of both attracting and retaining A players, even for "unattractive" jobs.

Rural headquarters far removed from major airports usually don't work. WalMart is an exception, in a tiny town in Arkansas. The relocation costs, "battle pay" for an unattractive location, and higher severances (to relocate people back to cities) add more. The sheer hassle in inaccessibility (additional 12 hours per week per upper manager wasted in one client company) is a killer. Sometimes moving a headquarters is most cost-effective.

1 0. "MY SUBORDINATES TEND TO GIVE 'THUMBS-DOWN' ON A PLAYERS."

Solution: Don't vote. Make the hiring decision yourself.

Having your subordinates interview a prospective peer of theirs is desirable, almost necessary. A-player candidates might insist on it. But don't forget obstacle #1 ("C players don't hire A players"), because a corollary is "A-player peers might not want the competition of other A players." So, get the peers' opinions, but don't give them a vote.

Your job is not to preserve the status quo. Get the A players in, help Bs to rise to the occasion, and remove the untrainable C players who drain the energy from your group. If your A players don't want competition, that's tough. Maybe you should change the compensation system so all are paid bonuses on team performance; maybe then A-player peers will be welcome. Always make it clear that hiring A players for your team is not a democracy—it's your responsibility and you will meet it.

1 1. "WE ARE DOWNSIZING AND MY JOB IS ON THE LINE; I NEED SHORT-TERM RESULTS AND DO NOT HAVE TIME TO TOPGRADE."

Solution: Improve short-term results *by* topgrading.

For years I have noticed a dangerous "death spiral" that can occur when organizations become leaner. Survivors of massive downsizings have more work to do; stress levels increase; the more marketable people, the A players, quit. Managers may not feel that there is time to find A players. A futile mistake is to try to squeeze A-player results out of the remaining B and C players. Stress increases even more and drives the best of the remaining talent to quit, causing the "death spiral" to continue. "Death spiral" is more than a metaphor; too many people have heart attacks and strokes under what could be avoidable pressure, had their organizations topgraded.

OK, if you are talking about keeping a C player for three more months until your new software is installed, fine. Perhaps that C player is lazy and disruptive, but is an expert in this particular software package. A replacement in "midstream" could be terribly disruptive. Coasting along with C players for more than six months is almost never justifiable, however.

CHAPTER 2 CHECKLIST:
DO YOU OVERCOME MAJOR OBSTACLES TO TOPGRADING?

Yes   No

❑   ❑   1. I understand that I should not have any C-player managers, but until I redeploy them I force them to hire only A players.

❑   ❑   2. If I'm a B player, I hire As who will help me function as an A player.

❑   ❑   3. I know the CIDS interview is the most powerful tool I can master to achieve a 90 percent or better success rate in hiring.

❑   ❑   4. I don't blame HR if I can't find A players to hire. I must be in the recruitment business all day, every day, with everyone I meet.

❑   ❑   5. If external recruiters fail to produce A-player candidates, I realize I must manage recruiters better.

❑   ❑   6. To avoid A players being "chewed up and spit out" by existing personnel, I provide them political protection or "air cover."

❑   ❑   7. I realize that if I say, "I can't afford to hire A players," I'm confused. A players exist at all compensation levels. Perhaps I mean that A players at a low salary are not good enough, and in order to attract the level of talent necessary, a higher salary will be required.

❑   ❑   8. I know that everyone can be an A player in *some* job.

❑   ❑   9. Although I may hate firing chronic C players, it is best for them that they move on to be A players elsewhere, best for the shareholders that As replace Cs, and best for my career to have a dream team, not a flawed team.

❑   ❑   10. I know that all management initiatives are ill-fated when carried out by C players and have the best chance for success when implemented by a team of A players.

❑ ❑ 11. To attract the level of talent I need to an unattractive location/industry/company, I pay a "battle-pay" premium in compensation.

❑ ❑ 12. I minimize "battle pay" in recruitment with a superpositive, superaggressive "full-court press."

❑ ❑ 13. To topgrade, I let my people interview a new member of the team, but I'm the one who decides whether the person will be offered a job.

Perhaps you intuitively embrace the topgrading philosophy, but wonder, "Can C players be *that* costly?" The next chapter addresses that question head-on.

THE TOUGHEST DECISIONS IN ORGANIZATIONS
ARE PEOPLE DECISIONS—HIRING, FIRING, PRO-
MOTION, ETC. THESE ARE THE DECISIONS THAT
RECEIVE THE LEAST ATTENTION AND ARE THE
HARDEST TO "UNMAKE."

PETER DRUCKER

3. The Astronomical Costs of Mis-Hires: Company Killers and Career Derailers

Hiring the wrong person, a C player, can cost you dearly. It costs your company dollars, BIG dollars. It can cost you in your career advancement. This chapter presents a groundbreaking quantification of the costs associated with making hiring mistakes. It is both a "heads up" for corporate and personal success and a call to arms for all managers to measure the costs of mis-hires.

At the "worker" level there are plenty of published statistics on turnover and even a few studies of the costs associated with mis-hires. A computer search of over 200 studies and articles produced a hodgepodge of single-company results, with costs of mis-hiring factory workers to be $1,500 in one company, sales people $6,000 in another.[1] Governmental studies have placed the costs of mis-hiring programmers at two to three times their annual compensation.[2] At the managerial and higher professional levels, the data are equally sparse. In a world inundated with metrics from smallpox incidence to the population of snail darters, from soft-drink consumption to the numbers of nuclear warheads, the topic of managerial hiring success has been strangely ignored.

---

[1] (Anonymous) "Retaining Top Salespeople: How to Motivate Star Performers," *Small Business Report* 13(2) (February 1988), pp. 23-27.

[2] F. L. Schmidt, J. E. Hunter, and K. Pearlman, "Assessing the Economic Impact of Personnel Programs on Workforce Productivity." *Personnel Psychology* 35 (1982), pp. 333-347.

Years ago I made a tiny effort to fill this research void. The first page of my 1989 book, *The Smart Interview: Tools and Techniques for Hiring the Best* (Wiley), includes a simple chart showing a few clients' estimates of the costs for having mis-hired people from $30,000 to $250,000 in annual salary. Nine years later an international publication featured that 1989 "quickie" study as its lead article. That research base was only eight (not 80, not 800) companies. The average mis-hire cost was five times the person's salary. A 1985 study by the Saratoga Institute claims that the average hiring mistake costs a company $15,000.[3] That's chicken feed, chump change.

Those numbers appear low and too sterile. Having interviewed over 4,000 managers in-depth, plus a couple thousand more in shorter career discussions, I know that many managers in my sample have *been* a mis-hire in at least one job. I've heard thousands of accounts of what it's like to make a major career decision that goes awry. Being a mis-hire, a C player who eventually is fired, is painful. Careers are set back and families disrupted; alcohol, drug, and ethics problems can result. In Chapter 2, I referred to a corporate "death spiral" in which poor senior hires result in lower-level A players "bailing out," leaving C players who hire more C players. The shareholders are left bleeding and wounded, and the company may become moribund. Mis-hires can kill companies, individual careers, and real people whose stress causes heart failure.

Remember—mis-hire means mis-selection from outside, mis-promotion, mis-placement. And ...

▶ Mis-placements become displacements, requiring replacements.

For this book Geoff Smart and I conducted a study of the costs associated with mis-hires, and here is the bottom line: With an average base salary of $114,000, the average total costs associated with "typical" mis-hires was $2,709,000—about *24 times the person's base compensation.* Wow! Those are by far the highest numbers I have seen on management mis-hires, but they certainly square with my experience. They ring true, but to see them in black and white is shocking.

Do you know annual costs of mis-hires for your group or your company? Maybe it's time to conduct your own cost of mis-hire research, every time you mis-hire someone. Following the principles in this book, you should mis-hire fewer than 10 percent of the time, but even so, calculating what it costs you for that one in ten will be instructive. Every company should do the same and provide incentives for managers to achieve a good hiring batting average.

---

[3] "Human Resources Effectiveness Survey," *1987 Annual Report*, ASPA/Saratoga Institute (Saratoga, CA: Saratoga Institute, Inc.).

In my experience, 50 percent of managers hired externally are mis-hires. Other authors[4] have used that same 50-percent figure. I did a little current research on the subject (see Chapter 5); 54 clients said that when using search firms, only 47 percent of the time were managers hired "good enough." Several dozen companies I know are very rigorous and professional at recruiting and screening managers, and experience only 10 percent mis-hires. Some, even less.

If roughly half of all external managerial hires are mis-hires, if rigorous topgrading approaches can increase the success rate from 50 percent to 90 percent, and if the costs in mis-hiring managers is 24 times their base compensation, there is an *enormous* opportunity for improvement at every level—yours, your company's, the nation's, and the world's.

A STUDY OF THE COSTS OF MIS-HIRES

Fifty-four clients supplied data on their costs of mis-hires. Some clients had begun to nail down the numbers with quite detailed research. Good for them, and all of us. There was no random selection of companies in my research, no experimental controls, not even large numbers. This is "quick-and-dirty" field research, but it's the best I've seen, and I truly hope it stimulates a lot more investigation.

Dr. Geoff Smart's research[5] connects two widely disparate bodies of knowledge—economics and applied psychology. He showed that hiring people is an investment, so why not calculate ROIs? Following Geoff Smart's lead, I have calculated ROIs on mis-hires in my study, with staggering results—ROIs of negative 500 percent!

My survey instrument instructs the respondent to generate estimates on a *typical mis-hire*, not the most costly, not the least. Of the 54 respondents to my survey, more than half are division presidents or above. Geoff Smart and I personally interviewed about half the respondents.

Some of the companies represented are shy. I have been encouraging them for years to hire better, and some don't want to publicly admit *any* hiring mistakes. The rest are more open, for they recognize that *all* companies occasionally mis-hire. Although many companies gave permission to attach their name to a specific mis-hire, I decided to group the data. So that you can judge how representative the data are, here are some of the companies whose executives participated in this study: Motorola, General Electric, General

---

[4] H. M. Fisher, "Select the Right Executive the First Time," *Personnel Journal* (July 1995).

[5] Geoffrey H. Smart, "Management Assessment Methods in Venture Capital: Towards a Theory of Human Capital Valuation," Ph.D. Dissertation, Claremont Graduate University, 1998.

Cable, General Signal, AlliedSignal, Con Agra, Gateway, Royal Bank of Canada, R. R. Donnelley, Office Depot, William M. Mercer, DSC Logistics, CompUSA, FMC, Viad, First of America, Carr Gottstein . . . and other well-known companies, as well as lesser-known companies.

Figure 3.1 is the survey document used.

Figure 3.1 Cost of Mis-Hires Survey

Job Title of Person Mis-Hired or Mis-Promoted: _____

Dates person was in position: _____ to _____
(If person was successful in previous job, but failed in a new job, just calculate costs for the years the person was in the new job.)

Reason for leaving:
Quit ___, Fired (or forced to resign) ___, Transferred ___, Retired ___, Died ___, Other ___.

This person is considered a mis-hire or mis-promotion because: _____

_____

_____

Notes: Adjust following costs for inflation (use your "best guess" for 1997 dollars).

1. Total costs in hiring the person: $_____
   - Recruitment/search fees (any guarantee; if so, money recovered?)
   - Outside testing, interviewing, record checking, physical exam
   - HR department time (for all candidates)
   - HR department administrative costs (all candidates)
   - Travel costs (for all candidates, spouses, other executives traveling to meet candidate)
   - Time/expenses of non-HR people (all candidates)
   - Relocation (moving household goods, purchasing house for candidate)
2. Compensation: (sum for all years person was in job) $_____
   - Base $_____ x number of years
   - Bonuses ("signing," performance, etc.) for all years
   - Stock options (realized for all years)
   - Benefits (life/health insurance, 401K, etc.) for all years
   - Clubs for all years
   - Car (incl. gas, insurance, etc.) for all years

3. Maintaining person in job: (sum for all years person was in job) $_____
   - Secretarial assistance for all years
   - Office "rental" (incl. electricity, etc.) for all years
   - Furniture, computer, equipment for all years
   - Travel (air, food, lodging, etc.) for all years
   - Training

4. Total severance: $_____
   - Severance fee (salary, benefits, use of office)
   - Outplacement counseling fee
   - Costs in negotiating separation
   - Costs in lawsuits caused by the person (EEOC, harassment, EPA, OSHA, etc.)
   - Administrative costs in separation
   - Wasted time of people in separation
   - "Bad press" (loss of corporate good will, reputation)

5. Mistakes/failures, missed and wasted business opportunities: $_____

   (Drove a key customer away, mis-hired three people at total cost of $300,000, impaired customer loyalty, failed to enter new "hot" market, wasted $10M on software that had to be scrapped, embezzled $1M, launched three "dog" products)

   Explain: _____

   _____

6. Disruption: $_____

   (Costs of inefficiency in the organization, lower morale, lower productivity, impaired teamwork)

7. Other: $_____

   (Specify) _____

8. SUM OF ALL COSTS (#1-#7) $_____

9. Estimated Value of Contributions of the mis-hire: $_____

   (Even if a $50,000-per-year store manager drove away customers and stole $1M, perhaps he contributed something—hired five excellent employees, came up with a merchandising idea worth $500K per year to the bottom line)

   Explain: _____

   _____

Quality Check: Does the ratio of total costs to estimated value of contributions seem correct? If not, please go back and make adjustments.

Figure 3.2 presents the results of the study. Rounding off, the most telling statistics are:

- In the sample of typical mis-hires earning less than $100,000, the average base compensation was $62,000 and the total costs were $840,000—14 times base, for average return on investment in those folks of -300 percent.
- In the sample of typical mis-hires earning $100,000–$250,000, the average base compensation was $168,000 and the total costs were $4,707,000—28 times base, for an average return on investment of -565 percent.
- For all 54 cases, mis-hires averaging $114,000 base compensation cost $2,709,000, or 24 times base, for a -500 percent ROI.

Figure 3.2 Cost of Mis-Hire Study Results

	Base Salary Less than $100,000	Base Salary $100,000 - $250,000	All Salaries
	N = 28	N = 26	N = 54
Base Compensation	$62,000	$168,000	$114,000
Number of Years in Job	2.5 years	1.75 years	2 years
1. Cost in Hiring	$13,000	$101,000	$55,000
2. Compensation (All Years)	$188,000	$555,000	$364,000
3. Cost of Maintaining Person in Job	$44,000	$99,000	$70,000
4. Severance	$17,000	$168,000	$90,000
5. Mistakes, Failures; Wasted and Missed Business Opportunities	$536,000	$3,559,000	$1,192,000
6. Cost of Disruption	$47,000	$226,000	$133,000
7. Sum of Costs (#1-#6)	**$840,000**	**$4,707,000**	**$2,709,000**
	(14 × salary)	(28 × salary)	(24 × salary)
Value of Contribution	$126,000	$436,000	$272,000
Investment *	$240,000	$756,000	$489,000
Return on Investment (ROI)**	-298%	-565%	-497%

Investment = #1 (cost in hiring) + #2 (compensation) + #3 (cost of maintaining)

$$**ROI = \frac{\text{Value of contribution - \#7 (Sum of Costs)}}{\text{Investment}} \times 100$$

These numbers are probably conservative for several reasons. For an ROI calculation, the costs of maintaining a manager (administrative assistant, office "rental," and so forth) are real. However, several respondents assigned zero or very low costs to "maintaining," figuring the administrative assistant would have been employed "anyway" (to serve others), and the office would have been there "anyway."

The biggest understated cost is the cost of disruption. More than half of the respondents registered the cost at $0. I called them to ask why, and they said assigning a dollar value of costs was too difficult, too subjective. They could ballpark all the other costs, but felt the cost of disruption would amount to a wild guess. Almost all respondents, however, indicated that they believe costs associated with disrupting the workplace are huge. C players make mistakes affecting and disrupting many people. Instead of removing business land mines, they inadvertently plant them. As the termination of a C player approaches, political jockeying takes place and more meetings waste time on internal issues, rather than on beating competitors. One company estimated the cost of disruption resulting from one mis-hire to be $50 million, and they could document it. I threw out the number because it was associated with a mis-hire that was not "typical" in costs.

A potentially disastrous CFO mis-hire resulted in very small costs. Instead of meeting with analysts the day of a stock offering, the CFO ran off with his mistress and began writing checks, stealing from the company. He hasn't been found, but damage-control procedures prevented any major problems. His check-writing authority was canceled, a trusted vice president controller was promoted, and the press never knew what happened. We record the mis-hire costs at only two times his base, but the costs could have been a lot higher.

Finally, the results of this study are probably conservative because many companies supplying the numbers are great companies. Some wrote "best practices," including those pertinent to topgrading. These companies are quick to identify mis-hires and nip them in the bud. Lesser companies have more mis-hires and live with the consequences many more years. My guess is that for average companies, the costs of mis-hires are perhaps 25 times base compensation for those under $100,000 and 40 times base for those earning $100,000–$250,000.

People frequently ask, "Doc, what's the most interesting mis-hire you have witnessed?" The most interesting mis-hire in my experience was one of my clients, the head of a global organization, owned by entities in over 60 countries. This story shows how mis-hires, if not identified and redeployed, can risk catastrophic consequences. A Soviet ambassador and I helped in the most dramatic multicultural corporate transformation I know of, a total conversion of a high-tech country club to a lean marketing company. The ambassador helped create the new strategy. My job was to assess and coach all senior managers; two-thirds stayed, one-third left. The only senior manager to not participate in my assessment and coaching was the top man, Alberto (not his real name), who said, "I won't, because you'll find out I have a dark side." After three years my assignment was completed, and Alberto took me to dinner at the Watergate Hotel in Washington, D.C. A few weeks later, fingered by the CFO, he was arrested for taking kickbacks on the construction of a fabulous office building. He went to jail, and repaid the company millions. The company got a black eye in the press, but because there was an instant replacement by a man with a global reputation for integrity, business did not suffer. The costs of this mis-hire? It's hard to say. Alberto cost the company a couple million dollars, but the losses could have been 20 times that, had a clever CFO not smelled a rat.

Each person mis-hired is a study in human nature. Alberto is quite a study. In an attempt to overthrow a Latin American dictator, Alberto was strung up by his hands, soon to be emasculated by the dictator's machete. Alberto urinated in the dictator's face. Rather than kill Alberto, the dictator tortured him—stuffed him in a casket-like box. For six months Alberto lived, barely, on bread and water. A coup then brought democracy to the country and Alberto became a hero. He became prominent and rich—worth $400 million. Alberto was wined and dined by kings and heads of state, and his personal stories were equally fascinating and shocking. He loved to shock. Some folks might tell a dictator, "piss on you!" but Alberto actually did it. Some later speculated that Alberto took kickbacks to fund a gambling habit. Who knows? I heard that there was major damage to his family, that his wife was so humiliated she attempted suicide.

Alberto's cost of mis-hire numbers are not included in my study because he could hardly be considered "typical." My figures do not include the human suffering of Alberto's family. There is not even a category for "family disruption," no dollar amounts to reflect the costs of an attempted suicide, in my study.

The single biggest estimable cost in mis-hiring is the wasted or missed business opportunity. For 27 years I have witnessed multimillion-dollar fiascoes that clearly could have been avoided had an A player been hired instead of a C player. Gross neglect by a C-player salesperson resulted in the loss of the #1 customer in one client company. In another, incompetent information technology consultants were hired. Why? Because they were friends of a C-player CIO. The losses in information technology bankrupted the company.

One of the most insidious elements of "wasted or missed business opportunity" goes to the heart of topgrading. C players hire C players and drive away A players. Several clients carefully tracked the costs of C players mis-hiring people, and the cumulative costs through an organization where there are a lot of C-player managers were astronomical.

Some companies are beginning to routinely calculate accurate costs of mis-hires. They are starting with big numbers—$35 million in severance costs in one year for one company in my sample, $55 million for another. As one senior executive put it, "Those mis-hire costs go right to the bottom line and lower the stock price."

The easiest costs to pin down are in autonomous units. A retailer can accurately measure a department manager's numbers in comparison with other department managers' results. All department managers had the same merchandise, advertising, and so forth. When a department that has always done well gets a C-player manager whose results plummet, and when a replacement manager gets results back on track, the losses are estimable in sales, margins, customer satisfaction (measured by survey results and complaints), unwanted employee turnover, EEO charges, and so on. At higher levels, entire divisions can reflect changes in president, particularly from A player to C player, then back to an A player. In one case, operating income was up a steady 15 percent per year six years in a row under an A player, declined to red ink in one year under a C player, and then returned to 15 percent the year a new A player entered. The CEO said there were no other performance factors of significance. These are not scientific experiments, but the mis-hire costs associated with autonomous business units can be reliable.

MIS-HIRES AT THE TOP

CEO mis-hires are the most serious. The media, if not behavioral scientists, cite at least some of the costs. Gilbert Amelio was generally considered a disastrous CEO of Apple, taking over at a pivotal time and plunging it into the muck. Although Apple's stock dropped 50 percent under Amelio, he left with a $9 million severance package. Ovitz was fired from Disney, and took $75 million in severance. Irani of Occidental Petroleum takes the prize. Occidental's returns were 15 percent when the oil industry's returns were 44 percent, but he was booted with $95 million in severance. Not only the stockholders are hurt, but all business suffers a black eye when senior executives reap great financial rewards despite destroying companies and jobs. Careers in business become less attractive, so bright young people are naturally inclined to pursue careers elsewhere. Mis-hires at the top cost the nation a lot.

AT&T fired Bob Allen the "nice guy" way. Under Allen, AT&T's stock missed the fabulous bull market of the 1990s. AT&T lost shares in long distance, failed in an attempt to acquire SBC, faltered in penetrating the $100 billion local business market, and suffered a PR nightmare when Allen laid off 40,000 employees while taking millions in undeserved pay. The C-player board of directors gave C-player Allen the authority to find his successor, and he went to a company one-tenth AT&T's size (R. R. Donnelley) and chose the CEO who achieved equally dismal stock performance in the 1990s. That man, John Walter, was forced out nine months later. The board could not attract an A player because Allen was to remain CEO for 18 months. What future CEO would take a job reporting to a failed CEO for 18 months? Walter was a second-tier candidate and did not last long at AT&T. His severance package was $25.8 million.

The right way to handle CEO succession is to give the failed CEO the boot *now*. AlliedSignal asked Larry Bossidy, then vice chairman of General Electric, to please come on board under a chairman who would depart in 18 months. Bossidy said no. I was with him three days before he joined AlliedSignal and he said, "I'm too old to be a trainee." The AlliedSignal stock sextupled in the next four years under Bossidy.

The world should *not* begrudge high pay for A player CEOs. The return on the shareholder investment in them is typically sky high. Successful CEOs create jobs and make retirement funds secure. From 1994 to 1996 the total value of stock owned by American households rose $1.8 trillion, with CEOs taking home far less than 1 percent of that.[6] The socialist press in Europe is particularly hard on CEO pay, but they don't get it. When the shareholders are happy to pay for A-player performance, what is "unfair"? Nothing. Boards deserve praise for granting large stock options to CEOs who deliver stock performance.

WHO'S RESPONSIBLE FOR MIS-HIRES?

Blame the boards of directors for not firing C-player CEOs, for not rigorously selecting A-player CEOs. Blame shareholders for not shouting "*topgrade or out!*" to boards. Of course, you the hiring manager must accept the lion's share of responsibility for mis-hires. Even if your company does not have topgrading policies in place, you can do the job right. (This book teaches you how.) If you accept blame for mis-hires, no doubt you will pass some of the blame along to search firms who found you C players, Human Resources professionals who dropped the ball, and management psychologists who failed to dig for the truth.

Mis-hired people should also take responsibility for accepting a job over their head. The mis-hired person should have studied the job description and the required competencies and should have asked lots of questions of a lot of prospective coworkers to see if there was a "match." Even if the company failed to spell out exactly what the first-year targets were, and the impact on bonus, the candidate should have nailed those down.

Blame CEOs, who should have put all those topgrading basics in place. When companies fail to perform the front-end basics (job descriptions, competencies, targets), they usually fail in the middle, too, with poor or nonexistent performance management practices. Years of neglect result in performance appraisals that lack content, fairness, and integrity. So, C players are given high performance ratings they don't deserve. A new mis-hire is apt to work in a feedback vacuum until the ax falls. The better way is for senior management to assure integrity in all performance ratings, to not put up with shallow "whitewashes." They should sit in meetings with managers and com-

---

[6] I. T. Kay, "CEO Pay and Shareholder Value" (1998), St. Lucie Press.

pare their people openly, with full discussion of what constitutes "Meets Job Requirements" or "Exceeds Job Requirements," then feed back honest conclusions to the people rated. Finally, after the company has failed to install the front and middle components of topgrading, it pays dearly on the back end in severance pay. People rated tops in performance and then fired for nonperformance soon find attorneys who—well, you know the rest. Outplacement and fair severance just add a few more costs.

So, who's counting? We all should, beginning *now*. We're all responsible.

CONDUCT YOUR OWN COST OF MIS-HIRE STUDIES

An intuitively appealing and immediately credible rationale for topgrading and for calculating costs of mis-hires goes like this:

> We should be as rigorous in hiring as we are in capital spending. For a piece of equipment costing $2,700,000 we're disciplined in calculating ROIs, in comparative shopping, and in planning installation. Up front we have a meticulous process to justify and specify the type and amount of equipment we need and the expected outcomes, to be sure we are paying for precisely what we need to do the job. After the equipment is installed we debug it and then we systematically review the purchase to be sure it met our expectations. Did we get the capabilities we projected? The measured results? Brad and Geoff Smart's study showed the average cost of a single mis-hire to be $2,700,000. But are we as rigorous in hiring as we are in capital spending? Nope. We "wing it" on the front end without specifying the competencies, we "wing it" in the hiring process with redundant, shallow interviews, and we let people sink or swim rather than debug any assimilation problems they experience. We never go back to calculate benefits of good hires or costs of mis-hires, and never systematically study how we could do better next time. So, let's apply as much rigor in hiring as we do in capital spending.

In several new-client situations, this rationale led to:

> Let's start by estimating the costs of our mis-hires. If the numbers are large, this will provide the impetus to design and implement rigorous and comprehensive topgrading processes.

A solid corporate topgrading system includes measurement of hiring effectiveness. Individual managers can take the Cost of Mis-Hires Survey (Figure 3.1), and "run the numbers" on their own mis-hires. Then corporate Human Resources can "roll up," aggregate the individual cases for an annual corporate profile.

But you don't have to wait for a corporate program. Perform the Figure 3.1 cost of mis-hire calculations on any of your mis-hires. In my two previous books on interviewing, I suggested that hiring managers also keep a Scorecard, with final ratings on the successful candidate on all competencies. I'd suggest that you do this, for your research on your hiring conclusions can help you improve. Appendix E lists 50 management competencies. Develop your own Scorecard and use it to summarize your final ratings of a candidate following your CIDS interview, reference check interviews, and all other interviews. Figure 3.3 offers a sample Candidate Assessment Scorecard.

Figure 3.3 CANDIDATE ASSESSMENT SCORECARD

Position: _____ Date: _____

Hiring Manager: _____
First-Year Bonus 1) _____
Accountabilities 2) _____
3) _____

6 = Excellent   5 = Very Good   4 = Good   3 = Only Fair   2 = Poor   1 = Very Poor

Competencies	Minimum Acceptable Rating	Rating by Hiring Manager	Comments
INTELLECTUAL			
1. Intelligence	❏	❏	
2. Analysis Skills	❏	❏	
3. Judgment/Decision Making	❏	❏	
4. Conceptual Ability	❏	❏	
5. Creativity	❏	❏	
6. Strategic Skills	❏	❏	
7. Pragmatism	❏	❏	
8. Risk Taking	❏	❏	
9. Leading Edge	❏	❏	
10. Education	❏	❏	
11. Experience	❏	❏	
12. "Track Record"	❏	❏	

Competencies	Minimum Acceptable Rating	Rating by Hiring Manager	Comments
PERSONAL			
13. Integrity	❏	❏	
14. Initiative	❏	❏	
15. Organization Planning	❏	❏	
16. Excellence	❏	❏	
17. Independence	❏	❏	
18. Stress Management	❏	❏	
19. Self-Awareness	❏	❏	
20. Adaptability	❏	❏	
INTERPERSONAL			
21. First Impression	❏	❏	
22. Likability	❏	❏	
23. Listening	❏	❏	
24. Customer Focus	❏	❏	
25. Team Player	❏	❏	
26. Assertiveness	❏	❏	
27. Communications—Oral	❏	❏	
28. Communications—Written	❏	❏	
29. Political Savvy	❏	❏	
30. Negotiation	❏	❏	
31. Persuasion	❏	❏	
MANAGEMENT			
32. Selecting A Players	❏	❏	
33. Coaching/Training	❏	❏	
34. Goal Setting	❏	❏	
35. Empowerment	❏	❏	
36. Performance Management	❏	❏	
37. Removing C Players	❏	❏	
38. Team Builder	❏	❏	
39. Diversity	❏	❏	
40. Running Meetings	❏	❏	
LEADERSHIP (Additional Competencies)			
41. Vision	❏	❏	
42. Change Leadership	❏	❏	
43. Inspiring "Followership"	❏	❏	
44. Conflict Management	❏	❏	

Competencies	Minimum Acceptable Rating	Rating by Hiring Manager	Comments
MOTIVATIONAL			
45. Energy	❏	❏	
46. Enthusiasm	❏	❏	
47. Ambition	❏	❏	
48. Compatibility of Needs	❏	❏	
49. Balance in Life	❏	❏	
50. Tenacity	❏	❏	
OTHER			

Pull the Scorecard out six months after the person is hired and then rate the person. Match your "interview" (Rating by Hiring Manager) and "actual" (six months later) ratings. Study your interview and reference check notes to see where you were on-target, and off.

Ask your subordinate managers to conduct the same sort of research with their Scorecards (Figure 3.3), and their estimated Cost of Mis-Hires (Figure 3.1), to fortify your topgrading efforts with important accountability metrics.

CHAPTER 3 CHECKLIST:
DO YOU KNOW YOUR COSTS OF MIS-HIRES?

Yes No

❏ ❏ 1. I calculate all the costs of my mis-hires.

❏ ❏ 2. I keep a Candidate Assessment Scorecard to record ratings on all competencies at the time a person is hired.

❏   ❏   3.   I use a Candidate Assessment Scorecard to learn where I accurately, and inaccurately, assessed candidates.

❏   ❏   4.   Upon reviewing a Candidate Assessment Scorecard six months after a person was hired, I revise my assessment techniques to improve, unless I was "right on target."

My vision is for individuals to be more responsible for their careers—to take jobs when they have intelligently analyzed the likelihood of being an A player. I want you, as a job candidate, to request job descriptions, competencies, first-year accountabilities. They don't exist? Then write them yourself and review them with your prospective employer. A players take that initiative. They also say:

> Thanks for the offer, but before I accept, I need to have frank discussions with others in the company and with some people who have left. And, I'd like to see the financials. Finally, I would need to know exactly what my first year's bonus will be based on—the measurable accountabilities and the resources I'll have to enable me to achieve them.

The prospective employer should be impressed with this initiative (and ashamed, if she hasn't done her homework). If a job offer would be withdrawn because of such requests, so what? You wouldn't want to take a job if the company hides such information.

My vision is for all hiring managers to conduct CIDS interviews, making few mis-hires, and conducting their own cost of mis-hire studies. I would hope every company would aggregate those costs of mis-hires. Armed with accurate ROI information on hires, teams can make better capital allocations, and all managers will embrace more rigorous selection. Why not give a higher bonus to a manager who hires and retains A players and who becomes a provider of talent to other parts of the company? Why not lower the bonus of a manager who costs the company $2 million in mis-hires in a year and who drives away two A players?

It is time for all managers, from the CEO throughout, to acknowledge:

- A 50-percent hiring success rate is common but wholly unacceptable.
- A 90-percent hiring success rate is achievable, and expected.
- Management mis-hires cost an average 24 times base salary.
- Topgrading methods, policies, and leadership reduce mis-hires.
- Mis-hires should be analyzed by individuals and companies, to improve interviewing skills and understand all of the true costs.

IT IS NOT GOOD TO BE BETTER THAN THE VERY
WORST.

SENECA, C. 4 B.C. – A.D. 65

4. Firing C Players: Is It Immoral?

If topgrading means packing teams, the entire company, with A players, then it usually involves removing chronic C players—those who are untrainable. Some chronic C players can be redeployed internally, into jobs where they can be A players. If this isn't feasible, the C players are redeployed externally. They're let go, "changed out." Topgrading requires some firing, or asking people to resign. It's painful, but is it immoral?

This chapter addresses the moral issues in firing C players. Topgrading also requires redeploying B players, but to make the central points, I'll refer in this chapter to the C-player issue. My purpose is to fortify your commitment to topgrading, including firing nonperformers, so that you can do it better and be a stronger advocate of a topgrading culture in your company. First I will discuss the pain in firing people and deal with blame. Next I offer a firing model, so you can see where you fit, in terms of the ease with which you make the decision to fire someone and the ease with which you implement it. I will support my conclusions on the basis of business necessity and conclude: It is immoral *not* to remove C players. A sample dialogue is provided to help you get the words and actions right. After offering legal cautions in firing people, I conclude with a checklist to help you determine if you are both a moral and legal topgrader, when you fire chronic C players.

As companies embrace topgrading, someone with a little too much creativity inevitably "invents" the word "bottomscraping," to mean one of two things—"hiring the dregs because we can't attract better candidates," or "firing the dregs, to make room for A players." Ugh! Bottomscraping has a particularly disdainful connotation. It evokes images of the 1800s, with general stores full of barrels that held crackers, pickles, you name it. Periodically the

60

barrels would have to be scraped, to remove the grunge. The bottom of the barrel contained the worst, the foulest-smelling grunge. There is a dehumanizing tone to "bottomscraping," as though what is being hired or removed is an object, and a foul one at that. I like to remind people that the fine Muscadets and Cognacs come from the scrapings at the bottom of the barrel. Deployed properly, the lees enable the fermentation of nectar of the Gods. Anyone can be an A player. Anyone. So, please discourage the invention of "bottomscraping" in your organization.

While we are discussing language, let me clarify what I mean by "firing." In management, people are technically "fired" only under extreme circumstances—theft, for example. Ordinarily, if a C player can't be redeployed internally, he is asked to resign in exchange for signing a severance agreement. A typical severance arrangement provides pay and benefits for half a year (or whatever, depending on length of employment and level in the company), along with requirements that the person not steal secrets, pirate employees, or sue. This is a forced resignation, which has almost the same psychological effect as a termination, since the person has no choice but to go. But at least the person forced to resign gets to say, "I resigned and the decision was mutual," a mildly face-saving sham. During the remainder of this chapter, please consider "firing" to include forcing resignations.

THE PAIN IN FIRING

Firing chronic C players need *not* be a major obstacle to topgrading, if a CEO or other senior manager says, "Do it!" and lower managers comply. Most managers are sensitive to the pain firing brings, however, and they hate it. The vast majority of managers I've interviewed told me that the hardest, most agonizing actions they take involve letting people go.

Many managers I've assessed have been fired at least once. They might have been relieved to finally be extricated from an unbearable boss, an untenable strategy, an unreasonable profit goal, or the like. However, the ego usually takes a significant hit. They know what it's like to announce to the family, "I'm no longer needed." The family pretends not to believe "You're a loser," but that thought enters everyone's mind. The kids say, "We understand," but if a relocation results, it means losing friends. A relocation could force an unwanted job change on the spouse. Depending on the severance agreement, the family's lifestyle may decline. Marital and family discord are more likely, as are drug and alcohol problems.

Firing your C players makes a powerful, and public, statement regarding who you are, and what you stand for—your character. Are you slashing and burning just to protect your skin? Are you scapegoating others, or executing (that's the right word) a stupid strategic plan because you don't have the guts to stand up and disagree? Or, are you doing the right thing, and doing it the right way? If not, your reputation may be painfully impaired.

Firing is a macro issue, a powerful determinant of the architecture of human society. Your firing a C player is a microcosm of how the human race defines itself. And, it all has to do with pain. Socialism declined with the Berlin wall, and free-enterprise democracy reigned supreme (with a few exceptions). Some former Eastern bloc states are thriving because, for the first time in decades, power flows from talent, not governmental power. The radical notion that talent be rewarded is a powerful lever for creating economically successful democracies all over the world. Permitting companies to topgrade has made Poland, the Czech Republic, and other countries vibrant and relatively new. But lifetime employment was replaced by employment at will, and some people were fired and remained unemployed. Countries such as India and China are trying to balance the economic gains of free-market capitalism with enough of a safety net that political leaders are not removed from office. As of this writing Russia still doesn't get it—the power of governmental bureaucrats has not been transfered to A-player capitalists, but to Mafioso thugs. More than a handful of unemployed workers would love some generals to stage a coup, returning both the former Russian glory and, of course, guaranteed jobs. Lifetime employment in Japan has evaporated. In China pockets of free enterprise are expanding across its vast landscape, but it is still ruled with an iron fist, in part because its leaders worry that unemployed masses might experience so much pain they would revolt.

If your company has fired or laid off a lot of people, treatment by the press can be brutal. It seems terribly wrong, even immoral, for powerful companies with rich executives to fire people just for what—more profit, more lucrative stock options? Firing as an option, a choice, is one of the most dramatic far-reaching issues facing the human race.

If you travel a bit, you will hear lots of folks say, "The U.S. is uncivilized" because our companies fire or lay off people, apparently without concern for the anguish inflicted. Responding, "Well, we now have to announce plant closings in advance, and portability of insurance is coming" sounds a bit feeble. Are we, are *you* uncivilized, or immoral, when you fire a C player?

When you fire someone you've mis-hired, you can expect to experience pain relief (C players drain your energy and effectiveness), but some residual pain. Your peers and bosses question your judgment in people. Perhaps your bonus will be eliminated, if you've mis-hired too many C players you've had to fire.

The firing component of topgrading should not be confused with downsizing. In my experience, topgraded companies rarely have to downsize. It can happen—even premier companies suffer losses when foreign economies go sour or when a competitor launches a new technology. Premier companies must alter strategy to survive, and as a result entire divisions are sold or disbanded; even A players are no longer needed. Downsizing is necessary and moral when it will permit a basically good company to recover or grow. But, downsizing has a bad name because too often it's a last ditch effort of a failed CEO; jobs of A, B, and C players are slashed, earnings pick up, and the CEO cashes in his stock and exits just before being fired. A successor is then hired to pick up the pieces. Please, don't call that topgrading! Al Dunlap ("Chainsaw Al") was fired by the board of Sunbeam, not because he fired people, but because he was destroying shareholder value.

Pain, pain, pain. It's not just the fired C player who suffers, but you as the hiring/firing manager, your company, and even the nation can experience collective pain as well. Any equal-opportunity finger pointer can find plenty of places to lay blame when preventable layoffs or terminations take place. There is just too much pain experienced by too many people, because of stupidity, incompetence, and dishonesty. But that does *not* mean that firing C players is immoral.

A FIRING MODEL

When firing your C player, how do you stack up in:

Ease of making the decision. Do you conscientiously take your C player through the appropriate steps of coaching, training, and looking for alternative jobs internally, and if all those steps have failed to produce an A player, do you then easily conclude, "He has to go"? Or, do you waver, procrastinate, avoid confronting the issues with the C player, or perhaps even ignore the fact that you have an underperformer?

Ease of implementing the decision. Once the decision to fire the C player is made and will be implemented shortly, how easy or hard is it for you to fire the person? Are you a cold ("Hey, this is business, nothing personal") sort, pulling the trigger on the C player without empathy? Or, do you sympathize and show human concern as you say, "Sorry, Charlie, but you have to go"?

		Ease of Making the Firing Decision	
		Easy	Hard
Ease of Implementing the Firing Decision	Easy	Hatchet Person	Ostrich
	Hard	Topgrader	Wimp

The Hatchet Person is thorough and fair in the decision to remove the C player, and the firing is conducted with surgical coolness and precision. No tears, no sympathy. Team members respect the Hatchet Person's decision, but are frightened by her callous, uncaring style and seeming lack of humanity.

Some A players might even find another job rather than work for that heartless robot. The Hatchet Person's lack of sympathy is most justifiable when the person fired has done something egregious—sell company secrets to a competitor or embezzle money, for example. Under such extreme circumstances coolness is appropriate, but vindictiveness or vengefulness are not.

The Wimp frets and avoids dealing with the C player. He knows he has a chronic underperformer, but he is so soft he procrastinates in making the decision to fire. He is extremely apologetic when the deed is finally done. Team members might like the Wimp as a neighbor but don't respect him in business because he's too soft. The whole team has suffered because the Wimp gave fifth and sixth chances to a chronic underperformer. They know the Wimp is a weak leader, not a winner. A players on the team get frustrated and look for jobs where they can be on winning teams. If there is an example where extreme softness is justifiable, perhaps it is in dealing with a beloved C player who also is an opinion leader. In an era of more common team-based bonuses, not many laggards are considered lovable. But, if one exists, special consideration, fairness, and caring must be evident, or the termination could result in a serious decline in morale, and then in organizational performance.

The Ostrich ignores signals that he has a C player, so he can't determine if the person can be salvaged. Softness is not his problem, it's naivete and lack of judgment. If the Ostrich has his head in the sand in making the firing decision, he leaves it there when firing C. Typically a boss will say, "Ostrich, you just don't get it. Your C player is killing us! Either you fire C or I'll fire you!" Firing C becomes easy, because it wasn't Ostrich's decision. And, Ostrich is so oblivious to reality and so wrapped up in himself, he tends to ignore the pain C will experience in being fired. Team members consider Ostrich a loser, and any A players he inherited soon look for better opportunities elsewhere.

The Topgrader is professional and caring. The C player's hopeless situation is recognized and dealt with properly. The Topgrader does not delay firing the C player, but she hates doing it. Topgrader is not soft, but she is humane. She conveys a moral sense, questioning what went wrong and wondering if she should have coached better or hired better. She is genuinely sympathetic to the C player's pain. Team members respect the Topgrader for her quick but fair decision, and they are happy she cared.

This model has a simple but clear message: Retain your moral sense and human caring while quickly and professionally ratcheting up talent by replacing C players with A players.

BUSINESS REALITY

Key questions are, "Does business necessity require removing chronic C players?" "Can the company afford to retain some C players?" and "If I retain C players, am I putting my company in jeopardy?"

Twenty-seven years of experience, serving over 100 companies and scrutinizing managers from close to 700 companies, have convinced me: The world is a much more painful place when companies *fail* to remove chronic C players. In an increasingly globalized economy, there is no place companies with many C players can hide. Companies packed with A players mercilessly annihilate companies burdened by C players. It's inevitable, and it's happening at an accelerated pace. As every company achieves high quality and streamlines processes, more and more businesses offer products and services that are commodities. Their processes are replicable. Stronger competitors can be copied. *People* truly make the difference between corporate winners and losers, so protecting incompetent people is corporate suicide. C players simply do not have the moral right to sentence companies to mediocrity or bankruptcy.

Corporate Darwinism is all-powerful today. Companies sprout, flourish, and die in a few years. A players become C players, not because they changed, but because the world changed around them and they failed to adapt and grow. People and companies need to flex quickly, or suffer. Is this bad? Is it immoral? No, this is reality. If you agree, then:

▶ It is immoral NOT to remove C players.

A new business reality seems to be emerging, a new short-term social contract for the workplace. It may eventually render this whole "firing-C-player" issue moot. Generation Xers tend not to want or expect long-term corporate relationships. Particularly in high tech, companies come and go with blistering speed. Companies are outsourcing more and more, and short-term consulting assignments are replacing full-time jobs. Xers surf the Net for short-term outsourced jobs, and find them. Xers are becoming free agents in the exciting, ever-changing world of technology. This is fun! They love learning neat new things and don't even talk about long-term job security with one employer.

If this short-term social contract blossoms in the twenty-first century, firings could be less painful than in the twentieth century. There could be fewer "victims" because individuals will take more responsibility for maximizing and marketing their abilities. Talent will flow seamlessly among well-publicized and ever-changing job opportunities. Everyone can benefit.

HOW PREMIER COMPANIES DO IT

Even if this future scenario becomes reality, it is not here for most of us . . . yet. So, we still have to deal with C players who are not so flexible, who might have to be dismissed, and who might experience a lot of pain. How do the most respected companies deal with the firing issue? In the first place, premier companies tend not to fire many people. And when they do, perhaps because of a necessary strategic transformation, they do it the right way.

When the boards of premier companies pick A-player CEOs and senior managers who get the strategy right and topgrade the whole company, there aren't many awful business decisions that have to be corrected by removing people. There are no C-player managers to immorally fire A players who might upstage them. Rigorous recruitment prevents many mis-hires. In Chapter 6 you will read case studies of topgraded companies that quietly redeploy B players to become A players internally and very rarely nudge a person out of the company. In excellent companies there are mostly A players who take responsibility for their career and want only to be in jobs where they can be an A player. HR systems measure and guide people so they don't become B or C players. Firings and forced resignations don't occur much, and when they do, they are done with integrity and class, and for credible, solid strategic reasons.

Premier companies protect those rare C players, just a little, to maintain a positive, human organization culture. When a lot of people have to be removed, normal attrition and early-retirement options are fully explored. If former A players near retirement become C players, they are given token jobs with prestige for a year or two. They no longer function in a key decision-making role, but do special projects and remain available to mentor up-and-coming managers. People who have an unusual personal crisis that hurts their performance are afforded slack. For example, letting someone decline from A player to C player during a period of mourning can produce an even more motivated A player when things are back to normal. At a minimum, such tolerance of temporarily lower performance gives a humane tone to the organization culture and usually inspires coworkers to pitch in and take up the slack. "After all," they say, "a crisis like that could happen to me."

Too often managers feel that a demotion will be humiliating for an individual. This is often true when rigid corporate hierarchies shout out everyone's status. Premier companies take a better approach by creating an organization culture in which there is fluidity of movement, connecting people's talents and needs to the organization's requirements smoothly, seamlessly. Although I personally have coached high-potential people to set their sights higher, I have also coached C players to accept lesser roles, where they could be A players. For example, several managers in a consulting firm were advised to return to an individual-contributor role. I coached them through the data gathering and thought processes regarding how *unlikely* it would be for them to become an A player if they remained in management. They concluded that career security and financial success were definitely more likely in the individual-consultant role—to which they returned, with no subsequent regrets. Good-performance management systems help people realize when the job is becoming too complex, too overwhelming.

Premier companies minimize the Peter Principle (getting promoted to one's level of incompetence). Topgrading is an antidote to the Peter Principle. In a premier, topgraded organization there are frequent career discussions. B players talk to their boss or HR about the need to be redeployed in a different position, where they can qualify as an A player. They want to get up each morning, confident that they will have fun, contribute, and grow. Federal Express is widely known to face the fact if they have promoted someone prematurely; they demote and retrain managers, later promoting many for a "second chance."

Ross Perot once told me that he liked to fire failed trainees in one of his businesses by removing them from the training center in the middle of the night. He thought that the remaining trainees would be more motivated if they awakened to the realization that a couple more trainees were axed. I doubt that this version of "business necessity" worked. In my experience, successful organizations do *not* publicly bludgeon the reputation of trainees who fail or A players who decline to C players because the company outgrew them. Smart CEOs and senior managers apply their creativity to find ways to retrain people, restructure jobs, and flex in order to permit loyal C and B players to become loyal, highly productive A players in other roles. They look for ways to protect honest people's dignity, not humiliate them to make an example.

In premier, topgraded companies, the immorality in firing people is a nonissue because people aren't fired often, and when they are, no one blames anyone. Firing C players thus becomes a rare, but necessary, business action.

FIRING C PLAYERS CAN FEEL RIGHT

What? Firing people and feeling good? Maybe not good, but right—certain that the right action is being taken, the right way. If you believe retaining C players is self-defeating, you must be able to look a C player in the eye and say, literally, "It's time to go."

Let me paint a picture from your entering a new job as a senior manager right up to saying, "C, it's time to move on." You are Vice President Operations and C is Plant Manager, very likable but failing. C was a very good financial analyst; he asked to transfer into Operations and has been struggling for two years as manager of a small plant. The problems in his plant are not being solved, yet C is eager to be named your successor as VP Operations.

In the dialogue that follows, a discussion lasting several hours is being compacted into paragraphs. Please assume there would be a lot more meaningful communication and fewer blunt statements by you, the "Manager."

January 5:

Manager: Hi, C, I'm Pat your new manager. I'd like to spend several hours with you next week in a CIDS interview, to get to know you—to review your background, accomplishments, and developmental needs and to hear what your goals are and what you'd like to see from me.

C: Great, a boss who wants to know all about what I can do!

The CIDS interview was conducted January 12, and you sensed C was a C player. You considered dozens of competencies in your diagnosis. C's level of commitment to doing well is high, his basic values (ethics, respect for people, high standards) are fine, and his confidence is normal—a bit low, but understandably so, because he's failing. The problem is skill, and you sense that there is no easy fix with C, that C cannot acquire the many competencies, the skills to succeed in this job in a reasonable amount of time. But you decide to observe C a month to be sure. If C cannot be salvaged, you want to nudge him out the right way. At the conclusion of your January 12 CIDS interview . . .

January 12:

Manager: C, you say that you hope to grow from Plant Manager to Vice President Operations. I don't want to wait for a year for a performance review to discuss how realistic your goals are. Do you?

C: No way! What do you have in mind?

Manager: Let's meet in a week. Here is the job description and competencies for Vice President Operations and for your job, Plant Manager. You rate yourself on all the competencies for both jobs. When we meet in a week, let's discuss your performance goals for this year—how realistic you feel they are, how you intend to achieve them—in relation to how strong you feel you are in the essential competencies. And, let's discuss your career goal of vice president and how you stack up on those competencies.

Consistent with legalities discussed in Chapter 13, you consulted with Human Resources and Counsel. They reminded you that the company policy manual requires you to give a written warning to a person, stating that termination can occur in 90 days if performance accountabilities, stated in writing, are not met. They asked you to document everything—accountabilities, every discussion about nonperformance.

January 19:

Manager: C, you've put a lot of time into preparing for this meeting by rating yourself on essential competencies and stating your performance goals for this year. We've been talking two hours and I think we've clarified a lot of things. Your and my ratings of you on the competencies for both Plant Manger and Vice President Operations are about the same, but based mostly on the CIDS interview, discussing your entire career in-depth, I rate you a little lower than you do on Assertiveness, Performance Management, Selecting A Players, and Initiative. Because you know you have slipped in your goal attainment, maybe we should stop talking about your becoming Vice President Operations and focus on this year and how you can improve and succeed in your present job as Plant Manager.

C: You're right. I haven't been on track to meet my performance goals. I need to learn some things to do a better job as Plant Manager. Only a couple of years ago I was a financial analyst, so I'm still learning. I agree I should hire better, and as for Performance Management, I just don't want to be an autocrat.

Manager: OK, let's see if we can make sense of all this. You agree you should hire better. I'll personally teach you CIDS interviewing so maybe we can eliminate those costly mis-hires.

C: I'd like that, and with two supervisory openings, I can use help now. I think I talk too much in interviews.

Manager: People like you a lot, and maybe I can help you use your winning personality to learn more about candidates' competencies.

C: Sounds good.

Manager: Let's talk about Assertiveness. My hunch is that you would come closer to meeting your production goals if you could schedule the shop better. To do that you need to engage the sales people so they get you the projections sooner.

C: But I ask, and they're just late and make excuses.

Manager: I could talk to the Vice President Sales, because you really need the projections on time. But my preference would be for you to show a little more Initiative and Assertiveness rather than relying on me.

C: I don't know. The VP Sales is pretty stubborn.

Manager: OK, I'll handle it, for now. Let's move on to Performance Management. I've observed your asking your people to do things.

C: I'm not an autocrat. I ask, not tell.

Manager: That's fine, but what I wonder about is if people feel really accountable. I heard a lot of excuses.

        C: Yeah, they say I ask two people to do the same thing, so I guess I should communicate better. Some crises have arisen, so we're not able to do as much. I don't know if those are excuses, but it's hard to keep everyone focused.

Manager: You don't conduct weekly staff meetings?

        C: No. I have had staff meetings, but there doesn't seem to be time to have them weekly. Not even monthly.

Manager: But if people are confused, crises are occurring, and your team isn't focused, I wonder if you might not save time by getting everyone coordinated in a weekly staff meeting.

        C: OK, I guess.

Manager: You're hesitating.

        C: Yeah, my meetings wander. We don't seem to get a lot done. Your staff meetings are really productive, but I just don't have the knack . . .

Manager: Would you like it if I were to co-lead one or two of your staff meetings, to get you started? I'm big on agendas, fast-moving discussions, participation, action plans. Consensus is desirable, but I call the shots if we stall out. For every decision someone is accountable to do something, and I follow up to be sure results are achieved. No excuses. If someone this week says they'll do an analysis by next week, they have to do it.

        C: Phew! You don't scream, don't threaten, and yet you are forceful. Yes, I'd like you as a partner, co-leading. Maybe you can set a better tone and then pass the baton to me. I have trouble pushing these guys, because, well, when I was in finance a couple were my drinking buddies. I'm Mr. Nice Guy, I guess.

Manager: I see. You're Mr. Nice Guy, not just because you need to be liked but because you have some social friends reporting to you.

This "data dump" in real life would have taken a couple of hours and there would have been a lot of give and take and better coaching form, in order to give C the very best chance to improve his skills. You want to also boost C's confidence, but not in a shallow, artificial way. My point here is that you, as a manager, need to be *both* positive and hard hitting. Take two hours, if necessary, but be sure your subordinate gets the message. Summarize this conversation in a memo, to be clear C understood, and to protect against a wrongful termination suit. Returning to your January 19 meeting with C . . .

C: I know, I know. I'm not leading so well.

Manager: Do you want to move to a different plant to get away from your buddies?

C: No, if I can't become a good leader with this bunch, I'm not cut out for leadership. Your standards are awfully high, though.

Manager: I guess so. I'm asking for you to achieve the targets you agreed to at the beginning of the year. Can you do it?

C: I don't know. You're trying to help me, and I appreciate it.

Manager: I'll continue to help any way I can. I haven't raised the bar, just held everyone to the existing bar. We have a plan to help you improve both skills and results. In addition to interviewing your finalists for those two open jobs, I'll co-lead a couple staff meetings to show you how to get more Performance Management. And I'll set up a weekly update with the Vice President Sales, so you can get sales projections sooner and adjust your production schedule more quickly. I'd like you to show more Initiative and Assertiveness in getting results. Is that a pretty complete summary?

C: Yes, and thanks a lot, Manager. I feel I'm letting you down, but I appreciate your help.

Manager: Let's follow up in one month to see how we're doing.

C: See you February nineteenth.

By February 19 you are fully convinced C is a chronic C player who has to leave the job. Perhaps he can return to his former job as financial analyst, which would be a demotion. If not, he'll have to leave the company. You have followed through on the plan to help C, but C is still Mr. Nice Guy, letting his team avoid accountability.

February 19:

Manager: Hi, C, let's look over the numbers and review your personal progress.

C: There's good and bad news. The good news is that I'm getting a much clearer understanding of what you expect and why. And thanks to you, Sales is giving me their projections on time. That's helped me schedule production better, so productivity is up, a little. You helped me hire better people than I would have. But I just wish I could hold people accountable like you do. That's really tough for me.

Manager: C, it sounds as though you've been doing some serious thinking.

C: I have. I'm still not back on track for getting the productivity and quality numbers for this year. The others on your team feel they can make the numbers this year if I don't drop the ball. Since January my numbers are a little better, but there is no way I'll meet the annual goals. I'm letting the whole team down. I hate getting up each morning, looking myself in the mirror, and saying I'm going to fail again today. I find myself wishing I were an analyst again. I should be back as an analyst, working toward becoming a division controller. I can see now I'm not cut out to be Plant Manager.

Manager: You have been honest with yourself, C. Good for you. Do you want to move back into Finance?

C: Let me think about it. Are you considering firing me?

Manager: I'd hate to, C. We have a progressive-performance-improvement policy, as you know, and here (hands document to C) is notice that you are on probation. You have 90 days to achieve those same accountabilities we've been discussing. I'm really sorry. Is there anything at all I can do to help you succeed as Plant Manager?

C: No, you've done more than I could have expected. Maybe I will go back to Finance. I'll think about it.

Manager: Don't wait long. You think you might be happier in Finance, and so do I. You're a whiz with numbers. If you earned a promotion to a financial-management job, you could hire other whizzes, and probably hire better ones because you've recently learned how to conduct a CIDS interview. And, the pace is less hectic there. You would be a technical manager, respected for your technical talents. You wouldn't have to motivate people the way you need to in the plant. You should keep working to fix your weaker points, but they would be less weak in Finance. You can be an A-player analyst and with developmental work I'll bet you could become an A-player division controller in a few years.

C: I agree, but what about pay? Even if they let me return, they won't pay me the $80,000 I now earn, and I can't afford a $60,000 analyst's pay.

Manager: Take a half day here or there to check on jobs outside the company if you want and I'll cover for you. You might be able to get a job as controller somewhere, but I wouldn't recommend it until you show more Initiative, more Performance Management. If you stay here, as a financial analyst, you might have to take a cut, although I'll see if we could take you down $10,000 next year and the rest during the following year. Let's say by March 5 we'll make a change, OK?

By March 5, C will have another job. This wasn't the prettiest, easiest scenario. C was a C player in Operations, and his short-term goal of becoming Vice President Operations was totally unrealistic. Manager was honest, helpful, and direct—a Topgrader in the Firing Model presented earlier in this chapter. If C quits for a job with a different company, there will be a nice going-away party, a cake at lunch, best wishes. Maybe C will suck it up—remain with the company as an analyst, live on a lower salary, and tell everyone he benefited from the cross training. If there is no job available for him in Finance, and no other position where C will be an A player, you as Manager have to fire him (or ask him to resign).

If C *really* works on improving, perhaps he will overcome fatal flaws in Assertiveness, Initiative, Selecting A Players, Removing C Players, and Performance Management. This could take years. If so, he could become a division controller. His career will be a lot more successful than if he had been "carried"—permitted to get by with nonperformance, poor accountability, frequent mis-hires, and Mr. Nice Guy softness.

Will C be jobless if he is fired? Probably not. Despite downsizing, the number of civilian workers in the United States *rose* by eight million between 1991 and 1996; furthermore, it took executives over the age of 50 an average of 3½ months to find a new job, with half earning *more* money.[1] This redeployment scenario contained the moral elements:

- Thorough and accurate assessment
- Reasonable performance goals
- Ongoing feedback
- Role modeling (CIDS interview, conduct of staff meetings) by manager
- Comprehensive coaching
- No hard feelings
- Increasing self-awareness by C
- Increasing skills by C
- Opportunities for ego protection

Everyone wins. C is better equipped to become an A player and to take responsibility for his self-development for future positions. You documented each discussion in memos, partly for legal protection and partly to be sure communications were clear. This is only fair. You, the manager, serve the shareholders and yourself by removing a chronic C player (and presumably

---

[1] J. M. Templeton, *Is Progress Speeding Up?* (Templeton Foundation Press, 1997).

by replacing C with an A player). The company is stronger, better able to preserve and grow jobs and to pay taxes.

I have interviewed more than 100 presidents and CEOs who attributed their failure to "carrying C players." In the CIDS interview they described the strengths and weaker points of each of their key managers; in the vast majority of cases, they said, "I should have moved quicker to get rid of C players."

Manager, in this scenario, is competent, professional, and humane. In "real life" managers all have flaws, and our firing C players is more moral if we are less flawed. Chapter 8 is devoted to minimizing our weaker points. In an ideal world Manager would be so inspiring, so perceptive, so fantastic in all respects that C players are magically converted to A players. In my experience, such super leaders number less than 1 percent. Coach Keady, Purdue's successful basketball coach (retired in 1998) had a reputation for converting a B team of talent to an A team. Good for him! Aspire to be like Coach Keady. But don't limp along with C players, if you are not such a talented coach and developer.

FIRING C PLAYERS LEGALLY

Chapter 13 includes common "do's" and "don'ts" in order to function within the law when firing C players or forcing their resignation. Performance-management systems these days have been time tested for legal protection. Job descriptions are written in behavioral terms, accountabilities are spelled out, and nonperformance is documented. When someone is in jeopardy of being fired, there is usually a formal "disciplinary process." Among my clients there have not been many lawsuits resulting from C-player managers being fired. Why? Because the proper, fair, and legal process is followed. Properly coached, chronic C players *want* to move out of a job where they are failing and into a job where they can succeed, even if that means leaving the company. As much as we moan and groan in the United States about legal barriers and costs, at managerial levels there really are not high legal barriers to redeploying a chronic nonperformer. Typically if a person does not quit, a severance is offered in return for a legal commitment to not sue the company (discrimination, wrongful discharge, and so on).

Countries with job-protection laws suffer, economically. Europe is more socialistic than the U.S. It is so hard to fire anyone in Germany that companies, both German and non-German, are fleeing Germany. That's a major reason unemployment became sky high in Germany in the late 1990s. Ditto in other European countries. How can companies compete in this global economy when they are legally bound to retain C players? They can't. Socialistic protection of C players is bad economic policy because it drives away taxpaying companies and jobs, and it is immoral. It makes helpless victims out of individuals who could otherwise succeed as A players in a competitive world.

What about firing members of protected groups in the United States? CEOs call those shots, and my client CEOs have a common perspective: "Diversity (or inclusivity) is a business necessity so embrace it, and if a chronic C player is in a legally protected group (age, race, and the like) don't retain the person just because a lawsuit is more likely." Those CEOs say, "Hire A players to begin with, but don't 'carry' chronic C players because you fear a lawsuit. Do your homework, work with Human Resources and Counsel to document nonperformance and its consequences, coach like crazy to help the person succeed, and if worse comes to worst, fire the person."

Indeed, permitting C-player members of protected groups to keep their jobs while C players who are not members of protected groups are redeployed is divisive. It smacks of tokenism and is deeply offensive to A players in that protected group, because it diminishes their value.

CHAPTER 4 CHECKLIST: ARE YOU A MORAL REDEPLOYER?

Yes   No

☐   ☐   1. I believe, deep in my soul, that redeploying chronic C players is moral.

☐   ☐   2. My company has a world-class performance-management system.

☐   ☐   3. Regardless of the quality of our performance-management system, I personally provide thorough, regular performance feedback to every one of my direct reports.

☐   ☐   4. My C players are given a fair chance to become A players.

☐   ☐   5. I give C players months, not years, to prove they can be A players.

☐   ☐   6. In redeploying chronic C players, I look hard for an internal role where they can be A players and be happy in their new role.

☐   ☐   7. In redeploying a C player internally, I look for creative ways to protect people's dignity.

☐   ☐   8. I protect C players a year or two from retirement.

☐   ☐   9. I consult with Human Resources and Legal Counsel to be sure I am functioning within the law in redeploying C players.

☐   ☐   10. I have never lost a lawsuit concerning actions covered by employment laws.

This entire chapter on firing C players would not be necessary in a book on screening candidates for the entertainment industry. Here it is obvious that "talent counts." Fans *demand* the heads of C-player athletes. No one buys the CDs of C-player musicians. A C-player news anchor in Chicago is quickly dispatched to be a weather reporter in Peoria. It is the rest of the business world (and not-for-profit world) that is sometimes considered "immoral" for firing a salesperson who can't sell, though her continued employment is not good for the company, not good for the shareholders, not good for any of the other team members, and not good for that salesperson, either.

IT IS A HECK OF A LOT EASIER TO HIRE THE
RIGHT PEOPLE TO BEGIN WITH THAN TO TRY TO
FIX THEM LATER.

BRAD SMART

5. Recruitment Best Practices: How to Avoid Mis-Hires

Recruiting is like dating. Overtures are extended, prospects play "hard to get," the relationship gets serious, a legally binding offer is made, and finally one is accepted. Sometimes the marriage is made in heaven. Oftentimes it's not, and a major reason is unsuccessful recruitment.

This chapter dissects recruitment approaches and offers improvements. If you think this is a chapter directed at Human Resources professionals, think again. The blame for poor external recruitment rests on your—the hiring manager's—shoulders, and those of your CEO. I begin with a "typical" recruitment scenario, a scenario flawed by C players or at best A players who don't know how to do it right. Then the results of a survey are presented, showing an unacceptable failure rate when expensive search firms are used. The "good news" begins with a "promote from within" model, but unfortunately ever-changing business strategy is forcing "promote from within" companies to recruit externally more often. The proper roles for external recruitment are spelled out—for CEOs, hiring managers, and Human Resources professionals. A "blueprint" for organizing recruitment processes is offered. Finally, the chapter checklist helps you focus on the essential components of recruitment that will help you achieve the 90-percent success rate enjoyed by premier firms.

A TYPICAL RECRUITMENT STORY

Consider the following scenario, to see how you stack up in terms of key elements in recruitment. Suppose you are Vice President Marketing. Your

Marketing Director just quit. She was superb at analyzing market data, developing product brochures, and coordinating advertising; she earned $90,000 base salary.

Your company experiences a typical 50-percent success rate in external hires, in part because your CEO has failed to set the recruitment bar high. There are no performance standards for hiring, no accountability, no policies that assure A players will be hired.

You run to Human Resources. "Find me a new director, quick!" There is no job analysis. A job description is thrown together and a few competencies specified, but these are done superficially. In a rush, a few internal candidates are considered, but without a thorough assessment of their talents. Your company made you attend a Diversity workshop and you promised yourself you would recruit more women, blacks, and Hispanics; however, in this crisis you forgot to make it a priority. You ask around to see if someone can recommend a good external candidate, thus saving a search fee. Nope. Neither you nor Human Resources has created a data base of external talent. And, very little thought is given as to whether the job needs filling; perhaps a sharp marketing analyst could perform the necessary functions, eliminating the need for a director.

A headhunter is called, an executive search consultant who meets with you and the Human Resources Director for two hours, to learn the job specs. Snickering at your poorly constructed job description, the search executive promises to do better, but the result is a boilerplate job description thrown together with boilerplate competencies. The true essence of what it will take to do the job (coping politically with the cantankerous Vice President Sales, for example) isn't discussed. It's not that you want to deceive the search firm or candidates, but why turn off candidates with negatives? So, you put your best foot forward, concealing the dirty linen that could make a director of marketing's job hell.

Since the headhunter works for one of the largest search firms, 40 percent of *Fortune* 500 companies are its clients. So, 200 of the largest firms are off limits, blocked, locked out of your search. You were not told the lock-out list was so large, eliminating A-player candidates from so many premier firms. You didn't think to ask.

The search executive delegates 90 percent of the work to lower-level associates who haven't even met the client. They screen résumés against the vague competencies. They lack the horsepower to penetrate premier companies and tenaciously sell A players on considering a different company. There is very little communication with HR or the hiring manager for two months— just periodic updates that are supposed to convince you that hundreds of people are being screened. Since the search fee is 33⅓ percent of the total compensation, the early work produces the epiphany that maybe you will have to go higher in compensation to attract the higher powered Marketing Director you need. There is a powerful financial incentive for search firms to say, "Gee, we're just not finding the level of talent you need at $90,000, so let's at least consider candidates in the $125,000 range."

Three or four finalists are trotted out for you to meet. The search firm partner has spent an hour with each, read his associates' reports, and scanned preliminary reference checks, which were all glowing (except for "sometimes too impatient with people who aren't doers"). The file on marketing director candidates appears too good to be true. Hmm.

You, the hiring manager, meet the candidates, perhaps for lunch, explain what the job needs are, ask a few questions about their experience and interests, sell the job a bit, and respond to questions. If it looks like a mutual "go" for one or more finalists, your assistant organizes a day of interviews with some key members of your team. Current practice for "organizing" the interview sequence is like a fourth-grade fire drill. On the day of the interviews, two scheduled interviewers have crises to address, and so substitutes are thrown in at the last minute. The candidate is asked to be flexible, interviewing with a partial group. Most interviewers are ill-prepared, fumbling through candidate résumés for the first time—"uh . . . tell me about yourself." Interviewees consider this day a hodgepodge of redundant, superficial, shallow interviews. But it's typical.

At the end of that disorganized day you talk for a couple of minutes with the other interviewers, but too often their thoughts are disjointed and contradictory. At best, questions touched on a few competencies (not all) and the scattergun interviews hardly provided deep, penetrating insights into *any* competency, except one—First Impression. The candidates don't seem as perfect as the search firm's assessments. So a second visit is organized, but it, too, is disorganized.

Throughout the entire process, HR was an escort service, coordinating visits; neither HR nor you, the hiring manager, required better service from the search firm. Neither you nor HR performed a CIDS interview. HR did not conduct a thorough background check on the new hire, nor did the search firm. If your new marketing director rapes an employee, and if a background check could have disclosed it, the company could be liable for negligent hiring. Don't blame HR or the search firm—*you* are the hiring manager, so the buck stops with you.

Reference checks were performed on finalists by the search firm that performed the preliminary reference checks. They found more of the same, revealing nothing other than that the finalist has lots of strengths and no serious shortcomings, except candy-coated strengths such as "extremely high performance expectations," "sometimes a little impatient," "and works too hard." Since you did not conduct a CIDS interview, you couldn't ask references the really probing questions. So, you accepted the search firm's reference-call summary.

After two company visits by two finalists, it's decision time. You are disappointed. The caliber was not high enough. Both finalists are out of work; the search firm did not exactly pry them loose from premier companies.

Instead of an A-player Marketing Director being hired, urgency "requires" taking the less bad (appearing), who now seems more apt to be a B player than an A player. Of course, half the time your external hires turn out to be C players. The management psychologist's report hinted at some shortcomings, but her process, consisting of a day of tests and a one-hour interview, wasn't expected to be definitive.

The final compensation escalated to $110,000 base plus $40,000 bonus, so the search firm pockets $50,000, not the $35,000 initially projected. Plus all expenses. You, the hiring manager, get headaches and a career black eye for a mis-hire (half the time) and HR ducks—avoids any complicity. No one, not the hiring manager, not HR, not the psychologist, not the search firm is really accountable, because people are presumably unfathomable, complex, and not completely honest in interviews.

It's as though C players were made for each other—C-player hiring managers, C-player search professionals, C-player HR professionals, and C-player management psychologists. And let's not forget the CEO who tolerates mass incompetence. I feel sorry for companies accustomed to excellent outcomes when promoting from within, yet suffering through the preceding scenario when they have to recruit outside. I'm amazed that so many companies that *have* recruited externally for years continue to tolerate an incredibly poor level of performance in this crucial endeavor.

THE STATISTICS ON SEARCHES

Having interviewed thousands of senior managers and having asked them how successful they were when hiring externally, I'm accustomed to hearing, "About half the time the headhunter didn't produce someone I hired, or if they did, the person turned out to be a disappointment." In preparation for this book, I asked more than 100 CEOs and presidents who's to blame for such a poor recruitment record, and 90 percent of them pointed the finger at search firms. I don't think that's fair, but I decided to research the topic a bit more formally. I asked six prominent search firms for their performance statistics, but none kept the statistics I wanted. One reported, "Eighty percent of the managers we place are still on the job four years later." OK, but what percent of retained searches result in someone hired? What percent of searches result in "good hires"? What percent result in A players hired? All six responded, "We don't have those statistics."

A distinction should now be made. "Retained searches" are conducted by executive search firms, who are paid (usually one-third of first-year salary and bonus) regardless of whether their client hires someone they found. Executive-search professionals are at the top of their profession; they help to fill senior-management positions. "Contingent-fee recruiters" get paid (usually 15 percent to 25 percent) only if they produce a candidate who is hired.

Contingent-fee recruiters usually work at lower levels—midmanagement, professional jobs, sales positions, administrative assistants. Both contingent-fee and retained-fee recruiters are "headhunters," the latter hunting for higher salary "heads" than the contingent-fee recruiter. Retained-search professionals rarely guarantee their work, but contingent recruiters usually offer to replace a mis-hire who quits or is fired within months at no additional charge. Since my practice involves assessing candidates for management positions, the headhunters referred to in the remainder of this chapter are retained, not contingency.

Returning to my quest for success statistics, I called the professional association for retained-fee recruiters and found they maintain statistics on numbers of searches done in various industries and jobs, but not on success rates. A representative of Association of Executive Search Consultants (AESC) said to me, "I don't know how we would determine success rates." How about—ask clients!? An organization publishing the Directory of Executive Recruiters has a research arm that told me, "I've never heard of client satisfaction research covering many search firms."

So I did my own survey. I sent a questionnaire and/or personally interviewed clients and assorted others—executives interviewed for clients, plus others in my network. Half the respondents are CEOs and presidents, one-fourth are HR executives, the rest are other senior functional executives. The first 50 responding to my survey letter were recorded. Varied industries and company size are represented, though the median-size company is about $1 billion in sales. The average experience of the person contacted is 25 years. The results are confidential, and respondents were asked to reflect on their *total* career experience and not just their experience with their current employer.

The respondents include long-term executives with well-known companies, such as General Electric, Gateway, Viad, Royal Bank of Canada, Boeing, General Signal, R.R. Donnelley, Snap-on, Inc., Ford Motor Company, Ingersoll Dresser Pump, T. J. Maxx, Amway, Airborne Express, Chicago Title and Trust, AlliedSignal, Citicorp, Rockwell International, Stanley Works, General Cable, and Idex. Although many in my sample are premier companies, several (anonymous) mediocre companies are represented in the survey—companies with poor financial results, slow growth, and loss of market share. How did they get into my sample? Search firms produced them as finalist candidates for my client companies, and during the CIDS interview I pushed the pause button and asked the questions for my study.

THE RESULTS

The three questions in my survey produced the following results:

1. Percentage of retained searches in which the search firm:

Generated a candidate hired:	68%
Failed to generate a candidate hired:	32%

2. Percentage of search engagements in which the search resulted in someone hired who was:

"Good enough"	49%
"Not good enough"	51%

3. Percentage of search engagements in which the search resulted in newly hired managers (produced by retained search firms) who turned out to be:

A players	17%
Less than A players	83%

My sample, disproportionately weighted with premier firms, showed about one-third of all searches resulted in no successful candidate produced by the search firm. The search firm is paid, but does not deliver. Sometimes an internal candidate gets the job.

Theoretically such a search might not be "failed"; if the company thinks it has an A player internal candidate and invests $100,000 in a search that confirms that he/she is among the top 10 percent available, fine. In my experience, however, the internal candidate is apt to be a B player and a search produced no A-player candidates. The search firm "discovers" the best candidate is internal. Most of these "exploratory" searches are a waste of money and qualify as failed. Occasionally the company restructures, eliminating the job. This is not the search firm's fault, but the search dollars were wasted.

In this survey about one-half of the time the search firms produce someone who is hired and is "good enough"; that means only one-half of searches are reasonably successful, and one-half are not. When search firms are retained, only 17 percent of the time A players are supposedly hired. I say "supposedly," because CEOs and presidents say the number is 10 percent, with human resources professionals reporting 40 percent were A players. In this little study, the HR people were happier with results of the search firms *they* hired.[1] At the risk of oversimplification, premier firms represented in my study tended to report much better results from search firms than did mediocre companies. The premier firms tended to follow the best practices reported in this chapter, whereas the mediocre companies tended to suffer from the "typical recruitment scenario" portrayed at the beginning of this chapter.

---

[1] A tendency for Human Resources people to be a little more lenient than CEOs regarding success of managers hired might be supported by a Center for Creative Leadership study. As reported in *Fortune* (June 22, 1998), p. 26. HR professionals said about 40 percent of new management hires fail in the first 18 months. "Fail" meant being terminated for performance, performing significantly below expectation, or voluntarily resigning—maybe with a discrete push from above.

Challenged with these dismal statistics, A-player search executives fire back:

- "Only half of marriages succeed, so why should our statistics be any better?"
- "B-player hiring managers say they want A players but won't hire one that threatens their status. This search firm shouldn't be blamed in this case."
- "Hiring managers initially say they will be flexible on budgets and other resources, but then restrict new hires who can't perform. When clients misrepresent the job, it's not the search firm's fault when there is a mis-hire."
- "We produce A-player candidates who have other job offers and need to meet our client *now*, but the client is too disorganized to schedule a visit and loses good candidates."
- "Many times I have tried to put the client through the paces of job analysis and construction of meaningful competencies, but the client is lazy. It's clear they haven't really thought through the job requirements, and when I try to pin them down they become evasive and defensive."
- "We in the search industry have done a poor job of instructing clients on how they can get the best results."

I believe A-player search executives accept assignments only where they are very confident they will succeed. It's the C-player search people who incur the wrath of CEOs who complain:

- "Large search firms are ethically prohibited from penetrating their client companies, but they don't tell you which ones are on their 'lock-out list' unless you ask."[2]
- "I asked for a lock-out list and found that the search firm was ethically forbidden to search in two-thirds of all *Fortune* 500 companies in our industry—their current clients. So, their pool of potential A players is one-third of what we expected."
- "Some large companies hire *every* large search firm for one search every other year, just to keep them from pirating their A players. You have to pay to keep the vultures away."
- "They know darned well a B-player manager won't hire an A, but they take the assignment anyway."

---

[2] The Association of Executive Search Consultants' (AESC) published Code of Ethics states: "Disclose to present and prospective clients information known to the member about relationships, circumstances or interests that might create actual or potential conflicts of interest. . . . "

- "Instead of pushing clients to figure out if the job is really needed, they take the fee and don't care if the search is canceled."

- "Their lock-out list contains only the divisions they worked in. If they found a manager for Division X, they feel entitled to steal a manager from Division Y. They say they need to ask about talent in other divisions to understand the total company and then go after our people in other divisions for their other clients."

- "The search partner is the salesperson; he closes the search deal and then low-level associates do all the work. But those associates aren't sharp enough to get to the executive A players and entice them away from good jobs."[3]

- "The search industry is the only industry I can think of that hasn't undergone a major transformation in 30 years. It attracts C players from the business world—sales types who can make a quarter of a million bucks a year selling searches while mostly playing golf."

- "They don't do thorough background checks and don't protect us from negligent hiring suits."

- "If they are hired by corporate HR, they don't view divisions as clients, so the division gets terrible service."

- "Reference calls by search firms are a joke. They never kill a candidate. They use reference calls to bolster, not screen, finalist candidates. They occasionally throw in an example of how reference calls eliminated a candidate, but the person was an obvious misfit to begin with."

- "The percentage of salary commission structure, 30 to 33 percent of first-year compensation, motivates search people to ignore superb talent that is cheaper in favor of acceptable talent that is much more expensive."

- "Search executives sometimes do long interviews, documenting accomplishments, but there is too much hype, no mention of failures, no mention of mistakes, and too much concealment of weaknesses that we see within weeks of hiring someone."[4]

Although CEOs are critical of the executive search industry, premier companies manage to find A-player search professionals and get good results. But there are many links in the recruitment chain, and one rusty or nonexistent link can result in a mis-hire. What's the solution? The remainder of this chapter offers several.

---

[3] The AESC Code of Ethics requires members to define "the scope and character of services to be provided."

[4] AESC Code of Ethics requires members to "thoroughly evaluate potential candidates, including careful assessment of the candidate's strengths and weaknesses."

PROMOTE FROM WITHIN

The most obvious and common alternative to external recruitment is to promote from within. Historically, premier companies have "grown their own." They promote people they have worked with, and these people know the company well and understand jobs to which they are promoted. So, "promote from within" results in a much higher success rate than can external recruitment.

Promote-from-within companies recruit externally, but their focus has typically been on recent college graduates or MBAs. Half of those recent college graduates and MBAs are gone within four years, but so what? These are trainees, and the consequences of high turnover and mistakes in the entry positions are not serious. There wasn't even a search fee, although executive time in campus recruitment is not negligible. As budding young managers grow in various assignments, their performance is carefully monitored. Chapter 6 describes the General Electric process for rigorous assessment of internal talent. Growing your own is still the best game in town.

Premier professional services firms do a particularly good job of initially recruiting entry-level professionals and later promoting from within. Consider the approach of a very private, very successful investment bank— I'll call it Acme. Acme screens hundreds of recent college graduates for each entry analyst it hires. Acme wants very smart, very driven team players. A senior partner told me with a grin, "We like insecure overachievers." Applicants would kill to join this prestigious firm, in which the average annual partner bonus can exceed $5 million. The analysts work up to 80 hours per week for the two-year job; almost all complete the two years, but some are wheezing and gasping and are happy to have Acme on their résumé and move on. All are scrutinized by Acme to determine who might be the long-term A players. After two years as an analyst, the next step is to get the finest MBA, at Harvard, Stanford, Wharton, or University of Chicago. During the MBA years, Acme is in touch, continuously recruiting the cream of the crop, the best of the best of their former analysts, their future partners. Acme not only has its pick among MBAs from the finest schools, it has a four-year dossier on most candidates. Acme hires the "best and brightest" who are A players at every level as they rise to partner.

Many professional-services firms embrace topgrading principles, "because our assets ride up and down the elevators every day." All they have is human capital and a few PCs, and they know it. The rest of the business world is waking up to that reality. Financial reports of manufacturers may list people as costs, and their capital equipment, real estate, and brand franchises may be listed as assets, but the truth is, human capital is all *any* company has. Coca-Cola and Nike may have powerful brand images, worth zillions, but parachute C players into their management ranks and watch how quickly the brand value dissipates.

SAY GOOD-BYE TO EXCLUSIVELY PROMOTING FROM WITHIN

Large companies in all industries and professional-services firms in particular will continue to promote from within, and they should. But the landscape is changing, forcing companies to "go outside" more and more. Fewer and fewer companies are certain what business they will be in five or ten years from now. Even if external hiring of managers increases from 5 percent to 20 percent, topgrading will become all the more critical. If companies enjoy a 75 percent to 80 percent success rate with internal promotions, and experience a typical 50 percent success rate through external recruitment and selection, the trend to go outside more could bludgeon earnings.

Sure, McDonald's will still need store managers ten years from now. And Boeing has already contracted to build planes far into the future, so hiring engineers and later recruiting internally for engineering managers is a good bet. But General Electric evolved from a small appliances company, to a heavy manufacturing conglomerate; by the time Jack Welch retires in the year 2000, GE will be much more of a financial and hi-tech services company. Royal Bank of Canada for 125 years grew managers to run "brick and mortar" branches; in the 1990s computerized banking was taking over, totally new banking skills were required, and the company began recruiting more externally than ever before. The Travelers Express case study in Chapter 6 is not at all unusual—CEO Bob Bohannon had to find a new strategy, and half the senior managers developed internally were removed. Hewitt Associates, cited in *100 Best Companies to Work for in America*, has changed strategy, moving into outsourcing. For the first time in its history, Hewitt is aggressively hiring outsiders. The point:

> ► Since strategy is changing faster for most companies, skills to implement it are new, thus requiring more external recruitment.

Confidential strategic plans for two dozen of my clients call for dramatic changes, requiring new competencies. To satisfy their need for new competencies some firms launch major training programs, hoping to continue promoting from within. Almost all, at a minimum, use external hiring to "salt the mines" with the skills to pursue a new strategy. Some look at outsourcing or tapping career "free agents" for extended consulting assignments. Some (Cisco Systems, for example) have acquired companies, mostly to buy the new talent. Silicon Valley companies, desperate for talent to accommodate a new strategy, growth, or both willingly pay three or four search firms $500,000 each, annually. It can be a feeding frenzy, this external hunt for talent.

Recruitment, of course, simply produces the bodies, the candidates for selection, whether the recruits come from internal or external sources. Superb recruitment is not sufficient, but it can improve the selection ratio from, say, 1 hired out of 10 candidates recruited, to 1 in 50 or even 1 in 500. But with an intolerably high failure rate in external hiring, the "selection" component of recruitment/selection is crucial. Chapters 11 and 12 present the CIDS interview for truly revealing insights into candidates. Some premier organizations have figured it out—how to recruit and select the right way, and that involves sorting out proper roles.

CEO ROLE IN RECRUITMENT

Until an organization is topgraded, B and C players will prevent the hiring of A players. As Chapter 2 indicated, this is the #1 obstacle to topgrading. Until there is a "critical mass" of A players who can overwhelm the mediocrity of C players in the hiring process, the CEO must be actively at the recruitment helm. The CEO role in recruitment is to:

- Take responsibility for topgrading success, including internal and external recruitment results, policies, and processes. The CEO must drive a recruitment best-practices blueprint.
- Set specific management hiring goals—numbers to be hired, diversity (I prefer "inclusivity") goals, and the requirement that only A players, or people with A potential will be hired.
- Hold all managers accountable for topgrading (including recruitment success).
- Monitor topgrading progress (hiring As, culling Cs).
- Devote one-quarter of work time to topgrading (Jack Welch estimates one-third of his time).
- Provide incentives for topgrading (some companies award one-third of the management bonus in part to topgrading).
- Minimize the use of external recruiters by personally encouraging everyone in management to build his or her networks, keep his or her Rolodexes updated, and recruit like mad.
- Occasionally call the big plays (override subordinate hiring decisions to be sure all A players are hired).
- Be sure all vendors (recruiters, management psychologists) understand that the CEO is the key client, so that if there are attempts to undercut topgrading, they are required to notify the CEO.

The CEO must make management recruitment a top priority and must keep it there. Ann Drake, CEO of DSC Logistics, generates one or two management candidates from most industry meetings she attends. She has exactly the right perspective, one to be emulated by every manager: "I recruit all day long, every day, with everybody I meet." Ted Waitt is Gateway's most effective recruiter. Bill Gates personally calls recent college graduates—"Hi, this is Bill Gates. I can sure use you at Microsoft."

The CEO can drive recruitment through regular (monthly in a corporate turnaround, quarterly otherwise) topgrading meetings. Whirlpool Corporation has the "bunker," a 15' × 25' room in which the only topic of discussion permissible is talent. This locked room has the A, B, C players' pictures, with ratings of promotability.

What happens in the CEO's topgrading meeting? Let's back up. Strategy produces an organization structure that results in organization charts with boxes—jobs—to fill, this year and maybe five years from now. A simple coding is A, B, C player in present job, with promotability indicated by numbers (1, 2, 3) or by color (yellow for promotable one or two levels, green for promotable to executive committee level, and red for someone who has plateaued).

In the topgrading meeting performance appraisals, psychologists' assessments and task-force accomplishments are introduced to compare people. This establishes a common standard across functions and divisions. "Intelligence" on competitors' teams is introduced, to compare talent. The CEO is the final arbiter of how strong a manager has to be to qualify as an A player, what happens to C players (termination, transfer, demotion, forced retirement), or exactly when someone is to be promoted.

In topgrading meetings the CEO asks, in any number of different ways:

- Do we have the talent to meet our strategic goals? Will we have it?
- How successful are we at recruiting people, internally and externally? What is our hiring batting average?
- Where are we strong and weak in management?
- Which A players should be promoted, and to what jobs, in order to retain and develop them, but not put them over their head?
- How many external searches should we do, for what jobs?
- Have we made progress in culling the chronic C players? Why not? Who's responsible?
- Should we consider acquiring a company mostly for its talent?
- Are we all in a full-court press for recruitment by developing and using our networks to generate candidates? Can we bypass search firms?
- Are we managing the search firms for our benefit?
- How are we progressing on developing an internal "bench," so we can have an optimal blend of promoting people from within and enriching the mix with talent from outside?
- For specific jobs, do we need A players at higher ($150,000) or lower ($100,000) levels, in bigger or smaller leagues?
- Do our HR systems (compensation, performance management) reinforce topgrading?

- How are we doing in all these areas? Do we have the right measurements? What do they tell us? Is there progress or not? Why not?
- Which managers are topgrading and which are not?

HIRING MANAGER'S ROLE IN RECRUITMENT

As the hiring manager, you must fully "own" your hiring decisions. You will be the boss, the manager who will conduct the performance appraisals of the people you hire and your overall performance will depend on your hiring success. Of course, any hiring manager can adopt the perspective of the CEO, but have authority over a smaller domain. Your company might not be topgraded, but your department, division, or function can be. Your topgrading meeting simply becomes a regular part of your staff meeting. Your recruitment role is to:

- Hire A players, at the right level. It's your job to overcome the obstacles. No excuses.
- Continually build your network of potential A-player candidates, lessening dependence on search firms. Keep a talent Rolodex of dozens of names. "Recruit like mad," for life. If Bill Gates and Ann Drake can make the time to do it, so can you.
- Work with HR to analyze the job and write behaviorally based job descriptions. Entire books are written on how to analyze a job, but the basic steps are straightforward—talk to incumbents and former incumbents, ask informed coworkers for their insights, obtain best practices information, ask HR consultants and search firms to contribute. See Appendix F for an example of behaviorally anchored competencies.
- Manage search firms.
- Conduct a CIDS interview of every finalist.
- Conduct three to six reference calls, with previous bosses (and perhaps peers, subordinates, customers) and try to talk with a peer or boss who left the present employer.
- Conduct candidate evaluation meetings at the end of visits.
- Evaluate yourself on your hiring success (bring out the Candidate Assessment Scorecard six months later to learn where assessments were accurate, or not, and conduct your own cost of mis-hire studies).

HOW TO MANAGE SEARCH FIRMS

The CEO should establish policy for managing recruiters, and HR typically screens search firms and negotiates contracts. However, each hiring manager is on the front line, the day-to-day client of a recruiter. For retained-fee recruiters (who get paid even if the job is not filled) there are many ways to achieve a high level of professionalism:

- Favor boutique firms of fewer than ten professionals. Large search firms have some A players, but if they can't invade their premier clients to attract A players for you, their value is diminished. Use large search firms to fill positions in which industry-specific competencies are not required: for example, functional positions such as director of human resources or vice president/controller. Be wary of firms specializing in an industry (computer software), because many top companies might be their clients and therefore locked out of your search.

- Require a written list of client companies they cannot penetrate—their "lock-out" list—before you or HR signs a contract.

- Check references of the key search executive before signing a contract.

- Sign a contract that requires the professionals you want to do the work (and not delegate it to underlings you haven't met or approved).

- Sign a fixed-fee contract, removing the incentive for the search firm to find more expensive candidates.

- Require original job descriptions plus several dozen competencies, written after a minimum of two full days of on-premise meetings with hiring managers and key team members.

- Expect the search executive to consider the CEO the major client, the 800-pound gorilla, but also to serve you (the hiring manager) and HR as clients.

- Require the firm to produce A-player candidates to help achieve your diversity (inclusivity) goals. For example, if your company needs more women in management, require that a certain percentage of candidates they present are female.

- Require weekly updates—names and discussions of prospects, not just statistics ("We screened 100 people").

- Insist on CIDS interviews of all finalists (including mistakes and failures, not just career accomplishments). Tell the search executive, "If you cannot motivate candidates to disclose failures and shortcomings, you're not the right professional for us." Be reasonable—don't punish search firms when they present candidates with shortcomings. After all, there is no perfect candidate.

- Require reports to disclose at least six *real* weaker points—everyone has at least that many.

- Require reference check summaries that disclose negatives, not just positives.

- Sign a contract requiring the search firm to not steal your company's employees for three years. Your entire company, not just your division, is locked out for them. So, if a search firm does a search for GE Capital, it cannot target managers at GE Medical Systems or any other GE entity, for three years.

- Evaluate some résumés and review some telephone screens early on to be sure you're "on the same page" with the search firm.
- Be accessible to meet with candidates.
- Be professional. Meet with search people to do job analyses, etc. Return their calls promptly.

So, who are A-player search executives? One is Fred Wackerle of Fred Wackerle, Inc., Chicago. *Business Week* noted that he was ranked by large company executives among the top five executive-search professionals in the United States. Interestingly, Wackerle has received awards by the search professional association AESC, yet he is far different from his fellow professionals. Fred Wackerle:

- Has 35 years' experience
- Signs fixed-fee contracts (no financial incentive to jack up the starting salary)
- Does the work himself (refreshing!)
- Takes on no more than three search assignments at one time
- Is ethically forbidden from penetrating only 10–12 firms in the world

HOW TO MANAGE MANAGEMENT PSYCHOLOGISTS

Are the management psychologists the good guys, riding to the rescue—sorting the As, Bs, Cs search firms produced so hiring managers can be sure only A players are hired? Sometimes. We are a mixed bag, however, with our A, B, C players. As in the search industry, C-player psychologists work in a sea of mediocrity. C-player managers find C-level management psychologists who will not recommend hiring A players who might get the C player's job. The CEO should be the main client, always, to guard against C-player managers manipulating HR, search firms, and psychologists in order to hire C players.

My personal bias is in favor of CIDS interviews and against reliance on psychological tests for upper-management hires. Tests, properly validated, are terrific predictors of job performance at the lowest levels—factory worker, salesperson, typist. For management jobs, tests such as Myers Briggs Type Indicator are fine in workshops—"thinkers" go to that corner and "feelers" go over there, and you all talk to each other to learn how people with different thinking styles can communicate better. But for management selection, tests are dull instruments. The psychologist should know the company strategy, culture, the hiring manager, the job, and the competencies, and then use the CIDS interview to reveal fit and no-fit factors. I have never heard of a psychologist relying on eight test profiles and a one-hour interview achieving a very good batting average in assessing managers.

In short, require your psychologist to use a CIDS interview. And, track the accuracy of the psychologist's report—pull it out six months after a person has been hired and require 90 percent (or better) accuracy.

HUMAN RESOURCES ROLE

A-player HR professionals are increasingly valuable. I know of 15 companies in which the HR person is the "right arm" of the president or CEO. In most premier companies the senior HR manager is on a par with peers in terms of overall influence, and pay. A major reason for HR's ascendancy in respect is their effectiveness in motivating managers to hire A players. They sell, cajole, challenge, coach, and browbeat their client managers to topgrade. The A-player HR role in recruitment is to:

- "Partner" with hiring managers, serving those managers to be sure A players are hired.
- Drive recruitment through upholding A-player standards, encouraging hiring managers to "recruit for life."
- Embody "recruit for life" as a role model.
- Topgrade HR with diversity (inclusivity), serving as a role model, recruiting all A players for HR.
- Coordinate job analyses and the creation of job descriptions that really describe the job, have up to 50 competencies, state major challenges, spell out first-year bonus accountabilities, and build Candidate Assessment Scorecards (Chapter 3).
- Create strong recruitment sources (prescreen search firms, find A-player search professionals, build powerful image in college-campus recruitment and Web sites, consider hiring full-time research firms—recruiters on an hourly pay contract). Many top HR professionals actually negotiate contracts with recruiters. My point in suggesting that the hiring manager *require* certain contractual terms is to make you, not HR, ultimately responsible for *your* hiring success. In practice after a CEO requires certain contractual terms, HR negotiates them and hiring managers like you simply check, to be sure the terms are met.
- Provide internal recruiters, when appropriate, for outside searches.
- Explore "bounty" systems ($1,000 to employee if an A-player referral is hired).
- Lead design of topgrading systems surrounding recruitment.
- Calibrate the level of pay for A players at the right level ("Is an A player at $100K necessary . . . or $150K?"); tap personal network and acquire pay surveys to get the money-talent ratio right.
- Coach team (peers and boss) on structure.
- Coach team on legalities of hiring/firing.
- Coach team on achieving diversity (inclusivity) goals.

- Organize interviewing training.
- Coordinate topgrading meetings.
- Coordinate visits of candidates.
- Coordinate assimilation of new hires.
- Coordinate psychological assessment/coaching.
- Assure background checks, drug tests, physical exams.
- Monitor topgrading success; track each hiring manager's "batting average" and summarize company results periodically.

HR managers are not the driving force behind recruitment, the CEO is, but HR can coach, educate, and support their internal clients. HR can further support recruitment by assuring that HR systems impacting recruitment are world-class. Those HR systems are:

- *Performance management*, to be sure it is fair and hard-hitting in identifying A, B, C players.

- *Management development*, to be sure Bs and As are powerfully developed, in order to qualify as A players when the bar is higher—when the company is bigger, when the jobs are more complex.

- *Succession planning*, to be sure promotions achieve what is intended— A players succeed in bigger jobs, the "system" is fair, A players are retained because they grow, C players are put in jobs where they can be As, and that the company has the right "bench strength."

- *Compensation*, to assure that packages (including benefits, stock, perks) reward desired behavior leading to the company's success (including pursuing the right strategy, achieving sufficient talent, and maintaining a high-performance organization culture).

- *Mid-year career review*, to adjust conclusions about each manager's career goals, strengths, and weaker points and to create a comprehensive development plan for the person's next 12 months. (The reason it is mid-year is to have career discussions separated from the tension of annual performance reviews, bonus awards, pay increases, and promotions).

HR must be a topgraded function, because the top HR executive will be in the limelight, driving integrity into each system that affects recruitment. Inequities in performance appraisals come to light in topgrading meetings. If a B player should be replaced through external recruitment or given another chance depends on the management development system's power. If someone is considered a C player because of being a poor team player, yet the compensation system rewards *not* cooperating with other departments, change the compensation system.

A RECRUITMENT BEST-PRACTICES BLUEPRINT

Let's get organized. Having discussed the roles of CEO, hiring manager, and HR, and having provided advice on how to get the best results from search firms, a blueprint for structuring the entire recruitment process can now be laid out. This blueprint:

- Further breaks down your responsibilities as hiring manager and those of your key partner, Human Resources
- Outlines a practical visit schedule, assuming two visits to the company by a finalist
- Proposes an interviewer-focus matrix, in which each interviewer delves into a competency rather than "wing it"
- Presents a sample structured interview guide for one of those shorter structured focused interviews

Exactly how to conduct good interviews, the CIDS interview or the shorter structured interviews, is covered in Chapters 11 and 12, and Chapter 13 spells out important legal considerations.

Let's begin with how responsibilities are typically "divvied up" between Human Resources and the hiring manager. Figure 5.1 summarizes it.

1. You, the hiring manager, determine that a job needs to be filled, so you complete the necessary requisition forms and submit them to HR.

2. Job analysis is performed, with HR working closely with you. For a new management job, three or four hours of analysis can produce a "real" job description, rather than "boilerplate." The two of you modify my generic list of 50 competencies in Appendix E, writing behavioral definitions of what it will take to do the job. If HR is to do preliminary screening, step #2 can assure that you are both "singing out of the same hymnal."

3. HR posts the job, to produce internal candidates.

4. Recruitment of outside candidates is apt to initially be done by you and HR. You will tap your personal network—oftentimes the *only* way to quickly hire an external A player. Keep your Rolodex full and updated. If this approach fails, HR might ask an internal recruiter to help you. Too often HR departments are *not* held accountable for success of new hires, and selection is not driven toward excellence. Your job is on the line, and an internal recruiter should feel accountable to *you* to find A-player candidates.

5. If recruitment of internal candidates (#3) and use of your network and other internal recruiters of outside candidates fails, a search firm is hired. The search firm should view the CEO as the main client, but on a day-

Figure 5.1 Responsibilities of Hiring Manager and Human Resources

	Hiring Manager	Human Resources
1. Requisition Forms ... completed by	x	
... submitted to		x
2. Job Analysis, Job Description, Competencies created by	x	x
3. Posting		x
4. Internal Recruitment	Network	Ads
5. Search Firms hired and managed by	x	x
6. Screen Résumés	x	x
7. Screen Career History Forms	x	x
8. Telephone Interview (in-person interview, if local)	Technical	Routine
9. Coordinate Visits		x
10. Visit #1: Structured Short Interviews coordinated by		x
Written Evaluations collected by		x
Decision to Continue or Reject Candidate	x	
11. Visit #2: Exchange of Perspectives Interviews coordinated by		x
CIDS Interview	x	
Written Evaluations collected by		x
Decision to Continue or Reject Candidate	x	
12. Factual Record Checks		x
13. In-Depth Reference Checks	x	
14. Psychological Appraisal coordinated by		x
15. Meeting to Decide Hire/Not Hire coordinated by		x
Decision to Hire/Not Hire	x	
16. Retain Records		x
17. Send Rejection Letters/Offers		x
18. Research Hiring Success	x	x

to-day basis you and HR are the key contacts and operational clients. You and HR both manage the search firm (using guidelines presented in this chapter).

6. Don't delegate all of the résumé screening to HR, or to a search firm. Share the responsibility initially, to be sure HR is screening internal and internally generated candidates the way *you* want. Same for search firms with external candidates.

7. Same as #6 with Career History Forms (application forms). How to use the Career History Form (Appendix B) is discussed in Chapter 11.

8. Search firms screen, but for internal searches (conducted by you and HR), initial telephone screens can be done by HR. However, if you are a lot better equipped to determine technical expertise (engineering, finance, and the like), you could screen quickly on this essential competency and HR could screen on other competencies. Short "verbal surgery" telephone interviews are appropriate here. If you are apt to be

"selling" the interviewee, try to arrange a face-to-face interview—more time consuming for an initial screen, but worth it if you are strapped for viable candidates. *All* interviewers should write a brief report, and HR should collect them. You decide if you want to proceed with each prospect.

9. HR can coordinate visits to the company. The two one-day visits are typically a month apart. If there is a decision to proceed with visit #2, it usually takes a month for calendars to align all of the interviews. In a time crunch, however, for an apparently outstanding candidate, visit #1 and visit #2 could be combined into a single two-day visit. The risk, of course, is that after the first day you may reject the candidate. Sending the candidate home in the middle of a two-day visit is more awkward than not inviting a person back after a one-day visit. And, the extraordinary effort to coordinate two days of interviews is wasted.

10. For the initial day of interviews, both HR and you are apt to be on the schedule. You will have already talked with the candidate, so you are on a first-name basis. By now you know how to balance your question asking versus question answering, your screening versus selling the candidate on you and the job. You are apt to take the candidate to breakfast, and at the end of the day talk with all interviewers and review their written reports. HR will be one of the interviews during the day and handle coordination of the schedule and collect reports. You decide whether to drop the candidate or continue.

11. In the second visit, a couple more short structured interviews are conducted, along with the CIDS interview—conducted by you. Some companies place the CIDS interview the morning of visit #1, so the hiring manager can cancel all subsequent interviews if the candidate "washes out." The visit #2 CIDS interview is for well-oiled topgrading machines, where very few visit #2 candidates are eliminated. The advantage is more data available, so the visit #2 CIDS interview is a little more revealing. Additional "sharing-perspectives" interviews are appropriate—no more grilling the candidate, but instead several prospective coworkers talking with the candidate as colleagues. Then HR collects the reports and, again, you decide to continue the selection process or reject the candidate.

12. Factual record checks should be done by HR (or the search firm). "Factual" means obtaining confirmation of education records, dates of employment, and so forth.

13. In-depth reference checks are conducted by you, the CIDS interviewer. Only you can bond with the candidate's previous bosses and only you can ask the really penetrating questions. The interviewee actually coordinates those interviews (see Chapter 12 on Reference Checking). Any reference checks conducted by internal recruiters or search firms are considered preliminary.

14. If a psychological appraisal is conducted, it is at this "final check" time.

15. A final meeting to hire/not hire and compare various candidates is coordinated by HR, but *you* make the decision.

16–18. HR retains all records (EEOC, and the like), and sends out rejection/offer letters. Top HR departments also track hiring success, so you and they and the company can continually refine the selection systems and achieve that 90–95 percent success rate. Even if HR does not, you should track your own success.

Figure 5.2 is a typical Candidate Visit Schedule. HR should coordinate it, but it usually requires the hiring manager—you—to motivate your peers to serve as interviewers, be on time, write a brief report, meet at the end of the day.

Figure 5.2 Candidate Visit Schedule

VISIT #1

2 weeks before:	*Hiring committee meets.* Hiring manager reviews status of search (how many prospects, how good they are), revisits importance of job to strategy, and organizes visit #1—who is available to interview, who should focus on what competencies, distributes paperwork (résumé, job description, Candidate Assessment Scorecard). HR is partner and "quality control coach," but also keeps the calendar, reminds interviewers of schedule, scrambles to replace interviewer if one becomes ill, etc.
7:30–9:00 A.M.	*Hiring manager* picks up candidate, goes to breakfast, drives candidate to offices, reviews schedule for day with candidate.
9:00–10:00	*Interview #1: Intellectual Competencies*
10:00–10:15	Interviewer completes written summary; candidate gets short break.
10:15–11:00	*Interview #2: Personal Competencies*
11:00–11:15	Summary/break
11:15 A.M.–12:15 P.M.	*Interview #3: Interpersonal Competencies*
12:15–12:30	Summary/break
12:30–2:00	*Interview #4: Management and Additional Leadership Competencies* (during lunch)
2:00–2:15	Summary/break
2:15–3:15	*Interview #5: Motivational Competencies*
3:15–3:30	Summary/break
3:30–4:15	*Meeting.* Hiring executive and candidate (Wrap-up—"Let's touch base tomorrow to talk about next steps"). Candidate takes tour of facility.
4:15–5:00	*Hiring committee meets.* Hiring manager reviews all interviewer summaries with Committee, to get all opinions on person's strengths, weaker points, fit, and consensus on whether to

proceed with visit #2. Discussion of how best to "sell" attractive candidates and how family needs of candidate can be addressed (help spouse get job, introduce kids to coaches, make real-estate agent available).

VISIT #2	
2 weeks before	(same as for Visit #1)
7:30–11:30 A.M.	*Interview #6:* Hiring manager conducts Chronological In-Depth Structured (CIDS) interview followed by answering questions by interviewee.
11:30–12:00	Interviewer completes Summary.
11:30–11:45	Candidate break
11:45 A.M.–1:30 P.M.	*Interview #7: Exchange of perspectives* (over lunch)
1:30–1:45	Summary/break
1:45–2:45	*Interview #8: Exchange of perspectives*
2:45–3:00	Summary/break
3:00–4:00	*Interview #9: Exchange of perspectives*
4:00–4:15	Summary
	Hiring executive and candidate meet for brief wrap-up.
4:15–5:15	*Hiring committee.* Hiring manager runs meeting to summarize all data from both visits, refine consensus on candidate strengths, weaker points and fit, decide whether to proceed with in-depth reference checks and psychological appraisal, and discuss how to best "sell" candidate on joining company.

An Interviewer Focus Matrix (Figure 5.3) may help to clarify what the one-hour shorter structured interviews cover in relation to the CIDS interviews. Both you and the management psychologist (if one is used) conduct the full CIDS interview, which as you see in Appendix A covers all competencies—intellectual, personal, interpersonal, and so forth. The shorter structured interviews focus on *one* group of competencies, although Figure 5.3 shows that *all* interviewers are apt to get some insights into interpersonal competencies.

What specific questions do the shorter structured interviews cover? These interview guides really should be created for each job—by you and HR. Appendix F presents a sample hiring process for Wm. M. Mercer, including the specific questions to be asked to investigate each competency—a short structured interview guide. Figure 5.4 is another example—all of the focused questions on intellectual competencies taken from focused questions section of the CIDS Interview Guide (Appendix A). And, let me repeat, Chapter 13 highlights simple but important legal guidelines.

Figure 5.3 Interviewer Focus Matrix

	Intellectual Competencies	Personal Competencies	Interpersonal Competencies	Management and Additional Leadership Competencies	Motivational Competencies	Exchange of Perspectives	Visit
#1 Chuck	X		X				#1
#2 Leslie		X	X				#1
#3 Geoff			X (major focus)				#1
#4 Bill			X	X			#1
#5 Chris			X		X		#1
#6 You (CIDS)	X	X	X	X	X	X	#2
#7 Mary			X			X	#2
#8 Pete			X			X	#2
#9 Kate			X			X	#2
#10 Psychologist	X	X	X	X	X	X	After visit #2

Figure 5.4 Sample Short Structured Interview Guide

Applicant _____ Interviewer _____

Date _____

Interview Focus: Intellectual Characteristics

Scale: 6 = Excellent; 5 = Very Good; 4 = Good; 3 = Only Fair; 2 = Poor; 1 = Very Poor

Rating _____

_____ **1. Intelligence**
   a. Please describe your **learning ability.**_____
   b. Describe a **complex situation** in which you had to learn a lot, quickly . . . how did you go about learning, and how successful were the outcomes?_____

_____ **2. Analysis skills**
   a. Please describe your **problem analysis** skills. _____
   b. Do people generally regard you as one who diligently pursues every **detail**, or do you tend to be more **broad brush**? Why? _____
   c. What will references indicate are your style and overall effectiveness in "**sorting**" the wheat from the chaff? _____
   d. What **analytic approaches** and tools do you use? _____
   e. Please give me an example of **digging** more **deeply** for facts than what was asked of you._____

_____ **3. Judgment/Decision Making**
   a. Please describe your **decision-making** approach when you are faced with difficult situations . . . in comparison with others . . . at about your level in the organization. Are you decisive and quick, but sometimes too quick, or are you more thorough but sometimes too slow? Are you intuitive or go purely with the facts? Do you involve many or few people in decisions? _____
   b. What are a couple of the **most difficult** or **challenging** decisions you have made recently? _____
   c. What are a couple of the **best** and **worst** decisions you have made in the past year? _____
   d. What **maxims** do you live by?_____

_____ **4. Conceptual Ability**
       Are you more comfortable dealing with concrete, tangible, short-term, or more abstract, **conceptual** long-term issues? Please explain._____

_____ **5. Creativity**
   a. How **creative** are you? What are the best examples of your creativity in processes, systems, methods, products, structure, services?_____
   b. Do you consider yourself a better **visionary** or implementer . . . and why? _____

_____ **6. Strategic Skills**

a. In the past year, what specifically have you done in order to remain **knowledgeable** about the competitive environment, market and trade dynamics, products (services) and technology trends, innovations, and patterns of consumer behavior? _____

b. Please describe your **experience** in strategic thinking, including successful and unsuccessful approaches. (Determine the individual's contribution to team strategic efforts.)_____

c. Where do you predict that your **(industry/competitors/function) is going** in the next three years? What is the "**conventional wisdom**" and what are your own thoughts? _____

_____ **7. Pragmatism**

Do you consider yourself a more **visionary** or a more **pragmatic** thinker . . . and why?_____

_____ **8. Risk Taking**

What are the **biggest risks** you have taken in recent years? Include ones that have worked out well and not so well. _____

_____ **9. Leading Edge**

a. How have you copied, created, or applied **best practices**? _____

b. Describe projects in which your **best-practice solutions** did and did not fully address customer/client needs. _____

c. How will references rate your **technical expertise** . . . are you truly leading edge, or do you fall a bit short in some areas? _____

d. How **computer literate** are you? _____

e. Please describe your professional **network**. _____

_____ **10. Education**

a. What **seminars** or formal **education** have you participated in (and when)? _____

b. Describe your **reading habits** (books and articles—global factors, general business, function, industry)._____

_____ **11. Experience**

a. (Compose a series of **open-ended questions**—"How would you rate yourself in _____, and what specifics can you cite?" For Finance, learn expertise in Treasury, Controller, Risk Management, etc., areas. For Human Resources, learn expertise in Selection, Training, Compensation, etc.

• Question:_____? _____
  _____

• Question:_____? _____
  _____

• Question:_____? _____
  _____

b. What are the most important **lessons** you have learned in your career (get specifics with respect to when, where, what, etc.)?_____

_____ **12. "Track Record"**
Looking back in your career, what were your **most and least successful** jobs? _____

Other Competencies Observed

Rating	Competency	Comments
_____	_____	_____
		_____
_____	_____	_____
		_____
_____	_____	_____
		_____
_____	_____	_____
		_____
_____	_____	_____
		_____

When do you "sell" a candidate? Always, from the very first contact, throughout every interview, and even after an offer has been accepted. Chapters 11 and 12 emphasize the importance of not interrupting the CIDS interview much to "sell," but instead asking all your questions and then inviting the candidate to ask you questions. There are no hard and fast rules, however, except one: You can best sell candidates by having keen insight into their needs, and that comes from CIDS interviews. The recruitment mating game fluctuates between selling and probing, selling and probing. Silicon Valley is in such a talent-hunt frenzy that selling is emphasized more than probing, assessing, screening. It's not a matter of either/or. You can do both. A players *want you* to assess them.

Your professionalism and thoroughness help sell candidates. You don't stop selling when the new hire arrives on the job, not these days. Employers the candidate rejected in favor of your company haven't necessarily given up. Maybe their full-court press is still on! So keep selling the candidate. The recruitment process is typically considered over *after* an assimilation process. A typical assimilation schedule, driven by HR, is:

1. *Before the first day.* You discuss any significant weaknesses noted on the Candidate Assessment Scorecard with your new hire. Attempt to diffuse problems or "debug" the person before he or she starts the job. This helps get the person off to a good start. A players want this.

2. *First week.* Discuss specifically (1) company strategy, (2) specific accountabilities of the new hire, and (3) potential culture-clash issues identified on the Candidate Assessment Scorecard.

3. *Week #12.* Have management psychologist debrief the person on his or her in-depth assessment. Identify successes and problems. Agree on items to go into developmental plan. Be sure the newly hired manager is both an A player and committed to the job.

4. *Week #14.* New hire meets with you, the hiring manager, to discuss the developmental plan, complete with (1) what will happen, (2) why, and (3) by when, and (4) how results will be measured. This is an important coaching opportunity (see Chapters 9 and 10) and it includes a 360-degree component. This assimilation coaching is the time to be 100 percent sure the newly hired manager is on board, to stay.

CHAPTER 5 CHECKLIST: ARE YOU A BEST-PRACTICES RECRUITER?

Yes	No		
❑	❑	1.	CEO drives topgrading, including recruitment.
❑	❑	2.	CEO holds managers accountable for hiring A players.
❑	❑	3.	CEO conducts periodic topgrading meeting, retaining final authority over who is hired, promoted, fired.
❑	❑	4.	CEO drives "recruitment as way of life."
❑	❑	5.	Everyone in management continuously updates his/her Rolodex with possible recruits; HR retains cumulative Rolodexes to be searched when jobs are to be filled.
❑	❑	6.	HR is topgraded, with strong recruitment staff/systems to produce an ample pool of A-player candidates.
❑	❑	7.	HR creates world-class processes for succession planning, performance management, compensation, and midyear career reviews.
❑	❑	8.	Entire senior team considers topgrading, including hiring, crucial to achieving strategic goals.
❑	❑	9.	Job descriptions are written by hiring manager (with HR input), including first year job accountabilities. Competencies, written into Candidate Assessment Scorecard, reflect reality (politics, budget constraints, etc.).
❑	❑	10.	Search firms are managed properly (acceptable list of target companies that cannot be penetrated, partner does the work, CIDS interviews ask for failures and mistakes, ref-

erence calls produce negatives, reports include negatives, weekly updates).

❑ ❑ 11. Hiring manager "owns" responsibility to hire A-player managers.

❑ ❑ 12. All interviewers are trained (in how to conduct valid interviews and stay within complex legal requirements).

❑ ❑ 13. Visits to the company are well organized (producing valid insights into candidates, "selling" them, and portraying high level of professionalism).

❑ ❑ 14. Hiring manager conducts Chronological In-Depth Structured (CIDS) interview.

❑ ❑ 15. Psychological appraisal is conducted.

❑ ❑ 16. Internal candidates are assessed with the same high level of rigor as external candidates.

❑ ❑ 17. Spouse/significant other/family are incorporated into process (dinners to make person feel welcome, help in job search, kids meet coaches, real-estate agent available).

❑ ❑ 18. Final reference calls are conducted by you, the hiring manager (after talking with all other interviewers and reading psychological assessment).

❑ ❑ 19. Assimilation activities take place before first day, first week, week #12, week #14.

❑ ❑ 20. Hiring success is "tracked" by HR and hiring manager, with feedback to hiring manager to help learning.

This recruitment "blueprint" is like a blueprint you would present the builder of your house. He would probably say, "This blueprint can be improved upon, so if you let me tweak it I can give you better quality, cheaper." OK. Start tweaking, and come up with your own recruitment blueprint and your own system that one way or another, help you topgrade.

6. Case Studies: How to Topgrade

Average organizations might view topgrading as hopelessly idealistic—an entire company of A players and no chronic C players? But examples abound. Global companies can topgrade, but so can tiny businesses and individual managers in any company. Chapter 6 provides examples of each: the "inside story" of how the major obstacles to topgrading described in Chapter 2 were overcome.

The first case study is of a medium-sized corporation that topgraded, with fabulous results ever since; the Travelers Express case study is more detailed than the others because it provides an easy-to-understand "blueprint" for topgrading. General Electric, the second case study, is an A-player talent machine. It "grows its own," internally. GE's approach to measuring and developing talent is powerful and instructive. Next, a tiny regional company that has topgraded for 25 years is showcased; HEB became one of the largest and most respected privately owned companies in America, and it has enjoyed positive morale—a lesson to those who think topgrading can hurt morale. For the reader who wants to topgrade without a company-wide process, an individual case study shows how a midmanager topgraded and earned a promotion. Finally, the "roots" of American topgrading are traced back almost 400 years, to William Bradford, America's first great leader. Had he and the Pilgrims merely upgraded rather than topgraded, the foundations of America would likely have crumbled.

TRAVELERS EXPRESS TOPGRADES IN ONE YEAR

Travelers Express was a division of Dial Corp., included in a spin-off into Viad. In 1992 Travelers Express was a $100 million company with 1,100 employees. Its business was unusual—it owned 40,000 money-order machines sprinkled throughout retailers in the United States. Sales and earnings were flat. A long-term president couldn't figure out what to do with his languishing "cash cow," and a replacement was recruited. Travelers Express needed fresh strategic thinking, a new vision, and new talent to make it work. That's when I entered.

The search firm had produced several C-player candidates for president. Job descriptions and competencies had been boilerplated and had completely missed the most important responsibilities. This wasn't a maintenance presidency, but a turnaround with no road map as to how to reach the destination—profitable growth. So, I suggested finding candidates who, in the past, had figured out new strategies and succeeded. And I suggested that the search firm target premier financial-services companies for candidates for president.

Bob Bohannon was hired, a true A-player president. He didn't have a fresh strategy for six months, but he knew he wanted a team of A players to devise it with him. CIDS-based assessments helped him peg A, B, C players at the senior levels. Feedback and coaching helped As remain As and Bs become As, but not one of the C-player senior managers improved enough to stay. Half of Bohannon's team was redeployed. Two remained with the company in jobs where they could be A players, and four left with normal severances (based on years of service). Replacements of the six executives were all screened with CIDS interviews; there were no mis-hires—all were A players, and jelled nicely with the team.

Shirley Kerfoot, a newly hired Vice President Human Resources, was an A player and topgraded her HR team. She became an excellent "partner" to the entire executive team as it topgraded. Unless HR is a topgraded function, it can hardly serve the rest of the organization. But Bob Bohannon was the engine behind topgrading. He knew topgrading could not be delegated, and it certainly could not be a HR program. Topgrading had to be a way of life, a new and essential component of what had been, for decades, a seniority-based, low-performance organization culture. Within six months Bohannon had his new team.

An off-site team-building meeting focused on two priorities: topgrading throughout the company and formulating a new winning strategy. The new team of compatible A players came together, ideas for strategy abounded and soon the company was pursuing profitable growth niches—payment systems, for example.

Bohannon asked the entire senior team to embrace topgrading. A quick glimpse at the new strategic goals produced an "Aha—we have a significant talent deficit!" Instead of replicating a topgrading model Bohannon used in the past, the team was asked to devise its own, within a few parameters:

- Everyone had to be both ranked (top to bottom) and rated (A, B, C player).
- The process would flow from the senior group down, level by level.
- Regular meetings would monitor and drive progress.

Bohannon wanted total commitment and buy-in, so he did not impose a strict definition of an A player, did not expand the list of core competencies to include some he liked. He wanted the team's pride of authorship to energize topgrading, and it did.

Figure 6.1 is an overview of the company's topgrading program. It essentially says the senior team will meet quarterly to drive the process. Rankings (best to worst) were required in every department to be sure no manager's ratings (A, B, C) were too generous. Vice presidents would meet with directors to rate their managers, putting the names of all of the As (by department), Bs (by department) and Cs (by department) up for all vice presidents to see. Illuminating discussions would take place. "Hey, if Julie in your department is an A player, then Sam in mine is, too." "Oh yeah, neither Sam nor Julie is an A—you guys are whitewashing!" Rankings helped separate the best As from the less impressive As, and in actuality it pushed some into B and C categories. Performance reviews, 360-degree surveys, task-force presentations—all the data were considered until a solid consensus was reached on exactly which managers were As, Bs, Cs. Then consensus was reached on supervisor, and finally those below supervisor.

The ranking and rating guidelines were simple, and dozens of competencies were reduced to the five most critical "core" for all jobs:

- **Innovative Outlook**—The ability to see new business opportunities that are not immediately evident to others; originality of thought; the inherent desire to seek new and more effective ways of doing things, and the initiative to implement them
- **Power of Analysis**—The ability to break complex problems down into simple elements and to solve them logically; sheer intellectual fire power
- **Ability to Communicate**—The ability to communicate, lucidly and forcefully, both verbally and on paper; then tailor the form and method of communication to the needs and perceptions of the recipient(s)
- **Leadership Capability**—A natural, unforced ability to inspire people to give their utmost toward a group objective
- **Ability to Manage Change**—The ability to create in others the willingness to ardently embrace and drive change

Figure 6.1 Travelers Express Topgrading Overview

GOAL:	*To create an organization comprised predominantly of A players.*
PURPOSE:	*To identify our A, B, and C players utilizing a forced ranking-and-rating process, 360-degree input, and performance review results.*

- Identify employees who are doing an outstanding job.
- Identify employees who have "plateaued."
- Identify critical keepers and future leaders (not synonymous with each other).
- Identify employees who are not doing an acceptable job.
- Ensure appropriate management actions are happening with our A, B, or C players.

RANKING AND RATING CRITERIA:
- Five core competencies
- Additional skills/abilities and knowledge
- Delivery to plan/goals and objectives

TOOLS TO CONDUCT MEETINGS:
- Ranking and rating guidelines
- 360-degree results on each individual being ranked
- Performance review results on each individual being ranked

TOPGRADING MEETING PARTICIPANTS:
- Senior team and president/CEO will participate in A/B/C ranking and rating for all upper-level employees in the company.
- Each manager/supervisor along with group/division VP will force rank and rate all employees within their group/division.
- Meetings will be conducted quarterly.
- Each participant brings his or her group/division ranking and rating information/results to the meeting.
- Review the actions taken regarding the previously identified C players.
- Begin to rank (A/B/C) and rate from highest to lowest grades.
- Begin discussion with the person who owns the individual being reviewed.
- After reaching consensus, each employee is rated an A, B, or C— there are no pluses, no minuses.
- Each employee is also assigned a ranking calibrator, which is used as a fine tuner to define contribution levels among ranked peers (i.e., greater than, equal to, or less than).
- VP human resources is responsible for documenting all data gathered.
- Each VP leaves the meeting owning the action item to address all C players (i.e., performance improvement plans).
- Each VP leaves the meeting owning the action item to ensure A players are being appropriately compensated and recognized.

For specific positions, the five core competencies were supplemented with additional competencies. For example, a senior sales management position required:

- Continuous Improvement
- Meeting Budgets, Schedules, Commitments
- Quality of Work
- Supervision Required
- Technical Knowledge (i.e., accounting, programming, etc.)
- Communications Skills
- Interpersonal Skills
- Creativity/Innovation
- Flexibility

- Initiative/Sense of Urgency
- Group Contribution/Teamwork
- Judgment and Decision Making
- Customer-Service Skills
- People-Management Skills
- Training and Development
- Accountability (self and employees)
- Clear Focus and Prioritization
- Change Management

Travelers Express defined A player as top 10 percent of talent available in its recruitment efforts. Initially, however, A/B/C player were designations for job performance:

A Player: Always exceeds established goals and objectives with an unusually high degree of initiative and success. Employee is recognized for exemplary demonstration of Travelers Express's five core competencies.

B Player: Consistently meets goals and objectives in all areas and may exceed them in a number of areas. Employee solidly demonstrates Travelers Express core competencies.

C Player: Job performance is not acceptable. Improvement is required in one or more significant area to satisfy the objective established for the positions. Employee fails to exhibits a satisfactory level of one or more of Travelers Express's five core competencies.

In order to maximize objectivity in assessments, each person was compared with others. Comparison groups included the following guidelines:

- Review HRIS reports and determine comparison groups.
- Maintain groups for like jobs and, if possible, include no more than three grade levels.
- Comparison groups should ideally include a minimum of nine employees.
- Separate individual contributors (i.e., nonmanagers) from supervisors and managers.

In each meeting to rank and rate people, key criteria to consider were:

- Supervision required (how "high maintenance" is the person?)
- Impact of errors on the company
- Budget impact demonstrates five core competencies

Prior to each group topgrading meeting, managers were given the following guidelines on their forced rankings and ratings:

- Each manager should come prepared to discuss and rank his or her upper-level staff.
- List all individuals to be ranked.
- Compare each individual with each of others. Identify the top contributors and then the bottom contributors; the middle will fall into place. Assign a value to each individual.
- Don't waste time differentiating between one or two positions (i.e., #2 vs. #4 or #5 vs. #6).
- Depending on the size of your group, you may manage this process by splitting groups into halves, quarters, thirds, etc.
- After ranking (best to worst), rate each person A player, B player, C player, and review rankings and ratings to be sure they make sense.
- Review all rankings and ratings one more time (supervision required, impact of errors, etc.).
- Ability is not a substitute for accomplishment.
- Quantity is not a substitute for quality.
- People-management skills and technical-management skills are of equal importance.
- Look at performance for whole review period, not just the most recent performance.
- Rank employees in comparable positions.

TRAVELERS EXPRESS TOPGRADING RESULTS

After four years of flat earnings, the company "took off." Record sales and earnings have been achieved every year since Bob Bohannon launched topgrading in 1992. In 1996 Viad was spun off from Dial, a separate $2.5 billion group of 11 companies. Bob Bohannon, who had grown Travelers Express from $100M to over $200M, was named Chairman and Chief Executive Officer of Viad. One of Travelers Express's vice president's, Phil Milne, replaced Bohannon as President of Travelers Express. At his first President's Retreat as CEO of Viad, Bohannon included a half-day segment on topgrading, using the

Travelers Express model for the other companies to emulate. Bohannon said, "Topgrading was essential to our success at Travelers Express."

Returning to the topgrading process—in Travelers Express's first year (1992–1993) 20 percent of the company (all C players) had been redeployed, with three-quarters of them leaving the company. In the second year, 10 percent were redeployed—a total of one-half of all employees within two years. Topgrading never ceases. Bohannon said, "Topgrading is a way of life, not a program; it never stops." Except for the lowest levels in the company, topgrading was accomplished in a year, even though it will never be "completed."

The term "topgrading" was and is frequently used. Senior executives discourage phrases such as "bottomscraping" and "organization strengthening," because they can be interpreted negatively. And of importance, of those who left the company, 50 percent quietly found other jobs, were given nice going-away parties, and left with their heads high. Half, despite a solid performance-management system with solid feedback, coaching and counseling, were fired. There have been zero lawsuits. As a result of the performance management system, one-third of those identified as C players improved sufficiently to stay, two-thirds did not. The performance-management system simultaneously helps people know what is expected and where they stand, and it provides all of the legal documentation necessary to convince a jury that a terminated employee was fairly treated.

In order to internally "sell" the organization on topgrading, a few articles on the subject were distributed, but mostly managers studied the approaches at General Electric, Intel, Hewlett Packard, and some small semiconductor companies. A common metaphor was used "This is like an athletic team, and we must have mostly first stringers and few second stringers, but we can't have any third stringers."

As is all too common, some C players had received favorable reviews for up to ten years and were shocked at the first truly honest forthright performance appraisals. These individuals established very aggressive developmental plans, which were reviewed monthly. The norm evolved in the company that despite a history of undeserved, positive reviews, a chronic C player should either show significant improvement within 90 days or be removed (externally or internally).

Morale is sky-high at Travelers Express today. During the first year of topgrading, morale was mixed—low for C players, but high for A players ("We're finally going to get moving!"). A lot of very conscientious, loyal Travelers Express employees are sorry some of their former coworkers had to leave, but there is a feeling of rock-solid integrity in the topgrading system. The company began growing again and would not have if those C players had remained. The incoming A players were not perceived as taking jobs that internal people deserved, after the first year. Some of those new A players were essential in creating a new strategic vision and strategy. Instead of just focusing on selling more retail chains or putting in a few more money-order machines, the new team is looking globally at such things as payroll systems; they are doing deals they never thought possible.

People at Travelers Express say, with total sincerity, that most (not all) former coworkers they have stayed in touch with are much happier in their new position. Some have progressed much farther than they would have, had they remained with Travelers Express.

Only seven people did not readily accept termination. Again, there were no lawsuits, but any company must expect human nature to prevail. Any company with 30 percent or 40 percent C players is bound to have some of them who, despite solid professional efforts to help them accept reality, continue to deceive themselves regarding their capabilities. Every company that rolls out a massive topgrading program will remove a person who, if given a seventh or eighth chance, would finally "come around." The real world rarely permits the luxury of giving seventh and eighth chances.

Travelers Express circumvented the Chapter 2 obstacles in fairly typical ways. CIDS interviews helped avoid the misassessment problem (hiring Cs instead of As or labeling internal people as As when they are Cs). There is a high degree of confidence that the correct "labels" were assigned internally, and there have been no mis-hires externally. Repeat—*no* mis-hires externally.

When Bohannon's senior team looked at their A, B, C players in relation to what would be needed to achieve their strategic goals, recruitment was elevated to a high priority for everyone. When A players came in and shook things up, not only Bohannon but each of his A-player vice presidents "protected" the new hires. Assimilation exercises were conducted by Human Resources—anonymous feedback to the manager two months after starting. Executives kept a keen eye out for attempts by remaining C or B players to undercut the new A players. Of course, the C players were redeployed eventually. A players were hired at the right salary—at a level for a $200 million company, rather than the $100 million company it was in 1992, in order to have the talent to grow the company faster, more successfully. Loyal C players were given a fair chance to perform, then offered jobs where they could perform, usually at a lower level. Bob Bohannon and Shirley Kerfoot (VP HR) imbued the company with a warm, humanistic quality: "These are our associates, our neighbors, and even if they are not A players, we treat them with respect."

Initially, before Bohannon topgraded, B and C players wanted "veto power" over their new peers. No way! Lesser managers pleaded for topgrading to proceed more slowly, saying "we're part of a public company, we'll sacrifice quarterly results by disrupting the company with new managers." Bohannon believes Travelers Express achieved good short-term results *because of* (not in spite of) topgrading. He said, "The day an A player replaced a C player was always a great day, with fewer problems, not more, and with more optimism and fun, not less."

GENERAL ELECTRIC, AN A-PLAYER TALENT MACHINE

Entire books and hundreds of articles have been written about GE's approaches to talent. GE under Chairman Jack Welch is oftentimes cited in the business press as the best-managed company in the United States, perhaps the world. As of this writing, GE is the world's most valuable company. I will discuss a part of the GE talent machine—internal assessment, because that is the part I know best.

A General Electric executive named Don Lester was asked by Jack Welch to find an interviewing expert to train GE's top Human Resources (they call them "Human Relations" or just "Relations") professionals in how to thoroughly and accurately assess GE officers. The in-depth assessment would serve as the foundation for deciding senior moves: promotions, transfers. Performance reviews would also be considered, but Welch wanted a second opinion on each officer. Lester found my first book (*Selection Interviewing: A Management Psychologist's Recommended Approach*, Wiley, 1983) in London, called me and said, "Where have you been? I've been scouring the world for someone who does such in-depth interviews!"

General Electric had been using an approach that reviewed key accomplishments in each job. The CIDS interview does that but also scrutinizes failures and mistakes, and much more. I redesigned GE's process and participated in a multiyear training program beginning with CIDS interviews, adding 360-degree interviews, then report preparation, and finally feedback and coaching.

Within weeks of my first training program I met Jack Welch and Larry Bossidy (then Vice Chairman of GE and now Chairman of AlliedSignal), who asked me to personally interview and coach GE's most senior executives. John Trani, who took Medical Systems to #1 market share in the world and now is Chairman of Stanley Works, was the first GE executive I coached. I wanted to perform internal 360-degree interviews with subordinates, peers, and bosses, both present and past. At GE it was considered OK to have a ten-minute phone interview with the present and past bosses, but *not* subordinates. "It's counterculture to ask a subordinate to rat on his boss," I was told, "so you better ask Jack Welch."

Instead I simply asked Trani to ask his subordinates to level with me. "Tell them you are participating in the executive assessment and development program, you'll get the report, and all of their comments are anonymous and confidential. Tell them that you really want to learn something and craft a meaningful developmental program, so no whitewash, please!"

Trani's staff cooperated, and GE experienced a small culture change, with 360-degree feedback added to the program. The Relations professionals liked having much more solid 360-degree data. Being asked to assess and coach a possible future boss was career threatening, but the CIDS interview gave them much better insights and 360-degree data gave them more credibility with their officer, so the developmental plans worked much better.

Initially Jack Welch figured development would come from "handing the guy the report, and if he's sharp, he'll fix his shortcomings." I expanded that into a half-day coaching session, taking the rich pot of CIDS and 360-degree data and converting it into a developmental plan that was followed up on by Welch and Bossidy. GE executives have earned promotions and careers have been salvaged because of two or three hours of this coaching—not just handing the guy his report. Chapters 9 and 10 deal with this power-packed coaching model.

For the next four years annual training sessions were held in Connecticut, and altogether I trained more than three dozen HR managers to perform the full program:

- CIDS interview (GE uses tandem interviews, with a primary interviewer and a primary note taker: five hours is not uncommon)
- 360-degree interviews (anonymous and confidential discussions with present and past subordinates, peers, bosses)
- Written reports (typically with more than 30 strengths and 15 weaker points)
- Developmental planning (half-day construction of a 10–15-point plan, to be embraced by Relations and the person's boss) to address the most important developmental needs

This approach is now used as a final check before someone is named an officer at GE. But GE does a lot more to assess internal talent. The famous Session C process places Jack Welch in meetings in which he personally discusses the top 250 officers, every year. (At AlliedSignal, Bossidy does the same with 150 senior managers.) Welch, Bill Conaty (head of Human Resources), Chuck Okasky (head of Executive Development), and the head of a business meet to discuss that business head's key managers. The raw data are:

- Résumé data (career history)
- Individual self-assessment (career interests, strengths and weaker points, developmental plans)
- CIDS-based assessment and development report
- Performance appraisal (including person's disagreement with the appraisal by the business head)
- Latest career potential assessment (by the manager two levels up)

There can be feisty give and take. Welch challenges assessments, driving to be sure the manager's "head," "heart," and "guts" competencies are accurately assessed. After the meeting, there is follow-up, to finalize developmental plans, and new job assignments are sometimes made.

GE is excellent at assessing talent. Their world-class "university" at Crotonville and careful assignment of responsibilities permit managers to grow while rarely suffering from the Peter Principle. Only 5 percent of GE executives are nudged out of the company in a typical year. After years of topgrading, with constant attention to assessment and development, not many errors are made. Even most of those asked to resign become A players elsewhere.

Welch has frequently said, "I'm the top personnel guy around here." Topgrading starts at the top, if shareholders are going to benefit fully. Welch says, "My job is to get the right players in the field and call the big plays." As stated, former GE Vice Chairman Larry Bossidy moved on to AlliedSignal as Chairman and CEO; the stock has quadrupled under his leadership. "If I could do it over, I'd topgrade faster," Bossidy told me, "and I'd replace C players with A players in the first year rather than stretching it out." Bossidy has a prominant Human Resources executive in Donald Redlinger, who is quick to embrace his boss's perspective. Bossidy believes "The responsibility to infuse the organization with A players is a role the CEO cannot delegate. The CEO must own the topgrading process if the organization is to understand it is a key priority. That means a visible, systematic, and persistent commitment of the CEO."

A SMALL COMPANY TOPGRADES TO THE TOP

What do you do if you have just taken over the company, a profitable little company sure to be attacked by 800-pound gorilla competitors? What if you are a real-estate manager, with no experience running a company, no strategic plan, too many C players in your management ranks, and no major competitive advantages? You topgrade.

Twenty-seven years ago an obscure $200 million company in South Texas began to topgrade. It has topgraded as a way of life ever since. HEB Grocery Company eventually became a $7 billion powerhouse. Without topgrading, the company would almost certainly have gone bankrupt. In industry rankings, HEB is consistently ranked first, or among the first. HEB is not only among the most highly respected companies in its industry, it's one of the largest privately held companies in America.

Charles Butt, who took over the business in 1971, wanted to become an A player, a successful CEO. He did. He is among the most admired CEOs in grocery retailing. Topgrading was an unrelenting, driving force helping HEB become premier and enabling Butt to achieve his stature. It wasn't easy. Indeed, the grocery business is one of the most prosaic and competitive in the world. Charles Butt could never hope for a patentable product, some unique strategic breakthrough. In the grocery business everyone can and does copy any good idea that comes along. As Larry Bossidy, Chairman of AlliedSignal said, "Strategy is simple; it's the execution that make the difference." Charles Butt's unique competitive advantage became talent. If the grocery world is full of blockers and tacklers, not visionary geniuses, HEB would have the best blockers and tacklers.

How did Charles Butt topgrade? Roughly every five years for two decades his entire management team, every manager up through every senior executive, participated in my CIDS interviews for two purposes—assessment and coaching. Year after year Butt asked:

- Who are the A, B, C players now?
- Who can become the A, B, C players when we are twice our present size?
- What developmental activities can help our managers grow to become A players in the future?

Topgrading was in a sense born on the dusty roads of South Texas. In my mid-twenties, I saw HEB store managers who seemed overpaid for their salary. Many were glorified stockers, ill-equipped to lead hundreds of associates in the larger stores of the future. Why not, for the same salary, have store managers who were sharper, better team builders, better with customers, receptive to new technology? Butt agreed—why not? Today HEB has A-player store managers, possibly the highest-powered group of store managers in the industry, anywhere in the world.

Charles Butt topgraded HEB with a combination of infusion of outside talent and development of inside managers.

Mid- and upper-management topgrading has always been extremely smooth. Ninety-eight percent of the hundreds of managers promoted or selected using the CIDS interview succeeded; a mis-hire or mis-promotion was extremely rare. Managers were chosen to be A players in their current job, but also when the company would be twice its size. Many managers have stayed with HEB for more than 10 years. Some A players declined to B players and were placed in smaller jobs where they could be A players. A few left. Employee attitude surveys have been conducted periodically. The most recent survey I saw showed 96 percent positive morale. For those who think topgrading would hurt morale, I would say look at HEB.

When the head of MIS retired, some of the top information technology executives in the industry were screened, but following my CIDS interviews I told Butt, "They're not good enough—for the same compensation, you can hire much smarter, forward looking, logistics experts." So, HEB went outside the industry and hired Bill Seltzer, who permitted HEB to lead the industry in this cost-saving initiative.

At the top, Charles Butt initially used professional management to simultaneously grow his company profitably and teach him. He was an eager, willing, totally dedicated student. In topgrading his senior team he chose not "just" A players, but A players he could fully trust, who would jell as a team, who would teach him, and who would recognize his growth and take direction from him. That's a tall order, but again CIDS-based assessment and coaching worked. Butt became the respected CEO he aspired to.

▶ "Topgrading has enabled us to beat the competition by hiring and developing A players for the next bigger league; identification of A players has afforded us smooth sailing through troubled waters."

Charles Butt

For two decades I was that CIDS assessor and coach. A critical mass of A players continues topgrading HEB today. Charles Butt has infused HEB with a topgrading mentality. He continues to grow A players internally, parachute in bigger-league A players to grow the company smoothly, redeploy chronic C players, and rigorously assess people to accurately peg them as A, B, C players.

Jack Welch and Larry Bossidy sing out of the same hymnal on topgrading. So does Bob Bohannon, and Charles Butt. So does every head of every premier organization, every world-class leader in every industry I have heard of. So can you, whether you are a CEO, senior manager, or first-level manager.

JEFF DILL TOPGRADES AND GETS PROMOTED

Meet Jeff Dill, promoted last year to Regional Manager at CompUSA. Earlier he turned around two CompUSA stores, and topgrading was a powerful lever for Jeff's promotion to Regional Manager.

After entering CompUSA in a training position, Jeff was named General Manager of a medium-sized (90 employee) store in Ohio. When he entered, the store was doing well in terms of its sales and earnings, but he managed to improve it. How? "Topgrading," he said. He had five managers reporting to him, three A players (two were subsequently promoted), one B player, and one C player.

Topgrading to Jeff means developing everybody, including the A-player managers, so that they grow and continue to be A players. He sets "stretch" goals, constantly reinforces a clear and consistent direction and, as he puts it, "communicates like crazy." There are monthly store meetings, memos, weekly team meetings, weekly one-to-one meetings with managers, and a very open door. There is mega-accountability, mega-feedback, and contagious energy helping people be the best they can.

Unfortunately, Jeff was new enough to CompUSA that he did not have a clear "fix" regarding what was an A player, B player, C player. Working with a person he thought was "probably" a C player, Jeff set the expectations high, tried coaching, and the person improved . . . but not enough. "Now, in exactly the same situation with an identical C player, I would aggressively move through the 90-day performance-improvement cycle toward removing him," he said. Jeff is a little embarrassed talking about that individual, but there was a happy ending. That person moved to a different location, in a different job where he is performing well.

At CompUSA General Managers have a great deal of autonomy. They essentially run their own business, with only the most obvious structure imposed—the name on the store, buying policies, and so forth. When a manager offered to train people on the Internet, Jeff did not have to get corporate approval. He simply did it. He has tremendous authority in hiring and never has to accept any subordinate he doesn't want. GMs at CompUSA even have pricing authority.

Next, Jeff was named General Manager of a turnaround store. In a store of 120 employees, he had five managers as direct reports—one A player, a B who became an A, and three C players. True to form, he began the topgrading process by defining clear objectives, "communicating like crazy," providing feedback and coaching, and clarifying exactly what would be necessary in order for people to stay in their job. A positive, firm approach to corrective action (that 90-day performance-improvement cycle) led the transfer of one C player to a smaller store, where the job was much simpler, and her performance much better. With one C player, Jeff had an early heart-to-heart conversation: "You're over your head, so how about hanging in there for 30 days and I'll find you a job where you can be an A player?" That is exactly what occurred. Jeff replaced one of the C players with (oops!) a C player, and this has been the only major mis-hire of his career. Coaching did not improve this C player's performance, and again while Jeff was looking for an opportunity to transfer her to a smaller job, she left the company.

With a team of all A players, or at least key managers with the short-term potentials to become A players, the store was well on the road to becoming "fixed." His managers topgraded throughout the store in a matter of months. Jeff's boss told him, "Jeff, one of the reasons for your success is your willingness and ability to recruit and hire managers who have a higher level of expertise than you in their area of responsibility." Results in both sales and earnings improved dramatically, earning Jeff a promotion in 1998 to Regional Manager.

Jeff's close-to-perfect "batting average" in hiring is attributable in part to his good interviewing skills. He uses a chronological, in-depth, structured interview approach, and he looks carefully at patterns. "I don't think people change a heck of a lot" he said, "so I want to be confident that a newly hired manager will function as an A player right away." CompUSA does a background check on all new hires, but Jeff does his own reference calls. "I want to talk with at least a couple of recent bosses and coworkers, to test my conclusions; I'm not afraid to ask the tough questions to see if the reference honestly believes the candidate can perform in what usually is a higher pressure, more complex job."

Jeff believes that if CompUSA dictated whom he could hire or promote, his effectiveness would be severely diminished. His basic philosophy is, "Hire the best, then get out of the way to let them do the job." Of course the company helps assure there is sharing of talent for new store openings. The overall topgrading perspective for the company is simple. A players at the top hire and promote A players for the mid-management levels, who hire and promote A players for all the rest of the company. It's a formula that works in the most valuable corporation in America (General Electric), or for any manager (Jeff Dill) who is serious about success.

THE WILLIAM BRADFORD CASE STUDY

Topgrading is very new—and very old. America's first great leader, William Bradford, was a topgrader.[1] Before telling his topgrading story, let me intrigue you with a brief assessment of a man you might not have heard of. William Bradford is one of a handful of leaders in history who was both pure of heart and very successful at changing the world. Ghandi and Lincoln were two others. It is an exclusive club.

Here's his background: After the Mayflower landed at Cape Cod in 1620, William Bradford was elected governor of Plymouth Colony; he was reelected 30 more times. Under his leadership America was truly founded, 150 years before the Revolutionary War. Bradford led his team of A players (Winslow, Brewster, Standish, and others) as he:

- **Established what John Quincy Adams called the world's first true democracy.** The Greeks had slaves. Puritans flooded the New World after the Pilgrims showed families could survive, but the Puritans had a theocracy. Bradford's creation of democracy led the way to our Revolution and the spread of democracy throughout the world.

- **Abandoned socialism for free-enterprise.** In 1621 the Pilgrims were near starvation. Their contract with European venture capitalists called for socialism—all Pilgrims would farm and send back almost all the money to Europe, to pay off the debt. People weren't motivated. Bradford, in America's first privatization, let each family sell a portion of

---

[1] Bradford D. Smart, "America's First Great Leader: William Bradford, Governor of Plymouth Colony," *The Mayflower Quarterly* 62 (1) (1996), pp. 6–19.

its goods on the open market after contributing their fair share to the common store. The GNP of Plymouth shot up.

- **Began the first family Thanksgiving.** Bradford's free-enterprise effort permitted the Pilgrims to survive in the New World (otherwise we'd all be speaking Spanish or French), and our holiday of Thanksgiving began with him.

- **Assured separation of church and state.** Devout but no religious fanatic, Bradford insisted that rule by law, civil law, be separate from religious edict.

One leader, William Bradford, led the Pilgrims to these foundations of our society 150 years before the signing of the Declaration of Independence! For fun let's see how Bradford's topgrading withstood common obstacles to topgrading listed in Chapter 2.

- **Misassessment.** Instead of CIDS assessments, the Pilgrims self-assessed. How's this for a selection test: risk your life fleeing a monarchy, face a horrible Atlantic crossing, survive disease that will wipe out 50 percent of your team in the first year, face a mutiny by some hired hands, risk war with the natives . . . and in your spare time build a town, a government, an entire society. Any takers? The Pilgrims who jumped aboard the Mayflower were all Michael Jordans. Bradford was the best and brightest—the A player most respected to lead this miracle. How rigorous are *your* assessment methods compared to this?

- **Inadequate recruitment.** Only 100 Pilgrims and hired hands volunteered and boarded the Mayflower. Quality, not quantity, permitted our nation to be founded. The Pilgrims recruited Mayflower passengers from among their ranks for more than a year. B and C players were asked to remain in Europe. Do *you* cop out and accept B players because you don't want to wait a couple more months for an A player?

- **New A players chewed up by C players.** To have enough people to launch a colony, the Pilgrims permitted societal rejects to be hired hands onboard the Mayflower, and upon arriving in the New World, they threatened mutiny. The hired hands were a mixed lot, including A and B players, but also some C players. The A-player Pilgrims were such a strong and capable team that they were sure their reason and pureness of spirit would win over the misfits. So, they offered the C players a revolutionary form of government—democracy. Even the C-player misfits were among those voting for Bradford as their leader 31 times! How good are *you* at creating policies that show such contagious belief in the reason and goodness of people?

- **Don't want to fire loyal C players.** Bradford was magistrate, and he banned repeated lawbreakers. Even this generous Christian removed C players who threatened the viability of Plymouth colony. He hung one man (in 40 years), a man who killed an Indian. He banished several crooks. Do *you* banish C players who wound your organization?

- **Topgrading isn't necessary with key initiatives determined by others.** The economic model the Pilgrims began with was trade, but the trading vessel leaked and never made it to the New World. So Bradford and his team altered strategy, introducing farming. Changes in strategy work best with teams of A players. Do *you* use internal A players to alter strategy?

- **But location makes finding A players difficult.** Finding A players is always possible, but you may have to pay more to get the level of talent you need. The Pilgrims had a burning vision of economic and religious freedom. Their pay was psychic, spiritual. It's hard to beat a team willing to risk all for a vision. How compelling is *your* vision?

OK, launching a new society is not exactly like running a business. But the principles are applicable. It is utterly amazing that America succeeded, because it required the first government to be original (democracy) and flexible (changed economic systems) and despite all odds (50 percent mortality in first year) serve as a beacon for the future of the world. The massive and constant problems required Bradford and his A players to make a lot of decisions on the fly, and they had to be right.

In the most prophetic words in American history, William Bradford wrote:

Thus, out of small beginnings greater things have been produced by His hand and as one small candle may light a thousand, so the light here kindled has shone to many, in some sort to our whole nation.

Bradford wrote these words to suggest that Plymouth Colony's democracy paved the way for democracy across the New World. Perhaps the quotation can also mean that a small topgraded organization grew to the most powerful in the world. This strange, truly unique topgrading case study of William Bradford set a very high standard. Jack Welch, Bob Bohannon, Charles Butt, Jeff Dill, and William Bradford know what it is to topgrade with a passion, with a vision that will prevail.

PART TWO

Topgrading
for
Individuals

THE STEPLADDER IS GONE, AND THERE IS NOT
EVEN AN IMPLIED STRUCTURE OF AN INDUSTRY'S
ROPE LADDER. IT'S MORE LIKE VINES, AND YOU
BRING YOUR OWN MACHETE. YOU DON'T KNOW
WHAT YOU'LL BE DOING NEXT OR WHETHER
YOU'LL WORK IN A PRIVATE OFFICE OR ONE BIG
AMPHITHEATER OR OUT OF YOUR HOUSE.

PETER DRUCKER
MANAGING IN TIMES OF GREAT CHANGE

7. Becoming an A Player: Have Your Cake and Eat It, Too

Everyone can be an A player, today, in the right job, in the right industry, in the right league. My job in this chapter is to help you figure out how to become an A player in the biggest league you can . . . and want.

As an A player, you will qualify as the "cream of the crop," "best of class." Your career options will be magnified. You will be sufficiently on top of your job to develop competencies needed in bigger jobs. Maybe, if you play your cards as I suggest in this chapter, you'll be happy. And I'll guarantee you, as an A player you will be better equipped than B players to judge As, Bs, and Cs, which will help you topgrade your organization. As a topgrader, you will perform to your peak and earn promotions faster than managers who don't topgrade. Remain an A player and a topgrader, and you will have the best chance of becoming an A-player senior manager.

Even if you are not in the career major leagues yet, this chapter will alert you as to how A players in that league look at talent, careers, and developmental planning. After citing commonplace bad advice in career planning, I present you with nine keys to becoming an A player at the highest level. It includes some unconventional wisdom. By enriching and deepening your insights into the entire spectrum of career success principles and patterns, you will simultaneously learn how to be a better topgrader and how to "have your cake and eat it, too," in your career.

HAVE YOUR CAKE AND EAT IT, TOO

When managers learn about the 27 file cabinets with over 4,000 career dossiers in my basement, a predictable dialogue ensues:

Question: Doc, you've assessed and coached thousands of people, from all over the globe and in all industries. So tell me, what's the fastest way I can become an A player?

Answer: Wrong question—"fastest"? Since an A player is among the top 10 percent of talent available (at a given salary), just about any B player can become an A player by taking a demotion, a salary cut. A C-player marketing executive might be an A-player marketing analyst. Not a satisfying answer, but your question wasn't the smartest!

Question: OK, I forgot your definition of A player. So, tell me the 10 secrets of becoming an A player in this league I'm in or in a bigger league. I'm accounting manager in a $100 million manufacturing company and want to become division controller in a $500 million company within seven years.

Answer: Good for you—a midrange goal. What then?

Question: I want to become chief financial officer of a *Fortune* 500 company, possibly transition to president, or even CEO, earn the most money, have the most power, enjoy the most respect, I want it all! How can I get there?

Answer: Wrong question, again, but at least the contents of the 4,000 career files in my basement hold the answers. Ten percent of the profiles—roughly 400—were people I screened or coached to become president or CEO. The ultimate brass ring. Total, absolute power. No more fear. No more sucking up to anybody. At least that's what most anticipated in their quest for the brass ring.

Question: How do I do it? How?

Answer: I know how. I can advise you. I've guided many a folk toward president or CEO. Work 80 hours per week and suck up to powerful bosses without seeming to suck up too much. Knowing what to do to get there, however, misses something important. Asking what are the steps, the career development steps, to get there still might not be the best question you can ask, however.

Question: I got it, Doc—tell me what *not* to do. What are the five biggest mistakes managers make in their career decisions?

Answer: You're getting warmer. Twenty-seven years ago I began "going to school" on that topic. I eagerly listened to what older (my age, now!) executives told me in their quiet, reflective moments, about their best and worst decisions in life. They told me their regrets, what they'd do differently. Even more interesting was studying younger managers who had heard the old guys' (they were almost all "guys" back in the 1970s) advice, and followed it. From them I learned what worked, and what didn't work. I molded my own life around these insights and coached others accordingly. What worked for me is much less important than the career advice that worked or didn't work for hundreds of others. The combination of what to do and what pitfalls to avoid became my model, my paradigm for career advice. I'm still polishing that model, but the basics are certainly in place. I hope you can benefit from learning this model.

Question: Me, too. Tell me, what truths lie in those 4,000 career files in your basement?

Answer: Your questions are getting better. I must warn you—a solid one-third of the 4,000 files in my basement are not very happy files. Roughly one-third are pretty satisfied with their life in general, one-third are not, and the rest are resoundingly neutral. More than half the managers, in their own opinion, suboptimized their success–happiness balance. Their career was progressing nicely when I interviewed them, but when asked about life overall, there were significant, preventable, major problems. Their lives were quite devoid of joy, deep love, real meaning, quality relationships, even wellness. Around 1985 I began hearing, "Brad, I did everything you suggested ten years ago, I'm president now, but I'm not happy." Defensively, I'd respond, "You didn't ask about how to achieve happiness, only the president's office!" That's when I began coaching managers to focus a little on balance, not just on a success trajectory that would leave deep regrets.

Question: Should the question be, "How can I be happy, at the expense of career success?"

Answer: No, like most ambitious managers, you are probably an insecure overachiever. Living in Tibet three years and returning to bond with your family and run soup kitchens probably won't work for you.

Question: How can I be both successful and happy?

Answer: Don't whisper the question, shout it! Hundreds of my client managers have become both successful and happy, and their examples can teach you. All the other questions are dumb. Look around—one-third of the "successful" managers have crummy lives. Oh, they look fine at work and keep up appearances at the club, and some aspects of their lives are just peachy. But when I ask how their life is going overall, one-third place themselves below "happy," either in a neutral or worse category. Do you want to trade places with them? Despite career success, they tell me, "My life's in the shitter." It's not a very elegant figure of speech, but I hear it quite often.

Since the mid 1980s, my coaching has sought to help high-achieving managers ask the one important question: How can I maximize both my success and happiness? In topgrading terminology:

> ▶ How can I become an A player in the biggest league, while maximizing my overall happiness in life?

Some of the happiest people I know are low achievers. They enjoy serenity, rock-solid character, wonderful friends and family, spiritual grounding, respect in the community, a job they like, reasonable health, a few bucks in the bank, and love. You aren't a low achiever. You *need* career success. You are ambitious, or you wouldn't be reading this book. *Topgrading* will help you achieve your maximum potential *and* balance—have your cake and eat it, too. Perhaps you have been focusing *much* more on how to succeed in business than in life. If so, you have probably bought into a career mythology that won't work. But you follow the bad career advice anyway.

BAD CAREER-PLANNING ADVICE

"New paradigms" for career success are popping up all over, but in most respects they are not new. The same old post–World War II career-development principles are dressed up in words such as "virtual," "global," and "temporary." The baby boomers bought into the same career myths of their Depression-era parents, merely "tweaking" the paradigm. Generation Xers are different in some respects. They don't trust marriage (their parents split up), companies (dear 'ol Dad was downsized out of one company, rightsized out of another), and want to be high-tech entrepreneurs. Some are career "free agents" in careers they control; most are still like their predecessors—career slaves.

The "new paradigms" for career success are based on compelling statistics. You have heard it all. For example:

* Only 16 of the largest 100 U.S. companies in the year 1900 survived until the late nineties.

- Manufacturing jobs have dropped from 73 percent in 1970 to 11 percent today.

- A Christmas card that sings "Jingle Bells" today contains a chip with more computer power than existed in the entire world in 1960.

With globalization, national boundaries disintegrate, with profound career implications. A farm kid in rural China will jump on the Internet and grab a chunk of business from a mega manufacturer in Europe. "Lean" is here, contract employees/managers are the wave of the future. There will be more career "free agents" in the future, experiencing a series of short-term employment relationships, without career-long job security. Intel's Andy Grove writes *Only the Paranoid Survive,* and he's right. Gary Wendt, CEO of GE Capital Services and a client as his company grew to contributing almost $3 billion in annual earnings to General Electric shareholders, has a speech that answers, "How do you do it, Gary?" His answer: "Running scared." No business, no manager, can rest comfortably for a second because the velocity of change is increasing. In high tech, some companies pump out an average of two new product innovations per day. How can old career-success principles be relevant today? Simple. The old, and in crucial ways, *flawed* principles are repackaged.

The Bad Career-Planning Advice Is:

1. *Work harder.* It's fine to talk about "balance," but in this increasingly competitive, globalized, marketplace bad advice #1 encourages you to focus almost totally on your career. After all, while you're attending a concert or participating in community service, your peer competitor might be running a spreadsheet that will earn her a promotion. Downsizing is here to stay, so do the work of two people and be happy you have a job. If you aren't willing to work 70 hours per week, someone else will. Delay gratification. Sacrifice balance in life now so that you and your family will later reap the rewards of your rising as far as you can.

2. *Live beyond your means.* Spend money, because it's the American way! Social Security will dry up, but retirement will be paid for through your 401k, profit sharing, IRA, and stock options. You work hard, so spend some dough. Besides, a nicer abode, cars, and clothes will enhance your business image, your career marketability. Living in a better neighborhood can open doors. If working so hard has caused some problem at home, purchase some domestic harmony. Heh, heh.

3. *Never pass up a job opportunity people say you can't refuse.* A really big jump in income and responsibility can put you in that bigger league. So what if your skills aren't fully "there," you're resourceful, you'll learn. Do it! Go for it! Don't be a wimp!

4. *In job interviews, hide negatives.* With job security a thing of the past, job mobility is in. You will be interviewed more, because you'll change

jobs more often. Don't blow it with a naive "come clean" attitude. Get the job offer and worry about doing the job later. You're more talented than some people who are concealing their shortcomings, so why shoot yourself in the foot?

5. *Develop your strengths to the max.* Bad advice #5 might seem to defy logic, but it assumes your success thus far has come from those strengths, so put all your developmental time and energy into maximizing them. What could be illogical about that?

6. *Don't waste time trying to overcome your shortcomings.* Face it, you're not going to change your weaknesses. Leopards don't change their spots. People don't really change.

Most high achievers continue embracing the paradigm underlying these six myths. So, they work harder, grasp at higher brass rings, sacrifice more for the future—the future out there when the pain will be gone. Good luck. Most senior managers lie awake at night, listening to their heart beat, thump-thump, thump-thump. Worrying. Worrying about their performance, about company politics. About that goddam bar being raised. About balance—"Screw balance, I'm in a survival mode."

A players have a much better chance than B and C players of achieving balance and happiness. After all, A players are the top 10 percent available for their job—the best and the brightest, the cream of the crop. They can *afford* to get their life in balance. But plenty of A players have screwed up their lives; they suffer sleepless nights worrying about how to get the next job. They can fritter away their golden opportunity to "have their cake and eat it, too." A players at least have more power to get control of their lives *and* be successful. Here's how . . .

NINE KEYS TO BECOMING A HAPPY A PLAYER AT THE HIGHEST LEVEL

1. PERFORM A PERIODIC LIFE-BALANCE REVIEW, AND FOCUS ON BECOMING "GOOD ENOUGH" IN ALL SEVEN CRITICAL LIFE DIMENSIONS

How are you doing on all the dimensions of greatest importance in your life? Score yourself in Figure 7.1.

This particular set of dimensions, "legs" on life's platform, is pretty close to universal. Achieve "good enough" in the seven dimensions, and additional ones are automatically constructed—freedom, opportunities for creative expression, and time for intellectual development. But, it may not be the perfect list for you. You might have a burning need for power, control, status, or individuality. You may want to add or delete legs on your life platform.

Figure 7.1 LIFE BALANCE SCORECARD

	Good Enough	Not Good Enough	Critical Life Dimensions
1.	❑	❑	Career success
2.	❑	❑	Wellness
3.	❑	❑	Relationships (family, friends)
4.	❑	❑	Giving something back
5.	❑	❑	Financial independence
6.	❑	❑	Spiritual grounding
7.	❑	❑	Recreation (pleasure, hobbies)

Score yourself, right now, and be honest. Then adjust your life to achieve Good Enough in all seven Critical Life Dimensions. Do that and you will embody the one most important "truth" lurking in the 27 file cabinets of client reports in my basement. Hundreds of senior managers, successful in their careers, have told me various ways they would give anything, anything, to be able to wind the clock back and have another chance to achieve better balance.

Completing the Life Balance Scorecard is just a first step. Self awareness usually is. You can rate yourself Good Enough on five legs but Not Good Enough on #2 (Wellness) and #3 (Relationships) and be destined for an unhappy life. If you think the Bad-Career Planning Advice is good advice, not myth, you will simply follow the same path, put career success *way* above the other six, and end up an unfulfilled jerk with an impressive title and half of an impressive bank account (your former spouse will get the other half).

You may not feel the need to "give something back." Then score yourself Good Enough on that dimension. Or eliminate it. But where there is a deep, soul-wrenching ache that says your relationships (#3) are Not Good Enough, you had better adjust your life. Estimate what it will take—converting a few minutes per week one-on-one with each child to an hour? Perhaps four (rather than two) hours of quality time with your spouse/significant other?

This is an amazingly quick exercise. It takes only ten minutes. Score yourself, and if two dimensions are weak, give a rough estimate of the adjusted time allocation necessary to achieve *all* Good Enoughs in a year. If someone put a gun to your head and said you absolutely must figure out how to achieve all seven Good Enoughs within a year, you could do it. Guess what—destiny has put a gun to your head. The result of this exercise could be a major reallocation of time and energy. It could incur risk, such as crafting a major career change, throttling back your lifestyle, spending more quality time with your spouse, exercising half an hour per day—any one change could be major. Don't bite off more than you can chew.

Will seven Good Enoughs make you happy?[1] For most high-achieving, ambitious managers, yes. That is the clearest, simplest operational definition of happiness I know. It's the absence of Not Good Enoughs.

Steven Covey, in *The Seven Habits of Highly Successful People*, articulates the importance of balance, with a strong emphasis on one's inner core—integrity. I'd recommend the book to anyone needing a character transplant, or even a reminder about balance. My goals are less lofty. Quick fixes sometimes work. Completing the Life Balance Scorecard takes a few minutes, as does determining the fix. The adjustments, made yearly, will take a lifetime, but so what? As long as the outcome is a deep, meaningful, heartfelt LIFE IS GOOD, hey, isn't that good enough? You win, every year, not just after you retire. Life is the stroll, not the goal—the self-defeating goal of being "happy" after six and one-half decades of sacrifice.

Balance is a complicated issue when husband and wife are high powered *and* career oriented. When both want to earn $250,000, it takes a lot of flexibility, creativity, and love to figure out whose career will take precedence. The solution I see in my files: "We'll move this time for your career, we'll move next for mine." It's a partial solution, with no guarantees.

What about children? Quality-time parenting is not sufficient to rear emotionally healthy children, but it is necessary. My hunch is it takes 30 hours per week of totally focused, loving, full-attention parenting. That means good parenting is possible with one high-powered, career-focused parent, and the other had better have a nine-to-five job, or less. High-powered career junkies in my files, husbands and wives who considered six weeks off to have a baby a sacrifice, almost all were later embarrassed when their children showed "behavior problems." The children were supposed to be a joy on Sundays between 10:00 A.M. and 4:00 P.M., and provide that ideal Christmas card photo. But, the rug rats constantly disappoint. During the work week the children are a distraction; it's not easy for parents to pretend to really care as they rush out the door to make an appointment, or when they cram a "quality moment" in at the children's bedtime before they get back to their PC. High-achieving parents are proactive in their jobs, anticipating and preventing problems. They typically invest the amount of time necessary for their children *after* problems erupt, however.

A solution is readily at hand: professions. Free agents, one and all. It is becoming easier and easier for one or both parents to work 20 hours per

---

[1] "Happy" means deep fulfillment in life, not shallow pleasure, and certainly not happy-go-lucky.

week for a few years, zero hours a couple of years, and later 70 hours one week and 15 the next. Professionals can work out of their home—tax attorneys, marketing consultants, psychologists, financial planners. One woman, who cut back to three days per week after a preschool threatened to expel her child, said, "You can have it all, *sequentially.*"

In short, put reasonable *balance* first in your life, by measuring all seven components and working to make all Good Enough every year. It's OK to list career success first, as long as you don't put it first, second, third, fourth, fifth, sixth, and seventh.

2. PERFORM A PERIODIC PERSONAL-CAREER REVIEW

There are major talent dislocations in which mediocre talent skyrockets in hot industries and superb talent languishes in "stagnant" industries. There are retail managers I know who are A players at $100,000 per year, when they could move to high tech and eventually earn 50 percent more. They would still qualify as A players in that higher paying league. Only about one-third of the thousands of managers I have interviewed in depth had a good handle on how to manage their career—knowing their strengths and weaker points and how they might proactively take advantage of career marketplace trends. Two-thirds focused on the job at hand and maybe the next promotion, but were in the dark about what to do to maximize attractive job options over time, what industries to join, and what companies to pursue.

It's all about supply and demand, and your career review should ask, "Where can my competencies achieve the biggest bucks in the foreseeable future?" You shouldn't necessarily go after *just* the biggest bucks, but you should constantly inform yourself about how the marketplace trends are valuing what you have to offer.

People finish school, take the best job offer, and stay in that function, that company, that industry, too long. By the time they realize it, the demand for their skills has declined. "Downsizing can't happen to me" . . . until it happens. Engineering was hot during the military buildup of the 1980s, and plummeted at the end of the Gulf War. I saw Gulf War generals thanking General Electric engineers for having designed 12 of 13 jet engines used in the war. Despite concerns about dust and sand, the engines worked superbly. After watching a general's appreciative speech, I returned to a conference room where plans were being made to lay off 7,000 talented engineers. The defense industry was tanking. The demand for superb aircraft engineering skills plummeted. You owe it to yourself to keep your antennae tuned to those forces that will impact your career options, your marketability.

Suppose you are Division Controller and want to become General Manager in five years. It's time for a quick Personal-Career Review. Create your own, using this model:

▶ PERSONAL-CAREER REVIEW

- What must I do to become marketable as an A-player candidate for General Manager?

- Is this the industry for me to stay in? Is it growing? Does it reward technical skills (engineering) I lack?

- Is this the right company for me? Can I rise in it? Will it grow profitably?

- What is the competition like for General Manager? What will it be like in five years? What skills (international experience?) do I lack that will be essential in five years? Is my company growing general managers, or is it apt to recruit general managers from premier companies?

- What are future A-player candidates for General Manager doing developmentally?

- How do I stack up now, and how will I stack up five years from now, on all competencies necessary to be an A-player candidate for General Manager?

How do you get career supply-and-demand information?

- Develop a network of at least 20 people "in the know," people on top of industry and job trends. Some should also be people who can kick open doors to help you get the ideal job.

- Read, read, read. Read your trade publications and general business magazines such as *Forbes, Fortune, Business Week*, and *The Wall Street Journal*. Use the Internet for tons of career information.

- Attend at least three seminars per year for one to three days each, plus a trade show or two. While learning technical or management skills, or industry trends, you can expand your professional network. At the same time you can be recruiting (remember Chapter 5?) and, hey, why not make some of these same people part of your personal network?

- Stay in touch with at least five of the highest-powered headhunters who will talk to you. There is a clear pecking order—senior partners at top executive search firms don't have time for $50,000-per-year salespeople. Pump your headhunter associates not just for job possibilities, but for feedback—how strong is your résumé, what are your career strengths and shortcomings, what do you need to do so they can market you best?

A Personal-Career Review conducted annually is a reality check. It nudges you to keep abreast of career-relevant trends, including supply and demand, through reading and by checking with your network. The Personal-Career Review can and should lead to action plans, so that you continue feeling "on track" when you conduct your next review, next year.

3. LIVE BELOW YOUR MEANS

What? Is #4, "brush your teeth regularly"? I'm serious, dead serious. Financial freedom is central to becoming an A player at the highest level, and being happy.

In our consumer-driven society, we spend like mad. Other nations save in the double digits, and our savings rate is low single digit. Rising managers spend like mad to show off, to "buy off" the neglected spouse or significant other. High-tech IPOs have actually created hundreds of millionaires, but they are still a tiny minority. Most rising managers are strapped for dough, and a career setback would be catastrophic, causing a significant decline in lifestyle. That sort of personal financial mismanagement leads to regrettable career choices.

At least a quarter of high-achieving managers I have worked with have caused themselves big problems because of financial desperation. They take jobs in which they can't succeed, because they have to have the income. They get caught up in a lifestyle that is hard to break out of. What would the neighbors think if they took a slightly lesser job in order to move into a higher growth industry, or spend more time with the family, or get healthy, or . . . get a life? They hardly know the neighbors, yet a frenetic compulsion to be successful is driven by a need for public show.

A *Fortune* 500 executive, Bruce, lived below his means. When his company was bought out, Bruce and others received lump-sum severances. Most of Bruce's peers jumped at the first decent job offer, but Bruce took nine months to make a job choice. He performed due diligence on a lot of job possibilities. He was slower than his peers to get the next job, but years later he is the most successful and happy. He had his cake and ate it, too. His peers were stretched financially and grasped for the highest paying jobs fast, and most have changed jobs three times since. They never screen jobs well, because they buy Bad Advice #2 (live beyond your means) and #3 (never pass up an opportunity people say you can't refuse). They are chronic B players if not worse, whereas Bruce can "afford" to be an A player.

Bruce's example is unusual, but not rare. Many A players live below their means but don't advertise it. They quietly build their nest egg and relish their growing freedom. Bruce became financially independent by 40 years of age. His peers' stories are commonplace: "I guess I didn't perform due diligence on the next job" is a tune I hear every week. How can a smart guy get into such a hopeless job? "I had to—my expenses were high and that was the only job offer I could live with." Bunk! That is saying, "I'm not smart enough to get my finances in order, so I destine myself to be a B or C player." You can "afford" to be an A player. Anyone can.

A measure of financial independence permits quitting jobs on principle. A division VP last year told me he "had to" tolerate felonies for a couple of years because the CEO didn't care and, "I had no other job choice." Bunk! If the conflicted manager had two years' savings, he could have easily quit rather than risk going to jail! Can *you* "afford" to be a person of high integrity?

How much should you save? Several hundred happy A players gave me a common rule of thumb:

> ▶ Save 25 percent of pretax income, including pension, profit sharing, 401k, and stock options.

Saving 25 percent is easy in high-growth companies. Stock appreciation alone can exceed 25 percent annually. I see more and more IPO millionaires making wonderful "adjustments" in their lives. There is an ever-so-slight but discernible trend for them to fill out their Life Balance Scorecard and make the necessary adjustments. They can "afford to." But really, anyone can. You've seen the numbers—anyone saving 25 percent and investing it conservatively, starting at age 25, can retire at 45. More luxuriously at 55.

Anyone can. You probably understand the magic of compounding, but I'll give an extreme example to make the point. Two hourly workers earning $20,000 per year ($40,000 total) can save $10,000 per year and live on a taxable $30,000. (Articles and books have shown how a family of four, with resourcefulness, can live on $25,000, comfortably.) For simplicity, let's say the $10,000 leaves $7,500 per year to save, after taxes. Let's assume a 10-percent ROI, achievable in their IRAs, but also achievable in a tax-managed index fund. That $7,500 per year accumulates to $.5 million in 21 years, and to $1 million in 28 years. OK, I didn't take out inflation, but I didn't assume our couple had earned or saved a penny more since they started saving 20 years earlier, either. This $40,000-per-year couple will become millionaires and get about $100,000 per year from their investments when they are in their mid-fifties. If these two can enjoy a comfortable life and achieve financial independence solely on conservative savings, with no windfall, you can, too.

The career benefits of living below one's means, and saving for financial independence, are:

- Ease in maintaining high integrity in your career (less temptation to cut ethical corners and rationalization)
- Flexibility in making job changes (easier to walk away from highly stressful jobs)
- Confidence in seeking and accepting jobs where you can be an A player (you can afford to look longer and scrutinize jobs more thoroughly) and grow more

- Quiet satisfaction in knowing you are doing something important to winning the game of life

The disadvantage is only one. You can't show off as much, materially, for a few years. You can show off after that *and* be financially independent, however. This is the deal: You get more integrity, flexibility, confidence, quiet satisfaction, and growth opportunities in exchange for less show for a few years.

4. ACCEPT JOBS WHERE YOU WILL BE AN A PLAYER

Turn down (almost all) those opportunities people say you simply "can't refuse." I hear the excuse for failure all the time—"It was an opportunity I couldn't refuse." Finish the sentence—"so I took the job, failed because I was a C player, and regretted it." Nice logic.

The "can't refuse" rationale typically means there was a big jump in money and title. As long as the Life Balance Scorecard registers Good Enough in all dimensions, as long as your Personal-Career Review questions are satisfactorily answered, and as long as you have the competencies to be an A player in the opportunity, fine—consider the job move. Perform exhaustive due diligence on the job—what challenges you'll encounter, your resources to fix things, and exactly what are the accountabilities you must achieve to earn your first year's bonus. Talk to prospective peers about the organization culture, the boss, the finances in the company. Talk to people who have left the company, too.

A bad job choice is an indication of bad judgment. You shouldn't blame the hiring company if you accept a job and you turn out to be a B or even a C player. It's your life, your responsibility. Trouble is, the greedy, stupid job moves tend to feed on themselves. Your compensation jumps, you buy a bigger house, and quickly get accustomed to that country club. It's hard to admit failure and go back—very hard if your spouse went along with a major relocation largely because of the income "bribe." So, as the bullet nears your head, you talk to your search network, "You gotta get me a job with $150K base, minimum!" Struggling to *not* get fired becomes a way of life. In that state of desperation, the Life Balance Scorecard becomes a joke. Forget family, forget working out, forget getting a life!

There is comfort and personal security in accepting bigger jobs only when you are sure that you will be an A player—among the top 10 percent of people available for the bucks you earn. Having personal security does not mean avoiding career risks. Becoming an entrepreneur, starting a company, is a career homerun for a lot of folks. In my experience, successful entrepreneurs are very secure, very confident. They may stumble once or twice, but they learn, adapt, and then succeed. They know they are or will be A players in the league they seek to play in. Their problem is recognizing when their company has outgrown their skills, when they need professional management. But that's a different story. My point here is: Accept jobs where you will be an A player, and that does not mean being highly conservative. Seizing opportunities on the fly can be damned foolish or can be calculated risks well within the scope of your A-player talents.

5. WORK ON OVERCOMING YOUR WEAKER POINTS MORE THAN MAXIMIZING YOUR STRENGTHS

That's heresy. In the career section of every bookstore the "ten-guaranteed-success-secrets" books say to forget working on your shortcomings. It's a waste of time and effort. Recognize the competencies that got you to your present level, and build on them. If you're a discus thrower, work on discus throwing and forget trying to be a sprinter. Square peg, avoid the round holes. Sound logical? It is, for individual contributors, early in their career. It is *not*, for anyone in management.

Career individual contributors such as tax attorney, compensation analyst, and medical researcher have technical expertise to develop throughout their careers. "Leadership" is not a high priority. They need to work on being organized, showing initiative, broadening their experience in their specialty. For those who will remain individual contributors, learning how to hire A players would be a waste of time, so they should keep maximizing their strengths. For them, this career myth is no myth.

For those pursuing management, however, the story is different. From first-level supervisor to CEO, the game is totally changed. You still need your strongest assets—brilliant creativity, fabulous sales ability, or whatever—but your career will be more affected by your serious shortcomings. The fabulous salesperson who can't be a team player is a bad bet for promotion to management.

Please glance through Appendix E, a list of 50 generic management competencies. You tell me on which of these 50 competencies you can, as a manager at any level, afford to be Very Poor. None? How about Poor? None again? How about Only Fair? OK, you might be promoted and succeed, despite being Only Fair in Education (take some classes), First Impression (your bosses can buff you up), Communications—Oral (get a coach), Communications—Written (get a good assistant), or Selecting A Players (read this book). But, if you are Very Poor, even in these competencies that can be "easily" compensated for, you may have an Achilles' heel, a fatal flaw, a career derailer.

At General Electric, Chairman Jack Welch shocked and impressed the world when he rolled out a simple model showing why super performers might be fired for being Poor or Very Poor on a few competencies.

Welch said if you both achieve your annual performance numbers *and* you exhibit the positive, empowering GE values, you stay. Miss on both, you

GE Model

Make Your Numbers

		No	Yes
Exhibit GE Values	Yes	Yes/No	Yes/Yes
	No	No/No	No/Yes

go. Miss the numbers but show the values, or make the numbers and not show GE values, and you get a second chance. My coaching work with GE executives helped show Jack Welch that if autocratic SOB number achievers learned to positively lead teams, the operating results would be even better. Some executives getting second chances succeeded. After some second chances failed, however, Welch fired chronic values violators. Arrogant, condescending managers destroy teamwork, stifle good ideas, and drive away A players. They fail to optimize shareholder value. So, the bullet catches them. Please note that the most valuable corporation in the world got that way in part by firing managers who were Very Good or Excellent on dozens of "hard, objective" competencies, but they were Poor or Very Poor on a handful of "soft" competencies.

On a common-sense basis, if you were CEO, could you afford any manager rated Very Poor on *any* of the 50 competencies? Probably not. It's not that you are a bureaucrat, mushing everyone together in a sea of mediocrity. You can, and probably should, delight in having a rich mix of diverse talents and personalities. But you can't afford raging egomaniacs, dirty politicians, sexual harassers, crooks, dummies, change fighters, lazy butts, and the like.

No A player in management can be awful on any of the 50 competencies. So, no matter how strong your strengths, working on developing your Very Poor, Poor, and Only Fair competencies so they are at least Good is time well spent.

▶ High-potential managers can better advance their career by devoting personal development time to fixing their weaker points than making strengths even stronger.

If you have 40 hours to devote to personal development, beyond learning day-to-day in the job, perhaps 30 hours should be allocated to fixing your one Poor and two Only Fair competencies. That leaves 10 hours to maintain or strengthen Good (or better) competencies. If you are Very Good in global manufacturing best practices, for example, and this is your job, then attending a two-day symposium on the subject might be an efficient way to stay abreast.

Chapter 8 is devoted to exactly how you can improve in various competencies, to fix your weaknesses. Chapters 9 and 10 (on Coaching), address when people can change, and when not, and how coaching can help. For now, I hope you can understand why all of those publications saying "ignore your shortcomings" are wrong, except for niche players, individual contributors, or fringe specialists. For managers, my advice is:

▶ Fix your Very Poor and Poor competencies, or get out of management.

6. DEVELOP A-PLAYER COMPETENCIES BEFORE YOU NEED THEM

If you have fatal flaws, key #5 says fix them, and forget key #6 until you do. But if you have no career derailers, key #6 becomes important. Just because you just accepted a promotion and you're sure you're an A player, don't be self-satisfied for a second. If your company is growing and you stop growing, C-player status is fast approaching. Here's why: If your company doubles in revenues, your salary will automatically grow from, say, $100K to $150K. It's inevitable, whether or not you've earned the increases. As the company grows, pretty soon you'll need to hire managers at $100K, so "obviously" your salary can't stay at $100,000. We all like Human Resources departments who perform salary surveys, because they keep us "current." A bigger company requires that you get paid more. Heh, heh. But, if you were an A player at $100K and haven't grown enough, you could easily be a B or C player at $150K. Oops. Companies outgrow some people's talents. So:

▶ Stay in the personal-development business forever.

If financial acumen is an essential competency to move to the next level, don't count on getting the job and then learning it. Take the courses and then offer yourself as a better candidate because you already meet the job specs.

If "understanding Asian/Pacific cultures" is an increasingly important competency in a global company, read about those cultures. Volunteer for a special project that will take you to Singapore. Take your vacation in Thailand and meet businesspeople there. Attend lectures on Asia/Pacific. Then let your bosses know you have prepared yourself to succeed in that first international job.

Such initiative is one mark of an A player. A players at $50,000 base salary just express that career development initiative differently from someone at $500,000. If you don't have any fatal flaws, use developmental time to acquire competencies early, not late.

7. IN JOB INTERVIEWS, REVEAL NEGATIVES

You're an A player now, have your life in balance, and need only consider offers for jobs where you can be pretty sure you will be an A player—in a bigger league. So, why would you deceive a prospective employer? The commonplace answer—because books, search firms, outplacement firms, and former employers all make it "convenient" to conceal your negatives. Your own greed and unbridled ambition could be contributors, too.

Publishers for years have tried to persuade me to write a book on how to pass the CIDS interview. I could write it in a weekend. *How to BS Your Way into a Much Bigger Job*—the Brad Smart (BS, get it?) method. Go to the career section of any bookstore and 95 percent of the books imply the advantages in hyping positives, while concealing negatives. There are dozens of books, but not one I've seen advises getting a job in which you will qualify among the top 10 percent (until *Topgrading*). They're all about getting more, moving higher, regardless of the consequences.

People are changing jobs more often, so they go through more selection interviews—the defining moments of job choice, the vehicles for communicating truth or fiction about one's self. More interviews, more deception, more lies. It becomes easier to "omit" that failed three-month job, and as long as no CIDS interview uncovers it, why disclose that little blip in career judgment?

Some headhunters believe that if you reveal your weaknesses, they might be criticized for not producing less-flawed candidates. Only the most ethical search executives (and there are some) would press you to reveal your full job history, warts and all. There are also many ethical outplacement firms but, frankly, some less ethical firms reward "moving inventory," not "helping people become A players." Ordinarily honest candidates become "packaged" with résumés that hide negatives and hype accomplishments, with references persuaded to be kind, with role plays that teach how to avoid disclosing failures.

So, there you have it, a massive societal imperative that creates too many miserable C players. A greedy, materialistic society induces people to live beyond their means, to accept jobs where they fail. Books and outplacement counselors reinforce deception, former employers help conceal negatives (for fear of lawsuits), and job failures occur—half the time. Note that search and outplacement firms benefit from that revolving door, that 50-percent failure rate for outside hires (so do management psychologists who screen finalists, by the way). It's a nasty, painful "death spiral."

You can break the cycle by "just saying no" to deception. Put your best foot forward, but reveal your shortcomings. Be positive, but 100-percent honest in job interviews. Accept job offers only when you anticipate being an A player, a happy one. Don't let search or outplacement firms twist your arm into accepting the wrong job or hiding negatives. Your refreshing honesty will help you get offers for jobs where you will be an A player.

8. QUESTION WHETHER BIG-COMPANY LIFE IS FOR YOU

Working life is too often no life, these days. Despite the media attention to "family-friendly" companies, it generally ain't happening. Managers work 60-70 hours per week, *not* including time for commuting, business traveling (getting there and back), general business reading, or casually pecking away at the computer. The pace is rapid, and even accelerating. Change is "on the fly," and that's good; companies are adapting and flexing, but stress is high. Reorganizations are nonstop. A client executive told me, "The only reason we don't reorganize more often is we're too disorganized." New structures. New people. Team dynamics change. Organization Darwinism is at work; less effort, less dedication won't cut it, unless the competitors suddenly go lax. Not very likely.

Are there jobs where people have it "knocked"—moderate stretch jobs where success is almost a "given," where spurts of frenetic activity are occasional, not a way of life? Sure. If you are CEO of a niche company with very high barriers to entry, you might be able to build a team of A players and perhaps spend your life as you want. An alternative for some might be to get out of management and go back to being an individual performer, be a consultant rather than office head, a key account sales representative rather than VP Sales. These are versions of #4 (Accept Jobs Where You Will Be an A Player). That's smart, because it will free you to address the other six legs on your life platform. Cutting back may be best for balance and happiness, but most high achievers want more.

The single biggest decision affecting the success-happiness ratio, for many managers, is whether to work in large companies or smaller firms. As I edited these paragraphs I got a call from a man (call him Ron) I believe could become chairman of his *Fortune* 500 company some day, if he could just put up with the company politics. He couldn't force himself to get along with two consecutive bosses he didn't respect. The second fired Ron, who four months later called to tell me he is thrilled to be joining a smaller ($350 million) firm, with a 5-percent equity stake. This is not a lose/lose outcome, but win/win.

The big company got outstanding results from Ron for ten years, but no longer could accept this "loaded cannon." Ron didn't need the further agony of "playing the game." Ron is not suited for big company life, not now anyway.

Large and complex organizations can consume people's lives. Some A players thrive on the complexity, the grand scale, the internal competition. Some A players don't. CEOs implore managers to figure out how to achieve balance, and they are remarkably tolerant of an afternoon off for a child's soccer game or concert. Some A players in large companies are successful and happy, cutting deals with coworkers to free up time to take the kids to school or enjoy an uninterrupted three-day weekend. But, some managers can't achieve balance in big-company life. Meetings, meetings, meetings are necessary, but involve 20 hours per week. Scrambling to squeeze out quarterly earnings requires an enormous amount of time, creativity, and energy. Relocations are on the decline, but they are still necessary every three or four years, for up and comers in many companies. Some thrive on this life, others don't. If you don't, plan your eventual exit.

Here's an increasingly popular and smart way to work smarter, not harder: Stay with premier companies long enough (a decade?) to get leading-edge skills and career marketability, then leave. Go to a smaller organization where your skills can make a difference, yet you can work 50 hours per week. Big company life was not for Ron, who was eventually going to end up in a death spiral of stress and burnout. As it turns out, Ron is richer, both financially and personally, working in a smaller company.

Some talented people work smarter by becoming entrepreneurs. Dozens have broken away from Intel and Microsoft to start their own company. Being an entrepreneur is *not* an easier life, but can be more satisfying than clawing one's way up the corporate ladder. "I'm working as hard, but at least it's all productive work," one entrepreneur told me. He's working smarter, but still has to "get a life." "After my IPO," he said. Uh huh.

In the 1980s a lot of B and C players were nudged out of large companies. Instead of disappearing into the corporate hinterlands, many achieved remarkable success. In initially lower-level (lower-paying) jobs, they were A players, and ones with terrific disciplines learned at Motorola, 3M, Citibank, or the like. Their title was usually bigger, their scope wider, but they were a bigger fish in a smaller pond. They stretched, succeeded, and eventually made more money then they would have at Motorola. One said, "I have control over my life; I can work out at noon, attend my daughter's softball game, have dinner with the family—and I'll do homework at 9:00 P.M. or Saturday." Another told me, "Brad, I knew I spent a lot of time in meetings (at Intel), but now I'm free! I have 10 meetings per week, not 20. All that coordinating crap is cut in half!"

In the 1990s the large premier companies began focusing on the challenge of retaining A players more and more for one simple reason: They had to. Search firms are calling their A players, offering a simpler, better life in a smaller firm, and oftentimes more money and equity. Many of those departed A players are not sacrificing anything—they are having their cake and eating it, too.

To retain their A players, initially big companies tried locking them in with challenging, growth-inducing assignments. That hasn't changed, but it's not enough. Next, incentives to stay were offered in the form of stock: The 1990s bull market put golden handcuffs on A players. It worked, but in a few years there were a lot of burned-out managers, A players declining to B and C players. Now companies are beginning to listen more to what A players want—"a life—one that's not in the shitter." So, relocations are becoming less mandatory, careers of spouses are put into the equation, and sabbaticals are actually encouraged. Lean organizations that require everyone to work 80 hours per week are beginning to loosen up; a few more managers are retained, so the workload is spread a bit more and everyone enjoys a more normal 50- to 60-hour work week.

Topgrading had better incorporate the *needs* of A players, not just their skills. Premier companies are slowly adapting, so that managers can work smarter, not harder, and enjoy reasonable balance in life. These favorable trends are just beginning to occur in most large companies, however. For those managers who just cannot achieve balance, moving to a simpler company might be best.

9. TOPGRADE, IN BUSINESS AND PERSONAL LIFE

This entire book is about topgrading in business, which can help you gain a competitive edge in your career. But what about topgrading in your personal life? Do you have trouble getting and keeping good help? Are the nannies you hire not good enough for your kids? Does your cleaning service rip you off? Does your dry cleaner trash compact your clothes? If so, it's time to topgrade.

I have noticed a high correlation between business and personal topgrading. Topgraders in business get all A players, so their career is successful and they enjoy going to work each day. They recruit rigorously, check references, hire in the top 10 percent of talent available. They treat their A players with respect and caring and are repaid in loyalty and superb performance. To assemble dream teams in their personal life, they follow the topgrading principles in this book. They hire A players. So, their personal lives run more smoothly. They aren't constantly frustrated with C player mechanics, accountants, and cleaning people.

In Chicago, my wife Mary and I are thankful we found Kim and Karen 15 years ago, for they not only clean but run special errands, coordinate repair people, even help relocate a family member. Up north, our cottage is totally taken care of by Hank and Annie Slaby; they fix things before big problems occur, and handle our investment construction projects. In Bonaire (population 12,000) if a broken pipe floods our place, Tamara and Alberto will spot the problem and fix it. We depend on all these A players. Topgrading in your personal life can help make that life a joy, not a burden.

CHAPTER 7 CHECKLIST: CAN YOU HAVE YOUR CAKE AND EAT IT, TOO?

Yes   No

❏   ❏   1. I have completed my Life Balance Scorecard and have a plan to achieve all "Good Enoughs."

❏   ❏   2. I have a plan to fix all Very Poor or Poor competencies in my present job.

❏   ❏   3. (For those with no Poor or Very Poor competencies) My developmental plan seeks to improve the Only Fair competencies.

❏   ❏   4. (For those with all Good or better competencies) My developmental plan seeks to develop A-player competencies I'll need in future jobs.

❏   ❏   5. I'm in the personal-development business for life.

❏   ❏   6. I have conducted a Personal-Career Review, and my developmental plan incorporates my needs to stay on top of career trends.

❏   ❏   7. In job interviews, I put my best foot forward, but I reveal my negatives.

❏   ❏   8. I enter jobs only where I can be an A player.

❏   ❏   9. I live below my means, saving 25 percent pretax.

❏   ❏   10. I carefully consider if I am suited to big-company life and plan my career accordingly.

❏   ❏   11. I topgrade in both my business and personal lives.

❏   ❏   12. All things considered, I am having my cake and I am eating it, too.

The nine career-development principles comprise a strategy that is unique; it flies in the face of the American "get-ahead-at-all-costs" mythology in which the costs—hollow lives, deep regrets—are excessive and preventable. The common advice for success really doesn't work. By playing your cards smart, you can win with happiness and success.

Job security no longer exists, but career security does, for A players. Follow the guidelines in this chapter, ignoring the bad advice infused in our society, and you can be in the ninety-ninth percentile—that rare 1 percent for whom "life is good, the career is going great, and I wouldn't trade places with anyone else!"

8. Fixing Your Weaknesses: The Straightest Path to Success

So you want to become an A player in the biggest league possible? After learning about career successes and failures from more than 4,000 managers, I concluded in Chapter 7 that the best way to become an A player is to fix your weaknesses. Executives make it to the big leagues when their strengths are solid and they have *no serious weaknesses*. Nothing derails management careers faster than one or two fatal flaws. Therefore, the time you spend on professional development should be spent more on overcoming Achilles heels, not attending yet another seminar on the functional area you have mastered. It's not all or nothing; allocating some (10 percent) developmental time to maximizing strengths will help you maintain them as strengths.

This chapter will:

- Help you figure out your potentials—in what league you might be an A player, and what it will take to get there
- Help you topgrade—more accurately, "peg" A, B, C players and better understand what people are capable of in their developmental efforts
- Give you insight into how to fix your weakness in any of 50 management competencies

This chapter is not assumed to be sufficient to inspire you to change, and makes no effort to coach you. It succinctly conveys opinions on what it takes to be an A player and which are the most important competencies. It blurts out blunt career advice. Its style is colloquial, the way people really talk when assessing talent—"No way he's gonna get promoted until he learns to stay on budget!"

146

HOW A PLAYERS ARE PICKED

Over the years I have sat in hundreds of meetings in which candidates for promotion or for hire were discussed, dissected, and then chosen—or not chosen. I don't get a vote, but I usually have conducted CIDS interviews and have coached the candidates, so I try to contribute content as well as process—how to validly, fairly compare talent. Consistent with the points made in Chapter 7 (Key #5—"Work on Overcoming Your Weaker Points More Than Maximizing Your Strengths"), here's what happens:

- Candidates with the fewest serious flaws get the job.
- Candidates with the most impressive strengths get the job only if they do not have any fatal flaws.

At the risk of repeating myself (but in the hope of not being considered too outrageous), yes, early in one's career, strength maximization is all-important for individual contributors. Investment banking analysts had better be extremely hard working, extremely good at analytics, and good team players. The super insurance salesperson should continue to develop sales skills to assure immediate success; spending time learning customers and markets might be much more important than learning M&A skills, for now. The world I'm talking about is management. That is where allocating time for fixing one's shortcomings is almost always more career enhancing than using that time to strengthen one's strengths.

"But," you ask, "shouldn't I develop all 50 competencies for management and keep developing them forever?" Yes, definitely.

▶ Companies outgrow people. Fast-growing companies can outgrow people fast.

A lot of the coaching I do is with A players who are developing themselves *like crazy*, across dozens of dimensions, so they remain A players as their jobs get bigger, more complex.

Fortunately, day-to-day working develops not just a few competencies, but many. You got yourself organized with a department of 10, and you'll figure out how to do it for 50. Your assistant will help. Your subordinates will tell you they need a staff meeting. You'll learn. If you used the CIDS interview to hire specialists, you'll use it to hire managers, adding the management questions. Managing managers requires a set of skills different from managing individual performers; that fact is obvious all day, every day, so you figure it out. You used to interact with customer managers, and you'll figure out how to comport yourself with customer vice presidents. Your boss will drop hints about which fork to use, and you will sense when your humor was appropriate. Experience is not always the best teacher, but survivors survive. Every day is a training course in all 50 competencies at the next higher level.

If you don't develop across all 50 competencies, your nondevelopment in any will stick out like a sore thumb. Your minor shortcomings will eventually be seen as major. If you fall far short on a competency—Only Fair for one in which Very Good is the minimum necessary, you will have a fatal flaw and that could be career stopping. Better fix it. If Communications—Oral is a real strength, but Team Player is a fatal flaw, do you want to devote your developmental time to taking public-speaking courses? If so, you had better plan to be a professional speaker after you're fired.

Fifty management competencies are listed in Appendix E, followed by 11 career derailers. Despite feedback, coaching, and training, these career derailers continue to overshadow a person's strengths, dropping ratings from A player, to B, to C . . . and sometimes result in termination. In hundreds of talent-assessment meetings over the years, several competencies, or lack of them, resulted in low performance ratings, plateaued growth, termination, or reassignment where there would not be a problem. The 11 career derailers, related to needed competencies, are:

1. *Selecting A Players*—"mis-hires too many," "has a team of B and C players," "afraid to hire someone better than he is," "just won't topgrade"
2. *Integrity*—"lies," "can't be trusted to keep promises," "breaks confidences," "gossips," "pushes legal boundaries too far"
3. *Initiative*—"too passive," "doesn't take advantage of opportunities," "always trying to delegate upward"
4. *Ambition*—"too ambitious," "always trying to get the promotion rather than serve the company"
5. *Political Savvy*—"a dirty politician," "backstabber"
6. *Adaptability*—"over her head," "can't adjust to our reorganization," "job is too complex for her"
7. *Team Builder*—"can't empower anyone," "control freak," "old-fashioned autocrat"
8. *Team Player*—"builds silos," "thinks his department is the only one," "won't coordinate across departments, causing major production waste"
9. *Track Record*—"missed her numbers again," "sandbagger," "more excuses than reasons"
10. *Intelligence*—"lacks the brainpower to adapt," "slow learner," "just doesn't get it"
11. *Likability*—"arrogant," "condescending," "egotistical," "doesn't treat people with respect," "makes a mockery of our people values," "know-it-all," "sarcastic," "demeaning," "acts superior"

Which competencies are the career *makers*? All 50, but a few stand out—Selecting A Players and Removing C Players (topgrading), Initiative, and Self-Awareness. With Self-Awareness, A players figure out what is needed for success, and with Initiative the engine of success is in place. A person with a lot of Initiative is also apt to be passionately motivated, a change agent, and one who takes responsibility for having good people skills. The topgrading competencies assure the delivery system is good—the engine (Initiative) is in the right vehicle (dream team). There are exceptions—that's why we have 50, not five, management competencies. With Initiative, Self-Awareness, Hiring A Players and Removing C Players, all the other 46 competencies can (won't necessarily, but can) fall into place.

A FIX-MY-WEAKNESSES PLAN

Let's draw these interrelated points together in a simple action plan.

First, think of the next job you want (or a longer-term job, if you prefer). Write the job description for it. Ask some A players to help you. Next, go to Appendix E and write behaviorally anchored descriptions for 30, 40, or all 50 competencies, whatever the job requires. On a six-point scale (Excellent, Very Good, Good, Only Fair, Poor, Very Poor), rate the *minimum* necessary to earn a promotion. This is important:

> ▶ A players need not be Excellent on all competencies, but they must meet the minimum standard on all of them.

If your goal is accounting manager, you probably can get by nicely if your writing skills are Good and your First Impression is Only Fair, as long as you are Excellent in Analysis Skills, and Very Good in Organization/Planning and Excellence Standards. You get the picture.

Next, rate yourself currently. Ask coworkers to rate you. Note the discrepancies between current ratings and the minimum necessary in the desired job. Where are you Only Fair and need to be Good? Where you are Poor and need to be, at a minimum, Only Fair? It's time for Self-Awareness. If you are Very Poor on four competencies and need to be Very Good, are you being unrealistic in your Ambition? Do you have too many fatal flaws? Never underestimate Initiative. If your passion is to start your own company, rise to president, or sing at the Met . . . God bless you and good luck. Perhaps your initiative can take you all the way.

Figure 8.1 is a sample Fix-My-Weakness plan. Where your current rating falls short of the minimum rating necessary, create action steps, your plan to overcome the deficit.

Figure 8.1 Sample Fix-My-Weakness Plan

			Job: Accounting Manager
Competency	*Minimum Rating Needed*	*My Current Rating*	*Plan*
1. Education	4	3	Complete BSBA nights.
2. Experience	5	3	Get it on the job. Visit two companies this year with best practices I need to know.
3. Hiring A Players	5	3	Ask HR for training. Volunteer to interview college hires.
4. Team Building	4	2	Volunteer and become officer of community organization. Read three books on team building. Perform 360-degree feedback survey to monitor progress.

Scale: 6 = Excellent, 5 = Very Good, 4 = Good, 3 = Only Fair, 2 = Poor, 1 = Very Poor

You can attend a five-day career assessment course that essentially performs this exercise. If you do a quick-and-dirty version in one hour, it probably will be 95 percent on target.

THE BOTTOM LINE ON 50 COMPETENCIES

The rest of this chapter addresses all 50 competencies, offering some bottom-line insight into each. A chapter could be written about each one—what it is, how important the competency is to becoming an A player, how amenable it is to development, and exactly how people fix a shortcoming in it. You can, however, get a little deeper insight, for your own career development as well as your capacity to topgrade, from this overview. I've chosen a self-assessment-and-advice format to capture as many truths as possible from my 4,000 files, with their 40,000 job case studies. To avoid platitudes, I opt for bluntness. I exaggerate to make the point. The advice is not good coaching technique, but it is the sort of language savvy executives blurt out when they were to state the unvarnished truth to a subordinate. That bluntness is also the way A players think about their developmental needs. The situations are designed to cross all levels of management, all industries.

INTELLECTUAL COMPETENCIES

1. Intelligence

Self-assessment: I'm not as smart as my peers.

Advice: Senior managers in complex, fast-changing industries must be smart as heck. Either aim for more of an implementer job, or change to more of a static, slow-moving industry.

Self-assessment: I'm too smart, too quick for people.

Advice: You probably confuse people, interrupt, or win every argument because you are too intense, not too smart. Surround yourself with equally smart people who have better people sense than you and who can buffer your intensity.

Self-assessment: I don't know how smart you have to be.

Advice: We could debate the nature of intelligence all day, but IQ is increasingly important. Super-smart techno nerds are getting rich, as a drive through Silicon Valley will show. To rise in management, initiative is still more important than IQ. The notion that EQ (Emotional Intelligence) is more important that IQ is nonsense; the higher you go, the more important *both* are.

Self-assessment: I'd like to compensate for not having quite the innate brainpower most A players have in the job I want.

Advice: If the job you want is investment banker or senior consultant at Booz•Allen, there isn't much you can do; everyone is super bright, able to learn on the fly, quick, and hard working. But for most jobs, loads of initiative, hard work, and going the extra mile will compensate. Perspiration can still be more important than inspiration. Use your initiative to become a better topgrader, a better team player, and someone trusted more by coworkers and customers.

2. Analysis Skills

Self-assessment: My boss says my analyses are shallow.

    Advice: Show your analyses to smart coworkers before showing them to your boss. Or, determine if you are smart enough for this job.

Self-assessment: My analyses are good when I take my time, but my boss wants them done quickly.
    Advice: *Make* the extra time you need—evenings, weekends, whenever.

Self-assessment: I'm quick as hell, but sometimes I miss things.
    Advice: You're hip-shooting. Slow down, or you won't get promoted. You can be off 10 percent, causing a tolerable $20K mistake at your present level. At the higher level, that mistake might cost $200K—enough reason to not promote you until you show more maturity and discipline.

Self-assessment: A 360-degree coworker survey says I'm not able to analyze people situations, but I got 1410 on my SAT.
    Advice: Smart people sometimes do very dumb things with people. IQ is not the issue. You're so smart you have rationalized your interpersonal deficiencies. It's time for more self-awareness.

3. Judgment/Decision Making

Self-assessment: My decisions are good 75 percent of the time, but my subordinates feel I exclude them.
    Advice: Your subordinates are probably confused; they don't buy into your decisions, and the A players feel stifled because they know they could help you on your bad 25-percent decisions. Allocate time for more participation. Do damage control. But always reserve the right to call the really big plays.

Self-assessment: I just can't get my people to make decisions. They keep asking what I want to do. Why do I need them?
    Advice: You don't. Maybe they are C players. If they were previously managed by an autocrat, give them a chance to become people whom you can empower. If they continue to delegate upward, remove them.

Self-assessment: I'm accused of making premature, unfairly negative judgments about my managers' subordinates. But, I'm right 90 percent of the time.

Advice: That 10 percent is a killer. Keep your early opinions to yourself. By incorrectly labeling 10 percent C players, you kill the integrity, fairness, and accuracy necessary for topgrading.

4. Conceptual Ability

Self-assessment: My boss says I just don't have the conceptual abilities necessary for my job.

Advice: Your boss is saying you're a C player, that you lack the brains. Overall intelligence and conceptual ability are highly correlated.

Self-assessment: I'm OK with concrete, tangible situations, but not vague concepts.

Advice: Senior-management jobs all have a strong conceptual component. Read a lot and pick the brains of good conceptual thinkers. Don't expect to improve a lot, however.

Self-assessment: To get ahead in line management I need to take a staff marketing job for a year or two. It's a conceptual job and I'm scared.

Advice: Compensate. Beg or hire smart conceptual types to back you up to do some of your thinking for you.

5. Creativity

Self-assessment: I'm criticized for not generating many ideas.

Advice: Lack of creativity is rarely a career derailer, but lack of initiative is. Attack problems 40 ways, not 4; steal best practices and tailor them to your needs. Conduct brainstorming sessions.

Self-assessment: I'm a great implementer, but not a creative idea person.

Advice: Avoid taking a job where you would have to independently write the script.

Self-assessment: I'm in a field requiring creativity, and I've just run out of ideas.

Advice: Change jobs, change companies, or take a long vacation.

Self-assessment: I feel it's my job as leader to think of the most creative ideas.

Advice: Think again. Your job is to build a team of A players with whom you can brainstorm and jointly produce creative ideas. Try to do it all yourself and you're a C player.

6. Strategic Skills

Self-assessment: I'm a VP and won't make Sr. VP until I'm considered a strategic thinker. But I'm not strategic.

Advice: Topgrade, so your A players include strategists. Or, hire a consultant. You can't afford McKinsey? Then hire a retired strategist, or a sharp strategist between jobs. And, read *Competitive Advantage* by Michael Porter.

Self-assessment: Six months ago I was named Division General Manager. My people say they're confused. They don't know my vision for the division.

Advice: You are probably confusing the heck out of them with contradictory goals, such as "increase profits but lower prices." Go off site with your team and hammer out a credible vision, which is necessary before you can have a credible strategy.

Self-assessment: I want to become a plant manager in charge of 350 people. Do I need to be strategic?

Advice: No, but chances are you will have to show foresight and plan well—capital plans, layouts, production, inventories. Stay abreast of best practices in manufacturing or people will say you are not strategic.

7. Pragmatism

Self-assessment: A 360-degree survey showed me to be lacking in street smarts.

Advice: No one will promote you until you are at least Good in pragmatism. Spend time with the most savvy opinion leaders and bounce any ideas off them.

Self-assessment: I'm an idea guy, and people say half my ideas are great, a quarter need work, and a quarter are lousy.

Advice: Separate brainstorming sessions, where no idea is bad, from decision-making sessions. Let your coworkers persuade you to scrap the nutty ideas after brainstorming, before decision making.

Self-assessment: I sometimes impose my impractical ideas on people.

Advice: Don't surround yourself with yes-people. Hire strong, practical people who will keep you from shooting yourself in the foot. Don't be a control freak—the combination of bad ideas and stubbornness is a career staller.

8. Risk Taking

Self-assessment: They say I'm too conservative for this gun-slinging, fast-growth high-tech company.

Advice: Maybe "they" should listen to your caution. If you are thorough but slow, then continue being thorough but speed up your analyses. If you are a chronic nay sayer, change companies.

Self-assessment: I'm a newly appointed VP who has achieved success taking chances, with an occasional big mistake. My new boss says I have to tone myself down.

Advice: Your boss could be right. Missing a $100,000 budget by 10 percent isn't so serious as missing a $20 million budget by 10 percent. Be more thorough and buttoned-up and your hip-shooter image will soften.

Self-assessment: My team thinks I'm too chicken to push back against the unachievable goals my boss requires. We've done well, but haven't achieved a bonus in three years.

Advice: Are you a gutless wonder? Your A players have probably already quit, lessening your team's ability to achieve goals. You should not stay in a job in which you enter each year knowing you and your team will fail again. Accept "stretch," but refuse to agree to "unachievable."

Self-assessment: The biggest risks I've taken have been in changing companies and not knowing what a rat's nest I'd enter.

Advice: Shame on you. Every company, every boss, every job can be checked out. Talk with people who left the company. Insist on seeing the financials before you accept an offer. Talk with your prospective coworkers about the culture. Know your first-year accountabilities and be sure you can achieve them.

9. Leading Edge

Self-assessment: "Best Practices" is a lot of baloney; its TQM one day, then reengineering. Now downsizing is out. Why learn all that crap?

Advice: To save your career, that's why. If you don't search the world for "best practices" to do your job, someone else will and will probably get your job. Read, build your network, use judgment in accepting leading-edge approaches, and stop acting like an opponent of change.

Self-assessment: The corporate office checks out leading-edge approaches. Their jobs are to benchmark and alert us in the field to best practices. So, why should I do their jobs?

Advice: You peg yourself as a change implementer, not a change agent if you wait for others to lead you. You're a "tell me how to do it" mid-manager, not a visionary future executive. Show some intellectual curiosity and thought leadership by searching for best practices yourself.

10. Education

Self-assessment: For 20 years I've learned on the job. Most executives here have MBAs, should I?

Advice: If you are working 70 hours per week, read a lot, know the financials cold, and have a reputation for leading-edge thinking, forget the MBA. You probably have the equivalent of two MBA degrees in your head. However, if you have the time for a weekend MBA and need more breadth and depth, get the degree—at the best MBA program you can attend. Otherwise, take selected courses and seminars.

Self-assessment: What business periodicals do managers read?

Advice: Everyone reads the trade rags. Executives and future executives read *The Wall Street Journal* (including Editorials), *Business Week, Forbes,* and *Fortune.* At least scan each issue for pertinent articles. *Harvard Business Review* or *Sloan Management Review* should be circulated. *International Herald Tribune* and *The Economist* give some international insight.

Self-assessment: Why should I work all day and then take evening finance courses?

Advice: If you are getting feedback that you are weak in finance, you'd better do it. Finance is the language of business. If you aren't keeping up, aren't showing keen awareness of all the financials, then you're a B player, maybe a C. To be an A-player candidate for any senior-management role, master the nontechnical aspects of finance. Ask your CFO or CEO what specific financial skills you should master. Courses in the evening are less of a pain than cozying up to a complex book on M&A at 9:00 P.M.

11. Experience

Self-assessment: I've risen to VP Controller but I've always wanted general management.

Advice: Be the most field-oriented controller you can. Learn operations, learn marketing, and help salespeople construct winning bids. Accept a lateral move into operations, sales, or marketing, to broaden your base. Work in a company with a history of moving finance people into general management.

Self-assessment: What types of experience are generic, and increasingly important?

Advice: To maximize your marketability, it's useful to have participated in successful growth, severe belt tightening, major transformations, and international. Ask A players in the job you want what experiences they feel are crucial.

Self-assessment: I have been in a functional specialty ten years. How can I break out? I've talked to my boss and HR, but they say I'm great where I am, and I keep getting promoted.

Advice: Learn all you can about the new responsibilities you want. If you're in finance and want a crack at marketing, prove it. Read all you can. Build relationships with A players in marketing in different companies. Show Initiative (there's that A-player competency again) by volunteering for a special project in marketing and blow everyone away with your value added. If worse comes to worse, quit. Take the next job on condition you will have broader responsibilities the day you start.

12. "Track Record"

Self-assessment: I'm much more talented than my track record indicates. I've had bad bosses, and economic downturns have hurt.

Advice: Bunk! Your track record *is* your talent manifested. Research prospective bosses more thoroughly. Even in recessions, talent shines. Maybe your talent lies in a narrower or lower-level domain.

Self-assessment: I have an excellent track record in a large company. What are the problems in moving to a small company?

Advice: Get a deep understanding of what resources will exist. Most people making such a change grossly underestimate the problems. They assume all sorts of talent exists, in all departments, and it usually ain't so. Be specific—check out exactly how many people, with what talent will be in your department and other departments; know your budgets. People talk too much in generalities, when understanding the hard core specifics will help you picture whether you will have all the skills, and the will, to make such a change.

Self-assessment: I hired someone with an excellent track record in Information Services and she couldn't do the job.

Advice: Improve your interviewing skills. The words on a résumé make it appear that she had succeeded in overhauling IS. But, she inherited the successful plan, and major decisions had already been made about software, hardware, and talent. All she had to do was implement. And, she had a strong boss who gave her air cover. You should have probed further in interviews to determine *her* roles in past accomplishments. She failed in the job because she had to start with a blank page, a political rats' nest, and too little air cover from you.

PERSONAL COMPETENCIES

13. Integrity

Self-assessment: My boss says people don't trust me because of white lies. So what, everyone lies, even U.S. Presidents.

Advice: Lack of integrity is a career derailer in the business world. Just the perception you tell white lies makes you a C player, at best. Read *The Seven Habits of Highly Effective People* (by Steven Covey).

Self-assessment: It's a lot easier to say I'll do it and then not do it, than admit I have no intention of doing it.

Advice: Your integrity will be questioned. If people can't trust you, you're dead.

Self-assessment: Everyone breaks a confidence now and then.

Advice: Wrong! It's your responsibility to let people know your boundaries of confidentiality. Say, "If I know the answer to your question and was sworn to confidentiality, I won't respond." Say, "I'm sorry, but I can't promise confidentiality in advance, but if you choose to tell me something, I'll tell you if I can maintain the confidence." Learn to avoid topics. Loose lips sink careers.

Self-assessment: I moved into a new job only to find people committing felonies.

Advice: Do not commit a felony. Tell your boss of the situation, and if he doesn't back you completely, quit. Don't break the law.

14. Initiative

Self-assessment: Given direction, I'm an excellent implementer, but to be honest, barriers thwart me.

Advice: You sound like a career midmanager, and a B player at best. One competency separating A players at all levels is figuring out how to get over, around, under, or through obstacles. Of 50 competencies, Initiative is the single most important, the single best distinguisher among A, B, C players.

Self-assessment: I have all sorts of ideas for making improvements. I work weekends to put the plans together. But my boss, and frankly the whole company, is risk averse—chicken, slow, and bureaucratic. The competition is killing us and we languish in old ways of doing everything.

Advice: Join one of those aggressive competitors. Then write at least one "white paper" each year, developing an orignal idea into an action plan for the company. Submit your white paper through your boss to senior management.

Self-assessment: I have enough to do without looking for additional ways to make a contribution. My boss says lack of initiative will hurt my bonus next year.

Advice: Your boss is telling you that you are not an A player. No matter how overworked they are, A players *always* look for ways to do things better, faster, cheaper.

15. Organization/Planning

Self-assessment: I was OK in my last job, but since my promotion I can't get organized.

Advice: Every promotion brings new complexity. Get to know the capabilities of your new team, using CIDS interviews. Then organize your time focusing on three top priorities, delegating a lot to your A players. Remove the chronic Cs or you'll never be on top of your job.

Self-assessment: I have no administrative assistant, and I'm dying.

Advice: Get one, *now*. A temp, anyone. You could get fired for not producing results and no one will accept the excuse that you didn't have an admin.

Self-assessment: I've taken time-management courses and sort things into different priorities, but my people say I keep changing priorities.

Advice: Then communicate a lot more with them. Go from biweekly to weekly staff meetings. Go to daily conference calls. A players do not confuse their teams with changing priorities that cause a lot of wasted time.

Self-assessment: How many "top priorities" can there be?

Advice: Determine three or four—the ones that will make, or break, the year. Then drive, drive, drive them to completion. For those four, make DO IT NOW the mantra. No excuses.

16. Excellence

Self-assessment: I've always been conscientious, but a 360-degree survey indicates people feel my standards are dropping.

Advice: Raise the bar. Competition is forcing higher standards in every industry; the Information Age means everyone can instantly know what products and services are best. When you stop performing at the highest level in the marketplace, your career is going to slip.

Self-assessment: My standards are too high, and I'm impatient and intolerant of C players.

Advice: Your standards for yourself are too low. You keep C players and beat them up, when you should nudge them out. Perhaps you also pound on A players, demeaning them and motivating them to quit. You accept behavior in yourself that brings out the worst in others, not their best. Fix your personality and people will embrace your high standards.

Self-assessment: I embrace high standards, but the velocity of our business precludes doing four drafts of documents.

Advice: You are not alone. When you had two weeks to polish a client report, fine. In one week, you get so close to the report you can't edit well. It's time to institute a peer-review process. And, to save some time, proofing and graphics perhaps should be done by specialists.

Self-assessment: The company won't permit such processes.

Advice: Then hire people part time to back you up. Pay for them yourself. It's either that or realize you are a B player, perhaps in job jeopardy.

17. Independence

Self-assessment: I've always been a rugged individualist, figuring all this team malarkey is for followers, not leaders.

Advice: Keep your individualism, and call the difficult plays yourself. But embrace teams because they aren't going away. The old hierarchy is gone forever, because it is beaten by a flat structure, with flexible teams.

Self-assessment: My manager says I'm high maintenance, always bugging her with questions.

Advice: With flat organizations, the span of control for managers is broader, with more subordinates. It sounds as though you'd better act more on your own. The wave of the future is for Independence to be a more important competency.

Self-assessment: I'm new and just need some coaching till I figure things out.

Advice: That's fair. Assuming you've talked directly to your boss about your needs (that's what A players do) and she's unresponsive, look to your peers for help. Ask them the questions first. Perhaps a couple of them went through the same awkward assimilation and will help you.

18. Stress Management

Self-assessment: I'm 50 and seem calm on the job, but I'm going nuts. Delayering gave me two jobs or none, so I'm working 70 hours per week. No time for exercise or family.

Advice: Yes there is. One-and-one-half hours for family, one-half hour for exercise, *every* day. Topgrade to be able to delegate more to A players and waste less time cleaning up after C players.

Self-assessment: Exercise burns off stress, but my hectic work schedule doesn't permit a good one-hour workout three times a week.

Advice: Yes it does. I studied 200 on-again, off-again exercisers who became regular exercisers. Their secret has worked for many others, including me. Their secret? *No pain, I gain.* Make a lifetime commitment to exercising and *never* experiencing pain. Exercise five times per week for half an hour, but start slowly. Take six months to get to an aerobic level, if that's what it takes to never feel the exercise is too hard. Have a cold? Then ease up. But *work out*. Chart your workouts; if you want 20 per month, and you fall behind, do double workouts (big deal, one hour on Saturday). Alternate aerobic and lightweight exercises.

Self-assessment: A players seem driven yet calm. How do they do it?

Advice: Most are not calm, but some of those who are calm practice some form of meditation. They avoid burnout and keep everything in perspective with one or two 15-minute quiet periods each day—eyes closed, total calm, not sleep.

19. Self-Awareness

Self-assessment: Every two years my company puts all managers through a 360-degree feedback exercise. Is this enough?

Advice: Because you're asking the question, I'll bet the answer is no. Senior managers all have "blindspots" and 5 percent or more of the perceptions about them are typically untrue. Regular feedback from a trusted subordinate and a trusted peer can help you manage perceptions. Isolate yourself only at risk to your career.

Self-assessment: I've worked in the same company 15 years and we're not good at giving feedback, so I wonder if . . .

Advice: Say no more. You are experiencing feedback deficit. You can't calibrate yourself in relation to the rest of the world. Build a network of A players outside the company, from seminars or professional organizations, trade shows, vendors. Find out what A players know and do by watching, talking, probing.

20. Adaptability

Self-assessment: Some change is OK, but I struggle with so much change.

Advice: Warning! Warning! Lack of adaptability is a career derailer. A players are Excellent in Adaptability. They tolerate ambiguity and make decisions on the fly. They not only tolerate changes in structure, processes, locations, but seek them out in order to gain a competitive advantage.

Self-assessment: I need to find a job or company with a lot of stability, structure, predictability, security.

Advice: If that's true, be prepared to steadily decline in authority and income. Careers reflect supply and demand, and demand for static managers is plummeting. Perhaps you should try harder to see the advantages of adaptability. Instead of trying to find security in rigid old ways, find career security in embracing change.

Self-assessment: I'm certain I am right, but people accuse me of being inflexible.

Advice: If ordinarily you are considered adaptable, then perhaps you *are* right, and the others are wrong. You owe the shareholders perseverance, not acquiescence. Show the others you fully understand their perspectives (use active listening a lot); get a solid, impartial, outside opinion; and stick to your guns.

INTERPERSONAL COMPETENCIES

21. First Impression

Self-assessment: I'm slow to get promoted because of my image—dress and slang, I guess. People say I lack "presence" but I get the job done.

Advice: Without being a phony, always cultivate an image appropriate for the next higher level—attire, bearing, hair style, and so forth. Don't upstage your boss. Look and act the part, and you might get promoted a little sooner.

Self-assessment: I'm in high tech, where substance, not image, counts. Every day is a casual day.

Advice: Great, but be careful. In management your jeans may hurt you. In an IPO, Wall Street might think your casual attire is flaky. If your stock price suffers because of sloppy processes and the senior team looks sloppy to analysts, well—the medium is the message.

22. Likability

Self-assessment: I'm not much of a people person.

Advice: Become a monk. Just kidding. Warmth and charm are wonderful, but rarely necessary. Sincerity, credibility, and willingness to listen are essential. You can become more likable without a personality transplant by holding "town meetings," brown-bag lunches, and managing by wandering around (MBWA). With all of these, you must really listen, tell people the truth, and follow through on any promises.

Self-assessment: I'm confident but people say I'm arrogant.

Advice: Arrogance is a career derailer. It motivates people to undercut you, to deliberately let you hang yourself. It destroys teamwork, insults everyone. You don't have to be Excellent in Likability, but below Good, you're in trouble.

23. Listening

Self-assessment: I finish people's sentences and interrupt, but I know where they are going.

Advice: Either let people finish or else tell them what you think they are getting at. Let them confirm you were on target. Use active listening; that is, play back to people what you think their point of view is, and when they feel listened to, you will find them more willing to listen to your point of view. To be considered empathetic, you have to play back some unstated feelings (frustration, anger) along with the content. Active listening really works. Read *People Skills* (by Robert Bolton) for good chapters on the subject.

Self-assessment: I listen, I understand, but then *I* usually do what I feel is best.

Advice: "Usually?" Then what are your subordinates needed for—carrying your bags? You're an autocrat, maybe a nice one, but you don't have much empathy for the plight of your people. A players will quit, saying you only think you listen, that your mind is made up.

24. Customer Focus

Self-assessment: I do exactly what my boss calls for—generate profit and expand market share. Yet I was passed over because customer complaints are up.

Advice: Good for you for stealing profitable business from competitors. With more sales, naturally there are more customers to complain. You sound defensive, however. Someone thinks you are screwing customers or taking some other short-sighted approach. *Never, ever* be accused of being out of touch with customers. It's career suicide. Visit customers, take surveys, run focus groups. Every meeting should bring up the customer.

Self-assessment: I know what customers are thinking without having to be out in the field with them.

Advice: Bunk! Surveys and other metrics (complaints) are insufficient. Senior managers are so busy, they try to justify being removed from the customer. A players must be Very Good, minimum, in this competency, and they make time for face-to-face customer interaction.

25. Team Player

Self-assessment: People say I'm too much a team player. That's impossible!

Advice: No, it's not. Are you so cooperative you are spineless? Do you lack independent opinions? Are you easily intimidated into abandoning your point of view? Do you hold five meetings when one should have been sufficient? Teams still need leaders. Are you one?

Self-assessment: In meetings with my peers and boss I'm kind of quiet because everyone else is trying to grandstand.

Advice: Sounds like defensiveness on your part. You have an obligation to make your opinions known. You have a responsibility to make the team a team—to reach out to help others, to actively tear down silos, to intervene in disputes to resolve differences. Read *The Wisdom of Teams* (by Jon Katzenbach).

Self-assessment: My boss says I'm not a team player because after a course of action is determined, I'm not always the most enthusiastic supporter.

Advice: You're *not* a team player. You should argue, disagree, fight for what you feel is best for the company, but only behind closed doors. If there is a major philosophical difference, A players will offer to resign. When a decision is made, you must support it 100 percent. Don't go to your people and say your boss has required X or Y. Get behind it. Make it work. Use your initiative!

26. Assertiveness

Self-assessment: I'm blunt, honest, direct, forceful. However, I'm told I have too many "rough edges" for a promotion.

Advice: Keep your openness, but eliminate the most outrageous 5 percent of your behavior (publicly embarrassing people, temper outbursts, anything smacking of meanness). Doing that can improve your image, not just 5 percent, but 50 percent.

Self-assessment: I'm the opposite—not assertive enough. I never have been.

Advice: Look for a five-year improvement plan at best. The hyper-assertive person tones himself down every day, in meetings with bosses and customers. He can easily increase his control of assertiveness. You must develop new muscles, and it takes a lot longer to show improvement. If you are Poor in this, management is probably not for you.

Self-assessment: I'm quietly assertive. In negotiations I'm never taken advantage of. I stand on principle. Should I be more demonstrative—shout, pound the table?

Advice: No, not unless you are in a company of screamers who consider you a wimp.

27. Communications—Oral

Self-assessment: I'm an organized but dry speaker in formal presentations.

Advice: Join Toastmasters or get a public-speaking coach, to gradually add charisma without phoniness. I've seen terrible speakers become great. Anyone can become Good. Anyone.

Self-assessment: I don't want some public-speaking coach to try to change my personality. I'll appear phony and too packaged, like a politician.

Advice: Good speaking coaches will study your style and leverage your strengths—using *your* humor with better timing and emphasizing *your* gestures for better emphasis.

Self-assessment: I say "like" when I should say "as though"—I feel like I should work harder versus I feel as though I should work harder.

Advice: Ask an assistant to point out this grammatical flaw, for $1 each time. Spend $15 this way and your grammar will improve.

28. Communications—Written

Self-assessment: I'm just not a polished writer.

Advice: This is one area where a formal course should help. Do reference checks to be sure the course gets rave reviews.

Self-assessment: I can't stand proofing documents and I'm not permitted to have an administrative assistant. The typos are getting embarrassing.

Advice: A players don't let typos kill their chances for promotion. Figure it out. Put up with the pain and proof better, beg your boss for help, or pay someone outside of work to proof the most important documents.

Self-assessment: I've taken a course but I'm still Only Fair; to get ahead I have to be Good or better.

Advice: It's time to find a coach, a mentor—an A player who will work with you. Persuade one to review three pages of documents per week with you for six months.

29. Political Savvy

Self-assessment: I'm not a gutter politician, but people say I'm naïve.

Advice: You need to become politically aware—in tune with political forces that can help or hinder you and your group. Have lunch once a month with someone who will clue you in.

Self-assessment: I'm sick of having to wire every decision with ten people before going into a big meeting. And I hate sucking up to top executives.

Advice: Welcome to corporate life. Wire or die. Suck up a little or get left in the dust. Figure out how to lay the groundwork honestly and efficiently. Figure out how to assertively advocate your opinions on big matters *and* defer to top execs on unimportant matters. Or consider moving to a smaller company or a smaller job in your company.

Self-assessment: I'm above politics.

Advice: Or, is your head in the sand? Develop at least one solid, trusting relationship in each area of the company that powerfully affects you—someone who will give you a "heads up" when you need it.

Self-assessment: My reputation is that I'm a politician, going around people, pushing and pulling levers. It's worked so far.

Advice: Some politicians manipulate all the way to becoming CEO. Most get caught. "Suck-ups" who advocate what bosses want even if it is wrong are "yes men (or women)," not worthy of promotion. What goes around comes around. Dirty politics indicates an integrity shortfall. Premier companies don't promote people who are not Very Good or Excellent in trust.

30. Negotiation

Self-assessment: I'm a win/win negotiator, but I'm criticized because banks get the best of me.

Advice: You're not win/win. You lose. For win/win you probably need a lot better information on the other person's hand and less puppy-dog gushiness in showing your hand.

Self-assessment: I'm just not quick on my feet in negotiations.

Advice: You don't have to be. A players are thoroughly, thoroughly prepared. Know everything about the other guy, his positions, needs, leverage, and vulnerabilities. Know thyself, too. Preparation beats flash every time.

31. Persuasion

Self-assessment: I'm not a dynamic, outgoing salesman. I've done well in manufacturing operations and asked for a key account sales position to show I can be a general manager. I got the sales job, but I worry that I'll fail.

Advice: Stop worrying. The most effective salespeople are usually not super people-oriented. Instead of "bonding," they listen carefully to what customers want, they study customers to know their marketing strategy cold, and then they deliver. This world rewards salespeople who are competent and driven, not bubbly.

Self-assessment: I'm not quick on my feet in sales situations.

Advice: See #30—preparation beats flash. Do your homework. Know your prospects' company strategy and marketing plans, their appraisal of other vendors, and their personality quirks. Listen. Then listen some more. Promise, but always, always deliver.

Self-assessment: I am silver-tongued. I can sell an Eskimo a block of ice. It's just a natural talent. People love me!

Advice: Thank God you are on this earth, Mr. Slick! But watch out! The twenty-first century will reward service and performance. Hard work, sweat, going the extra mile. Tickets to a ball game and charisma are not unimportant, but even in industries where these have been important, the trend is toward impartial business decisions based on performance.

MANAGEMENT COMPETENCIES

32. Selecting A Players

Self-assessment: I have a mediocre hiring batting average.

Advice: Read this book and follow the advice. There is no more powerful lever for career success than topgrading. It's an A player's secret weapon. If you try to topgrade by removing Cs, but inadvertently replace them with more Cs, you will create a mess. Use CIDS interviews to hire As.

33. Coaching/Training

Self-assessment: I'm a compulsive doer, too impatient for coaching.

Advice: You can still coach after hiring people using a CIDS interview. Chapters 9 and 10 will help.

Self-assessment: I hire A players who don't need much coaching.

Advice: Good for you. But sometimes managers can get more talent for the buck with less experienced hires. Their potential is high, but they need coaching.

Self-assessment: A 360-degree feedback survey showed that my people are frustrated; they rated me Only Fair as a coach.

Advice: Meet with each, discuss the survey, and work out a program with each one—a plan you and they can live with. Maybe a few group sessions would efficiently meet their needs. Once-per-month one-on-one meetings might help. Find out what are their legitimate needs to perform and to grow. Respond, or you will have a big strike against you.

34. Goal Setting

Self-assessment: Subordinates say my goals for them change too much. I am just being flexible.

Advice: You are probably flighty, too. Your people should sense your driving toward completion of three top priorities, and it's OK to flex around ways to achieve them. If you change your mind because of new data, communicate it!

Self-assessment: I'm very participative and empowering; I think my subordinates will set higher goals than I could impose.

Advice: You sound passive and naïve. Your goals must be congruent with overall corporate goals, so you can't delegate setting them. Your team has to be coordinated to achieve their combined goals, so you must be engaged. If bonuses are tied to individual performance, their incentive is to sandbag.

Self-assessment: I love stretch goals—they bring out everyone's best, even if they are unachievable. I go along with them because I'm a good team player.

Advice: Be careful. When you think a 10-percent increase in sales is achievable but agree to a 20-percent goal, budgets for staff, capital equipment—everything in SG&A—skyrocket. Earnings will plummet, the stock will tank, your boss will be fired, and so will you. Your obligation is to be 100 percent clear in stating what you feel is achievable. Stretch goals are fine. "Yes man" acquiescence is cowardly and not good team play. It also can frustrate the hell out of your people (see #8).

35. Empowerment

Self-assessment: With each promotion I'm hesitant to empower people until I know whom I can trust to do the job.

Advice: Use the CIDS interview for new hires, to learn whom you can empower, to coach As and Bs, to quickly redeploy chronic Cs. The alternative—work 100 hours per week and frustrate your A players.

Self-assessment: I've learned to empower my people, but it still scares me. Our organization culture punishes mistakes, and I'm afraid this empowerment could blow up.

Advice: Find a middle ground—e-mails from your people on their decisions before they act, or discussion of key decisions in your staff meetings.

36. Performance Management

Self-assessment: My new boss is moving from operating reviews every six months to every three months, because we are in a turnaround crisis. Quarterly reviews require preparation and I'd rather do the work, not prepare for so many meetings. Who's right?

Advice: Could be you're both wrong. Operating reviews every six months is for smooth-running teams of A players. Quarterly reviews are for mild turnarounds. Monthly mini ORs are for turnarounds.

Self-assessment: I like my people to learn from mistakes.

Advice: Fine, but that doesn't mean you don't hold them accountable. If there is a promise to do X by a certain date, follow up. Build a team culture in which everyone holds everyone accountable.

Self-assessment: What do A players measure?

Advice: Everything, all the time. Constant feedback.

37. Removing C Players

Self-assessment: I inherited C players, but at least they know how things operate around here. How long should I keep them?

Advice: Historical knowledge is overrated. Almost always topgraders say they should have moved quicker to remove C players. Parachute As in and retain the C players until the As feel the Cs are no longer needed. Then redeploy the Cs. Almost any team can be topgraded in six months.

38. Team Builder

Self-assessment: My people are scattered throughout the world. Monthly staff meetings seem too costly.

Advice: Try meeting in person twice per year, and twice monthly by teleconference or videoconference. At the end of each meeting, do a "process check" to see if you need to meet more or less often. Key team questions are: Do we need better teamwork and, if so, what can we *all* do (not just you) to produce a more cohesive, effective team effort?

Self-assessment: OK, I've topgraded and half my team is new. But, we're disjointed.

Advice: Go off site for team building.

39. Diversity

Self-assessment: Frankly, we're a white male senior group, but we've done OK with diversity down in the organization. We've had no legal charges, so why sweat it?

Advice: If your strategy is to branch out beyond Duluth or Peoria, diversity isn't a nicety, or a legal insurance policy, it's a necessity. Globalization requires diversity, so get with it.

Self-assessment: I don't believe in quotas or tokens, but we need more minorities in management.

Advice: Then recruit like crazy. Require recruiters to produce A-player candidates including blacks and women, for *every* opening. Get the numbers not through lowering the bar but through creatively and aggressively recruiting.

40. Running Meetings

Self-assessment: My people complain that my staff meetings aren't very productive. I've tried preparing better agendas and moving people along, but if I cut people off, I'm accused of being domineering.

Advice: Read two current books on meeting effectiveness—any two. They all say to empower the participants to take full responsibility. You speak as though it's all your responsibility, and it's not. *They* are copping out. Hold a "meeting on meetings"; attack all of the factors listed in the books (clear goals, high commitment, widespread participation, mutual trust, timing, separate note-taker, tight follow-up on actions, and so forth). If it doesn't improve, hire a facilitator.

Self-assessment: How often do A players hold staff meetings?

Advice: Weekly. At a minimum, everyone can say what's going on so everyone is aware of others' activities. Better yet, participants interact for better coordination. Better yet, key decisions are made.

Self-assessment: I don't know what an A-player staff meeting looks like—friendly and professional?

Advice: Intense and chaotic is more typical. Everyone is active. The manager makes sure every meeting addresses all four key priorities for the year. Every issue gets out on the table and is addressed. Commitments are made. Follow-up is guaranteed, so everyone holds everyone accountable. They are fast paced. No one attacks anyone personally, but no one avoids attacking an issue just to be nice.

ADDITIONAL LEADERSHIP COMPETENCIES

41. Vision

Self-assessment: Should vision be the ideal or the practical?

Advice: Both. The balance must be credible. To be credible, it must be understandable and then understood by all. It must be alive—constantly reinforced, brought into decision making. When it is a mockery, hypocritical, or ridiculously unrealistic, scrap the vision and start over to create a better one.

42. Change Leadership

Self-assessment: I drive change pretty hard, and I'm told too many people are confused and scared.

Advice: You probably need to communicate 300 percent more. That means listening to people's concerns, responding, explaining, and involving people more in the change efforts. Kotter's book (*Leading Change*) is good, but perhaps you need a workshop (National Training Laboratories, phone: 703-548-1500) or the help of a change consultant.

Self-assessment: I'm a change agent; I love it when I can show that I welcome a new structure that will beat the competition. More than just accepting it, I make it work.

Advice: You sound like a wonderful change implementer, taking others' initiatives and making them happen. A players are more apt to be true change masters, *authoring* changes *and* making them happen.

43. Inspiring "Followership"

Self-assessment: I'm not a natural leader, and my people seem to go off in their own directions.

Advice: So-called natural leaders are 1 percent, and all the other successful leaders are *made*. Get a credible strategy (#6) and vision (#41), topgrade your organization (#32, #37), conduct good meetings (#40), and people will follow.

Self-assessment: Peter Drucker writes that charisma is not as important as substance.

Advice: He's right, but even he agrees that charisma can help in times of great change—"selling" hundreds or thousands on accepting a new direction. A quiet, cold leader won't be very effective in the constant communications necessary to drive change; a dynamic, positive, charismatic leader has an advantage.

44. Conflict Management

Self-assessment: Two of my subordinates can't resolve a major difference, and they have reluctantly brought the issue to me to resolve.

Advice: Bring them together NOW. Ask each individually to explain (a) her point of view, (b) the other's point of view, (c) what she will "give" for a solution, (d) what she asks the other to give. Go through all four lists with a major goal of mutual understanding, and that's all—*not* necessarily a resolution. There is one ground rule: On any points of disagreement, X must state Y's point of view to Y's satisfaction, before stating her (X's) point of view. You are the referee. This is powerful: It *assures* mutual understanding. *Then* resolution might be finally achieved.

Self-assessment: I'm an A player, newly introduced into a C organization that fights everything I try to do. I get no air cover.

Advice: Shame on you for bad judgment in accepting an offer for a job in which you will probably fail. After getting a lot of scars, you'll either quit or get fired. In the meantime, talk to your boss about getting protection.

MOTIVATIONAL COMPETENCIES

45. Energy

Self-assessment: My energy level is declining. I eat right and take vitamin and mineral supplements, but I just can't find the time to exercise. My doc says make the time.

Advice: Listen to your doc. See #18 (Stress Management).

Self-assessment: I don't take much vacation. We're so delayered, everyone is doing at least two jobs.

Advice: Sounds as though your life is out of control. I've never known a manager who could not take full vacation, barring a crisis, if he or she had topgraded. No vacation means C players are killing you.

46. Enthusiasm

Self-assessment: I feel enthusiastic, but don't show it.

Advice: If rah, rah is important, like in selling change, and if you are low key, express your enthusiasm in other ways—videos that capture you at your best, celebrations of success in which others play effusive roles, well-written pieces for the house organ, and so on. Public-relations coaches can sometimes "tweak" a presentation style, adding enthusiasm without attempting to remake a person's personality. Phony, plastic "techniques" backfire.

Self-assessment: I'm not really passionate. I just do my job, and damned well. I'm serious, purposeful, and I'm an A player. Except for enthusiasm.

Advice: Chances are you don't need to change. But progressing from Poor to Only Fair in Enthusiasm could spark the organization culture a bit. Without changing your personality, you can probably give a few more deserved pats on the back, say a few more positive things in staff meetings, and smile a bit more.

Self-assessment: I'm the nay sayer who keeps the nuts around here from going off in foolish directions.

Advice: You'd also better be a yea sayer. Any attorney or financial controller can say no, even a C player. A players have to add value to the yeses.

47. Ambition

Self-assessment: I'm considered a "high-potential" manager, only 45 years of age, but everyone sees me as a future CEO of a public company. Trouble is, I want my health and a real family life more than the CEO title.

Advice: Good for you. Follow your heart and you'll be happier than 90 percent of the ambitious strivers. Read Chapter 7 carefully. You can have your cake and eat it, too. Either forget the CEO title in a large company, or if you decide you want it but can "get a life" only in a smaller company, leave. You probably have 20 years of experience, so get 15-percent equity in a small company where you can be CEO *and* go to your kid's soccer game *and* eat dinners with the family *and* work out regularly. This could be more satisfying, more fun, more autonomous, and more lucrative.

Self-assessment: People say I'm too ambitious, too eager to get ahead.

Advice: Don't trip over your ego. Let the powers above you know your desires, but your peers and subordinates should see only your deep commitment to your *current* job. If people see you as sacrificing future results to look good now, you are sucking up way too much; your integrity becomes suspect.

48. Compatibility of Needs

Self-assessment: My leading candidate for VP Marketing really wants a GM job. She had one, but then her company relocated, and she didn't go. She says she can be happy as VP Marketing but maybe she's just saying that to get a job. I'm afraid that if she joins me as VP Marketing, she'll continue looking for a GM job.

Advice: Cut a deal . . . if she does an excellent job as VP Marketing, you'll help her get positioned again for general management in, say, three years. Special projects, a task force, a couple of seminars, acting as GM for a vacationing GM can be part of the plan. Promise her only development, not a GM job. If your company cannot credibly develop her, don't hire her—she'll be "trolling" for that GM spot from the day she begins as VP Marketing for you.

Self-assessment: You can't find out what a job or company is really like until you get there.

Advice: Yes you can. A players do it. They perform due diligence, thoroughly. Organize multiple visits (see Chapter 5).

49. Balance in Life

Self-assessment: What balance?

Advice: Life is a process, not a 40-year career goal. Most senior managers who sacrificed balance for more than a year or so every five years gave up too much. They ultimately regret it. Balance . . . work, family, wellness, community, spiritual expression . . . that *is* the endgame. Balanced people are the most fulfilled. If your organization uses people up, QUIT.

50. Tenacity

Self-assessment: A talented subordinate of mine gives up too easily, saying that frantic pursuit of work goals sacrifices his balance in life.

Advice: That's a cop-out. Of 50 competencies, Tenacity, the passion to succeed, is not last, but right up at the top, close to Initiative *and* Self-Awareness. Tenacious people figure out how to serve customers and get quality time with the family. People generally low in tenacity should not be hired, except for the few mechanical, low-level jobs.

Did you see yourself and your subordinates in many of these situations? I suspect so.

Is such a focus on fixing weaknesses "negative thinking"? I hope you don't feel so. If you were an otherwise great surgeon, but your surgical knots were just a bit sloppy, unnecessarily stressing the adjoining skin, what would you do? You're Only Fair at knot tying, and you really want to be Very Good. Let your assistants suture for you? OK. Not bad—that's like a manager hiring people to compensate for his shortcomings. Or you could focus on knot tying and become Very Good at it. Is that negative thinking? A players don't think so. This is reality. Fixing weaker points separates a lot of us from Bs and Cs. That's reality.

CHAPTER 8 CHECKLIST: DO YOU HAVE WEAKNESSES TO FIX?

Yes No

❑ ❑ 1. I recognize that my developmental time is better allocated to overcoming a potential fatal flaw than maximizing an existing strength.

❑ ❑ 2. I know what are the 11 most common career derailers.

❑ ❑ 3. I am particularly interested in developing the most important competencies—Initiative, Self-Awareness, Selecting A Players, Removing C Players.

❑ ❑ 4. I have a fix-my-weaknesses plan in progress.

With this groundwork laid on how As differ from others, how A players are picked, what competencies are most important, and how fatal flaws are fixed, let's move to how you can coach your people to maximize *their* strengths and, yes, fix *their* weaknesses.

9. Coaching 101: The CIDS-Based Model

Coaching is hot, hot, hot! Everyone is doing it. Since human capital is hot, coaching to get the most out of human capital is searing. Companies such as Microsoft, IBM, Wm. M. Mercer, and Herman Miller are "into" coaching.

Coaching is dealt with in this chapter and in Chapter 10, not just because it is an important topgrading skill (though it is), but because CIDS interviewing can enable you to dramatically improve your coaching of new hires.

This chapter begins with a definition of coaching and then presents statistics showing that many, if not most, managers are deficient coaches. Next, CIDS-based coaching is explained, and luckily, the CIDS interview "automatically" helps you acquire "super-coach" characteristics, to be used during the new hire's "honeymoon period." Next, the tough issues in coaching are dealt with: can people change, what competencies are amenable to change, why do and don't people change, and what are the necessary psychological steps taken that assure change (including the "crocodile theory of motivation"), for the better. This may sound theoretical, but it will lay the foundation for the examples, real-life case studies, presented in Chapter 10. From these two chapters, you will learn to be a more effective coach, and this skill will make you a more effective topgrader.

DEFINITION OF COACHING

Coaching is a one-to-one-dialogue in which the coach helps a person understand his or her strengths and weaker points and build commitment to

180

improve performance. Coaching helps unlock someone's potentials. But is it any of the following?

- **Counseling**—to help someone improve self-awareness and change points of view
- **Mentoring**—sharing sage advice to help someone become more savvy in matters of organization culture, networking, and career planning
- **Teaching**—instructing someone in order to improve expertise
- **Confronting**—addressing nonperformance to help someone either achieve performance goals or accept the necessity of redeployment

Yes. It's all of the above. Naturally, someone skilled in "all of the above" is no common mortal.

THE COACHING CHALLENGE

Most managers are lousy coaches. Surveys of over 50,000 people conducted by Smart & Associates in the past 20 years show that 75 percent of employees rate their managers Only Fair or Poor as coaches. In my files of thousands of finalist candidates for senior management, only 25 percent qualify as having coaching as a stand-out strength. That leaves most of my senior-management sample in need of improved coaching skills.

When people describe coaching deficiencies, they commonly describe their managers as:

- Inaccessible to me
- More results-oriented than people-oriented
- Too impatient to coach
- Hypercritical
- Stingy with praise
- Unconcerned with my career development
- Poor at listening
- Late and or/shallow in performance reviews

The hundreds and hundreds of managers I have coached have common excuses:

- *"I'm just too busy."* Downsizing and constant reorganizations require 70 hours per week. Delayering produces more subordinates, too many to coach.

- *"I don't know how to criticize without seeming hypercritical."* It's management by exception; in the crunch of time you learn to criticize, not praise.

- *"I just don't have those great coaching qualities—empathy, sensitivity."* Besides, the shareholder wants results from aggressive leadership. You don't rise in management by being Mother Teresa.

I've found that even the excuse makers find the promise of coaching alluring. Most senior managers I've interviewed have known at least one super coach, and that coach led a charmed life. Coaching turbo-boosts talent, so the manager doesn't have to fight fires. With a trusting, supportive partnership forged with each subordinate, the coach is a nonstop inspiration to greatness. Each member of the team is coached to be better at problem solving, decision making, team building. Are you short on time? Coaching is the answer—delegate more to people who have grown through good coaching. Are you hypercritical? No problem for a super coach, who has so minimized his people's shortcomings; criticisms are positive tweaks, little nudges here or there. The non coach is impaired, stifling his people through inattention, sentencing himself to having a group of passive, dependent, nitpicked, low-morale, perpetual trainees.

The super coach is the genius—initially coaching a lot, then empowering more and eventually coaching less; she is able to play golf more because the job is done better. Super coach is the talent magnet: "Susan doesn't use up talent, she grows it." A players flock to her to realize their full potentials. Her well-coached flock flies on to bigger and better jobs, opening up slots for the lucky few who will reap the benefits of her coaching wisdom. Susan is a net provider of talent to other parts of the organization, which earns her accolades from the CEO. In times of fast, complex organizational change, Susan's folks are the change agents, the fully developed leaders.

Some weak coaches burn out from trying to do it all themselves. Meanwhile, super coach has balance in life. Because she coaches regularly and effectively, she has time for herself—for thinking more strategically, for special projects that give her visibility and promotability. On rare occasions super coach can't salvage a C player. Her coaching skills are so good, however, she rarely has to fire someone. Chronic C players thank her for her sincere coaching and find another job.

Some managers experience a death spiral. There is no time to coach, so they micromanage and nitpick, which fails to grow people, leaving less time for the "luxury" of coaching. So they micromanage more, drive away A players, have even less time to coach, and so on. As for those inspirational human qualities—forget it! No time. No time.

THE MAGIC OF CIDS-BASED ASSIMILATION COACHING

Put simply, if you have conducted a CIDS interview as this book suggests, you automatically possess super-coach advantages. Really. You can sit down and coach your new hire and earn Very Good ratings with about two hours of preparation. Pull it off as this chapter teaches, and you will find yourself improving as a coach with the other members of your team. This chapter is the equivalent of teaching you a good five-iron swing. Master it, and the principles will transfer to other clubs. Learn CIDS-based assimilation coaching, coaching your new hire to "fit" and to begin a long-term development plan, and it's like mastering a five-iron shot. Then transfer your assimilation coaching to other venues such as confronting nonperformance and teaching new approaches.

Of course, with CIDS interviews, your hiring should improve so that you have 90 percent good hires to coach. A players are more coachable than C players! Encourage your subordinate managers to use CIDS-based assimilation coaching and pretty soon your entire team will be a hotbed of super coaches, maximizing the talents of A players on your dream team.

> ▶ It's a lot easier to be a super coach when you've done a super job of CIDS interviewing and have hired an A player.

Your improved coaching skills can come a few weeks after you have hired someone using the CIDS interview. Assimilation coaching is mostly to help the new hire adapt to the new job, but it can lock in a new hire who, after learning what the job is *really* like, might be tempted to accept that other job offer that remains open. It provides a marvelous opportunity to begin heavy-duty coaching, helping the new hire perform short-term and to grow, long-term. Assimilation coaching can be hard-hitting, addressing strengths to be maximized and weaker points to be fixed. You know my opinion: Development time is most productively allocated to fixing shortcomings for anyone in management. Your coaching efforts are turbo boosted, of course, because A players are not only more willing to be coached, they have stronger talents to grow.

CHARACTERISTICS OF A SUPER COACH

Coaching is important to, perhaps even the essence of, good leadership. What exactly are the characteristics of a good or super coach?

1. **A partner.** "Hey, you've got a problem, let's work on it together." Interested, engaged, respected.

2. **Promotes autonomy.** Helps coachee to independently diagnose problems, consider solutions; makes informed choices regarding development.

3. **Positive.** Supportive, builds confidence, an enthusiastic motivator. Uses praise and recognition for progress and accomplishment. Never ridicules. Passionate. Has a sense of humor. Invariably respectful.

4. **Trustworthy.** Honest. Maintains confidences. Open. Admits when wrong. Doesn't overpromise.

5. **Caring.** Compassionate and empathetic. Sincere.

6. **Patient.** Understands how hard it is to change. Tolerant. Reasonable.

7. **Results-oriented.** Focuses only on important issues. Proactive. Infectiously committed to helping coachee perform. Follows through on promises.

8. **Perceptive.** Understands coachee's strengths, shortcomings, goals, needs.

9. **Authoritative.** Knowledgeable. Wise. Clear and specific in feedback. Has common sense. Generates valid measures of improvement.

10. **Active listener.** Plays back content and underlying feelings. Summarizes, clarifies.

If such superb human qualities are necessary for coaching, it's no wonder most managers are found deficient.

HOW YOU STACK UP DURING THE HONEYMOON PERIOD

During the first few weeks after starting to work, the new hire mostly is listening and getting to know people. The shortcomings you know exist in your new hire aren't apparent . . . yet. It's like a honeymoon. How does your new management hire regard you? Chances are you stack up extremely well against the ten characteristics of a super coach.

Remember, you conducted the CIDS interview and half a dozen revealing reference checks. Your newly hired manager is almost certainly an A player and was not shy about asking you penetrating questions. You both concluded this is a good match. At the beginning of your CIDS interview you promised assimilation coaching, and this is it. The CIDS-interview introduction promised coaching for short-term performance and long-term development. This is it. Several weeks after the new hire started, you are meeting to begin fulfilling these promises. This is it!

Of course, you're regarded by your new hire as a *partner*, super-coach characteristic #1. Extending the job offer was a vote of confidence by you and an indication of respect for you. You are the *authoritative* boss, in charge, which is super-coach characteristic #9. The CIDS interview provided extremely thorough insights into your new hire; assuming you performed a 360-degree survey within the past few days, your new hire is eager to learn "How am I doing?" You know the hiree's strengths and weaker points better than anyone, making you *perceptive* (#8). You accurately perceive the hiree's needs because you've already asked dozens of ways. You have shown you understand. So, in this honeymoon period there is no doubt you are *caring* (#5) and *trustworthy* (#4). You both want that new hire to achieve high-performance goals; you both are *results-oriented* (#7) in this coaching. You've hired an A player, who wants not dependency on you, so you are regarded as *promoting autonomy* (#2). If there have been missteps in the first few weeks, now is the perfect time to nip problems in the bud. If you have insights and a willingness to coach for long-term growth, hey, that's what A players want.

"Bonding" naturally occurs in CIDS interviewing and hiring A players, so it's pretty hard for you *not* to be *patient* (#6), a good *active listener* (#10), even if these generally are not your strengths. Without being a psychologist, you already have a good idea of the thinking style (intuitive, analytical, participative, experimental, emotional) of the hiree and how compatible you are. You know what the hiree *expects* in a manager—you've checked it out multiple ways. You both know you can work together. Your new hire is all ears, open and responsive, truly in a "teachable moment." You are *positive* (#3) and perceived to be positive by your new hire.

Hey, it doesn't get any better than this. The combination of the CIDS interview and the honeymoon period endows you with super-coach characteristics. Take advantage of this golden moment!

The typical 50-percent success rate in hires makes an assimilation-coaching meeting awkward, half the time. Mis-hiring destroys a mutually trusting "partnership" and usually triggers mutual blaming. "You didn't tell me about all these problems." "Oh, yeah, you didn't tell me you had so little project-management experience." So much for the honeymoon. But CIDS interviews produce good hires, A players.

First-time CIDS interviewers have fun in assimilation coaching, a rare high-powered, positive coaching session. You feel empowered, so it is relatively easy to empower the new hire. There are fewer problems to fix with A players than with C players, so there is little inclination to push, cajole, demand certain changes. With an initial coaching meeting a success, you become positively reinforced to polish your skills, to extend coaching to other subordinates, with other purposes.

CAN LEOPARDS CHANGE THEIR SPOTS?

Coaching requires a complex interplay of assumptions regarding:

- Whether people in general can change
- Whether this individual can change
- How amenable specific competencies are to change
- What circumstances trigger unusual change

As an interviewer you should bet that people will change only when they already have demonstrated an ability to improve in a particular competency; that is, assume people can change when they already have changed. If someone is improving teamwork skills, believing further improvement will be possibly justified. Don't be naïve and assume someone will finally get organized when every boss in the past ten years has criticized the person for being disorganized. You can be sure at every job change, the person promised "I'll improve, I'll improve, I really mean it this time!" Sure.

Let's investigate this subject in more depth. We all know that we have changed, for the better. We mellow, become wiser, acquire maturity and judgment. We all know individuals who dramatically changed—a hard charger that slows down after a heart attack, an autocratic SOB who becomes more positive after a child contracts leukemia. However, no hiring manager, no coach, can count on life-altering epiphanies.

CIDS-based coaching meetings, whether for assimilation or another purpose, is not a love-in. It's not always warm and fuzzy. Even A players have weaker points, and plenty of them. Coaching need not be acrimonious, but to be effective it must be hard-hitting.

My advice is not simplistic. But it can simplify the complexity of trying to figure out how amenable 50 different competencies are to change. Let's take a look at those 50.

The positioning of competencies in the three columns in Figure 9.1 is not carved in stone. Specific competencies are "relaively easy to change" or "harder but doable" for different individuals and in different circumstances. The "very difficult to change" list fits almost everyone, in my experience. No matter how much we might want to change, there is simply no way an adult can acquire significantly more Intelligence, more IQ points. We may learn to stretch our intelligence through hard work and listening to smarter people, but it is rare for people to transform shallow Analysis Skills into deep ones, dullness into Creativity, lack of Conceptual Ability into a strength. There aren't many places to go for a character transplant to improve one's Integrity. Some sort of religious conversion might do it, but that is hard to incorporate in a developmental plan. So-called "natural" leadership components of

Figure 9.1 The Amenability of Competencies to Change

Relatively Easy to Change	*Harder But Doable*	*Very Difficult to Change*
Risk Taking	Judgment	Intelligence
Leading Edge	Strategic Skills	Analysis Skills
Education	Pragmatism	Creativity
Experience	"Track Record"	Conceptual Ability
Organization/Planning	Initiative	Integrity
Self-Awareness	Excellence Standards	Assertiveness
Communications—Oral	Independence	Inspiring "Followership"
Communications—Written	Stress Management	Energy
First Impression	Adaptability	Enthusiasm
Customer Focus	Likability	Ambition
Political Savvy	Listening	Tenacity
Selecting A Players	Team Player	
Removing C Players	Negotiation Skills	
Coaching/Training	Persuasiveness	
Goal Setting	Team Builder	
Empowerment	Change Leadership	
Performance Management	Diversity	
Running Meetings	Conflict Management	
Compatibility of Needs	Credible Vision	
	Balance in Life	

Assertiveness and Inspiring Followership take years and years of serious work to improve from weaknesses to strengths.

Tough SOBs, short on Likability, can be coached to be nicer; they are "nicer" every day with their boss and customers, so it's a matter of figuring out how to broaden the range of already existing skills. "Meek Mike" is always lacking in Assertiveness and if he suddenly tries to be forceful, he blows it. It takes him a long time to develop muscles he has never used. Better wellness and Balance can jack up Energy a bit, but both require major commitments and real discipline. Enthusiasm can be faked a little better, but in general the motivational competencies—Energy, Enthusiasm, Ambition, Tenacity—are ingrained, hard wired.

All the other competencies are more fixable—that is, for most people, a conscientious effort can correct an Only Fair rating to Good. Is change from Very Poor to Good possible? Anything is possible, but the only Very Poor competencies I have frequently seen become Good are Education (take the courses), Experience (take the job), Communications—Oral and Written (take classes or get a tutor), Political Savvy (after getting burned), Selecting A Players (use CIDS interviews), Removing C Players (you can order it), and Compatibility of Needs (take the right job).

WHY PEOPLE CHANGE

The crocodile theory of change is sophisticated, so pay attention. We all live on tiny islands separated from danger. If a big, nasty crocodile comes ashore, we become highly motivated to change, to escape. But, jumping in the water with more crocs is also scary. Without a credible way to get to safety, why risk changing? If more crocs come ashore, we'll just go nuts. Welcome to the business world! The more responsibility you get, the more crocs come ashore, first nipping at your feet, then your ankles, then higher.

You discover a rowboat, a way to escape! But, it's leaky, so why risk it? Aha, now you find a speedboat, gassed and ready to go! That makes change easy.

People change when the avoidance of pain seems worth the risk. If one baby croc crawls ashore and you offer me a speedboat to escape, my decision is easy to make—I'll do it, I'll change. If 15 full-grown crocs come ashore and you offer only a leaky rowboat, I might risk leaving the island, because I have to. But no boat, no change. No crocs, no change. It's all a calculus—a balancing of developmental options (boats) in relation to anticipated pain (size and number of crocs) if I don't change. Anticipated career failure is ten big crocs, but if I don't see any escape boats, what can I do? The coach provides boats. If I don't know there are crocs on my island, I won't be motivated to change. The coach points out the crocs—a 360-degree survey showing arrogance combined with a "not promotable" rating because of it, for example.

Rational belief is frequently insufficient to effect real change. There are a few baby crocs on my island, and I know they will grow bigger and I know that my boat is beginning to leak and will only rot more, so I suppose I should change, one of these days. Or maybe I'll depart next year, when the crocs are bigger. Everyone tells me I should listen better, get organized, but why should I? After all, I'm getting top performance reviews. There are only baby crocs motivating me to get better organized. But when they are suddenly full grown, my emotions enter. Real fear. What a great motivator! If my boss tells me my 50-percent bonus will be zero if I don't get organized, that's like having ten hungry crocs licking their lips (do they have lips?).

The crocodile theory of change applies to negative motivation. Another sophisticated theory handles positive motivation. It's called the "fast-food paradigm." I'm getting along adequately living on my island because I have a lot of bananas to eat. One day I'm looking through my binoculars and see on the mainland—McDonald's. Mmmm! As a fast-food freak, I'll jump in my speedboat, race over, and pig out. But I wouldn't risk rowing a leaky boat three miles across treacherous waters. I want to improve my knowledge of investments, I really do, but in this bull market trying to improve my returns from 25 percent to 27 percent, well, it's not quite worth the effort. Now I look through the binocs and see—oh, by gosh, a new Pizza Hut, Burger King, and

White Castle! I gotta risk it. In my leaky boat I go. The lure of improving my investment returns from 25 percent to 50 percent is just so enticing.

You get it. Coaches point out the fast-food restaurants (the vision of an exciting, better life), the crocs (pain for not changing), and the boats (developmental avenues). In 27 years of coaching I have found the most significant and enduring change to take place when the manager perceives a lot of fast-food stores, a lot of crocs, and a lot of speedboats.

WHY PEOPLE DON'T CHANGE ON THEIR OWN

Why don't we, you and I, change on *our own?* Even when we realize we will be happier making a change, why don't we? Would coaching help us?

People don't change because:

- **It's impossible.** A subordinate may correctly conclude that he lacks the innate capacity to play for the Chicago Bulls or become a CPA. No coaching needed.

- **Blind spots.** Sue simply doesn't know what it takes to succeed, what career paths would match her talents and interests. Charlie does not realize how offensive he can be barking out orders. Coaching can help.

- **Normal defense mechanisms.** We all rationalize failures, blame others, project our own foibles into others, deny that an "idiosyncrasy" could be a career derailer. Coaching, not therapy, can help here.

- **Neurotic need to not change.** We all become hard-wired early in life. A part of us might want to fail, to perpetuate distance from others, to snatch defeat out of the jaws of success. Coaching can help if people have already begun changing. If not, clinical psychology is appropriate.

PSYCHOLOGICAL STAGES IN CHANGE

Whether for coaching a new hire, addressing a newly observed problem, or facilitating change in any performance-management or career-development system, the steps are the same:

1. *Awareness.* "I seem to have a need to change."
2. *Acceptance.* "I definitely need to change."
3. *Commitment.* "I not only own the problem, I own responsibility to fix it."
4. *Program for development.* "I fully embrace this program, with specific activities."

5. *Reinforcement.* "I need internal and/or external reinforcement—feedback, crocodiles and fast food—for maximum growth."
6. *Monitoring progress.* "I embrace measurement of my progress."
7. *Conclusion.* "I've fixed this problem; while recognizing that for some issues a lifelong effort is necessary, I have achieved the specific goal of eliminating a potential career derailer."

Let's consider the context, the implicit psychological contract in a constructive coaching session.

> ▶ Implied in all seven steps is who's in charge—not you, but your coachee.

Even if you have to confront nonperformance in a C player, the most constructive outcome (even if it is a friendly termination) comes not from a trash compactor, beating a person with failure, but from a dialogue in which the person arrives at self-awareness and the conclusions necessary to change. A players usually say, "Give me the unvarnished truth, don't beat around the bush, and I'll figure out how to fix myself." Great! All seven steps might be addressed in five minutes. With C players it's slower, much slower, but the basic principle is the same: We *all* change fastest and deepest when *we own the process.*

If you buy the assumption that you as a coach are a change facilitator, not a change intimidator, a lot of super-coach qualities emerge. Instead of blame, you problem solve. Instead of focusing on the person, you focus on the problem. You address, not criticize. You come across as I'm OK, you're OK, and never, ever the condescending, I'm OK, you're NOT OK.

Questions help the coachee diagnose and fix problems, rather than respond defensively. Instead of, "Why weren't you generating more leads?" it's "How many leads did you generate in relation to the performance standard?" If you already know the answer, ask, "How do you feel about last month's performance?"

A wonderful technique for communicating those super-coach qualities is *active listening*—playing back what you hear and the feelings underlying it. Active listening is more than simply echoing back what you have heard. It involves paraphrasing the essence of the person's point of view. An active listener grasps and reflects back people's intent, reading between the lines. Body language is observed, and unstated feelings are accurately interpreted. It is much more helpful to reflect content and feelings by saying, "You're stumped by that problem" than to fake understanding ("I think I know what you're saying"), feign empathy ("I feel your pain"), or talk about yourself ("That reminds me of a time . . .").

Active listening is a powerful coaching tool when you want to avoid an argument, help a person become more dispassionate and objective, or guide the person to diagnose and solve a problem without giving your solution. Forget trying to use active listening when you are angry at the person, when trust is an issue in your relationship, or when you are too hassled or frustrated to calmly tune in to both the other person's feelings and your own.

Summarizing the three reasons why the goal was not met does not mean you agree with "excuses," but simply that you care, you are listening, you understand. Saying, "You missed quota three months in a row, and one more month and you're fired" is clear, but a more motivational coaching approach might be, "Joe, you've indicated three reasons for not making quota, you've shared how difficult and frustrating this is, and you just can't see how you will make quota in the future." This opens the door for the salesperson to take responsibility for either changing the results or considering job options. Putting the coachee in control means a chronic C player will be more apt to fix his behavior or, if not, more apt to depart as friends (no lawsuit).

CIDS-based assimilation coaching builds in all seven of the psychological stages in change. Let's pause on each step for some coaching tips.

1. AWARENESS

This is the biggie. Even marginally effective coaches can easily coach an ambitious A player to do something she is eager for, to improve her experience. "Mary, I know you want both international and marketing experience, so how about representing our group at the Global Marketing Conference in Paris?" Yes, Yes! What a great coaching intervention!

Awareness is a "biggie" in coaching because of defensiveness, which occurs when a person either doesn't recognize a need to change or does, but can't. Even in an assimilation exercise, a subordinate might be so eager to impress you that your pointing out minor shortcomings could meet a little resistance. Coach a person toward awareness and minimize defensiveness by:

- *Encouraging the person to generate feedback.* If you have heard customer complaints, present your data and perhaps the salesperson will suggest a customer survey.

- *Granting that 5 percent of negative perceptions of a person may not be true.* Negative self-fulfilling perceptions of people are common if they aren't liked. An unliked gossip can easily be accused of breaking confidences, and people will believe it, even if it is not true. Unless you are certain the person broke confidences, don't point your finger accusingly. Your coachee will be less defensive if you concede that at least a small percentage of the time, perception is *not* reality. What passes for fact in the business world is not, necessarily. However . . .

- *Conveying that the higher the management position, the more true is the statement "perception is reality."* Even if the person is not lazy, if that is the perception it is worth being aware of it. Then a program must manage the perception, even if the perception is inaccurate.

- *Doing a "data dump" on resilient, confident A players ("I don't think you are fitting in very well yet") but inching into it more gradually with C players ("How do you feel you are fitting in?").* The more defensive the person, the more dialogue is necessary in order to know when there is receptivity to more negatives.

- *Being prepared with good data—specific (not general), descriptive (not evaluative), objective (not subjective), conveys "I" (rather than blame), and well timed.* Bad data would be: "I know you're running to catch a plane (poorly timed) but you've (blame) screwed up (evaluative) on that software project (general), and I think you are deliberately undermining a project you never wanted (subjective)." A better approach: "Jan, thanks for carving out half an hour to discuss the software project (well timed); the flow chart (objective) shows three weeks of slippage (specific), and I ("I") can't deliver on my goals without it."

- *Suggesting that any data can be checked for accuracy.* If there is disagreement, you will be happy to help the person test the data further. In fact, you are not on a witch hunt, and if the negative data are invalid, you want to know it.

2. ACCEPTANCE

- *Connect the Awareness of the person's stated short-term performance goals and long-term ambitions.* If a person is hesitant to take the CPA examination, ask "How much more marketable will you be with the CPA?"

- *"Visualize" what the person's life (job, career) would be with improvement. Be colorful, enthusiastic.* Visualize what consequences will be without change, the pain (crocodile). The video generations respond to scenes vividly described, so paint word pictures with crocodiles, Big Macs, rowboats, and speedboats.

- *Explain interaction effects among weaker points.* "The 360-degree feedback shows your team considers you aloof, uncommunicative, inaccessible, unconcerned with teamwork, and uncaring. When you fail to return phone calls promptly, all five negatives are exacerbated. A death spiral ensues. On the other hand, if you fix one, the perception might be that you are fixing others. If you return calls promptly, you show caring, demonstrate communicativeness, and so on."

3. COMMITMENT

- *Show understanding of how difficult it is to change.* Build commitment by acknowledging that some changes take years, that it's normal to take two steps forward and one backward.

- *If interpersonal changes are needed, say that a 5-percent change in behavior can improve ratings from Only Fair to Good.* For example, when hypercritical, condescending volatile managers eliminate the most outrageous 5 percent of their behavior, coworkers genuinely feel the manager has improved a lot. Coworkers of the manager then become less defensive and are more willing to admit mistakes. Teamwork improves because there is less inclination to point fingers. A manager I have coached every three years for the past decade saved his job by eliminating the most outrageous, offensive 5 percent of his behavior. Instead of A players fleeing from him, he attracted them. His business has improved from contributing $50 million in profits to more than $500 million yearly.

- *Don't try to change anyone's character or basic personality.* People can accept being coached, helped, and facilitated, but resent being changed, manipulated, "saved." Even people who have improved dramatically in their relationships when they have become a heck of a lot more considerate and human as a result of coaching, say, "OK, I changed my behavior, I've mellowed and improved my listening skills, but I'm basically the same person." People are more committed when *they're* in charge, not when you have "made them" more committed. We all thrive best on free, informed choice.

- *Avoid overload.* An eager beaver might initially be committed to a 20-point personal development program, but loses commitment when things start to slip. Focus on the most important issues, particularly potential fatal flaws.

4. PROGRAM FOR DEVELOPMENT

- *Encourage the person to write it.* It's not your program. To be a program it must answer what activities will be performed, why, by when, and how the results will be measured. I have found over the years that three-quarters of the people who compose their own plan following my coaching interview follow through. Of those who do not impose their own plan, only one-third follow through.

- *Stimulate multifaceted activities.* One-shot fixes rarely work. Suggest or be supportive when the person plans to involve many avenues—learning a skill from one person, observing another, reading, taking a seminar.

- *Involve role playing.* Don't shy away from dress rehearsals if presentations have been sloppy. Be willing to observe the person experimenting with being more assertive.

- *Add your suggestions.* It's a matter of emphasis. Although you want the person to design a solid program, you have more experience. It won't kill the person's initiative if you offer to toss out a couple of ideas. The important thing is for the person to want them in the program, not feel manipulated into including your ideas.

- *Use an annual calendar.* For a fairly comprehensive plan, covering three or four issues, an annual calendar works best. One intensive learning experience (seminar) is OK, but continuing the learning process by visits with experts and readings spread out over a year can make it "stick" better.

5. REINFORCEMENT

- *Recommend 360-degree surveys.*[1] Anonymous, confidential survey feedback need not be expensive or time consuming. Frequently a ten-item survey (seven positive, three negative items), with a 1–10 scale, conducted by Human Resources, will be perfect. Done quarterly, progress becomes reinforcing. "Hey, I'm not a 7 yet, but I'm getting there." Three-hundred-sixty-degree surveys are also great for monitoring (#6).

- *Suggest keeping a log.* People rarely think of this on their own. Interpersonal (giving praise), emotional (blowing up), and organizational (time spent on top priorities) improvement are reinforced by a daily log. Recording successes and failures need take only five minutes a day. More successes over time fortify commitment, because the act of recording more successes and fewer failures is self-reinforcing ("Hey, I'm really improving").

- *Include some easy fixes.* Although the program should mostly address the most important developmental needs, include some activities to tweak minor shortcomings in order to boost motivation. "Take PC class" is the simple activity—checking it off is a reinforcer of the entire developmental program.

- *Offer a reminder card.* I give people laminated reminder cards, credit-card size. Million-dollar-a-year executives have said, "I pull the card out with my credit cards, and it reminds me to stay on the program." Here's an example:

---

[1] In case you didn't see the earlier footnote—they are called 360-degree surveys because usually feedback comes from many directions—bosses, peers, subordinates.

Management Development Plan
Pat Jones

- Hold weekly staff meetings
- E-mail boss monthly results
- Give praise ten times each day
- Read *The Wall Street Journal* daily
- Take one peer to lunch each week

- *Offer regular coaching.* You can be the most powerful reinforcer, meeting weekly (serious people problem) or quarterly (all other issues) to review progress, praise accomplishment, tweak the program. Regular meetings for feedback from a customer, a peer, a subordinate who will tell the truth in feedback sessions can also be useful. Remind your coachee to *never* punish honest feedback—to accept it appreciatively, or else the feedback sources will "dry up."

6. MONITORING PROGRESS

- *Convey a bias for metrics.* You love data. Your coachee will, too—measurements of production, quality, customer complaints, teamwork (survey), and other indications of good achievement. It could be useful for the person to measure herself— moods, frustration, satisfaction. A players thrive on metrics, but C players have to be nudged toward objective measurement of reality. If measurement and mood are both spiraling downward, it could be time for a job change.

7. CONCLUSION

- *Celebrate wins!* Don't let your A players move on to the next developmental plan (they always seem to be doing that) without popping the champagne to celebrate big improvements. C players who have "hung in there" and fixed a fatal flaw deserve to have not only a sincere pat on the back, but assurances that the fixed issues will not be brought up as a negative again and again.

CHAPTER 9 CHECKLIST: ARE YOU BECOMING SUPER COACH?

Yes No

❏ ❏ 1. I conduct CIDS interviews, so I hire A players at least 90 percent of the time.

❏ ❏ 2. While introducing the CIDS interview, I promise coaching for assimilation, short-term performance, and long-term growth.

❏ ❏ 3. I conduct 360-degree interviews in preparation for CIDS-based assimilation coaching.

❏ ❏ 4. I understand which competencies are relatively easy to change, harder but doable, and very difficult to change.

❏ ❏ 5. I understand the crocodile and fast-food theories of why people change.

❏ ❏ 6. I can list four reasons why people do not change.

❏ ❏ 7. I can list the seven stages in change.

❏ ❏ 8. I understand that the most dramatic and enduring change occurs when the coachee is in charge.

❏ ❏ 9. Following coaching interviews, my coachees write their own developmental plans and follow-up reports.

The next chapter converts this theory into practice, beginning with a hypothetical case study for your first CIDS-based assimilation coaching session.

IT IS NOT THE STRONGEST OF THE SPECIES
THAT SURVIVES, NOR THE MOST INTELLIGENT; IT
IS THE ONE THAT IS MOST ADAPTABLE TO
CHANGE.

CHARLES DARWIN, 1809–1882

10. Case Studies: Coaching to Fix Weaknesses

Applying the theory of coaching is easier than you think. As promised in Chapter 9 and elsewhere in *Topgrading*, having conducted a CIDS interview gives you instant coaching skills. It is like using oversized club heads in golf, or parabolic skis. Suddenly you are 20 percent better.

But not 50 percent. So this chapter puts it all together, beginning with a simple case study outlining the steps in conducting a CIDS-based assimilation coaching session. Two additional case studies show how the CIDS-based coaching model is put to the test, with a C player mis-hire, and a leadership style turnaround challenge. Case studies are presented in three levels:

1. *CIDS-based Assimilation Coaching Model*—Pat, a Retail Store Manager
2. *Coaching a Mis-hire*—Phil, a Division Controller
3. *Coaching to Improve Leadership Style*—Tom Brock, newly promoted General Manager at General Electric

I assume that you have passed Coaching 101 (Chapter 9). This chapter lays out the structure, the sequence of actual coaching sessions. It's like a videotape of what actually happens during successful coaching meetings.

CIDS-BASED ASSIMILATION COACHING MODEL

In this fictitious case study, you are the Vice President Store Operations who hired Pat, a Store Manager. Pat was brought in to turn around an underperforming store with high theft, poor sales, lousy morale, C players, red ink. Although she appears to be an A player, she is ruffling some feathers. It's time for CIDS-based assimilation coaching, six weeks after she started. The goals are:

- Smooth the transition into her new job as Store Manager
- Create a developmental plan to maximize her strengths and minimize her weaknesses in order for her to achieve the highest level of performance NOW
- Include in her developmental plan activities to help her reach her long-term goal of Vice President Operations (your present job)
- Protect you and your company legally

Why not begin a comprehensive, hard-hitting developmental-planning process now, during the honeymoon period (or in Pat's case, toward the end of it?). This is when problems can be nipped in the bud. Why wait for more serious problems to occur? Pat is coming on strong, as you hoped and expected, but in bulldozing her way toward achieving business goals she is too pushy with some corporate people and irritating her staff enough that they are complaining to merchandisers visiting the store.

This is a perfect time to put your rich, full CIDS-interview data, plus your extensive reference check notes, to work. You know Pat, you predicted she would come on too strong. You provided some "air cover" by warning Corporate that in changing red to black ink she would be demanding, even brusque. You briefly coached her, noting that she comes from a "rough-and-tumble," high-performing retail chain, entering the kinder and gentler organization culture of your company. You told her she was being hired to be a change agent, and you advised her to use you to help with the politics. She heard, but didn't really hear. So, six weeks into her job you asked her if she was interested in assimilation coaching, and she said "Of course!" A players are eager for coaching. You asked her if she would like 360-degree feedback, from confidential interviews conducted by you with her department managers and corporate people to check their perceptions of how she's doing. She replied, "Yes, but I'm not here to win a popularity contest with C players I'm about to demote or with thieves I'll fire," and you assured her you were not looking for her to tolerate mediocrity.

You conducted the 360-degree survey and now are preparing for an assimilation coaching interview with Pat. You have reviewed your CIDS interview notes, the notes from structured shorter interviews, the Candidate Assessment Scorecard, your confidential reference notes, and, of course, the 360-degree survey comments. Let's begin.

1. **Greet** Pat, offer her something to drink and chitchat a minute to "bond" a little.

2. Restate the general **purposes**—assimilation and developmental planning for short-term performance and longer-term career success.

3. Restate your intent to have a **Mid-year Career Review** in five months (six months after she started), separate from the formal performance-management system. The purpose of the Mid-year Career Review is to update her development plan and career goals in an atmosphere less charged with emotion than an annual performance review (when pay and bonus are discussed).

4. Begin with your **conclusions**—you believe Pat can turn the store around, be an A-player Store Manager, and eventually become a good candidate for Vice President Operations.

5. State your first **recommendation**, which is for her to take the information from today and write her own plan saying what she intends to do, and why, when, and how the results will be measured. *Her* plan, written in *her* words, will be implemented more conscientiously than your recommendation in your words.

6. Review her **strengths.** Your list is apt to be long—two dozen competencies. Include a couple of "easy" developmental items to address strengths to be maximized. For example, she is smart and wants to learn the total business, so she can attend the upcoming trade show and can represent her district in a "best-practices" conference in three months. Easy!

7. With a warm glow beginning from discussion of her strengths, insert a **weaker point** that might be an overused strength, such as her sense of urgency that becomes pushiness at times. Discuss the shortcoming knowing *she* acknowledged it in the CIDS interview; she predicted references would comment on it. While protecting confidentiality, advise Pat on how to best approach various Corporate people. Let *her* come up with ideas to improve, such as initiating lunches with some corporate people to build more mutual understanding and respect.

8. Discuss the **remaining weaker points**, leveraging off her self-insights. "In the CIDS interview you said you thought previous bosses would say you can be too insistent on doing things *your* way. Even the strongest on your staff are feeling you don't value their ideas enough." Let her generate ideas for involving them more, such as asking them to participate on an in-store task force. This is the meat of this coaching interview. Ninety percent of her personal development time should be spent on fixing her weaknesses, only 10 percent on maximizing her strengths. As suggested in Chapter 9, it can be appropriate to make a few suggestions: "How about keeping a weekly log on how you're doing controlling pushiness?" or "How about making up a wallet-size card with three or four reminders?"

9. **Conclude** the meeting. Pat should summarize all the key points—her conclusions, her strengths, her weaker points. The two of you have discussed perhaps 15 developmental activities, and she has already indicated which ones she embraces. Her plan is only in draft form, to be finalized soon, by her. You should document your discussions too, to be sure Pat has heard you, and "just in case," for your legal protection. This brief summary will help her and you sense if it is a comprehensive and workable plan. Did she bite off more than she can chew?

10. Conduct a **Mid-year Career Review** in five months. Pat will prepare for it with a summary of the first six months as Store Manager—her accomplishments, her failures, her progress on achieving the turnaround. She will restate her career goals, summarize her strengths and weaker points, and assess her progress on her developmental plan. Then you chime in, adding your thoughts, observations, insights, and advice. This is her meeting, but it is a partnership dialogue. This is not her performance review. You don't adjust her pay or inform her if she will get a bonus. It will be easy for you to discuss monitoring her progress, because her results are apt to be good. Praise and recognition are apt to flow from you, because she deserves it. And she is making you look good. As an A player, Pat will naturally move to the next step, which is a revised, updated developmental plan. She promises to give you the final plan, in writing, in a week.

One final step in that Mid-year Career Review is Pat's rating of you. You ask her for feedback and discuss what she feels are your strengths and weaker points as a boss and coach and how you can best manage her. Maybe by now she would like less air cover, less of your running interference, so she can more easily build teamwork relationships with Corporate.

This rather typical assimilation-coaching session progressed through the seven psychological stages in change (Chapter 9) of Awareness, Acceptance, Commitment, Program for Development, and even some Reinforcement. Pat accepts the Monitoring, because she will write the plan to include it. And you and she will assure a favorable Conclusion.

You don't have to be a "natural," warm and fuzzy counselor to make CIDS-interview-based assimilation coaching really potent. You are armed with compelling data. No doubt you are a very credible source of insight for Pat. Leadership involves coaching—surfacing opportunities and problems, getting ownership, setting goals, planning, empowering, and implementing the plans. It is *much* more difficult to *not* have a coaching relationship for a year and then attempt to deal with a nasty, negative issue during the formal annual performance review.

If you require your managers to embrace this recommended coaching process, your team will be among the top 10 percent I know of in coaching effectiveness. CIDS-based assimilation coaching bolsters topgrading by turbo-boosting A players from the start. If you mistakenly thought you were hiring an A player, but that person turns out to be a C player, at least there will be early recognition of a "fatal flaw," so the person can be redeployed sooner, not later.

COACHING A MIS-HIRE

Phil, Division Controller, had impeccable credentials and a winning personality. He is tough-minded but warm, friendly, self-effacing. Unfortunately, the Division President had conducted a superficial screening process, consisting of round-robin shallow interviews and nothing close to a CIDS interview. The Division President conducted no reference-check interviews (the search firm did those). I was brought in to assess whether Phil (a real case study, name changed) could make it, and either way, coach him. I used the CIDS interview plus confidential 360-degree interviews with his seven peers and six subordinates. If this case study seems reminiscent of the Chapter 4 dialogue with the C player, it's because many of the same approaches and principles apply. The different developmental issues will be illuminating for you, reinforcing techniques for successfully coping with underperformers.

To make this case study more relevant to your needs as a hiring manager, picture yourself as the newly appointed Division President inheriting Phil, a recently hired Controller. You are both new, but Phil had been on board two months when you arrived. In order to get to know your staff, you conducted CIDS interviews with all of them, plus 360-degree interviews.[1] (You quickly learn that A players welcome your interviewing them.).

So, you are the hiring manager, replacing Brad Smart as assessor and coach. *You* interviewed Phil during your first month as Division President, conducted the 360-degree interviews, and concluded that Phil was a chronic C player, over his head in this turnaround situation. The CIDS interview showed Phil to be OK maintaining a solid department, but previously at 3M he had failed twice—once in a complex corporate function and later in a division-controller job. Phil was open and honest with you in the CIDS interview; it's too bad those revealing CIDS interview questions weren't asked before he was hired! Phil had been nudged out of 3M, and in order to maintain his income he foolishly accepted an offer for a job he couldn't perform. Here is your assessment of Phil:

---

[1] Specifically, you asked each of your subordinates about each other, and each of the subordinates about them, saying, "So I can get to know the whole team, please give me your frank, confidential opinions about each team member's strengths and areas for improvement."

STRENGTHS

- "Stretches" intelligence through effort
- Listens to others' ideas
- Experienced, savvy business perspective
- Not apt to hip-shoot
- Willing to try new ideas
- BA in Business and Economics
- Ten years' experience, all with 3M
- Well grounded in 3M disciplines (planning)
- Down-to-earth
- Expressive
- Widely liked
- Exhibits a positive "can-do" attitude
- Extremely hard worker (15 hours per day)
- Results-oriented
- Responsible
- Honest and open
- Trying to improve systems and accuracy of monthly reports
- Accessible
- Willing to remove chronic C players

WEAKER POINTS

- Below-average intelligence, compared with midmanagers; indecisive
- Technically deficient (weak in all aspects of basic accounting)
- Shallow analytic approaches
- Not creative
- Slow to learn our business
- Unable to get a handle on our software mess ("it's just too complex for me")
- Monthly reports still inaccurate; blames staff but has no fix in place
- Very limited experience improving talent; has not hired/fired many people; relied on 3M in this regard
- Asks two people to do the same task, without telling each the other is involved
- Frazzled; overreacts ("Phil's temper could get him in trouble")
- Has not yet won the respect of his team; not empowering anyone (even his strongest subordinates)
- At times overwhelms subordinates with requests for detail

Your plan is to give Phil a chance to succeed, a fair chance, with your serving as a partner, a positive coach. If he surprises you and succeeds, great. If not, he will either quit or you will nudge him out. In any event, the organization culture (nervous in this turnaround as it is) will be enhanced if Phil is widely perceived to be treated fairly, with integrity and compassion. Morale will be harmed if Phil is a C player and remains in the job, or if he is mistreated.

So, you set up the assimilation coaching session, similar to what was done with Pat; you have your CIDS-interview notes and 360-degree comments, but no reference check notes (Phil was already on board when you started as Division President). You greet Phil, chat a moment, and restate the purposes, which are assimilation and developmental planning, both to improve present performance and to help Phil achieve his long-term goal of becoming a chief financial officer (CFO) of a small company. Please assume several hours of bonding already took place and that 50 percent more positive coaching skills were used "in real life." The following script is abbreviated for ease of reading, but it reads much more blunt and harsh than what took place. Now for the coaching dialogue, starting from when you present your Conclusions:

Manager: Phil, we're both new and struggling, and we both are eager to succeed. Thank you again for being so honest with me in the CIDS interview the other day. Based on that, if you were my next door neighbor considering a job offer here, I'd advise you to turn it down. You were happy and successful in three different jobs at 3M, but you struggled with your last two jobs as complex as this one, and I'm doubtful this is a good match here.

Phil: I just can't afford to fail in this job. Are you letting me go?

Manager: Let's give it the good ol' college try. Our purpose for meeting this morning really is coaching. Let's work toward developing a plan to help you succeed. If we're both satisfied with the plan, let's forge ahead. Within a couple of months we'll know if the plan is working.

Phil: That's fair. I need help. I can't figure out which software package to purchase, and I don't have time to study it because my team keeps pumping out incorrect monthly reports. I'm fire fighting. How can you run the business without reliable metrics?

Manager: I can't, but let's not start with analyzing the problems. From the CIDS interview and 360-degree interviews with your peers and direct reports, I've concluded you have a lot of strengths, Phil. Today we're going to also discuss how you can maximize your long-term career success, so getting a consensus on your strengths is really important.

Phil: Great!

This is a hard-hitting beginning, exactly what I did with Phil in "real life." Bonding in the CIDS interview assured that Phil would not be too defensive. You spend the next 45 minutes going through your list of Phil's 20 strengths. It's a dialogue; Phil is taking notes. This session is not for you to bludgeon him with his nonperformance and weaker points. It's coaching. A partnership.

You ask Phil for additional strengths, and he lists "family man." This is a good addition, for the career coaching might lead to a conclusion Phil should pursue a smaller, less complex job, one that affords him more time for family.

Manager: That is an impressive list of strengths, Phil! In the right job you can be an A player. Now, if you are feeling all warm and fuzzy and appreciated, you know what's next.

Phil: Here come the SCUD missiles!

Manager: Not really. You know your weaker points pretty well. Most of your peers are extremely smart, and you recognize that you have to work harder to learn and analyze things. Good for you for being so conscientious, but in this very complex job you're in, you have no other life. It has to be hard on your family.

Phil: It is. It's hard on me to come home after the kids are in bed. But, I've got to get on top of things.

Manager: You're not a technical accountant, and you don't really want to be one.

Phil: Right, I want to be a manager, not a technician.

Manager: That's OK if you have A players who are doing a great job.

Phil: And I don't. I've got a couple As, but mostly B and C players.

Manager: A players can offset your lack of experience in the industry and lack of accounting expertise. They can also offer creative ideas.

Phil: Right. I'm trying to get all their ideas, to learn as much as I can and check to see who's screwing up.

Manager: It'll come as no surprise, Phil, that the 360-degree interviews show you're driving them a little batty. They know you're still new and learning, but . . .

Phil: I know, I'm micromanaging.

Manager: Even the A players.

Phil: I guess so.

Manager: Careful, you don't want to drive them away.

Phil: But I don't want to show favoritism.

Manager: Phil, the frustration level is really pretty high. Just like what you told me occurred in the division controller job at 3M, you're overwhelming your people with requests for detail. People started transferring out of your area at 3M because of your micromanaging.

Phil: OK, item #1 on my plan will be to empower people more, particularly the A players. Damn! I swore I'd trust people more. I'll ease up, and at least stop micromanaging the A players.

Manager: There was another thing you swore you'd stop doing after you were removed from the division controller job at 3M. Remember?

Phil: Yeah, stop asking two people to do the same thing. I ask X, but if X drops the ball I'll ask Y and not tell X.

Manager: Right.

Phil: OK, item #2 on my plan will be to discuss the situation with X and if I decide to give the task to Y, I'll tell X. It's an excuse, but I figure I can save time if I just give it to Y. X will find out soon enough, anyway. But I'll talk with X and try to find other ways to save time. I really am drowning in the problems; that's why I need help.

Manager: Come to me, Phil, with your key decisions. For now, anyway. Maybe you can seem more decisive to your people if I help you sort things out. I have the experience you lack here. I'll be sort of a quality check, a sounding board.

Phil: That's item #3.

Manager: Good, let's talk about talent next. 3M promoted from within and we're in a turnaround without much promotable talent. External hiring is now necessary, and this is new territory for you.

Phil: It sure is. I can use some help. Maybe I've been hard on the C players, but at least they know where they stand. I don't have replacements internally or externally.

Manager: Let's ask your peers for names of people to replace your C players. Work with Susan in HR, who can partner with you. I want to interview finalists.

Phil: Sounds good.

Manager: I have a lot more experience interviewing. I don't want to do three-hour interviews of candidates for jobs reporting to you, but I have a 90-percent success rate. Probably the single best thing I can do for you is help you pack your team with A players.

Phil: Got it. Can Susan recommend an interviewing course?

Manager: Good idea. Yes. That's another good item for your plan.

Phil: Is that it?

Manager: Not quite. In all your jobs you have been a great team player with peers.

Phil: I know what you're gonna say. I get frazzled when these guys get on me about the inaccurate reports. But C players are pumping out crap. I exploded a couple of times, but I apologized.

Manager: They like you and sort of forgive you. I see an interaction effect here, Phil. You're over your head, so you work harder trying to do the jobs of your staff. Even the C players know more than you in some technical areas, but in order to get results you inundate them with requests for detail. You work harder trying to learn, you get impatient and frustrated, and you lose your cool. People lose a little respect for you. Instead of helping you with solutions, they give you data, data, data. You work even harder, get more frustrated, request more data. It's a death spiral, and lashing out at people will eventually turn them against you. Your winning personality won't win if you blow up at people.

Phil: You're right. I hardly know these guys and I'm acting like a jerk.

Manager: Your personality is a strength. How can you win them over other than fixing the problems in the department? You did it at 3M.

Phil: Yes. When I was doing the best job I was in the service business, asking my internal clients how we could better serve them. I've just been swamped here.

Manager: And in the two jobs at 3M, you weren't so successful at it.

Phil: I'd better schedule meetings with each internal client, to say I really want to help them, to show I'm trying, and to ask them to be patient with me as I learn. And to listen to them.

Manager: Listen! Aha! That's a strength of yours!

Phil: So . . . additional items are to stay calm, offer service to peers, and listen more.

Manager: Sounds like a comprehensive plan for the next two months that includes maximizing some underutilized strengths and minimizing some weaknesses. Let's see a written copy of your plan in a couple days.

Phil orally summarizes his plan and promises to write it out—what he intends to do and, why, when, and how the results will be monitored. (You write a memo summarizing these discussions, providing the legal documentation HR and legal counsel expect of you.) Phil is committed. You still don't think there will be a conclusion that saves Phil, but at least you can start topgrading his department now. Before you conclude the meeting you want to be sure Phil has more realistic career goals than that of becoming CFO of your large company.

Manager: One more thing. Let's talk about your career goals.

Phil: I have only one—succeed in this job. I'm not looking so good for CFO, am I?

Manager: Let's look at two scenarios, one if you remain in your job, one if you don't. If six months from now you are happy and successful, and you are working 60 rather than 80 hours, what would you think?

Phil: That becoming CFO is a possibility.

Manager: CFO of what? How complex a job?

Phil: Hmm. I see what you're getting at. Id' be silly to go after another complex job, like CFO. What do you think, should I go back to a staff-planning job?

Manager: At 3M you were a terrific planner, not a creative strategic planner, but a great tactical planner. You rolled up the numbers A players generated. If a division controller was late, you would appeal nicely, and they'd cooperate. You weren't a cop. That certainly is an option, even something to consider here, at Corporate.

Phil: What else? You've got broader experience than me.

Manager: I can envision your succeeding as CFO of a small company, one in good shape, not too complex. In an industry you know. Maybe a supplier to a company like 3M would be an alternative where you could be an A player.

One more summary by Phil concludes the coaching session. He reviews the lists of his strengths and weaker points, sincerely commits to each developmental item, and even summarizes the career options that make sense. He knows that his job is on the line. He has to get the financial numbers right, install a good software package, build a team, and earn the respect of coworkers. With weekly check points written into Phil's plan, Phil's lack of progress will result in more "heart-to-heart" talks. (No doubt HR will insist on retaining these records to show the company has been fair and legal, if Phil is fired and sues.) It becomes obvious he is *not* going to succeed in this job. You offer to cover for him if he wants to take a day here or there to check out other jobs, jobs where he can be an A player.

Let's review the structure of the coaching session with Phil, following your CIDS interview and confidential 360-degree discussions with Phil's peers subordinates:

1. Stated purposes (coaching for short-term results and longer-term career moves)
2. Conclusions ("I'm doubtful there is a good match here.")
3. Strengths (so Phil feels appreciated and understood)

4. Weaker points (positive, through frank dialogue)
5. Plan summarized by Phil
   a. empower more
   b. stop asking two people to do X
   c. use manager for key decisions
   d. manager does CIDS interviews
   e. stay calm
   f. offer service to peers
   g. listen a lot more
6. Career discussion (seeking complex CFO job was discouraged, but two options where Phil could be an A player were explored)
7. Summary of career options by Phil

You didn't have to be super coach, just a conscientious manager armed with CIDS data on Phil's background and 360-degree data on present perceptions of him. A solid, credible, fair developmental plan was created and implemented by Phil, but his job performance continued to be poor. In "real life" Phil was asked to resign six months after he was hired. He was given a six-month severance. There were "no hard feelings" (and no lawsuits) because he was coached positively. In fact, he called to thank me for coaching him to recognize he should find a CFO job in a smaller, less-complex company.

COACHING TO IMPROVE LEADERHIP STYLE

The Tom Brock case study does not repeat much of what was covered in the Pat and Phil cases. Instead I'll show how leopards can change their spots, thus expanding your range as a coach.

After 20 years with General Electric, Tom Brock was the #2 executive at a troubled division. With a reputation as a smart, hard-driving leader who quickly turns operations around, Brock was the obvious choice to replace the retiring General Manager. The division was profitable, but in jeopardy because:

- No credible strategic plan ("everything including R&D is sacrificed for short-term results") existed
- Morale at all levels was poor; people felt treated like machines, unloved, unvalued
- Finger-pointing, bickering, politics were rampant
- Customers threatened to take their business elsewhere
- A top-down culture with little or no empowerment

Brock was a controversial candidate for president. There was concern that Tom was not a good listener (in general), not a good team player (with corporate), and not a team builder with subordinates (because he insisted on doing things his way). Some rated Tom only a B-player candidate for GM. CEO Jack Welch said, "Get Brad Smart's opinion." I performed the CIDS interview plus 360-degree interviews. On a plant tour, I asked a group of workers several questions, the responses to which were:

- "Senior management can't be trusted."
- "Tom Brock is unknown."
- "Jobs are boring."
- "The only job security comes from that guy—over there—the union steward."

My report—all 22 pages—on Tom Brock went to Jack Welch. Following are excerpts from my Executive Summary:

EXECUTIVE SUMMARY

- Mr. Brock is an excellent candidate for immediate promotion to General Manager. He is an extremely bright, broadly based technologist/executive, with extraordinary drive, creativity, vision, and resourcefulness.
- His strengths *far* outweigh his shortcomings. Although it ordinarily would seem that a person with such interpersonal shortcomings as his could not succeed, he will.
- Mr. Brock is long on substance, short on packaging. He also has too much integrity to play politics the usual ways.
- Mr. Brock is the sort of talented executive who can beat the competition at their own game. The challenge for Jack Welch, however, is to prevent the bureaucracy and Mr. Brock's own shortcomings from killing him.
- A 10-percent improvement in his behavior will improve his image 50 percent. Even without any improvement, however, he is a good bet to succeed.
- He can function best if reporting to an individual whom he respects and who manages loosely. A highly structured, hierarchical executive would, at a minimum, cause Mr. Brock a lot of frustration and, at worst, drive him away.
- Mr. Brock should be encouraged to continue his development and told directly that promotion to Vice President (a title change, but at GE it means a lot to move from GM to VP) will be contingent upon his demonstrating considerably more maturity and interpersonal flexibility.

STRENGTHS

- Superior intelligence
- A quick study
- Accurately "calibrates" people's technical expertise
- Has unquenchable thirst for knowledge
- Adept at figuring out the business equation
- Excellent analytic and logical abilities
- Strong conceptual skills
- Decisive
- Strategic visionary
- Intellectually flexible
- Revolutionary change agent
- Respected by senior team
- Sets high goals
- Successful turnaround leader
- Maturing
- Becoming less intimidating
- Very confident
- Focuses on key priorities
- Listens to A players
- Powerful, dynamic leader
- Eager to be coached
- Cares about people (though doesn't always show it)
- A "doer" (do it now)
- Topgrader
- Principled
- Can make favorable first impression
- Open, direct person
- Leads with long-term perspective
- BSE from Georgia Tech
- 21 years' experience with GE
- Exceptional technical expertise; strong in manufacturing, finance; learning marketing
- Achieves "scheduled invention"
- High integrity; trustworthy
- Extremely independent
- Can be charming, smooth, and likable (socially, for example)
- Effectively manages across functions
- Highly energetic; passionate about success
- Customer-oriented

WEAKER POINTS

- Confuses people with quick thinking
- Does not "wire" change with communications nearly enough
- At times appears arrogant, combative, tactless
- Breaks down C players rather than positively nudge them out
- Interrupts people; at times poor listener; dominates discussions
- Refers excessively to past successes
- Politically insensitive
- Stingy with praise; hypercritical (hurting people's esteem and teamwork)

Welch called to discuss Tom Brock. I predicted that Tom would succeed, but I would need a year to help Tom file down his rough edges. The team was solid with A players who needed leadership. Tom was respected, and no one in his career had quit because of his arrogance or impatience. OK, Welch said, Brock gets the GM job.

Six months later I met with Welch on several topics. Welch said, "By the way, Brad, I think you lost your marbles on Brock—he's as arrogant as ever with customers, employees, his team." I said, "One year, Jack. Remember Tom would need one year to show significant change, and he has six more months." Exactly one year since the CIDS-interview-based coaching began, Welch was so impressed with Tom's progress, he praised him in a public meeting.

At that one-year mark, an internal General Electric assessment of Brock's progress was made:

ONE YEAR INTO COACHING

What Brock Did—Is Doing

- Partnered with B. Smart and Roger Farley (human resources)
- Created a vision, a new synergistic culture . . . a positive future-oriented culture
- His deep involvement, love for, belief in . . . business, technology, and people shows (very genuine and sincere)
- Focusing on crucial—real things (process—listening to customers—people . . . *now*, his theme)
- Building internal, real job security (no lows for significant productivity improvements)
- Symbols everywhere . . .
  - radios permitted and no ties required in shop
  - rewards/recognition
  - honest, open "blunt communication" (even painful ones)
  - weekly productivity—best practices meeting (union involved)
- "Showcasing"—creativity, cooperation, teamwork . . . looking for *good* in business people

People's Reaction—Impact

- Building people's self-worth, pride, self-esteem, resulting in:
  - less protective silos
  - less defensive behavior
  - fewer excuses
  - less selfish action
  - better teamwork
  - less rivalry
  - less political game playing

- less individual focus
- less backbiting
- People are saying of Tom:
  - "authentic," "real"
  - "open"; "we trust Tom"
  - "understands my problems"
  - "most excitement I've had in years"
  - "was going to retire (will wait now)"
  - "relates well to business/marketplace"
  - "safe to express; Tom listens"
  - "love the adventure"
  - "I'm not bored"
  - "values teamwork"
  - "never been happier, wanted to transfer but no longer want to"
- Visible signs of teamwork:
  - people reaching out to help each other/other teams
  - hunger for results, measurements, targets
  - having fun
  - walls are coming down
  - people are becoming inspired
  - real creativity, magic in the air
  - new leaders and "old dogs with new tricks" are emerging; people are following

Business Results

- Business results are beginning to show, and easier than ever (27 percent earnings growth over previous year)
- Ideas are flowing at a rapid pace, piggybacking off each other
- Partnerships with other GE businesses are at record heights

> ▶ Describing what's happening is exciting. Tom Brock's time has come. He's risen to the challenge. A new culture, leadership is being born, encouraged, cultivated.

Eighteen months after Brock began CIDS-interview-based coaching, Brock's boss wrote to Jack Welch, in high praise of Brock:

I have rarely, in my many plant and office visits, experienced such tremendous enthusiasm for employee involvement or teamwork. The dedicated leadership of Tom and his head of operations was clearly visible throughout our visit . . . they are to be commended for their realistic viewpoint as well as their huge accomplishments.

COACHING TOM BROCK

A key to Brock's leadership transformation was an unusually comprehensive, detailed, hard-hitting developmental plan. Wade through this with me, and you will get valuable insights into how you can coach a leopard to change it spots.

Following the CIDS interview and 360-degree data gathering, I met with Tom for four hours in person. He received my 22-page report and five-page suggested developmental plan, and we touched base almost monthly for a year. For fast-paced managers who think they lack the patience to coach, take note: Most CIDS-interview-based coaching may require periodic one-hour follow-up sessions, but the basic psychological steps (Awareness, Acceptance, Commitment, and so forth) can be accomplished in three to four hours (with Monitoring, Reinforcement, and Conclusion occurring later). The Brock coaching model can work for you, whether you are coaching a new hire, conducting a career assessment and development program for all your managers, or singling out a person for special coaching.

In Tom's case, initially he had general "Awareness" of shortcomings as perceived by his bosses, but he was not committed to change, until we met. In the four-hour coaching interview we began with a restatement of goals:

- At a minimum, I would help Tom better understand how he is perceived by me, coworkers at all levels, and key customers.
- Together we would compose a draft of a developmental plan aimed at helping Tom maximize his results and leadership effectiveness over the next two years.

Next I shared with Tom my overall Conclusions. He took a lot of notes, but I promised to send him my written report anyway. The bulk of our time was devoted to reviewing the bullet points for his strengths and weaker points—strengths first. I gave Tom my opinion, but then quoted coworkers and customers (anonymously). Some strengths ("socially very likable") were underutilized and resulted in specific action steps for his developmental plan (more informal interactions). Some strengths ("very quick thinker") were overused ("confuses people"), resulting in action plans to correct them.

Instead of my recommending all the developmental activities, I presented data and conclusions so Tom would propose action steps to improve. I supported them, or suggested an alternative.

Throughout, I used basic coaching techniques:

- **Be honest.** If I didn't think Tom could succeed at something, I'd say so. No phony praise. I care about Tom. I wouldn't insult him with insincerity.

- **I'm OK—You're OK.** Tom and I are colleagues. In a coaching interview there is no pulling rank. We're problem solving together, partners in Tom's development. No arguing. No criticism. My role is to be positive, even when discussing negative issues.

- **No overload.** Most people eventually say, "OK, that's enough for now—I'll implement this plan and see if I need to do more." It's better for Tom to commit to a shorter plan but do it than to a longer plan that is not completed.

- **Involve others.** Build a network of support for the plan. Tom met quarterly with his boss but twice weekly with his Human Resources professional, to give Tom feedback on his progress, reinforce positive steps, bolster him when he was frustrated, and modify the plan as necessary. Phone calls to me were encouraged "at any time."

- **Expect slow progress, and some backsliding.** It's normal to progress two steps, then slip back one. Long-term progress is the goal. Indeed, a dramatic change in personality would scare people and make them wonder, "When is that phony warmth going to disappear?"

- **Look for "quick fixes."** In Tom's case, eliminating just a few behavioral negatives (poor listening, interrupting) dramatically improved his overall image.

- **The best plan is authored by the counselee.** Tom's plan (Figure 10.1) is similar to the one I sent him following our half-day coaching session. By *his* writing *what* he intended to do, *why*, by *when*, and how *results* would be monitored, his commitment was locked in. His autonomy was fortified. Sharing that plan with his boss made it "management by objectives (MBO) for development."

- **Acknowledge carrots and sticks.** This is part of being honest. Some coaches believe only positive communications can be helpful. I feel that positively acknowledging negative consequences is essential for success. Remember the crocodiles (Chapter 9). For Tom, success would earn him at least another promotion (which he received in two years). Failure to show improvement from his plan would result in his plateauing or even being forced out of GE. That's reality. Don't dwell on the negatives, but don't think a lot of saccharine and smiley faces will suffice.

- **Have fun.** Coaching is serious, but improvement can sometimes be bolstered with whimsy. Tom was so quick to criticize coworkers, we addressed it several ways—including his framing and hanging a cartoon (a dead ringer for Tom Brock) I commissioned showing Tom "counting to 10." The joke—that his career development plan consisted of many of the same item—"count to 10"—is on him. Displaying it in his office, Tom was publicly promising not to jump on someone, criticize unfairly, or lose his temper. It worked. Tom keeps his word.

- **Don't neglect topgrading.** Tom was lucky. GE had already packed his team with A players. Leadership at the top—Tom—was needed, not a new team. Don't expect your coachee to change if C players constantly drag the team down.

- **Use active listening.** I played back to Tom not only the content but the unstated feelings sensed.

- **Encourage keeping a log.** The log records successes and failures in the development plan. Tom made entries for five minutes at the end of each day. Recording those "best behaviors" and slips for 18 months helped lock in his changes. Today, Tom is quite naturally a more sensitive, likable person.

Figure 10.1 Tom Brock's Developmental Plan
          Part A: Do's and Don'ts   Part B: Specific Action Items

---

Part A: Do's and Don'ts

Do's

- Articulate my vision for the business everywhere I go, every time I have an audience (hammer-repeat-repeat)
- Let go somewhat, depend on and "empower" A players
- Think before speaking and package comments better . . . be sensitive to new image (*the leader*)
- Play politics upward better . . .
- Show and express vulnerability, flaws, and shortcomings (shows realness—working to improve—it's contagious—*if he can, "so can I"*)
- Be consistent, predictable, encourage and recognize "teamwork"
- Be loose, show flexibility, keen sense of humor, "pick up" people who *are* struggling with new culture or a business challenge
- "Stroke," reward, and recognize people constantly
- Communicate more effectively (town meetings, brown-bag meetings)
- Start a *new* "Brock Mythology" (let go of past image)
- Above all, listen . . . listen . . . and *listen* more

Don'ts

- Change what people admire and respect most of me for GEDS (technology, product, people, customer driven)
- "Gloat" in reversing people or challenging corporate
- Kill messengers
- EVER . . . demean
- Talk so much . . . get on a "roll" and dominate the conversations, be an expert on everything

Figure 10.1 cont.

Part B: Specific Action Items

Items or Ideas	Purpose	Timing	Notes
A. Brad Smart discussions	Utilize Brad's expertise, get suggestions, feedback, and development ideas	Quarterly	Respect Brad's knowledge in the field and value his inputs
B. Solicit staff's organizational ideas	Get their ideas. Obtain their "buy in"	2/10 and 3/1 (done)	Most felt good about my new style
C. Social with wives at country club	Ice breaker and fellowship/team builder	2/23 (done)	Very timely and well received. Myth erased . . . some
D. Career discussion with each old/new staff members	Honest and real discussion on their role in new organization, potential and future roles in the business	3/9 (done)	Buy into their new position. Some "pain," but minimal
E. Six-month *"Walk the Plant"* plan	Expose me, one-on-one, to hourly associates	*First 3 months:* 10-15 mins. daily thru 9 different office or plant areas. *Second 3 months:* every other day ongoing once a week	I "pressed flesh" with everyone just to see how they're doing
F. Monthly *"Breakfast with Tom"*	Expose people to me, initially from areas where my "press" may be less positive or into less-known areas	Monthly	Could include a very short icebreaker questionnaire given out in advance and then discussed at breakfast

Figure 10.1 cont.

Items or Ideas	Purpose	Timing	Notes
			Samples: • "What do you like that we're now doing?" • "How can we do better?" • "What really irritates you on the job?" • "How do you feel about our new direction?"
G. *"Your Nickel"* 10-min. one-on-one's with me	Show that I *can* listen to others' inputs Expose me to many other key people (in the business)	Monthly on ongoing basis w/my staff; randomly w/others	Use a one-sheet questionnaire
H. Second quarter 1990—feature video with me	Establish benchmark of my objectives/vision for the business Show me "at my best"—animated, enthused, interested, wanting to motivate and lead others Revisit . . . why's of recent organizational changes	Release mid-April	Talk about "shortcomings and misconceptions of me"—and indicate my understanding of them and my intent and commitment to work on them Shows realness
I. *"Climate Council"*—establish an ongoing council of 6 or 7 thought leaders—people who can read the pulse of the work force and are candid	Meet every other month to discuss a continuing set of questions about the environment/climate Provide anonymous report to me Could include "what can I do to improve or enhance my effectiveness?" Involve human resources (Roger Farley) as partner in my development	Either monthly or every other month	Must be anonymous Must be chaired by someone highly respected by me so no concern about killing the messenger Suggest report be written

Items or Ideas	Purpose	Timing	Notes
J. My "In-Plant" Employee Press Conference: have 3 or 4 different employees each time w/questions thought out in advance to ask; after 10 mins. or so of above, open to ?'s from the floor	Establish open forum for employees to ask me questions directly. Hold in auditorium at different times—open to any interested employees • Some noontime • Some 4:45 P.M. • Some off-shift	Every other month	Capitalize on my open, enthusiastic, and contagious style
K. My "Report to Employees"	Report on ongoing basis on key business indicators/goals—progress and problems. Do through "Reporter". Format could be like a report card (A-F) on ongoing key items . . . or like an open letter	Every other month	Take concept of "sharing everything" one step further in a structured manner that is ongoing and "state of the art"
L. Attend at least next couple General Electric social functions	Mingle with people. Exhibit intent to "be with people" in a real way. Would make strong positive initial impression of "caring" attitude of new leadership	Next year	To show my "real" or approachable side
M. Speaking coach	Polish my skills		That I attend a seminar on "how *not* to alienate people" . . . "how to avoid pressing people's 'hot buttons'"

Two years after I began coaching Tom he was promoted from General Manager to Vice President, the coveted officer level at GE. Tom really improved his leadership skills himself. The CIDS interview provided compelling data that Tom was at a crucial juncture in his career—plateau or move to the next level. He insisted on a "full-court press" developmental plan, and he was unusually disciplined and courageous in implementing it.

Having turned his company around and built it, and having matured into a truly fine leader, Tom opted to "give something back." He resigned his position at General Electric and has been devoting his extraordinary energy and talents to various civic activities. He is one of the rare 10 percent of managers I have worked with who managed his career to fit into a life plan (Chapter 7) that would assure him both short-term success and long-term fulfillment. Perhaps he will accept an offer to be CEO of a company. He certainly has the talent. Perhaps not. But he has managed his career to permit a lot of attractive options.

FINAL COMMENT

All three of these case studies relied heavily on the CIDS interview. Three-hundred-sixty-degree survey data are helpful, but only as a backup to CIDS-interview conclusions. Absent CIDS-interview conclusions, 360-degree survey data are incomplete, confusing, contradictory. Three-hundred-sixty-degree comments lend credibility to coaching ("I know you talked to my peers so if you say they think I'm too political and self-serving, I'd better listen"). I hope you use CIDS-based skills to qualify as super coach.

For the last time I'll ask you to think of fixing weakness as positive, not negative. A good teacher will think of fun games to help children learn to read. If verb tenses are difficult for Susie, the teacher doesn't pound negatively on Susie, criticizing her verb tenses, but instead finds ways to help Suzie get them right.

Athletic coaches can be seen on sidelines going berserk over players' mistakes, focusing heatedly on players' weaknesses. This is *not* what I would recommend for 98 percent of managers, teachers, or even athletic coaches. Maybe—just maybe—when a linebacker with a 75 IQ hears his coach screaming to hit harder, he'll hit harder. Sports requiring intellectual capital, brains, in the athletes don't have many successful coaches who scream, demean, and criticize negatively.

As I write this I am the reigning world-champion three-meter springboard diver for my age group.[2] After a 27-year hiatus I reentered this demand-

---

[2] World Masters Swimming and Diving Championship, Sheffield, England, 1996.

ing sport at the Master's level, not just because it's a great way to stay in shape (it is), not just because it's a heck of a lot of fun to compete with has-beens from all over the world (it is, and we all are), but mostly to confirm that psychologists have a loose screw or two (you knew that). A few months ago I was coached in a diving clinic by Ron O'Brien, the eight-times Olympic coach who so often has brought home medals. Ron is positive, not negative, as he focuses on correcting every diver's biggest weaknesses. People say I won the world championship by getting 9's and 9½'s on my last dive, a forward one-and-a-half somersault with two twists. Nope. That's my bread-and-butter dive, one I can hit without much practice. For weeks before the championship I practiced all my dives, but worked hardest on my two-and-a-half pike, a dive I could easily "blow," my potential fatal flaw. Working on the weakest part of your game . . . is that negative thinking?

Can you imagine Tiger Woods's coach (his dad) yelling, "Damn it, Tiger, can't you remember anything?" Mike Ditka, when he was Chicago Bears coach, pounded mercilessly on quarterbacks, chewing them up and spitting them out. Ditka didn't get it—most players who have to think don't respond well to verbal abuse. Several Chicago Bears quarterbacks went on to succeed with other teams, with coaches who understood that fixing weaknesses is a positive "head game."

By now you know I am not recommending a soft, mushy coaching style. The business world is too fast paced, too demanding for quiet, gentle little hints, except for a rare subordinate requiring your most flexible and sensitive care. No, this world requires hard-hitting constructive criticism, not pussy-footing. You want the straight scoop, no beating around the bush if your boss is dissatisfied, right? But you want to be treated with respect, and you respond best when you are presented positively with an opportunity to improve, right?

This chapter has presented case studies in coaching others' weaknesses, but has simultaneously given you insight into how to fix your own (will some of Tom Brock's developmental activities work for you?). Overcoming fatal flaws is not just satisfying, but thrilling. Being a hard-hitting but positive coach to help others grow is not merely a skill, but the essence of good leadership.

PART THREE

CIDS

Interviewing

11. Your Most Powerful Tool: The CIDS Interview Guide

After reading Chapters 1–10, I hope you believe a 90 percent or better success rate in hiring is possible, and the assessment tool to achieve it is the Chronological In-Depth Structured (CIDS) Interview Guide (Appendix A). CIDS is a crucial component of topgrading. If you remove C players and suffer from a common 50-percent mis-hire rate using weak interviewing methods, you will fail. You will appear to be a hatchet man flailing away, since you fire C players and half the time replace them with C players. Morale will plummet and you're A players are apt to quit. CIDS promises a 90 percent or better success rate. With A players replacing Cs, positive morale mushrooms among your most talented people. Thus CIDS can make the difference between a clumsy, brutal, crude, ineffective hatchet job and a smooth, positive, exciting effort to topgrade.

Part Three presents the CIDS model in its entirety—what it is (this chapter), advanced interviewing tactics (Chapter 12), and how to avoid employment-related legal problems (Chapter 13). This chapter begins with a short version of the CIDS interview, to briefly explain its central core. Then I spell out the advantages in using the full guide, take you on a colorful tour through it, and explain its rationale. Finally, the question, "But is it valid?" is posed, with recent research that says, "Yes!"

By the time you read these three chapters, you will be much better able to:

1. Immediately conduct the most valid selection interview of your career
2. Comfortably use the CIDS interview guide
3. Appreciate the validity of the CIDS interview

225

4. Glean important insights from the Career History Form
5. Build a higher level of rapport
6. Effectively take notes
7. Spot "red flags"
8. Get the "negatives"
9. Interpret interview responses accurately
10. "Sell" the job
11. Effectively conduct short, structured interviews on a group of competencies (intellectual, or whatever)
12. Conduct truly revealing reference calls
13. Continue polishing interview skills

A SHORT VERSION OF CIDS

Suppose we were to meet on an airplane and, with the pilot about to land, you said, "I'll conduct the most important selection interview of my career in an hour. If I mis-hire this person my career will be in jeopardy!" I'd say, "Look, you don't have time to read my books on interviewing, so I'll help you improve your interviewing skills 25 percent in the next five minutes. Here is one page out of my Chronological In-Depth Structured (CIDS) Interview Guide (Appendix A). It's a Work History Form (Figure 11.1), covering a single job. Ask all the questions on this form for *every* full-time job your candidate has had, spending most of your time on the most recent years. The full wording is in the CIDS Interview Guide (see pages 325 and 326). Take good notes. Your interview will take three hours but I assure you, you'll learn more job relevant information about a selection candidate than ever before."

Is it that simple? Yes and no. No, because interviewing is an extremely difficult art. Some people are untrainable as interviewers because they lack the smarts, perceptiveness, personal discipline, and business perspective. But yes, there is a mechanical core base to CIDS interviewing. The science of interviewing has confirmed the importance of structure, even if the world has yet to see a study of an interview approach as thorough as the CIDS interview. Some talented interviewers, including CEOs of major companies, keep this Work History Form handy when they are interviewing. Essentially it is the miniversion of the CIDS Interview Guide. It works.

McLuhan proclaimed, "The medium is the message," and to a significant degree, so it is with interviewing. Thoroughness is the message, the passageway to truth. If you ask the right questions, if you use the CIDS Interview Guide, if you *at least* use the Work History Form for each job, you'll improve as an interviewer. If you want to improve more than 25 percent, don't just use the Work History Form, but instead open to Appendix A and use the full CIDS Interview Guide.

Figure 11.1 Work History Form

1. _____
   Employer   Starting date (mo./yr.)   Final (mo./yr.)

   _____
   Location   Type of business

   Description _____
2. Title _____
3. Salary (Starting)_____(Final) _____
4. Expectations _____
   _____

5. Responsibilities/Accountabilities_____
   _____

6. "Found" (Major Challenges) _____
   _____

7. Successes/Accomplishments _____
8. Failures/Mistakes_____
9. Most Enjoyable _____
10. Least Enjoyable _____
11. Talent _____
12. Reasons for Leaving _____

SUPERVISOR

13. _____
    Supervisor's name   Title

    _____
    Where now   Permission to contact?
14. Appraisal of Supervisor
    His/Her Strengths _____
    His/Her Shortcomings _____
15. Best guess as to what he/she really felt at that time were your:

STRENGTHS	WEAKER POINTS

Overall Performance Rating _____

ADVANTAGES OF USING THE CIDS INTERVIEW GUIDE

The CIDS Interview Guide (Appendix A) works better than highly "canned" structured interviews that omit a lot of crucial questions. It produces much more valid results than so-called "targeted" interviews that ignore the chronology, the crucial data on how the interviewee developed throughout his or her career that gives deep insights into how he or she will function in the next job. Those "targeted" interviews are typically shorter than CIDS, so only a few questions are asked on about one-quarter of the competencies, leaving huge gaps in understanding the interviewee's competencies. It's like a preflight check in which the pilot checks only 25 percent of the items on his list—ignoring checks for fuel, brakes, excessive weight, and so on. CIDS is a complete preflight check. Despite the size of the CIDS Interview Guide, it is like a manual that, once understood, permits you to perform a complex task easily, smoothly, and with an aura of confidence. The only disadvantage of using the CIDS Interview Guide is that it takes longer than other interviews. With an improved hiring "batting average," however, in the long run you *save* an enormous amount of time, not only in the entire selection process but in managing A players rather than C players. Managers who say, "I don't have three hours for a CIDS interview" should finish the sentence . . . "so I will waste hundreds of hours when half the time I mis-hire people." Some logic!

As I said, interviewing isn't easy. In any given moment you naturally want to listen carefully to the response to a question and in doing so you might wonder if further clarification is necessary. If so, you might want to compose an original question, so you need to figure out the wording to it ("try to make it open-ended, don't bias the response, and so forth"). You perform a quick memory scan, to see if the current response possibly contradicts a previous response. You are trying to tune in to your "gut feelings" in order to develop the intuitive sense that can only be valid if anchored in facts. All the while you are trying to maintain eye contact and a high level of rapport while taking appropriate notes and, by the way, carefully observing the candidate's body language. Phew!

The Guide simplifies this highly complex intellectual exercise by providing a clear, logical sequence of questions. The time-tested wording is presented, and there is space to take notes. If there is a blank after a question, this is a visual signal for you to ask the question (unless there is a good reason not to). By mechanizing the interview just enough, but not too much, you can look and feel professional and devote your energies to analyzing the candidate.

The Work History questions follow a logical pattern—what the expectations were coming into the job, what occurred, and why the person left. Chronology is all-important. Any interview process that asks what a person did in only the most recent job, or what would be done under hypothetical situations, misses the boat, big time. By tracing how a person *developed* over an entire career history, predicting the future becomes a lot easier. It's not that asking five questions about how a person relates to bosses is irrelevant; indeed, the latter half of the CIDS Interview Guide is devoted to dozens of such focused questions. My point is, by asking about bosses a person has had *over time* and by asking how those bosses would appraise the candidate, revealing *patterns* of relationships emerge and current competencies are assessed with much greater accuracy.

The focused questions at the end of the Guide are used only to "fill in the holes." If a very thorough job of interviewing was done throughout the chronology, only a handful of additional questions is worth asking.

The Guide permits tremendous flexibility. It has been used for interviewing candidates for CEO of multibillion-dollar companies, and for clerks. It looks as though it is designed for three-hour interviews, and sometimes they extend to five hours. It can also be shortened to a 30-minute or 45-minute interview for a lower-level person, a recent college graduate, for example. Its sole use is *not* just for assessment of candidates for external candidates for hire and internal candidates for promotion. It can also be used to "get to know" your team when you move into a new job. Finally, if there is a performance problem, the CIDS interview can serve as a solid foundation for you to really understand the strengths and weaker points of your subordinate, permitting the powerful coaching described in Chapters 9 and 10.

For your own growth, keeping track of your notes in the Guide, plus the Candidate Assessment Scorecard at the end of the Guide, can help you learn. As suggested in Chapter 3, pull out the completed Guide six months after a new hire is on board and match your predicted ratings on the various competencies in relation to the "actual." Then figure out how to improve your assessments ("Gee, I asked how many hours per week he typically worked and he said 'a lot.' I should have required more specificity because he works only 40 hours, and we work 50.")

Each of the questions in the Guide has been filtered for legal acceptability. Anyone can sue for any purpose, but this Guide has been constructed to minimize risk. Chapter 13 (Avoiding Legal Problems) says, "Stick to the Guide, take notes, and you should be in pretty good shape."

PREPARING FOR THE CIDS INTERVIEW

Let's assume that you will enter the CIDS interview having gone through the various preparatory steps you have read about in Chapter 5. A thorough job analysis has been done, and a job description has been written that includes first-year accountabilities. Extensive competencies have been spelled out, written in behavioral terms, and assigned a minimum acceptable rating. Interviewing without valid competencies is like fishing without knowing if you want to catch a:

- Barracuda (looks fearsome on the wall, easy to catch, okay to eat)
- Bonefish (puts up a fierce struggle, tastes like a porcupine, not much to mount)
- Bluegill (easy to catch, mount only as a joke, great to fry up for breakfast)

Unfortunately, organizations end up landing the wrong fish, because the hiring manager has not made the effort to spell out what should be looked for in job candidates. For most technical or staff positions, approximately 15 competencies should suffice. Any interview for a management position, however, should deal with at least four dozen competencies (see Appendix E).

Let's assume that you have "partnered" nicely with Human Resources and the recruiter (if one is used), so you are all singing out of the same hymnal. You met a week or two before the first visit by the candidate, convening a meeting with the other interviewers in order to "divvy up" who will do what short structured interview on a component—Intellectual Competencies, for example—of the full CIDS interview. The first visit resulted in your decision to have a second day of interviews. Your CIDS interview is scheduled on that second day. Just prior to the CIDS interview you review the individual's résumé and Career History Form. Let's push the pause button.

CAREER HISTORY FORM

The Career History Form (Appendix B) looks and acts like an application form. These days, however, A players are in such demand they don't want to think of themselves as out looking for a job. You have to go after them. They will fax you a résumé, if they have one, but some are quite hesitant to complete an "application form." If your previous interactions have lured the person into a full-day visit, however, and the candidate is willing to return for a second full day of interviews including your CIDS interview, you can probably induce the individual to kindly complete the Career History Form. Say something like,

> Thanks very much for sending your résumé, but now would you please complete the enclosed Career History Form? It asks for about 30 things not included in a typical résumé, and it will permit the CIDS interview to take three hours rather than four. I won't have to ask you a lot of detailed questions answered in the Form, so your interview will go a lot smoother. We'll then have plenty of time for you to ask me questions.

This Career History Form is a marvelously revealing document. Résumés are constructed with the help of others and are typically "sanitized" versions of the person's career history. This Career History Form accounts for every year and month since the person began working full-time jobs. That makes "hiding" an extremely short-term job or two very difficult. Compensation is specifically requested, and it is broken down into "base," "bonus," "other." The name and title of each boss is requested, along with a clear statement that reference checks might be done (with the individual's permission); this helps inspire honesty. Dozens of inches of space are devoted to asking what was liked most and least about jobs. Educational performance and SAT/ACT scores are requested. Several feet of space are allotted to asking not only what a person's strengths are, but weaker points and areas for improvement. There's more, but you get the picture. Perhaps one of the more revealing aspects of the Career History Form is an opportunity for you to understand chronological patterns even before conducting the CIDS interview. Sit back and look at the picture portrayed: In the 20 years (or whatever) since the individual started working full time, what have been the patterns for growth in title, compensation, likes, and dislikes?

The Career History Form in Appendix B requests dates for all full-time jobs, but *not* attendance or graduation dates for high school, college, or graduate school. This important issue is dealt with in Chapter 13. Suffice it to say here that a company that discriminates against people over 40 would be foolish to request education dates in interviews or application forms, since it is easy to calculate age from that information. The argument that requiring education dates is necessary to avoid negligent hiring suits ("We want to record-check the person for every job since high school") has some merit, but is a little weak, because an alternative is to require dates for *all* jobs. A Keystone Cop could determine most people's ages from dates recorded for all jobs, part time and full time.

Some companies, however, do require education dates. They do not discriminate against people over 40 and they believe requiring candidates to supply all employment dates along with all education dates inspires more completeness. The main reason these companies require education dates from high school on is to begin the CIDS interview during the education years and get a fuller picture of how a candidate developed various competencies. They also want to be sure no years are "missing" in the candidate's chronological history. Don't necessarily conclude that a candidate today is weak in a necessary competency because she was weak in it during high school. What happened back then is almost irrelevant in and of itself. However, the candidate reveals *current* competencies when reflecting on those early experiences. Some companies (and I) find, for example, candidates' reflections on what they did during high school and college produce insights into *current* decision-making modes, current needs. This book and its Appendices suggest a cautious approach, beginning the CIDS interview with college, but tracking dates only from the first full-time job. Bottom line: Don't discriminate on the basis of age, do track dates as rigorously as your CEO will allow, and do read Chapter 13.

I like to keep the Career History Form and résumé at hand when conducting the CIDS interview. There are a lot of papers to shuffle, but after a half-dozen interviews you can get to be pretty smooth at it. Having the Career History Form and résumé data at hand equips you to speed up or slow down the interview, ask more probing questions or more generalities, and essentially zero-in on what will add even more depth to your understanding. If for some reason the candidate cannot complete the Career History Form, at least an hour of additional interview time is usually necessary. So, don't browbeat a super-desirable candidate into completing every item in the Form. However, make the request, and if that sought-after individual wants to blow off the exercise, that's possible by just leaving a lot of blanks. The vast majority, however, conscientiously completes the form.

Since you have reviewed the résumé and Career History Form, you might be conscientious and enter some of the basic data in the CIDS Interview Guide—name of college, first employer, and so forth. This can make the interview proceed a little more smoothly.

HOW TO ALLOCATE TIME

First-time CIDS interviewers sometimes find so much revealing in early positions or education that they do not apportion their time appropriately. As interesting and job-relevant as an experience 15 years ago might be, it is not sensible to spend 20 minutes talking about it, leaving only 5 minutes for your discussion of the present job. Here are some rough guidelines:

	3-Hour Interview	*2-Hour Interview*	*45-Minute Interview*
Opening "Chit-Chat"	5 minutes	5 minutes	4 minutes
Education	10 minutes	7 minutes	4 minutes
Work History	110 minutes	70 minutes	20 minutes
Plans and Goals	10 minutes	8 minutes	4 minutes
Self-Appraisal	15 minutes	10 minutes	4 minutes
Targeted Questions: Intellectual Competencies Personal Competencies Interpersonal Competencies Leadership/Management Motivational Competencies	30 minutes	20 minutes	9 minutes

OPENING "CHIT-CHAT"

You're an experienced businessperson, so you know how to break the ice, or do you? Thousands of interviewees have told me that they, and even CEOs, their interviews at my client companies, don't always do the "obvious." After a couple of minutes of chit-chat about the weather or yesterday's football game, don't forget to extend the common courtesy of offering the candidate something to drink. In this interview, the interviewee does most of the talking, so his mouth will get dry. Add a little bit of nervousness, and dryness is exacerbated. People don't smoke anymore in interviews, but if the interviewee would like a moment to collect some thoughts, taking a sip of something provides a welcome "crutch."

Some interviewers make a big point of sitting side by side with the interviewee rather than behind a desk. Do whatever is natural for you. If you manage behind the desk, interview behind the desk. That physical barrier does *not* necessarily constitute a psychological barrier. Indeed, interviewees like a physical barrier. If they want to cross their legs, or scratch their knee, the desk provides a little privacy. Twenty-five books on interviewing say you will have to go to detention if you interview from behind a desk, but those authors never asked interviewees their preference.

WHEN TO "SELL" THE CANDIDATE

You never stop selling! A players are in demand, so every step of the selection process should be designed to sell the candidate. That includes the CIDS interview. Prior to the CIDS interview you might have had a preliminary telephone interview, and in addition to gathering information about each other, you no doubt gave a little sales pitch on why the opportunity is terrific, what a wonderful manager you are, and so forth. Then you met the candidate for breakfast, the day of visit #1, where you did a little more "selling." All interviews in visits #1 and #2 contain some selling, not so much a sales pitch but indirect selling through your being professional, alert, open, friendly, and very interested in understanding the interviewee's needs.

During the actual CIDS interview, you do not want to go too far afield in touting the features and benefits of your industry, company, job, personality, and the like. The single best thing you can do to sell the interviewee is to get to know her competencies and career needs in depth, and on the basis of that information later structure your "sales pitch." Too often interviewers make the huge mistake of trying to sell the candidate on something she couldn't care less about. You are not apt to know what the real "hot buttons" are of an individual until completion of the CIDS interview. Although your company's stock options have been extremely lucrative, don't talk too much about them until you know if the individual is money-motivated. Perhaps the person really wants flexibility, independence, and job challenge and is not so money-motivated. All your talk about stock appreciation might make you sound greedy and turn the individual off.

Selection is like a mating dance. You spark the person's interest, then get information, return to intriguing the individual with the opportunity, then get some more information. You give information to the candidate, get some, and it's really a two-way street. It's important to prepare the individual for the CIDS interview, however, because during that two-and-one-half-hour (or whatever) interview, you get to ask the questions. At the completion of the interview, you should allot plenty of time for the interviewee to ask you the penetrating, in-depth questions.

Even if the person is prepared for the CIDS interview, after the chit-chat say something like:

> Jan, I appreciate your time today to review your background, interests, and goals to see if there is a good fit here at Acme Corporation. If there is and we offer you a job and you accept it, this interview and subsequent reference checks will help me figure out how to help you enjoy a smooth assimilation here. Also, by getting to know your strengths and areas for improvement, I'll be able to work with you better to help construct a developmental plan right away. This is a two-way street, of course, so after I have interviewed you, you get to ask me all the questions you want. We both need to perform our due diligence, to see if working together makes sense. How does that sound?

"Terrific!" is the response of most interviewees. A players like the thoroughness and professionalism of the CIDS interview. Naturally, they will expect reciprocity when they get to probe you.

USE A NOTEBOOK

We're just about to the point of your asking your first CIDS question, so let's deal with note taking. Many books on interviewing suggest that taking notes will impair eye contact, destroying rapport. Nonsense! Ask interviewees, and they say they very much appreciate your taking notes. Recording accomplishments and interests of the candidate shows you are conscientious and thorough. Momentarily losing eye contact to record the details of an accomplishment will give the interviewee an appreciated "break." Note taking, done with a little finesse, is definitely a rapport builder.

▶ "He listens well . . . who takes notes."

Dante

I like to use a notebook—you know, a leather-bound (or vinyl will do) portfolio you open up and there is an 8½" × 11" ruled pad on the right, and a flap on the left to hold the résumé, completed Career History Form, and job description. This arrangement permits you to take notes unobtrusively. Plopping the Guide down on a desk or a table makes it obtrusive; as soon as you write anything the slightest bit negative, the interviewee's eyes will be drawn to the paper. Simply put the notebook on your lap and make no attempt to hide note taking.

The CIDS Interview Guide is easily placed on the open notebook. You write on the Guide, and the notebook provides a firm backing. If any questions require more elaboration than the Guide has room for, simply make the notes on the 8½" × 11" tablet. When you go out for a break, you close the notebook and hide the Guide without making a big point of it.

As you use the Guide you ask the questions you want answered and skip the rest. Proceed to the next page after a glance tells you that the questions of interest on a page have been answered. Certainly for all the Work History Form questions, don't go to the next page until there is something jotted after *every one* of the questions. You'll naturally spend more time on the more recent jobs, so there will be more notes following each question on each page.

A TOUR THROUGH THE CIDS INTERVIEW GUIDE

Please stop here and take ten minutes now to read through the Chronological In-Depth Structured (CIDS) Interview Guide, Appendix A. It will be impossible to follow our "tour" if you don't review it.

Did you read Appendix A? Good. Let's begin a CIDS interview. Ever the gracious host, you have your interviewee at ease, ready to disclose all. You have prepared thoroughly. The first questions have to do with education. In order to fully understand why this oak tree looks the way it does, with its strength, its damage from lightning, its unique configuration of limbs, you want to begin early and come forward chronologically. Some interviewers actually like to begin interviewing 25-year veterans with a discussion of high school days. I do. High school days are important developmental years. (If you prefer, start with college.) For example, Team Player might be an important competency. Asking about career influences in high school, you might hear:

> My basketball coach taught me an important lesson. I was a loner, a great shooter, but a lousy team player. He benched me for a couple games when I hogged the ball. I learned the lesson, and we won more games that season when I became a good team player. It was a tough lesson to learn, but it's stuck with me ever since. Now I'm chosen to head so many task forces I have trouble doing my regular job!

When answering questions about education years, it is common for interviewees to switch to the present tense, helping you generate hypotheses about the present strength of various competencies. In the preceding scenario, is this applicant too hesitant to say, "No, I can't take on any more task forces without sacrificing my key goals"? With the person's full educational and career history to be explored, you will have multiple opportunities to confirm or disconfirm your hypotheses. By the time you are discussing the current job, you should feel confident you have this person "pegged."

Again, we're not so interested in what happened during the high school days as we are in career influences and, more important, how the interviewee reveals *current* strengths and weaker points when reflecting on those sometimes traumatic developmental years. Some psychologists feel that two-thirds of all people's careers can be accounted for in terms of living up to, or living down, one's high school reputation. That rings true in my experience. If you are interviewing someone fresh out of high school, with no college, then there is no choice—modify the college section to fit high school, and begin with those high school experiences.

The CIDS Interview Guide begins with college, because most interviewers, although they see value in starting with high school, feel squeamish doing so. OK. Let's assume you are interviewing a manager and begin with college. The opening question makes your investigation of the college years seem quite job-relevant. You ask:

Would you please expand on the Career History Form information and give me a *brief rundown* on your college years . . . particularly events that might have affected later career decisions. I'd be interested in knowing about *work experiences*, what the school was like, what you were like back then, the curriculum, activities, how you did in school, high and low points, and so forth.

This "smorgasbord" question lays out what you want, and the interviewee reveals a lot by what is answered, in what order, what is avoided, and what relative emphases are. Overly structured interview approaches amount to question-answer, question-answer, question-answer. You might as well have a computerized interview (which I have developed for low-level employees, and it works very well). For management, and *Topgrading* is a book for managers, the smorgasbord question is most appropriate. It makes the interview more an ongoing dialogue than question-answer, question-answer.

Just fill in the responses to the questions in the College section of the CIDS Interview Guide, as the interviewee talks. Naturally, the interviewee will forget some of the components of the smorgasbord question, so go back and ask them again, and jot in the responses. When the two pages are full, it's time to go on to work history.

If the candidate has completed the Career History Form and loads the college section up with accomplishments, this walk down memory lane will be quite positive. If there are a lot of blanks in this section, then you should assume that college was not the most positive time for the individual. Don't harm rapport by spending a lot of time on a negative part of the person's life, but at a minimum, ask for high points and low points, successes and failures. This is the pattern throughout the entire CIDS Interview Guide: Get successes, then failures—high points, then low points. This provides the "meat" for valid assessment. If the individual attended college 20 years ago and was a "goof-off," but has been very successful since and takes full responsibility for immaturity back then, you might conclude that the candidate today is quite a mature individual. That's the whole point. This is a guided escort through the candidate's complete career history, and as you learn what this unique individual liked and disliked, succeeded at and failed at, across dozens of different competencies and no doubt several jobs, with lots of different challenges and people to interact with, you learn—the "truth."

SAT and ACT scores are not pure measures of intelligence, but they are close enough to be of value to you. The ACT scores range from 1 to 36, with almost half of all test takers scoring between 27 and 23. Percentiles vary at different dates but the following are representative:

ACT Score	Percentile
31	99th
26	90th
23	76th
20	54th
17	28th

The SAT is scored from 200 to 800 for both verbal and math sections. As of April 1995 the scoring was adjusted so that the average for all tests taken is 500 for both math and verbal sections. The eightieth percentile on math is a score of 600; the ninetieth percentile on verbal is 600. With a combined score of 1600 perfect, my experience tells me that 1200 is fairly typical for corporate executives, 1400 is about average for partners in consulting firms, and 1000 is a score that is low, extremely low for a successful senior manager.

If the candidate attended graduate school, request the information, but do it in chronological order. If the MBA was acquired 15 years into the person's career, ask the MBA questions after completing questions about the first 15 years of the person's work history.

WORK HISTORY

This is the "guts" of the CIDS interview. It comprises about two hours of a three-hour interview. Work History Forms 1-6 are all the same. If the person has had ten jobs, or five jobs within two employers, you will need to either add Work History Forms or take more notes on your yellow pad. If a person entered a large company that had job rotation consisting of four jobs in two years, and those all occurred 15 years ago, group all four together into Work History Form 1. If the person is now in the second year of that job rotation, you might as well hear a little bit about each six-month job, using a separate Work History Form for each. If the candidate has a 15-year work history, spend at least half of the work history time on the most recent five or six years.

Ask every question in the Work History section for every job. Even if you allocate only three minutes for a very early job, nonetheless ask every question and jot a short response. With the later jobs you will be probing more, asking for more clarification, challenging apparent inconsistencies, getting examples.

The Work History section of the CIDS Interview Guide begins with another smorgasbord question (see pages 325–326). The purpose is exactly as it was for college. You learn more if an individual has to organize the entire career history and present it, emphasizing this, excluding that, and so on, than if you conduct an interview in rapid-fire question-answer, question-answer, question-answer. The latter format would probably take twice as long, too.

So, the opening question is:

> Now I would like you to tell me about your work history. There are a lot of things I would like to know about each position. Let me tell you what these things are now, so I won't have to interrupt you so often. We already have some of this information from your Career History Form and previous discussions. Of course, I need to know the employer, location, dates of employment, your titles, and salary history. I would also be interested in knowing what your expectations were for each job , your responsibilities and accountabilities, what you found upon entering the job, what major challenges you faced, and how they were handled. What were your most significant accomplishments as well as mistakes, and what were the most enjoyable and least enjoyable aspects of each job? What was each supervisor like and what would you guess each really felt were your strengths and weaker points? Finally, I would like to know the circumstances under which you left each position.

You might have heard the story about Picasso. He was in a restaurant and a lady came up to him and asked if he would draw something on her napkin. He did, and she said, "Thank you," triggering his response, "That will be $20,000, please." The lady said, "But that took you only 30 seconds to draw!" Picasso replied, "No, my dear, it took a lifetime." Comparing this Work History Form to a Picasso painting is a bit of a stretch, but there is something in common—it took a career for me to "draw" this form. If you want to know something about an individual's job, this has it all, and in an extremely efficient and logical format.

Question 3 regarding compensation is important, because compensation is the single most common standard measure by which we can gauge employee value. It is the most important component of "availability" in determining if a person is an A, B, or C player. Books on how to get a job tell people to conceal compensation information, but by the time you get to the CIDS interview, sufficient trust should exist that the individual will not "play games." Suppose someone balks. Simply say, "Compensation is a standard gauge of value, and in your case perhaps you were underpaid or overpaid. I don't want to either underpay or overpay you, but if we get together I would view it as an important obligation on my part to get your pay right. And, I would hope that by now you would trust me enough to not feel you have to conceal something as basic as pay."

Question 4 asks what the person expected going into the job. This is a wonderful question, because if you hire the candidate, knowing her expectations in going to work for you will be crucial. Knowing the pattern of how her expectations met with reality across many jobs will tell you a lot about the individual's values, due diligence, ability to assimilate into a new job, and overall performance.

Question 5 asks for not just responsibilities, but also accountabilities—the metrics that determine bonus, for example. Question 6 asks what was "found" upon entering the job—the talent inherited, performance of the unit, resources available, the problems, and the major challenges. The next questions have to do with what happened—successes and accomplishments, failures and mistakes, what was most enjoyable about the job and what was least enjoyable.

After conducting half a dozen CIDS interviews, you will not need to refer much to where each of the Work History Form questions is spelled out, with full wording. The "smorgasbord" question is so logical that you will remember it after a few tries. If you need a refresher on specific wording, on any of the questions, you can easily flip back to it. For example, in any of the Work History Forms you can see that item 11 has one word: Talent. If you forget the question, you can flip back to and read: "(For management jobs) What sort of talent did you inherit and what changes did you make? (For most recent two jobs, get A, B, C ratings and strengths/weaker points of each subordinate.)"

Notice the smooth chronological flow guiding the interview. You have heard why the candidate left the previous job and what the expectations were for the next job. You learned the responsibilities and accountabilities, what the person "found" upon arriving, and then what the person did—specifically successes and accomplishments, failures and mistakes, and what was most and least enjoyable. It's hard to ask all those questions without learning quite a bit about what talent the person inherited and what changes in people occurred (item #11), but if you need more information, you ask it. Then you ask reasons for leaving. Before going on to the next job, however, it's time to ask the TORC (Threat of Reference Check) questions, numbers 13–15. In the following chapter I go into quite a bit of detail about the incredible power of TORC for inspiring "truth" from interviewees, even those who might be inclined to hide something.

RFTER THE WORH HISTORY

Most of the interview is Education and Work History. We are still in chronology, however, asking the person to leap from the present into the future. Under Plans and Goals for th Future (see page 333), question 1 asks about the next job. It's straightforward. Question 2 could be interpreted as an inappropriate question, asking the candidate to divulge other private job discussions. If the interviewee balks, you respond, "I don't need to know the specific employers you have met with, but it would be helpful if you could tell me how the job opportunity here stacks up against those other opportunities—you know, what you're looking for and what is less important to you."

Question 3 asks about the ideal position, and Question 4 asks the candidate to compare that ideal with the job you are filling. Keep in mind, you've probably had at least a preliminary telephone interview, maybe a second preliminary interview, a breakfast with the individual, and the candidate has been interviewed by some of your coworkers. You talked with the other interviewers about your candidate and read their reports. There has also been a tour of the facility. You already have a pretty good idea of how your job appeals to the candidate before your CIDS interview. But, after completing the Work History chronology, hearing why a person left each job to pursue the next, you should have an *excellent* understanding of exactly what turns this person on, what the candidate is really interested in. The advantages and disadvantages of your career opportunity should make a heck of a lot of sense, with no surprises. By discussing this topic for a few minutes, however, you are bound to get a few additional insights into the candidate's "hot buttons." From this you should have "missile lock" on the importance of money, independence on the job, new responsibilities, location, or whatever.

The Self-Appraisal follows (see page 334). If you only had 10 minutes to interview someone, you would jump to this page and ask the questions. First ask for the pluses, since you are a positive thinker. Question 1 asks for "strengths, assets, things you like about yourself, and things you do well." That's four ways of asking for strengths. Get the "grocery list" of 10 or 12 strengths, and then go back and get elaboration, digging for specifics on ones that are unclear.

Do exactly the same for the weaker points. Question 2 asks for shortcomings, weaker points, or areas for improvement. The word "liabilities" seems a bit harsh. Again, get the grocery list of five or six weaker points, urging the person to produce at least that many. Then go back and get the specifics. If impatience is a shortcoming, challenge the person on it. Almost every book on how to pass interviews suggests that candidates say that impatience is a shortcoming, "because my standards are very high and I mostly am just impatient with myself." Fire back at the person, "Exactly how is impatience a shortcoming, because it sounds as though it's a strength to me!"

Get specifics, get specifics. Figure 11.2 explains what I mean. The first target shows, "I sometimes procrastinate," as an example of an unclear shortcoming or weaker point. Everyone *sometimes* procrastinate, right? Level 2 is a bit more specific. Missing three deadlines last year is precise, and if you already know that the person had 30 deadlines to meet and was given an overall performance appraisal of "outstanding," you might leave it at that. If not, it's time to go for the bull's-eye. You will want to know:

- You missed three out of three, or three out of three hundred deadlines? Was missing the deadlines your fault, or not?
- How late were you? What were the dollar consequences of missing the deadlines?
- What were the career consequences?

Level 1 hits the bull's-eye. The response convinces you that procrastination is not a major shortcoming. But suppose a level 1 response was, "I missed all three out of three deadlines, and it was totally my fault; I got the reports in eight weeks late; consequently, we lost our best customer and I both lost my bonus and was told that I could lose my job." This probing to level 1 would reveal that procrastination is possibly a fatal flaw. The *pattern* of successes and failures revealed through a series of level-1 responses will surely permit you to rate the candidate accurately on many competencies.

Next are Leadership/Management questions (see page 335). In each Work History section, you asked about talent. If you pass pretty quickly through this talent section of each Work History Form and haven't pinned down a lot of specifics on talent, asking all of the questions in the Leadership/Management section would be extremely important. Question 1 is a warm-up question—"Describe your leadership philosophy and style." Since you probably already have some good insights into the answer, the response to this question will be mostly a "hype test." Question 2 gets a little closer to the mark, because it's like a 360-degree survey completed by subordinates. Question 3 is a pretty good test of a person's willingness to grow as a man-

Figure 11.2

Interviewer Specificity

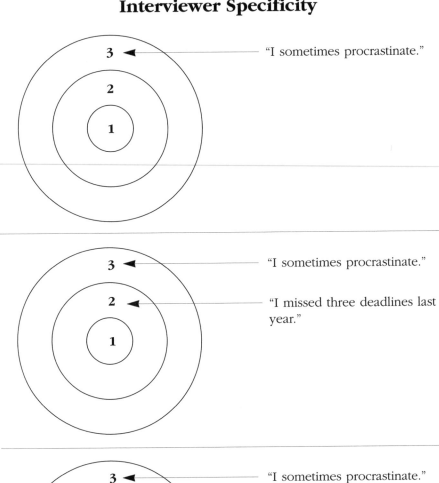

"I sometimes procrastinate."

"I sometimes procrastinate."

"I missed three deadlines last year."

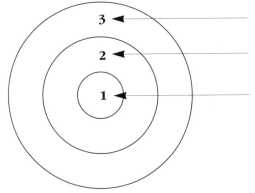

"I sometimes procrastinate."

"I missed three deadlines last year."

"I missed only three deadlines, and not by much. Most people missed more than 10, so I was given a bonus of $10,000, and a promotion to VP MIS."

ager or leader. Question 4 is the most revealing and productive of all, however. It asks for a thorough account of the total flow of talent in and out of the last two jobs. You ask for a one-paragraph assessment of each subordinate, including his or her strengths and weaker points. Were weak people coached and developed thoroughly, simply tolerated as C players, or coldly tossed overboard? What kind of recruitment efforts were there? These are the topgrading questions, so take your time. Get a good feel for what talent comprised the team, what changes were made, and what talent resulted. Is this manager inclined to topgrade, or not? In order to get some sense of patterns, the talent question is included in all of the Work History Forms, but I strongly encourage you to delve in depth, getting the names, titles, and all the other information suggested for at least two recent jobs.

Candidates might sing a pretty tune when responding to Question 1 regarding their leadership philosophy and style. They absolutely have no idea how revealing the responses to Question 4 are, however. People can honestly think they are topgraders, but when you hear the long lists of terrible weaknesses in most of the subordinates and how this candidate carried C players, you get the "true story." I have never seen an interviewing publication that suggested the interviewer pursue such detail about subordinates. Believe me, there is a "mother lode" of rich, revealing data in Question 4.

The Focused Questions begin next (see pages 336–355). If you have done a thorough job throughout the chronological interview and Self-Appraisal, chances are you do not need to ask many more questions. Some interviewers prefer to have an "insurance policy," slicing and dicing the data different ways to be sure the conclusions are valid. I'm one of those interviewers. You should be able to accurately predict responses to the Focused Questions. Then you know you are on target.

There are asterisks around the questions I tend to ask of almost all candidates. One way to approach the Focused Questions is to say, "I have remaining 19 pages of my favorite interview questions, and fortunately you have already answered most of them while discussing your career history. Why don't you relax a minute, and I'll read through these questions, asking only those where I feel I need a little bit more information."

After reviewing all of the Focused Questions, you might go to the last three pages of the guide where all 50 competencies are listed. If you have any questions, any questions at all, regarding whether the person meets your Minimum Acceptable Rating on any competency, ask another question or two. A typical one will be, "After spending three hours together, Pat, I'm still not quite sure how creative you are. How creative are you? What are the best examples of your creativity in processes, systems, methods, products, structure, or services?" (This is question 5a under Intellectual Competencies.)

These days, 360-degree surveys are so common, you might even ask to see the results. Or, if you have a question regarding any specific competency that comes up you might say, "Have you gotten any 360-degree feedback on this skill?"

YOU'RE DONE!

Well, not really. Even if the CIDS interview has lasted three hours, if you have promised that you would respond to the candidate's questions at this time, do it. Some interviewers plan for a lunch break and suggest that the candidate use this more relaxed time for asking you more probing questions.

In any event, you're still not "done." Clients figure that after thousands and thousands of interviews, I should be able to complete an interview and immediately pick up the phone to give them an assessment report. Sometimes I can, but I frequently say, "If I don't review my data two or three times, I'll probably be so off I will embarrass myself, so how about giving me a couple of hours to do my homework?"

I'd suggest for you what I do—take three passes through the data. One pass is just a refresher. Few of us took a shorthand course, so we simply scribble, scribble, scribble. Deciphering those scribbles immediately following an interview makes sense, because four days later they can look like hieroglyphics. After the first pass, go to the competencies (last three pages of the CIDS Guide) and make a preliminary rating, in pencil. Begin jotting cryptic comments in the space. Then take another pass through the data, to see if your preliminary ratings hold up. Next set the data aside for a few hours, or overnight, and come back one more time to review your notes and be sure you are confident of your ratings.

But what if you are not? Remember, the CIDS interview typically comes during the second day of interviews, and you have already heard from many coworkers following their short, structured interviews on different components of the Guide. That's not enough? In the following chapter I'll instruct you on how to conduct the most revealing reference calls ever, and this should help a lot. In the meantime, you might pick up the phone a day later and tell the candidate, "Jan, thank you again for our visit yesterday. I wonder if I could ask you a couple more questions?"

You should write a report, although some people like to conduct the reference calls first. Both topics are covered in the next chapter.

BUT, IS CIDS VALID?

When I completed my Ph.D. in 1970, I had read every study on interviewing validity, and the results were pathetic—interviews did not predict job success. In preparation for my 1983 book, research continued to show interviews to be invalid; they still did not predict job success. And yet, I was sure I had created a magic bullet.[1] I was sure that the CIDS interview could routinely achieve 90–95 percent "good hires." Beginning around the early 1980s, research began confirming that interviews not only can be valid, but done properly can be *the* most valid predictor of job performance.

Research, for example, showed job analysis is essential. During World War II armies (literally) of psychologists took job analysis to stratospheric heights. At lower levels of organizations, job analysts, industrial engineers, and systems professionals joined with compensation specialists to promote efficiency and productivity. Years later job evaluation specialists such as Hay Associates, who became quite proficient at assigning pay "points" to job "grades," found themselves competing with McKinsey MBAs looking to reengineer processes. But, somehow, job analysis rarely crept into the most senior management positions. It is still a casual undertaking in most companies. Nonetheless, all current research supports the importance of pinning down exactly what the job is (through job analysis).

"State of the art" today is commonly a process consisting of a job analysis, behaviorally anchored competencies, and then some sort of semi-structured interview format, so that questions focus on what is important to do the job. Topgrading offers even better approaches, but in most companies assessment consists solely of invalid, *unstructured* interviews. Unstructured interviews include one or more of the following characteristics: lack a question format, short (less than an hour), casual questioning ("Tell me about yourself"), unplanned (no job analysis, no job description, no written competencies), and no systematic analysis of data (the hire/no hire conclusion is made in minutes).

In 1988 Weisner and Cronshaw[2] found structured interviews over three times more valid than unstructured, in a review of 150 studies. Structured interviews are most valid when interviewers are trained, according to Pulakos et al.[3] Psychological testing is less valid than structured interviews, according to Van Clieaf.[4]

---

[1] One book on interviewing influenced me early-on: *The Evaluation Interview*, Fourth Edition, by R. A. Fear and R. J. Chiron, McGraw-Hill, 1990. It's still a classic, but seriously flawed. For example, whereas I might recommend a three-hour interview, Fear says one and one-half hours are too long, producing "a lot of unnecessary and irrelevant information" (p. 71). Furthermore, by discouraging asking about performance appraisals for every job (p. 107), Fear misses the most powerful lever for understanding negatives—the TORC technique.

[2] W. H. Wiesner and S. F. Cronshaw, "A Meta-Analytic Investigation of the Impact of Interview Format and Degree of Structure on the Validity of the Employment Interview," *Journal of Occupational Psychology* 61(4) (1988), pp. 270-290.

[3] E. D. Pulakos, N. Schmitt, D. Whitney, and M. Smith. "Individual Differences in Interviewer Ratings: The Impact of Standardization, Consensus Discussion, and Sampling Error on the Validity of a Structured Interview," *Personnel Psychology* 49(1) (1996), pp. 85-102.

[4] M. S. Van Clieaf, "In Search of Competence: Structured Behavior Interviews," *Business Horizons* 34(2) (1991), pp. 51-55.

A study by McDaniel et al.,[5] analyzing 86,000 interviews by leading researchers in 1994 concluded, "Structured interviews were found to have higher interview validity than unstructured interviews." My graduate school colleague Frank Schmidt was an author of this study; he has done many meta-analytic studies of interviewing and tells me that the jury is definitely in: Interviews must be structured if they are to predict job performance.

Perhaps you "wing it" in interviews because a tightly structured interview seems unbecoming, not as collegial as top-level interviews should be. Trouble is, the "wing it" interviews can't address all of the competencies, so 250 of such interviews might be necessary for valid conclusions about a single interviewee!

Let me cite two more studies. Pulakos and Schmitt[6] found historical experience-based questions ("What were your accomplishments and failures in that job?") to be better predictors of job performance than hypothetical situational questions ("How would you restructure the finance department here?"). The CIDS interview approach does both, and why not? Campion, Campion and Hudson[7] report a respectable validity coefficient (.50), with a 30-item interview, half-historical, half-future questions. An interview consisting of 30 questions could take half an hour. Add half an hour to "sell" the candidate, and the interview would take an hour, which is the length of time scheduled for 90 percent of all management interviews. The one-hour time frames exist because interviewers don't know how to interview and because lawyers have frightened managers into avoiding so many questions. The CIDS-interview approach, originated almost 30 years ago and described meticulously in the two earlier versions of this book[8] can easily ask 200 questions. In this book I argue that there are more than four dozen competencies *nec-*

---

[5] M. McDaniel, D. Whetzel, F. Schmidt, and S. Maurer, "The Validity of Employment Interviews: A Comprehensive Review and Meta-analysis," *Journal of Applied Psychology* 79(4) (1984), pp. 599-616.

[6] Pulakos, Schmitt, Whitney, and Smith, *op cit.*

[7] M. A. Campion, J. A. Campion, and J. P. Hudson, "Structured Interviewing: A Note on Incremental Validity and Alternative Question Types," *Journal of Applied Psychology* 79(6) (1984), pp. 998-1002.

[8] Bradford D. Smart, *Selection Interviewing: A Management Psychologist's Recommended Approach* (John Wiley & Sons, 1983), and Bradford D. Smart, *The Smart Interviewer: Tools and Techniques for Hiring the Best* (John Wiley & Sons, 1989).

essary (not just desirable) in any management job, so asking a lot more than 30 questions is necessary.

There are two interviewing approaches gaining in popularity, one good, one poor. The poor one is a panel of, say, ten interviewers listening to candidates respond to the same 10 or 12 questions. The reliability of such an approach is tops; the validity is terrible. Why? Because they confuse reliability with validity. That is, by observing exactly the same behavior—low voice volume and poor grammar, for example—interviewers at least have a chance to predict voice volume and command of grammar on the job. But with only 12 questions, the interviewers are like Olympic judges who observe only seconds of a gymnast's routine. Or, it's like ten weather forecasters trying to predict the weather when they can consider only one factor—current temperature. They may all agree on the temperature, so they have a "reliable" approach in that limited sense, but their prediction stinks because they did not reliably consider all the other data necessary to forecast the weather.

This is not to say "panels" are not a good idea. I have trained dozens of senior managers at General Electric, AlliedSignal, Federal Government of Canada, and other organizations to use a tandem (panel of two) CIDS-interview approach. I'm certain that individual biases are minimized with multiple interviewers. One interviewer is the principal question asker, the other the "note taker," but both can ask questions and take notes. A rich discussion of the interview data after the interview infuses the process with objectivity, rationality, and fairness. The downside? Time. It can take five hours for the tandem interview to be conducted and another three hours for the interviewers to review the Career History Form, plan who will do what in the interview, review the data, and finally write a brief report. Also, there is an organizational challenge of determining pairings (two introverts or two extroverts could be problematic) and finding convenient times to convene the pair with the interviewee.

My opinion is that a "solo" CIDS interviewer who is very experienced can be more valid than a tandem of moderately experienced interviewers. Pulakos et al.[9] found multiple interviewers to reduce harmful effects of interviewer bias, but only if the interviewers did not share the same biases.

I hope this short stroll down research lane has convinced you that structured interviews are the only interviews that predict success for dozens of competencies.

---

[9] Pulakos, Schmitt, Whitney, and Smith, *op. cit.*

CHAPTER 11 CHECKLIST:
ARE YOU A CIDS INTERVIEWER?

Yes	No		
❏	❏	1.	I use CIDS interviews for assessing external and internal candidates for selection, getting to know my team in a new job, and coaching.
❏	❏	2.	I sell the candidate on completing the Career History Form.
❏	❏	3.	I sell the candidate on the CIDS interview by offering smooth assimilation and career coaching that rely on it.
❏	❏	4.	I ask all the CIDS Interview Guide's questions until the section on Focused Questions.
❏	❏	5.	I ask all the Focused Questions with asterisks and any remaining Focused Questions unanswered previously.
❏	❏	6.	I take copious notes.
❏	❏	7.	I ask all the Work History questions for every full-time job, but spend a lot more time on the more recent job history.
❏	❏	8.	I apportion my time so I am not caught short at the end of the interview.
❏	❏	9.	I "get the specifics" so as to be able to make judgments on all competencies for the job.
❏	❏	10.	After the CIDS interview, I invite the candidate to ask me probing questions about the industry, company, job, or me.
❏	❏	11.	I review my CIDS notes a minimum of three times, rating the person on each competency.

After completing the CIDS interview, you should feel good about the validity of the process, regardless of how attractive the candidate is. Time and time again I have heard people say, "The first time I used the CIDS Interview Guide I felt I had conducted the best interview of my career, by far." Instead of conducting the usual brief insurance physical, you have conducted the equivalent of a thorough Mayo Clinic examination. Instead of buying a million-dollar piece of equipment after a cursory look at the numbers, you have performed a rigorous analysis of all the options. Instead of jumping in the cockpit and skipping three-quarters of the items on the preflight checklist, you have patiently made all of the checks. This really feels good. You know that if the candidate looks good now, this is an A player who is going to make you look good. The shareholders will benefit. Your career will be enhanced. Chances are if you have assessed several candidates, you will be absolutely certain that at least one of the others would have been a disaster in the job, creating misery for everyone—the candidate, you, your boss, your employer, the shareholders. Avoiding mis-hires while simultaneously hiring A players is nothing short of thrilling. At night, as you are reviewing your notes for the third time, you can finish with a shout, "Yes! I have this candidate pegged!"

THERE'S SOMETHING RARE, SOMETHING FINER
FAR, SOMETHING MUCH MORE SCARCE THAN
ABILITY. IT'S THE ABILITY TO RECOGNIZE
ABILITY.

ELBERT HUBBARD, 1856–1915

12. Mastering CIDS Interviewing: Advanced Interviewing Tactics

With the mechanics of how to conduct a CIDS interview understood, it's time to move on to the more advanced tactics.

This chapter begins with techniques for bonding with the interviewee; CIDS interviews elicit more negatives than other interviews, so it is important to do more than the usual rapport building. Next I describe the TORC technique, the most powerful lever I know to motivate interviewees to reveal their shortcomings. TORC convinces people that probing reference calls are imminent. The next section teaches you a technique that inspires 85 percent of references to accept your call and to tell you the truth. With the rich mother lode of CIDS and other data on your candidate, you need to make sense of it all. So, I'll explain ten principles for interpretation. I encourage you to write a brief report on your finalist, and this chapter gives you a sample. As a little bonus, I finish this chapter with some suggestions for easy ways to continue to hone your interviewing skills.

BONDING

This section might be called "building rapport," but simple rapport building doesn't seem to be enough in our interview that asks for negatives (failures, mistakes, disappointments) as much as positives (successes, accomplishments, likes). If we had only five minutes on the phone and you wanted my advice on how to improve your ability to build rapport, I would refer you to

250

Appendix D, the Interviewer Feedback Form. I would suggest that you study it, apply the principles, and maybe have someone observe one of your interviews and fill out the form on you. Done.

Let me walk you through Appendix D, but please take a couple of minutes to read it now. I'll assume that you have some experience as a manager, so this is not an elementary lesson.

Initial rapport-building components include "idle chit-chat" for a couple of minutes, offering the candidate something to drink and stating the purposes and expected timing. Even if you are not the most outgoing person, it is very important to get yourself in the mood to greet your candidate with a warm, friendly smile and a firm handshake. You are thoroughly prepared, so needless to say your notebook, job description, résumé, Career History Form, and CIDS Interview Guide are all neatly laid out. And please—no interruptions.

Throughout the interview, be sure to ask all appropriate questions. As obvious as that seems, I find many finance and technical people very good at this, but some sales and marketing people tend to fall in love with candidates, deviate from the Guide, and get into big trouble: They form invalid conclusions. I find that interviewers, particularly those just learning the CIDS interview approach, are so conscientious and purposeful they can appear cold to the candidate. So, I'll offer a number of suggestions to warm you up (if you need it).

There are a lot of techniques for connecting or "bonding" with the candidate at a human level. Some books on interviewing suggest that you have constant eye contact, but this is nonsense. Twenty percent is probably the minimum, and 50 percent is just fine. If there is much more than 50 percent eye contact you will be accused of staring. Remember, your mom told you, "Don't stare!" Friendliness, warmth, and enthusiasm are important, and it is certainly appropriate for you to use your sense of humor.

Bonding and maintaining control are complementary goals, though some interviewees need to be reminded of that. Books on "how to get a job" tell job seekers, "Interviewers don't know how to interview, so if you are going to get hired you have to take control of the interview and talk about your strengths." CIDS interviewees realize from the start they will have all the time they want to talk about accomplishments and strengths, so control becomes less of an issue. Indeed, A-player interviewees want *you* to have all the data you need. For an interviewee to schmooze in a buddy-buddy fashion and leave you without enough data on several competencies hurts everyone. You won't extend a job offer without "missile lock," and the interviewee won't get an offer. You must remain a friendly professional, in charge. Bond warmly with the interviewee, but if you find yourself losing control:

- Interrupt the interviewee who is going off on a tangent and say, "Please finish that thought, Pat, and forgive me for interrupting, but we're on a pretty tight schedule and I want to be sure to hear about your more recent jobs."

- Tell the candidate, "We're having a little trouble staying on the topic at hand here, Pat, and I'm wondering if this has been something you have been told in the past." If so, then say, "Let's do a little experiment to see if you can stick closer to the topic at hand during this interview."

This latter approach is appropriate only when the interviewer has a clear psychological edge over the candidate. The former approach works with everyone. These are wonderful tests. If they regain your control, you will be favorably impressed. If you can't regain control, you know you have given the interviewee a fair test, which has been flunked. You will probably reject this candidate.

It's important to appear sincere and genuinely interested in the interview. If the candidate is obviously thrilled about an accomplishment, it would be insulting to not at least acknowledge it with a statement, "That must have been a real high point of that job!" You are telling the truth.

I've discussed the importance of note taking in Chapter 11, so I will add only a couple of comments. Take a lot of notes and record not just the content (what is said) but the context (long pauses, loss of eye contact, and so on). Don't try to conceal note taking, but be unobtrusive. If the candidate is revealing something extremely negative, don't take any notes at all at the time. Instead, put your pen down, maintain eye contact, and be sympathetic. Then, when the topic is more positive, go back and write, "Sucker punched his boss!"

The CIDS Interview Guide does not bias the responses. However, toward the end of the interview if you are seriously concerned about some topic and open-ended questions ("Please give me examples of _____") don't work, it's time to introduce some deliberate bias. Say, "I get the feeling, Joe, that you're a little disorganized in your work, is that right?" This might trigger an open discussion and produce enough specifics that you feel confident you can rate the candidate on Organization/Planning. By being so direct, even blunt, you give the person a fair chance to convert your unclear assessment into a clear, positive conclusion.

The notion that an interview should involve equal amounts of talking by you and your interviewee is another common myth. Just prior to the CIDS interview you might have had lunch and the interviewee might have talked 90 percent of the time. Fine. After the CIDS interview you might be answering questions, and you talk 90 percent of the time. Fine. But *during* the CIDS interview itself, the interviewee should talk 90 percent.

Adjust your vocabulary level, vocal clarity, range, pace, and expressiveness to be able to communicate. If you are at a significantly higher level than the candidate, you might need to dumb down your communications style or you will intimidate the interviewee into unnatural responses. That can lead to invalid conclusions by you.

A CIDS interview, or just about any interview for that matter, has a cold tone to it if the interviewer does not use the candidate's name once every ten minutes or so. If it's more frequent than that, you will sound like an insurance salesman ("Hi, Sally, what a wonderful outfit you have, Sally, and, Sally, I'm looking forward to this mutually beneficial conversation."). If a half hour passes and you have not addressed your candidate by name, almost certainly your style is "blah," with a monotone, lack of expressiveness, a question-answer, question-answer, mechanical aura. If this is a real A player, you had better infuse some life, vibrancy, and humanness into this interview.

Candidates with healthy egos don't need a lot of ego protection, but those who are unsure of themselves need a lot of ego protection. Psychologically, a healthy ego exists in modest, quietly confident people. Ironically, the so-called "big-ego" types, arrogant and cocksure, actually are insecure and have teeny-weeny egos. So, rather than saying, "That was a colossal error," you should say, "Could it be that you might have made a mistake there, something that you wished you had done differently?" I'm exaggerating, but you get the point. The first time you are blunt with someone and you witness a "withering" reaction, you know to start bringing out the "weasel words."

You absolutely must control shock, dismay, negative surprise, or anger. You can always reject the candidate, but if you express some negative emotions prematurely, you can bias the rest of the interview, leaving you with insufficient confirmation of competencies to feel comfortable offering the person a job. If you become visibly annoyed, your candidate may withdraw. People use language differently. One company might use very violent metaphors, another gentle ones. You might be talking with a very gentle person, someone who in six months at your company would not be the slightest bit vulgar, but who says, "My boss slammed a hatchet through my head, popped out my eyeballs, and then stomped on them just for fun." Give the interviewee a chance to pick up your tone, your metaphors.

You know the CIDS interview might take three hours, and you told the candidate the timing. You might be able to last for a couple of hours without a washroom break, but don't assume your interviewee can. Every 45 minutes or so, say, "How about a break?" The casual interaction, walking around to get a cup of coffee can be revealing. You run into people, there are opportunities for introductions, humor is brought out, and the candidate is thrown a couple more "curve balls." It's all very instructive.

Partners in certain law firms and general management-consulting firms I know feel they have every right to split a candidate's head open, jump on their eyeballs . . . whatever. They are blunt, aggressive, demeaning, and sometimes downright nasty. They justify their behavior, saying, "The opposing attorney won't be gentle with you, so a high-pressure interview is appropriate," or "Client executives will rip the heck out of your presentations, so I want to see how you will hold up." Sure. There are plenty of other ways to test these competencies, but if there is a 20-minute segment that is to be allotted for grilling, be sure to do a lot of bonding with the candidate before and after.

Rejected candidates become prospective customers and clients in the future—sufficient reason to avoid abusive treatment of interviewees. If there is a single, overriding principle in interviewing style, it is this: Always, always, always *show respect for the interviewee*. Do you think there is an exception? A murderer? A crazy person? No way. I interviewed a convicted murderer, and believe me, by the end of the interview I was showing even more respect than usual.

There are a number of probes that help stimulate people to tell you more, to get to those specifics I discussed in the last chapter. Everyone does the easy ones. The affirmation of understanding ("uh huh," the nod). The more advanced probes include a summary. Once every 10 or 15 minutes summarize what the person has just said—the three reasons for leaving, the four accomplishments in that job. It shows that you are paying attention and are taking serious notes, not doodling. Immediately the rapport level shoots up, and you are "bonding."

After asking for a failure or mistake, zip it up. Simply don't talk until the interviewee responds. If you interrupt a pause after asking for an example of a failure, you tell the interviewee, "This interviewer is so uncomfortable asking for negatives, I'll help out by avoiding disclosing any!"

Repeating all or part of a response by the candidate is called the "echo," and it's an efficient way to stimulate more discussion. Active listening is a lot more subtle and potentially more powerful, however. I like the definition of active listening that includes not just paraphrasing what the interviewee said, but reflecting some unstated feelings. Active listening can boost mediocre rapport to very high. Be careful, however.

Suppose an interviewee's unstated feeling is too deep, due to unresolved guilt from having been rejected by parents. If you say, "Alice, I wonder if some problems you experienced with that boss might have been because he reminded you of your father, who rejected you because he wanted a boy, not a girl." If you are wrong, the candidate will get up and leave, thinking you are a nut case. If you are right, the candidate will get up and leave, thinking you are a nut case. Like levels of an onion, we all have our depths of unconscious and conscious motivation. Most of us like it when people seem to intuit our feelings, when they peel away one level of the onion. But, we don't want to be exposed, naked, particularly to a boss. If someone peels away five levels, they scare us. So my recommendation is this: Use active listening, and if you assume that your candidate has ten levels of psychic depth, aim your "unstated feelings" comments only one or two levels below the surface. That's all.

Techniques for "bonding" do not work if they are too artificial. You might review the Interviewer Feedback Form before each interview as a reminder, and think of it this way—be yourself, but don't overlook some rapport building and bonding techniques that will help you assess and sell the candidate.

THE TORC TECHNIQUE

TORC is an acronym for Threat of Reference Check, and it is by far the most powerful technique to "get the negatives." Candidates come to interviews well prepared to state accomplishments, strengths, and their needs. Although A-player candidates are more willing to disclose the negatives than are B or C players, it is really your responsibility as an interviewer to provide the "climate" for truth for all candidates. This is somewhat complicated psychologically. Even A-player candidates might not readily share negatives because:

- Your opportunity is fantastic, they want it, and they fear that disclosing their weaker points will hurt their chances for getting a job offer.
- Like all human beings, they have their defenses, and various individuals have a tendency toward denial, rationalization, and projection.
- Every book on job hunting encourages readers to be less than totally honest (a topic I keep hammering on).
- Outplacement firms tend to prepare people, sometimes too well, to put their best foot forward (and conceal negatives).
- Unskilled interviewers inadvertently invite candidates to minimize negatives by asking too few questions about failures and mistakes, failing to observe revealing patterns, and losing control of the interview.

The TORC Technique overcomes all that. It works, because the interviewee becomes convinced that extremely thorough reference checking will be done, and that you as the interviewer *will* know so much about all aspects of recent jobs that honest disclosure is the best way to get a job offer. The TORC Technique is appropriate, legitimate, legal, professional, and fair.

Put simply, the TORC Technique says, "I'll be talking with your bosses, so tell me what they will say." What's the big deal? By beginning the TORC Technique early in a person's career, the interviewee becomes accustomed to the questions. As you come into more recent history, your follow-up questions are more detailed and probing, achieving greater specificity (some to level 1), revealing more of what the person is really like today.

Candidates rarely ask about this line of questioning. However, if one asks, "Why are you so interested in what my bosses thought of me," you could respond:

I owe it to you, John, as well as to my company and myself, to be as thorough and professional as I can in determining if there

is a job match here and, if so, how I can help you succeed. In order to do that, I really need to know as much as possible about your strengths, and how I can maximize those. I also need to know your weaker points and anything I can do to manage around them and help you minimize them. By talking candidly and extensively with not only your bosses but perhaps other coworkers, I will be able to understand you and your needs. This is not one-sided, either, John. Assuming we move ahead in this selection process, I want to provide every opportunity for you to perform your due diligence on me and the company. In addition to answering your questions, I will invite you to talk with others who will be your peers and really anyone else you wish. In other words, we both have a lot at stake. You cannot afford to make a wrong job choice and neither can we. So I have a real obligation to make those reference calls, and I think it's only fair to you to ask what I am going to hear first.

The TORC Technique works in a very gentle fashion. You ask the questions, candidates respond, and you move on to the next questions. Question 13 under Work History in the CIDS Interview Guide (Appendix A) simply identifies the boss by name, title, and current location. "Current location" reminds the candidate that a reference might be done with this person. It's really most appropriate for jobs in the past ten years. With that information, including, "May I have permission to contact him/her?" TORC is underway.

Question 14 in the Guide is: "What was your supervisor's name and title? Where is that person now? May I contact him/her?" It's an amazingly revealing question, in and of itself. In order to accurately interpret what references might say, it is helpful to have an appraisal of that reference source. Beyond that, however, by asking your candidate about half a dozen different bosses, the patterns in responses tell you a great deal about what that candidate needs in you—the prospective boss. Suppose your candidate appraises various bosses as follows:

Boss #1: "A real moron with no brains."
Boss #2: "Real turkey—ten years behind, definitely trailing edge, not leading edge."
Boss #3: "A moron."
Boss #4: "Lacks basic common sense."
Boss #5: "Stupid—doesn't even read the latest periodicals."
Boss #6: "A nice guy, but technically a dud."

It does not take a Ph.D. in psychology to define this individual's mind-set—not just ten years ago, not five years ago, but today, now. If you aren't a technical wizard, you are going to be considered a "turkey," "idiot," and so forth. This candidate can only respect a boss with very strong technical expertise. You might have wanted to hire someone to compensate for your lack of technical expertise, but it probably should not be this particular candidate. Ask yourself, "Can I effectively manage this candidate, and if so, what is the best approach?"

Question 15 in the Guide is the guts of the TORC Technique—"What is your best guess as to what (supervisor's name) honestly felt were/are your strengths, weaker points, and overall performance?" Deviate from that wording at your peril. Believe me, the wording of that question has been massaged over decades, through mistake after mistake on my part. If you omit "best guess," many interviewees will say, "I don't know" and you will regret having to explain that, "Yes, I know, I don't expect you to be a mind reader."

Some interviewees are remarkably self-critical, and one might say, "My boss was critical of my on-time performance, relationships with peers, and technical development." Leave it at that, and you might arrive at an erroneously negative conclusion. When you hear that the overall performance rating was "outstanding," and that only 5 percent of people get "outstanding" ratings, you will inquire further, to learn that the strengths far outweighed the weaker points, and the weaker points were really quite minor.

Despite gently nudging the person into the TORC Technique, if he wants to conceal a significant negative, an amazing amount of creativity will go into trying to outfox you. When an interviewee attempts to sidestep the question, the most common response I have is to simply repeat it. Don't let the interviewee go on to another topic, but instead come back and say, "What is your best guess as to what he really felt at that time were your strengths, weaker points, and overall performance?" Simply repeating the question will convince any desirable candidate, "This interviewer is dead serious about my answering this question."

After asking the question, use that "pregnant pause." Your silence will shout, "Please respond!" If the interviewee says, "My boss was sick so much at the time, we hardly ever interacted," respond with: "Okay, what do *you* feel were your strengths, weaker points, and overall performance back then?"

Avoidance of the TORC questions is tantamount to the person saying, "I am withdrawing my candidacy." You owe it to yourself and your company to get honest responses, for only then will you be able to confidently rate the candidate on all of the competencies.

If an avoider says, "You will have to call her to find out what she thought of my performance," you can respond, "I'll do that, but I'm really interested in your insights into an important relationship—with your boss. I don't expect you to read your boss's mind, but do try to guess what she felt were your strengths, weaker points, and overall performance back then."

If a candidate seems genuinely confused by your probing, you might offer the long paragraph explanation at the beginning of this TORC section (pages 255–256). If a strong candidate is feisty and challenging, you might draw all the rationale for the TORC Technique together in this succinct, compelling fashion:

> By responding thoughtfully and honestly to this question, you show that you are *interested in what bosses think*, you not only are interested but you are *perceptive* and understand their perceptions of you, and you show me that you *trust me* and my judgment.

A slightly more negative way to state that is:

> If you can't answer this question, it suggests that you *aren't interested in what bosses think*, and since I am a prospective boss, that would be a concern. Or, perhaps you are interested in what bosses think, but you are *a bit dense* and simply don't get it. Or, you care what bosses think and you are perceptive, but you simply *don't trust me* enough to tell me the truth. As a prospective boss, that would worry me. Putting these all together, if you don't respond to the question I will consider you *uninterested* in what I will think of your performance, *dense*, or *untrusting*, or perhaps all three, and then I would conclude that maybe we don't have a good match here.

I give you this hypothetical explanation not so much because you will ever use it, but to help you get comfortable with the TORC Technique. It's true, if someone is tap dancing with you, avoiding truthful responses, and if reference checks are somewhat negative, your conclusions will be all the more negative about the candidate. If the references on candidates X and Y were identical, but if candidate X was very open and honest with you, and candidate Y was closed, your ratings of candidate X are apt to be higher. And, if an individual simply does not come forth with honest responses and you have used these various explanations to inspire truth, what else can you conclude but that the person would be very hard to manage?

A candidate I recently interviewed had no immediate boss in the past seven years. The person was moved from job to job with an open hole on the organization chart above him, and references from people two levels up would have been of only limited value. The TORC Technique under that circumstance was every bit as useful by just including peers, subordinates, and customers.

What about the current employer? There is always turnover, and it is up to you to determine who among bosses, peers, and subordinates might have left and would make good reference sources. And, a final offer in any event should be contingent upon "no surprises" in reference checks. If a candidate is nervous about that you might say:

Sara, if an offer is made in writing and you formally accept it, I'll naturally want to talk with your current boss. Now, don't worry—no offer has ever to my knowledge been withdrawn because of the current-employer reference check. But in talking with a current boss, I frequently get additional insights into how I can help a person succeed.

Follow that statement by reasking Question 15.

CONDUCTING REVEALING REFERENCE CHECKS

Many laws discourage you and your company from disclosing much of anything when people call for references on your previous employees. You know the drill—you are supposed to refer them to Human Resources who, with written authorization, will disclose employment dates, job titles, and probably little else.

As Chapter 13 points out, companies are penalized for giving out reference information only when they are determined to have disclosed false information or expressed malice. Most companies discourage managers, particularly lower-level supervisors and managers, from giving out reference information; they prefer that Human Resources maintain tight control, to be sure what is revealed is factual and devoid of malice. Carte blanche for managers to take reference calls could too easily lead a former employee to conclude a reference said something false or malicious.

But companies cannot stonewall, cannot refuse to give negative reference information without legal risks. If your company fired Joe for fighting, Human Resources had better reveal that to a prospective employer who asks. Otherwise, if Joe is hired and kills someone, your company might be found liable for not disclosing Joe's violence.

The courts are increasingly finding companies liable for hiring bad guys (rapists, for example), because the company failed to perform reference checks. So, it's understandable that companies withhold information on former employees, but those same companies are vulnerable to litigation if they don't check their own prospective employees' records.

Donald Weiss, who coauthored Chapter 13 on legalities with me, put it succinctly: "Asking for reference information is perfectly legal, giving out false or malicious information is illegal, and withholding certain negative reference information can be illegal." No individual manager is legally required to accept a reference call, so if a company is willing or legally obligated to disclose reference information, Human Resources is the usual designated source.

Some companies are fairly loose in permitting upper managers to take reference calls. They say, "If you take a reference call, say you will give your *personal* opinion, not speak for the company; be truthful and nonmalicious, and be sure the reference source can be trusted to maintain confidentiality and not distort the truth."

Human Resources people should check records from schools, credit bureaus, and the courts; the legal protection for sources and candidates is appropriately solid. The real barriers exist for reference discussions with former coworkers and bosses, who are understandably hesitant to say anything negative about a previous employee. Fortunately, those barriers are surmountable.

About 85 percent of the time, the technique I suggest works. As you review the candidate's work history and move into the most recent ten years, each Work History Form suggests that you not only identify who the boss was, but ask, "Is it okay if I contact him/her?" My suggestion to you is to determine if you really would like to talk to that individual, perhaps toward the end of the interview. Then, prior to wrapping up the interview say, "There are four of your previous bosses I would like to talk with, so would *you* arrange those interviews?" That puts the burden back on the interviewee's shoulders and makes it perfectly clear (from a legal standpoint) that you have not contacted a present or former employer without "permission." Sure, there's a chance that the interviewee will ask the previous bosses, "Would you please be generous in your assessment?" The downside risk associated with that is definitely offset by the pluses. The candidate will call you back with names, phone numbers, and availability times (preferably in the evening or on a weekend), so that when you call the individual, not only will the call be taken, but the individual will have prepared a bit for it. Telephone tag is minimized.

References called will not only talk, but talk quite openly. You should talk with bosses, but also a sample of peers, subordinates, and customers. Half a dozen reference calls could include three present and former bosses, and three "others."

Those calls are received because people will trust you. It's amazing, in our untrusting, litigation-minded society, but it "works." Appendix C is a form specially devised to make your reference calling even easier. Read it carefully. Here is a summary of the major principles stated in the Guide:

- You, the hiring manager, conduct the in-depth reference calls. After conducting the CIDS interview, no one knows the interviewee better, no one is better equipped to build rapport with the reference source. It's okay if, early in the selection process, Human Resources conduct preliminary checks with employers, credit agencies, and so forth (with written approval by the candidate). You as the hiring manager are apt to be the only one, however, with enough stature to call previous bosses (your peer level) and earn credibility.

- Conduct in-depth reference checks *after* the CIDS interview. In the CIDS interview you asked the candidate to appraise the person you are calling, and this is enormously helpful in your later building trust and rapport with that individual.

- Obtain written permission from the candidate to conduct reference calls. The Career History Form has such a request, but some attorneys want to have something more powerful.

- As previously mentioned , ask the candidate to contact the present and previous supervisors, plus two or three peers, subordinates, or customers, asking to accept a call from you some evening or weekend soon. (It makes it easier for a person working for a company that has a policy against disclosing reference information to take the call away from the office.)

- Promise those contacted total confidentiality and honor that promise. Take notes, just in case someone's going to accuse you of "making up" a story.

- Create the tone that you are a trusted colleague, a fellow professional who knows the applicant very well, who just might hire that candidate, and who is apt to help the individual be successful with insights coming from this reference call.

The In-Depth Reference-Check Guide (Appendix C) takes you through:

- Suggested introductory comments
- Comprehensive appraisal of the candidate
- Responsibilities/accountabilities of the candidate when working for the reference source
- Overall performance rating
- Confirmation of dates/compensation
- Your description of the opening you have
- Good/bad-fit appraisal
- Comprehensive ratings (covering more than four dozen competencies, grouped)
- Questions for you, the hiring manager
- Final comments
- Thanks! . . . with double-check on confidentiality expected

If you really need to disclose to your boss what this reference source said, don't do it, unless that person says it's okay. It's amazing, but if you say, "Is it all right if I share this confidential information only with my boss?" the person on the other end of the phone typically says, "I'll trust your judgment on that."

If your time is extremely limited and if the candidate is extremely eager to get the job, you can conduct five reference calls in a morning. Here's how: Establish half-hour time slots for the upcoming Saturday morning and ask the candidate to try to persuade people to take one. Many will, and the others will have to be contacted at a different time.

Just follow these guidelines, and in-depth reference checking will go smoothly. One caution: Do not ask references for prohibited information—on race, religion, and the like. You must operate within legal guidelines.

Are you still feeling a little guilty about requesting confidential reference information, while simultaneously being unwilling to give it out? Okay, think of it this way: Maybe these calls are not reference calls at all. Maybe these are "coaching" calls to help you assure a smooth assimilation for the candidate into the new job and equip you with some information to begin a comprehensive developmental program right away. Or, refer to the discussions not as reference checks but as 360-degree inputs. If you have done a thorough CIDS interview, and if all of the other interviews during two days of visits have been performed reasonably well, you almost certainly are *not* going to eliminate your candidate on the basis of these final, in-depth reference-check calls. In fact, these will be "coaching calls." I've never heard of a company prohibiting managers from participating in "coaching calls." So that's what you are asking—not for references, but for coaching sources. Feel better?

INTERPRETING ALL OF THE DATA

Let's review the data sources at your disposal just prior to your extending a formal offer of employment:

* Résumé analysis
* Career History Form analysis
* Preliminary telephone interview
* Five to seven one-hour structured interviews spread across two in-person visits
* Informal interactions during two visits
* CIDS interview, conducted by you
* Possibly a psychological appraisal (another CIDS interview, conducted by a psychologist)
* Preliminary record checks (by Human Resources)
* In-depth reference-check calls (or "coaching calls") conducted by you

You are now equipped to provide valid assessments of your candidate across dozens (if necessary) of competencies. At this point, there is absolutely no excuse for unsubstantiated "hunches." To validly interpret data, you don't need experience having conducted 100 CIDS interviews, but you frankly do need some life experiences and work experiences. Since this book is for managers, not receptionists who conduct screening interviews, let's assume that you have considerable experience.

Having trained several hundred people in the CIDS-interview technique, I have always tried to teach some of the most important principles for valid interpretation, which include the following:

1. ADHERE TO THE BASICS

Truth comes from doing everything advocated in this book—performing thorough job analyses, creating elaborate competencies, using the CIDS Interview Guide, taking thorough notes, reviewing the notes three times, probing for specificity (remember those targets?), and so on.

Okay, suppose you have performed the mechanics and you have all of the data a skilled interviewer should in order to arrive at valid interpretation. Then . . .

2. LOOK FOR PATTERNS

This is the magic of the chronological interview, the disclosure of *patterns* from school to first job, to second job, to third job . . . to the tenth job, followed by discussions of the future and substantiated with a few focused questions.

A sea cucumber is a very primitive animal about a foot and a half long, and biologists joke that it is a "mouth and anus, wrapped in cardboard." As brainless as this animal is, even it can accurately interpret patterns on the sea floor. You can do even better. Response patterns in a CIDS interview are a hiring manager's Rosetta Stone, translating the hieroglyphics into language you understand.

Go to Las Vegas (or any other sports-betting venue), and you won't find anyone making money who just considers performance in the most recent athletic event—a basketball game, a horse race, you name it. Earthquakes are predicted with accuracy when not just the most recent history is concerned but the pattern of quakes across decades. It's pretty difficult to predict when a bridge will collapse, unless you go back to the original drawings and note the various stress measurements across the years. A single cardiogram is not so revealing, in most cases, as the pattern of a series of cardiograms. *Patterns* reveal.

It is exactly the same with people. Discussing college days, a person will say, "I was quite a procrastinator, cramming at the last minute, and come to think of it, that's a problem I have now." A pattern is disclosed. Across a series of jobs, an individual can communicate in various ways that she is team-oriented—liking a special task force she was on, achieving a particular success as a result of wiring things cross-functionally, repeatedly earning praise from bosses (the TORC Technique) that she is an excellent team player. By the time you get to the current job, there is no doubt about her commitment to teamwork.

This is equally true for all of the 50 competencies listed in Appendix E. You don't have to conduct 50 chronological interviews, each covering one of 50 competencies. Starting with education and progressing through the entire career history, every job will provide fresh new insights into a couple dozen competencies. By the time you get to the current job, you should have sufficient data on all 50. If not, you have the Focused Questions to generate more insights. But that is unusual. Typically the data are so compelling about all 50 competencies that the Focused Questions merely jam the cork into the bottle, giving you some comfort that, indeed, you are on target, that you are being fair to the candidate, to yourself, to your employer in your valid assessments of various competencies. When you delve into specifics (remember the specificity targets, Figure 11.2) you can not only pin down data on a specific competency, but simultaneously generate data on others.

For example, if a person's guess is that his boss ten years ago would say that he is "creative," you should not be satisfied with that. You'd pin him down, to get specific examples of Creativity. And, when a candidate mentions a great idea, be sure to get the specifics—whose idea was it (candidate's or some else's), how good an idea was it? By the time you do this across three or four jobs, chances are you will have considerable information not just about Creativity, but also about Initiative, Team Player, Energy, Conflict Management, and many other competencies. Naturally you will be particularly attuned to patterns for the most critical competencies.

Arriving at correct interpretations is like an impressionist painting that morphs into realistic art. With every bit of data, the fuzziness of the landscape becomes a little more defined. Well into the selection process, you might be absolutely certain that an individual is not Very Poor, not Poor, not Only Fair with respect to a particular competency, so the remainder of the selection process is fine-tuning conclusions, to determine if the person is Good, Very Good, or Excellent.

Integrity is a "must" with my clients. A person must be Very Good or Excellent in Integrity in order to get or keep the job. It is extremely difficult to assess *without* relying on patterns of data that emerge in a CIDS interview. The impressionistic painting becomes realistic on this (and frankly, all) competencies starting at the beginning of the selection process. What a wonderful résumé, I wonder if it's all true? The CIDS interview provides the best opportunity to nail down exactly how much "hype" there is in the accomplishments listed on the résumé. The TORC Technique is a powerful lever for assessing Integrity. "When I talk to your boss, Mary, will her opinion be that the increase in sales was largely due to your efforts, or perhaps were there shared accomplishments?" Knowing that the boss will probably say, "Really, it was a full-court press by Marketing and Product Development that triggered massive sales increases across the world, not just in Mary's area," the candidate experiences pressure to be honest. As you nudge for more specific (the targets again) information, is a person naturally honest and open, or devious and manipulative? Are there flat-out untruths on the résumé or Career History Form? (If so, eliminate the candidate *now*.) When you finally conduct the in-depth reference calls, do you find compelling information to show that during the interviews your candidate was trying to pull the wool over yours (and others') eyes? In those reference calls, when you ask about Integrity, you really should hear "ironclad," and similar praise. When you hear, "kind of political," "sometimes a gossip," or "a little too ambitious," you know that you might have a values violator in your selection pipeline, with questionable Integrity.

> ▶ **"Use what words you will, you can never say anything but what you are."**
>
> Ralph Waldo Emerson

A fantastic psychiatrist or psychologist might be able to interpret a 30-second video of a candidate and accurately rate the person on a couple dozen competencies. You and I are not so gifted. That's okay—we have lots of 30-second segments in a CIDS interview. The *patterns* of those statements given today, reflecting on an entire career history, give multiple vantage points from which to find out what makes a person tick, what are the person's strengths and weaker points.

In order to calibrate a person's language, you need specific examples that cross chronology. A candidate for Sales Engineer might honestly describe herself as "creative," and the TORC Technique as well as reference interviews confirm it. "Creative" for Sales Engineer might mean listening to customers and taking their ideas back to our engineers so they can design the products and modifications necessary. A "creative" Brand Manager might develop a line extension (a different flavor), or originate a totally new product—candy for eraser heads on pencils, or whatever. On an absolute scale, the "creative" Sales Engineer is only a 2, where the inventive Brand Manager is a 9. The Sales Engineer might be extremely creative in relation to sales engineers, but far less creative than the Brand Manager. It is quite impossible to rate people accurately on competencies unless you glean specifics—specifics across many jobs, many situations, many opportunities to "say what you are."

3. ASSUME THAT STRENGTHS CAN BECOME SHORTCOMINGS

Under pressure, we all tend to overuse our strengths, and they can become shortcomings. During interviews, entertain this hypothesis frequently. For example:

- An ambitious person might sacrifice job performance in order to take additional classes and devote too much time to professional activities and expanding his professional network.
- A very conscientious, meticulous planner can become slow and indecisive.
- The friendly, affable customer-service representative might be easily dominated by assertive customers.
- Glib salespeople who are "quick on their feet" can manipulate bosses and be "high-maintenance."
- The highly cautious financial analyst or attorney might avoid fabulous business opportunities.

4. ASSUME RECENT PAST BEHAVIOR IS THE BEST PREDICTOR OF NEAR-FUTURE BEHAVIOR

Competencies have inertia. Success and failure patterns both persist. As you review an individual's chronological history, weigh the most recent behaviors most heavily. If the person was a goof-off in college but has been extremely conscientious and mature during the past five years, the previous adolescent immaturity can usually be disregarded. On the other hand, if a person was very mature and self-disciplined 15 years ago, but has undergone a midlife crisis that has resulted in four job changes in three years, watch out.

When people are learning the CIDS interview approach, there is a tendency to spend too much time on the early history—college, first couple of jobs—leaving too little time for the most recent positions. If this occurs, there are simply more data on early history, and it tends to be weighted disproportionately. Allocating time to different interview sections, as recommended in Chapter 11, will help you capture enough recent past behavior to predict near-future behavior.

5. ASSUME ALL BEHAVIOR IS MOTIVATED

Ralph Waldo Emerson's quote suggests that every word, perhaps every gesture and vocal tone, reveals the soul. Even Freud joked, "Sometimes a cigar is just a cigar," implying it is not always a phallic symbol. Do unresolved adolescent conflicts manifest themselves in behaviors 25 years later, without the individual's being aware of such controlling influences? Did my toilet training make me a better controller or a messy impressionistic painter?

You don't need to necessarily alter your philosophy of life, but I'll guarantee you that you will make more accurate predictions of job performance if you operate on the hunch, "all behavior is motivated." I have studied hundreds of hours of videotaped interviews, from start to finish. I believe that all behavior is motivated, but in studying the first half hour of the interview, I miss a lot of things. I know I miss a lot of things, because I watch the rest of the interview, and then observe how the person actually functions on the job. Time and time again it is apparent that every pause, every inflection, every choice of words, every omission, every inclusion, is motivated. Even if the same person might have a good day or a bad day, it all "fits." If it doesn't "fit," I feel I have not done my job as a CIDS interviewer.

Watch body language, but don't overinterpret. Sometimes a candidate folds his arms because they have begun to ache a bit, *not* because he is motivated to withdraw.

Occasionally people ask if video taping or audio recording interviews is a good idea. For terrible note takers, it probably is. For pretty good note takers, the disadvantages would outweigh the advantages. As soon as you start touching on negative topics, the obtrusiveness of the recording device creates a new motivation in the interviewee—to clam up!

6. SPOT RED FLAGS AND LOOK FOR EXPLANATIONS

"Red flags" are warning signals to the interviewer that something has gone wrong. Rapport suddenly declines, something changes in the interview to suggest that you have touched on a raw nerve. Either that, or it's time for a break. The signals are:

- Blushing
- Suddenly complex responses, when previously they were more straightforward
- Loss of eye contact that had been quite good
- A significant change in pace (speeding up or slowing down)
- A significantly higher or lower voice
- Inappropriate use of humor
- Sudden changes in voice volume
- Twitching, stammering, drumming fingers when there had been none of that behavior
- Formality in style or vocabulary, when the individual had been informal
- Inconsistency between nonverbal behavior and words (saying "I was very happy in that job," while frowning)
- Heavy perspiring, when the person had been calm
- Suddenly long pauses, when they hadn't occurred previously

It is the sudden change in the rhythm, style, rapport of the interview that should tell you, "Pay attention, something is going on here." Certainly make note of it in your Guide. Then go on a "fishing expedition," using follow-up questions to get additional information. "Could you tell me a little bit more about that?" or "Could you give me a specific example of what went on then?"

If it is early in the interview, don't destroy rapport by probing too aggressively. You can always come back later in the interview, after you have more information that will help you figure it out.

Later in the interview your bonding with the interviewee should be at a high level, to give you the "idiosyncrasy credit" necessary to risk a more in-depth probe. If this is your most attractive A-player candidate, you do not want to put the person off by appearing to go on a "witch hunt." However, after the CIDS interview, when you are finally putting all of your thoughts together and making the ratings, you will reflect on those "red flags." You probably will not feel comfortable offering the person a job until you know what the heck was going on, why rapport seemed to plummet so dramatically, why that particular topic seemed so sensitive for the individual.

So, as a last resort, at the end of the interview you can confront the individual directly, saying, "Joe, when we talked about your job at General Motors, you seemed extremely uncomfortable. I want to talk with your boss there, but I wonder if there might be something more you want to tell me about that job?"

You would not believe the flood of "truth" such a question has triggered. That murderer I mentioned earlier "confessed" in response to that question. It's usually something very negative, a failure, a political battle. But not always. In one case the hesitancy to talk about a boss was because the highly respected boss was killed in an auto accident and the individual did not want to become emotional during the interview. One humble person became very quiet and closed when asked about accomplishments because there were so many. Sometimes there was a significantly negative occurrence, but it is not particularly pertinent to the job at hand. The only way you know is to probe, ask, clear up the matter.

7. ASSUME THAT PEOPLE CAN CHANGE, WHEN THEY HAVE CHANGED

Can leopards change their spots? Do people really change? Everyone has a strong opinion on the topic. At least three-quarters of the managers I have interviewed have said, in various ways, "People don't really change." And yet, 95 percent of the managers I have interviewed give convincing examples of how *they* have changed. What that means is that when young and naïve, we tend to trust that people will change to better meet our needs, but they, too, often let us down. So, we become cynical.

In Chapters 8 and 9 I delved into exactly when and how people change. For now, let me repeat a bit of advice: Bet on change occurring only after there has been a strong trend in that direction. When people change jobs, they inevitably promise themselves they will minimize those shortcomings that existed in the last job, regardless of whether they failed or were successful. The new job brings new pressures, however, and people tend to regress to their former behaviors. In interviews people can sound sincere about their commitment to change, because they are. With rose-colored glasses on, people tend to hype their constructive change and downplay previous backsliding.

You are more justified in counting on the person changing when you see a general pattern of success in life, a willingness to disclose not just strengths but shortcomings, nondefensiveness, a high level of intelligence (but watch out, extremely bright people can rationalize like mad), achievement motivation (an incentive to change), and a pattern of having "fixed" other shortcomings. Bet that a person will turn over a new leaf when the person has a recent history of turning over new leaves.

8. LOOK FOR ATTRIBUTIONS AND EVALUATIONS

Understanding that a person has worked 15 hours a day, seven days a week can be important, but even more important is understanding how the person felt about such a workload. Did she feel burned out after a few days or motivated to keep going at that pace even after half a year?

As an interviewer, you need to know the basics (hours per week) but you also need to know how a person reacted to them. That's why, from education through the entire work history, the CIDS Interview Guide asks what the person did, what were successes, what were failures, what were disappointments, what were high points, what were low points, and what were reasons for leaving. Each Work History Form asks the TORC questions, which triggers more evaluation of what was liked (the boss's style, and so on), and how the candidate reacted to the estimated evaluation by bosses. All these questions produce rich, meaningful data because they require the candidate to express feelings, real needs. Candidates might be "prepped" for the typical "tell me about yourself" interview, but there is hardly any way someone can "prep" for a three-hour CIDS interview. If you ask the questions, you will find out what makes the interviewee tick. A great deal of that information comes from these evaluations.

Do not confuse a pattern of disliking something with a shortcoming. Many managers hate administration, but some are so conscientious they do it well.

Pay attention to attributions. To what does the individual attribute success or failure? Those with an external locus of control tend to blame. Such individuals do not feel in control of their destiny, and it becomes obvious in the patterns of responses to the questions, "Why did that happen, who or what was responsible?" What strengths, weaker points, and motives does the interviewee attribute to coworkers and customers? Nailing down attributions provides a rich source of interpretive data.

9. WEIGH NEGATIVES MORE HEAVILY THAN POSITIVES

I devoted a lot of Chapter 7 to the importance of fixing shortcomings in order that they not fall into that fatal flaw, Achilles'-heel, career-derailer category. Naturally, as an interviewer, you should incorporate this perspective:

> ▶ Good-fit factors do not assure success, but no-fit factors can assure failure.

Clients frequently ask if I favor overall talent or experience—superior overall potential, or lesser potential but more current savvy. Should they hire a super sales manager of medical products for their heavy machinery business, or hire an average sales manager in the industry? My short answer is to be sure the sales team has enough experience, but hire the manager stronger on talent/potential than on specific industry experience. Sharp people learn a new industry, a new product line.

10. WATCH OUT FOR STRONG FEELINGS AND BELIEFS

If you were at a party talking with someone who seemed to dwell on the topic of how volatile people are, after awhile you would begin to develop a hunch about this person. Is he volatile? Is he hyper-controlled, in order to deal with his extreme fear of volatility?

> ▶ "Methinks the lady doth protest too much . . ."
>
> William Shakespeare

Naturally, strong beliefs can be an asset for any candidate. It's when the beliefs are accompanied by rigidity, intolerance, and extreme emotionality that you begin to wonder if there might be accompanying shortcomings. The person who vehemently and repeatedly says, "Insensitive people drive me nuts," might be insensitive. How tolerant is the individual who screams, "If there's one damn thing I can't stand, it's intolerance."

Frequently at the end of a CIDS interview a person says, "That was really interesting, I learned a lot about myself." I think it's true. It would probably be beneficial for all of us to sit by the seashore for an afternoon, CIDS interviewing ourselves and listening to the responses. If we videotaped ourselves and then edited the tape to capture only what we feel most strongly about, there would be a—you guessed it—pattern. We might wonder what is underlying that pattern, and figure it out. Chances are it has something to do with insecurity, a nasty little pocket of insecurity that bubbles up to the surface in the form of an excessively strong and rigid opinion.

From an interviewer standpoint, we don't necessarily have to "figure it out." All we need to know is the "it" is there, that there is inertia to this behavior. Then, toward the end of the interview ask the person directly what this mysterious pattern of strong feelings is about. For example, a few years ago I interviewed the vice president of distribution of one of the largest companies in the United States, and I thought it was just a coaching interview, since the individual was an incumbent. Throughout the interview the man referred to the Mafia. He didn't say he had any dealings with the Mafia, but he told a couple of Mafia jokes, mimicked a Mafioso, and deplored their influence on society. Following my advice to pay attention to that, I did, but I wasn't getting to any conclusions. So, toward the end of the interview I said, "Dave, you have made repeated references to the Mafia, and I'm just wondering, have you had any recent contact?" As it turned out, he had invited two reputed hit men from the Mob to come to the corporate offices and discuss ways to control labor costs. For $100,000 a month, the company could hire a particular "labor-relations consulting firm" that would assure a much improved labor contract for the company.

We marched into the chairman's office to discuss it, and the chairman quickly chopped off the discussions. A particularly meaningful moment was the vice president's response to the question from the chairman, "But what if the local does not want to go along with our contacts at the national level?" "They'll be shot."

So, when there is some pattern of very strong feelings or beliefs, step back mentally to ask what the interviewee might be disclosing, assume these strongly held beliefs are not amenable to change, and then begin testing hunches about what the job-relevant behaviors and consequences might be.

WRITING A REPORT

With all the data at hand, and with basic principles of interpretation in mind, you are ready to assign your final ratings. I'll suggest several different ways to do this.

First, be sure you have all the information necessary to validly rate the candidate on all the competencies. If after gathering all the information you cannot interpret some of it, you haven't asked enough questions, haven't made enough reference calls, haven't dug deeply enough into the specifics. Pick up the phone, call the person, and gather some more information. My personal batting average is in excess of 95 percent, and I simply don't complete the interview until there is that comfortable little feeling in my belly that it all "fits." Toward the end of the interview I glance through all of the competencies to be sure I have sufficient data to accurately rate the person on the competency. If not, I'll ask more questions—probably some of the Focused Questions.

The last three pages of the CIDS Guide represent a Candidate Assessment Scorecard. In Chapter 2, I presented a different version. In both, assign Minimal Acceptable Ratings; after reviewing your notes three times assign final ratings, and squeeze in a few comments by each competency. There is not a whole lot of room to write on Scorecards, however.

You might create a different Scorecard allowing more room for comments. If you are extremely conscientious, you might write a ten-page report. I do it and so do CIDS assessors I have trained. It's a lot of work, however.

What seems to "work" for most hiring managers is what is portrayed in Figure 12.1. It consists of a conscientiously crafted Executive Summary plus the competencies spread across Strengths and Weaker Points. If the Minimum Acceptable Rating is met, it is a Strength. If not, it is a Weaker Point.

CONTINUING TO DEVELOP INTERVIEWING SKILLS

If CIDS interviewing is a "silver bullet," capable of launching you to ever-higher career heights, what are the best ways to master the skill? Reading this book is a pretty good start. After that, I do have some suggestions:

- Practice, practice, practice. If you are not hiring these days, offer yourself as an interviewer for others. Do the shorter, one-hour interviews, but also volunteer to perform a CIDS interview. Because the entire process is so time-consuming, you are volunteering close to a full day by the time you meet beforehand, and understand the job and competencies to conduct a CIDS interview and write the report. Doing this twice per year is about all most managers can or need do.

- Get feedback. The Interviewer Feedback Form (Appendix D) was designed for this purpose. Someone need not sit in on an entire interview, but merely half an hour of one. Do this a couple of times per year, and you will continue to improve.

- Conduct your first CIDS interviews on candidates over whom you have psychological leverage. It takes only a few CIDS interviews for most people to get the hang of it, but I wouldn't recommend trying it out on a likely A player who is far from being "sold" on joining you.

Figure 12.1 Sample Assessment Report

GLOBAL COMPENSATION CONSULTANTS, INC.

NAME OF CANDIDATE: Patrick Smith

POSITION APPLIED FOR: Senior Compensation Consultant, Europe

INTERVIEWER: Alan Jones

DATE: August 15, 1998

TYPE OF INTERVIEW: _____ Short Structured Interview

                          ____√____ CIDS Interview

EXECUTIVE SUMMARY

Mr. Smith can relate credibly with Fortune 500 CFOs and VPs of HR and can become a recognized compensation specialist in Europe. He is a savvy businessman with a very professional image and plenty of substance as well. I like him and would be proud to have him as a professional associate . . . if . . . . . . if he can prove he has the fortitude and drive to do the total job. Despite his "Exceeds" performance rating at General Motors, Mr. Smith acknowledges that senior GM executives would criticize him for not taking firm leadership stands on HR policy and for taking far too long to remove C players in his HR organization.

Mr. Smith is being nudged out of GM by a new, dynamic division president, determined to produce much better earnings. I'll call that division president for a confidential 360 degree discussion, but I fear he considers Mr. Smith weak . . . perhaps in the top 10 percent of GM's division HR VPs but *not* a sufficiently dynamic leader for a company undergoing a major transformation. I'm concerned that Mr. Smith feels 45-hour work weeks are "too much," because we need him to double our European executive compensation practice in the next three years. Furthermore, he is, as he put it, "not an aggressive salesman."

In short, I feel Mr. Smith lacks some of the "right stuff" to serve as senior compensation consultant. For the compensation he requires, I judge him (prior to my reference calls) a B player, with only B potentials.

Figure 12.1 *cont.*

STRENGTHS

- Smart; 1460 SAT
- "Quick on his feet" in conversation
- Fluent; articulate
- BA in Economics from Dartmouth
- MBA from Stanford
- Strong general business perspective
- 12 years' work experience
- Very strong analytic abilities
- Quick and deep at "sorting"
- Good writer; published two articles on compensation
- Member of top 50 HR group (ASTD); knows best practices of premier companies
- Prominent in HR community; was president of SHRM
- Consistently earned top performance ratings at General Motors
- Excellent record in project planning and implementation
- Reoriented HR to be service-oriented at GM
- Poised; at ease with senior executives
- Sophisticated, yet "down to earth"
- Strong team player
- Positive, effective manager; sets clear direction, assures accountability, attracts talent

WEAKER POINTS

- "Tired" of 45-hour work weeks
- May be too "above" nitty-gritty details
- More interested in strategic discussions than hands-on activity
- Slightly soft manager; does not confront negatives as he should
- A relationship builder in sales, but not a closer ("I'm not an aggressive salesman.")
- May be "running from" politics that exist in any company

- Watch your biorhythms. Research has demonstrated that some people are more generous on Fridays than on Mondays, on mornings than on afternoons. Once you recognize your patterns, that alone will help you prevent a timing bias.

- Watch your stereotypes. More research has shown that like favors like (race, age, gender, and so on), which should come as no surprise. At a more subtle level, I find it useful to write down the name of a person the candidate reminds me of. I know that in the first five minutes of an interview I cannot possibly arrive at a valid conclusion about his or her candidacy, across 50 competencies. However, I can be smart enough to know that we all have a gut-level liking or disliking for people based upon the first impression. Again, simply noting that this person reminds me of my neighbor, whom I like, warns me not to be overly generous in my questioning and rating period.

- Read books on management and applied psychology. The publishing world rewards good books and culls lesser works very quickly these days. Thumbing through books at the bookstore, or on AMAZON.COM, can give you good clues. Reading one book per month over a career will add to the richness of your perspective, helping you to "calibrate" the A players, B players, C players.

CHAPTER 12 CHECKLIST: ARE YOU A SKILLFUL INTERVIEWER?

Yes	No		
❑	❑	1.	I ask someone to observe me and rate me on the Interviewer Feedback Form at least once per year.
❑	❑	2.	Because the CIDS interview addresses negatives, not just positives, I know I must make special efforts to bond with the candidates.
❑	❑	3.	I convey respect for the interview 100 percent of the time. No exceptions.
❑	❑	4.	I use a summary every 10 or 15 minutes.
❑	❑	5.	I use active listening, but aim only one level down in the "onion" in conveying my understanding of the person's unstated feelings.
❑	❑	6.	I feel the TORC Technique is appropriate, legitimate, legal, fair, and powerful in getting the negatives.
❑	❑	7.	When interviewees avoid answering TORC questions, I always come back with a follow-up TORC question.

❏ ❏ 8. If the interviewee balks at TORC Question #14, my first follow-up attempt is to simply repeat the question.

❏ ❏ 9. After conducting the CIDS interview, I personally conduct the in-depth reference calls.

❏ ❏ 10. I realize that understanding patterns of behavior reveals the most valid insights into an interviewee.

❏ ❏ 11. I understand that strengths, overused, can become short-comings.

❏ ❏ 12. I believe that recent past behavior is the best predictor of near-future behavior.

❏ ❏ 13. I hypothesize throughout the CIDS interview that all behavior is motivated.

❏ ❏ 14. When "red flags" shoot up, I go on a "fishing expedition."

❏ ❏ 15. As a last resort, I resolve my confusion by asking very direct questions.

❏ ❏ 16. I count on people improving a competency only when they have already demonstrated the ability to improve it.

❏ ❏ 17. When a candidate has very strong feelings about something, I ask enough questions to figure out why.

❏ ❏ 18. I write reports on all successful candidates I interview.

❏ ❏ 19. I note and then consciously control my biorhythms and inclinations to stereotype.

CONCLUSION

CIDS interviewing is not a perfect science, and you will never be perfect at it. Nor will I. The tremendous saving grace of the CIDS-interview approach is that it is resilient. You can "miss" the body language indication of a red flag, fail to delve into the specifics as deeply as you should have, bias responses to a question or two unintentionally, or even blunder into harming rapport. Because this is not a short interview, you have time to regain your insight and bond with the interviewee. Because so much stock is put on patterns, you can flat-out miss some important pieces in that jigsaw puzzle and still figure out if the candidate is an A player, B player, C player. The resilience of the CIDS interview explains, in large part, why interviewers like it, A-player candidates like it, and shareholders benefit from its use.

13. Avoiding Legal Problems: A "Bulletproof" Approach

INTRODUCTION

I am pleased Donald H. Weiss, Ph.D., a leading author of management books on employment, has collaborated with me to write Chapter 13. Every manager should own Don's readable, understandable book entitled *Fair, Square and Legal: Safe Hiring, Managing and Firing Practices to Keep You and Your Company Out of Court*, Second Ed., Rev. (New York: AMACOM, 1995). Don updates his book periodically, to remain current with ever-evolving employment law.

Many thanks to the law firm Laser, Pokorny, Schwartz, Friedman & Economos, P.C., of Chicago, for reviewing this chapter. The firm serves business clients including closely held and public companies and specializes in corporate negotiations, mergers and acquisitions, employment law, commercial litigation, tax matters, and all phases of complex real-estate transactions. Brad Levin, a partner of the firm who specializes in employment law, not only added valuable case examples, but recommended improved language and creative legal approaches.

Discussion of legalities inspires me to declare that neither the authors, nor Laser, Pokorny, Schwartz, Friedman & Economos,

P.C., nor Prentice Hall assume any liability in connection with the information conveyed in this chapter or the prudence of its stated or implied advice. Nothing contained in this chapter constitutes legal advice. Legal counsel should be consulted with respect to the issues discussed herein, which should always be addressed on a case-by-case basis. Sound like legal CYA? Welcome to the new millennium, for it sounds like the old litigation-crazed millennium, doesn't it?

SAFE HIRING, MANAGING, AND FIRING PRACTICES

"Bulletproof" is in quotes in the title of this chapter because bulletproofing, or certain protection, is only an ideal.

In a perfect world, we probably would not need this chapter, but our world is far from perfect. *Topgrading* can embrace the spirit and letter of employment law or it can be abused. An effort to remove chronic C players can incur big risk, if care is not taken to avoid a charge of discrimination—age discrimination, for example. Developing future A players can trigger litigation, if disabled people protected by the Americans with Disabilities Act are overlooked. The EEOC will be knocking on your door if your infusion of new A players systematically excludes minorities. Employees and managers have discovered not only their civil rights, but also their contract and tort rights. Unless your company protects itself, it could face serious employment related claims, including claims of wrongful discharge, breach of contract, discrimination, negligent hiring, or harassment.

Two forms used in topgrading—The Chronological In-Depth Selection Interview Guide (Appendix A) and Career History Form (Appendix B)—will help you meet legal requirements during the hiring process. The leading-edge practices in recruitment and selection we advocate—job analyses, behaviorally anchored competencies, structured interviews, note taking, and so forth, must be coupled with working hand in hand with your partner in Human Resources and your Legal Counsel, to avoid shooting yourself in the foot. This chapter presents a general overview of legal considerations of topgrading. But, state laws vary and your company might be vulnerable in ways that would prudently require more "don'ts" and fewer "do's" than this chapter suggests. So, check with your attorney before acting, or failing to act.

Chapter 13 includes sections on safe hiring, safe firing, and a summary of risky versus less risky actions. The material in this chapter reflects many different pieces of legislation. You will gain particular insight into what you can and cannot do from points we raise regarding:

- Title VII of the Civil Rights Act of 1964

- Civil Rights Act of 1991
- Age Discrimination in Employment Act of 1967 (ADEA)
- The Americans with Disabilities Act of 1990 (ADA)

We are seeing more and more out-of-court settlements that reduce legal fees and the possibility of higher jury awards. Indeed, we argue that companies with a strong culture of topgrading (1) experience fewer reductions in force than companies run by C players, and (2) when they must lay off or otherwise remove employees, they treat them with more humanity, sensitivity, and generosity. They provide outplacement counseling, initiatives to find other jobs, early retirement packages, and generous severances. The attitude is, "why fight in court; we'll be fair and can part friends."

In these litigious times, it seems that almost anyone can sue. In one case, filed in 1991 and still going on, the *customers* of a well-known restaurant in Florida, *not rejected employment applicants*, brought a complaint before the Equal Employment Opportunity Commission (EEOC). They complained that the serving staff *seemed* to be nearly all male. It took six years before a U.S. District Court in Florida decided the case in 1997. The company appears likely to spend a few more years sending the decision through other courts. Although not yet completely settled, the case will likely set a precedent that will affect many hiring practices.[1] If your employment practices appear to grant preferential treatment on the basis of race, gender, age, or national origin, they can be challenged by those classes of individuals who are adversely impacted, that is, by white males claiming reverse discrimination, unless the preferred characteristic is a Bona Fide Occupational Qualification (BFOQ).[2]

Despite employment law contradictions, you can function reasonably easily in the United States. Learn the law, treat people fairly, and run your business—but check with HR and Counsel to avoid land mines. That's all.

SAFE HIRING PRACTICES

When hiring, there are three basic steps that make sense as business practices, as described in Chapter 5, but that also give you a measure of legal protection: perform a thorough job analysis, write a job description with behavioral competencies, and use nondiscriminatory language in all communications.

---

[1] Linda Micco, "EEOC: Employers Should Heed Restaurant Bias Case," *HR News* (August 1997), p. 7.

[2] Race cannot be a BFOQ under Title VII. Additionally, BFOQs are very narrow exceptions to the laws prohibiting discrimination. For example, a mandatory age cutoff is a permitted BFOQ in the case of a firefighter.

1. PERFORM A THOROUGH JOB ANALYSIS

Determine if the job is necessary. If you conclude it is, ask if it needs some tweaking, some reengineering before you hire someone. It is good business practice to streamline and simplify jobs to save time and money, but it is also important for legal reasons. To comply with the Americans with Disabilities Act (ADA), it is important to focus on the *essential functions* of each position and to document those essential functions as part of your ADA compliance. In identifying the essential functions of a job, it is important to distinguish between "fundamental" and "marginal" job duties.

Suppose you have an opening for an accounting manager. You might feel that an essential function of the accounting manager's job is to communicate frequently, in order to successfully change processes in the department. You might conclude from your analysis that Managing By Wandering Around (MBWA) is essential, but maybe it's not. "Wandering" might imply "walking," when reasonable accommodations for a wheelchair-bound person could permit meetings in a central location, or by telephone and e-mail discussions, video-taped communications, or the like. Always remember, the key to ADA compliance is not whether a disabled individual could perform the job, but whether that individual could perform the "essential functions" of the job when reasonably accommodated.

When hiring the accounting manager, ask people trained and experienced in doing the job you are filling to describe each function, in detail. Ask the incumbent to write out all tasks, observe the person performing them, and ask others (internal clients, internal accountants, outside CPA firm) their opinions. Probe to determine what is *not* essential.

Consider, for example, how easy it was to reengineer a job, eliminating a nonessential function for distribution center manager. "Tradition" required managers in a distribution function to load 100-pound boxes for five minutes at the beginning of a shift. It ostensibly would show workers the manager is hands-on, not "above" manual labor. The job analysis showed the workers felt it was a silly tradition; they wanted their manager managing, planning better, streamlining processes. Lugging was eliminated, simultaneously permitting the distribution center manager job to be more productive and opening the position up to women and candidates with disabilities. Whether massive reengineering of hundreds of jobs is necessary, or simply tweaking one position, the principles are the same: Cut out the nonessentials, focus on what is absolutely necessary, reengineer for efficiency, and strive to include (not exclude) protected classes.[3]

---

[3] A "protected class" is a classification that has received protection from discrimination under federal and/or state law. Classifications and characteristics that have received federal protection include:
- People of race or color other than white
- People of any bona-fide religious persuasion

2. WRITE JOB DESCRIPTIONS WITH BEHAVIORAL COMPETENCIES

Job descriptions can assure that both the job applicant and everyone involved in the hiring process are "on the same page," understanding what the job is. However, it is also important that a well-prepared job description retain flexibility by including not only a listing of the duties, responsibilities, and competencies entailed in the job, but also a catchall phrase: "and other duties as assigned by the employer."

Describe the job in terms of only the knowledge, skills, and abilities (KSAs) that are necessary for a trained or trainable person to perform the job. If the job analysis leads you to include peripheral activities that cannot be reengineered out, that's OK. But, you need to consider that possibility. It is also critical for ADA-compliance purposes that the job description state what you, the employer, consider to be the "essential functions" of the job.[4]

Where possible, job descriptions should include objective, measurable performance accountabilities. For management jobs, this might mean specifying the achievements necessary to achieve the first-year bonus—production metrics, quality goals, productivity improvements, number of product launches, maintaining nonunion status, and so on. Specifying first-year accountabilities may offer some legal protection as well, by forcing a more detailed job analysis, a clearer job description, and a focus on most essential competencies.

Most courts and the EEOC agree with the Fourth Circuit Court of Appeals[5] that competencies based on soft or subjective criteria such as personal, interpersonal, and motivational competencies are acceptable where they are applied evenhandedly to all applicants for a position and when subjective competencies are job-related; that is, they meet the standard of business necessity.

---

[3] *cont.*
- Members of either sex
- People over 40
- People with disabilities
- National origin classifications
- Veterans, current members, or applicants of the uniformed services or National Guard
- Pregnancy

Some of these classifications, as well as others, have also received legal protection under the laws of various states; therefore, it is important to check with your attorney to fully comply with such laws.

[4] Although the employer's view is not determinative as to what is considered an essential function of the job, the employer's view is taken into account under the EEOC Regulations.

[5] 757 F.2d 1504, 37 F.E.P. Cases (BNA) 633 (4th Circuit Court).

Appendix A offers 50 management competencies, many of them "soft." Subjective competencies should be made as objective as possible. Avoid "feels comfortable talking with strangers" and instead say "builds credibility quickly with customers." You can measure, in surveys, whether customers feel the salesperson is a good listener, passionate about learning customer needs, knowledgeable, prepared, trustworthy, and conscientious in following up on promises. Customers would have more difficulty assessing how "comfortable" a salesperson actually felt, and who cares? So what if the salesperson is not very comfortable but customers buy because she is passionate about learning their needs and preferances and is credible?

"Good attitude" is too vague and is hard to defend legally. Specify the behaviors necessary, the behavioral competencies necessary to do the job. Use active verbs and observable results expected. Appendices E and F include pretty good examples of behavioral competencies.

Civil rights laws do *not* say that you must hire women, or minorities, people over 40, disabled applicants, or war veterans. In fact, they do not say you have to hire them in proportion to their numbers in the community. But, if you do not hire protected classes, you must exercise sound business judgment and base your decisions on how the candidates compared on necessary job-related qualifications or other valid business reasons. If practicing a particular religion, for example, Catholicism, is essential to being an officer in, say, a Catholic charity, then you may ask if the officer is Catholic.

3. USE NONDISCRIMINATORY LANGUAGE

Wording ads, interview questions, and even conversational comments to focus only on specific, necessary job qualifications will help protect you legally.

Phrase information you publish (in ads, to search firms, job descriptions, e-mails, or word of mouth) to prevent intentionally or unintentionally excluding a protected class under the major EEO laws (Title VII of the Civil Rights Law of 1964 and its amendments, The Age Discrimination in Employment Act of 1967, The Uniform Services Employment and Reemployment Act of 1994, and the Americans with Disabilities Act of 1990). Don't stop at what the words mean to you; consider also what they might *suggest to someone else*—that you are discriminating against any one of several protected groups in terms of race, color, gender, age, disability, military status, national origin, or religion. Appearances sometimes fuel the desire to sue.

Application Forms   Following these three basic steps will help bullet-proof the basic foundations of any hiring decision. With the job analyzed and described with behavioral competencies and with various communications broadcasting your recruitment, the next chronological step is scrutiny of completed application forms. Is your application form legal? The Career History Form (Appendix B) is, in our opinion, legally acceptable. It is designed to be completed by managers, who are not apt to feel that doing so represents an offer of employment; for entry levels an application form including a disclaimer ("completion of this form does not constitute an offer of employment") is useful.

The Career History Form is not tailored for use in any particular state, but if your state allows you to express that "employment at will" is your policy, then an acknowledgment provision conspicuously stating "I understand and agree that if hired my employment is of no definite period and may be terminated at any time with or without cause or prior notice" provides important additional protection in connection with "at will" employees. For additional protection, after the disclaimer we suggest you ask applicants to sign an acknowledgment that reads, "I read and fully understand the terms set out in this application for employment and I certify that all statements contained in this application are true and complete to the best of my knowledge." Since disclaimer laws vary from state to state, check with your Legal Counsel. The last section of this chapter spells out in more detail what should not be included on application or career-history forms, but Appendix B is a pretty good sample.

Interviews With résumés and application (career history) forms screened, interviews come next. The CIDS Interview Guide is well-structured, requires notes, and focuses on behaviors and results without asking forbidden questions. No interview guide assures that the interviewer won't deviate and ask a forbidden question or make an unacceptable comment, because interviews are conversations. Chapter 5 discusses the different kinds of interviews, and legal concerns pertaining to *all* interviews. The EEOC recommends interview guides, so stick with them. But when you make conversation and probe deeper, you should be very careful. The final section of this chapter presents quite detailed do's and don'ts, but untrained interviewers violate them too often. Train your interviewers.

The EEOC accepts structured interviews, but suppose your company uses more *than one* structured interview, say one for men and one for women? The Eighth Circuit Court ruled[6] that an airline discriminated against women for that reason, that the interview *process* treated women differently from the way it treated men. If the airline decided not to hire the woman based on her answers to questions about child care and pregnancy, it would have blatantly violated Title VII of the Civil Rights Act of 1964. But more important, in this case (with which some Circuit Courts disagree), it violated the law by asking one set of questions of men and a different set of questions of women. Needless to say, use one structured interview guide (like the CIDS Interview Guide) for both men and women. (Some courts disagree with the

---

[6] 738 F.2d 255, 35 F.E.P. Cases (BNA) 102 (8th Circuit Court, 1984).

Eighth Circuit Court. For example, the Seventh Circuit Court says "merely showing the questions were asked is *not* sufficient to prove intentional discrimination."[7])

You'd think that by now, after all the years since 1964 and with all that's written on the subject, interviewers wouldn't make the kinds of mistakes they often do. Some male and even some female interviewers ask female applicants:

- How many children do you have?
- Are you pregnant now?
- What arrangements do you have for child care?

None of these questions is job-related, and they are of no concern to the employer. EEOC guidelines say it is not permissible to ask such questions of women if you don't ask them of men, but many state laws strictly forbid them. Even if your state allows asking such questions, doing so could lead to evidence of sex discrimination under federal law. And, besides, if it is possible a female applicant *thinks* they are illegal, why risk offending her? If you want to know if she can work the scheduled hours of 7:00 A.M. to 4:00 P.M., ask that, and avoid intruding into the way she organizes her private life to meet her work responsibilities.

Each step of the hiring process carries with it possibilities for mistakes, not only with regard to EEOC issues but also to those related to employment contracts. In each step avoid asking questions and making comments that can land you in trouble.

Whether for a telephone screening interview, a short structured interview, or the Chronological In-Depth Structured (CIDS) Interview, the rules are the same. Questions you cannot ask or comments you cannot make pertain to:

1. Age or date of birth (unless it's a BFOQ)
2. Gender (unless it's a BFOQ)
3. Group affiliation
4. Religion (unless it's a BFOQ)
5. Where born (unless national origin is a BFOQ)
6. Language in the home
7. Transportation
8. Arrests
9. Sued an employer (never ask)

And never, ever *code* your interview notes, interview guides, or Career History Form for race or any other protected characteristic.

---

[7] 950 F. 2d 355 (7th Circuit Court, 1991).

Chapter 5 advises you *not* to hire someone after one interview, and indeed we emphatically recommend that for management hires you begin with telephone-screening interviews, followed by two full days of on-site interviews. It is safest not to hire on the basis of one interview—for both legal and sound business reasons.

Questions you can't ever ask and comments you can't ever make during a selection interview are identified by EEO laws, including the ADEA, and the ADA. All questions and comments must meet one simple criterion: *They pertain to the essential functions of the job and qualifications that indicate a person's ability and willingness to perform those functions.* Besides, why would you want to know anything else? If you wander from an interview guide, what exactly can you or shouldn't you ask?

Age. Avoid obvious age-related questions (that some people still ask), and beware of indirect questions that suggest age, for example, "Where were you when President Kennedy was killed?" Finally, watch out for "smoking guns": "We need young blood here." They can imply that you're looking for young people and that older people need not apply.

Arrest Records. Arrests without convictions can be irrelevant. Anyone "under suspicion" can be arrested for a crime he or she didn't commit. On the other hand, you do need to protect yourself if a person has been arrested *and convicted* of a crime that affects his or her ability to perform a specific job. You shouldn't hire a convicted embezzler as CFO.

In fact, if you don't pursue conviction records, hiring a convicted felon can leave you vulnerable to a repeat crime or can lead to lawsuits charging "negligent hiring." However, be sure you have a good business reason for asking about convictions: "Have you ever been convicted of a crime related to this kind of work?" and "Have you ever been convicted of a violent crime?" are legitimate questions. That doesn't mean you can never hire an ex-convict, but if you do, it's wise to assign that person to work that reduces the potential for the individual to repeat the offenses or injure other people. It is important that you discuss such questions with your legal counsel because state laws regarding such questions vary; many states, in fact, require that questions about convictions must be accompanied by a statement on the employment application that a conviction will not necessarily disqualify the applicant.

Religious Affiliation or Group Membership. Only if religious affiliation is a BFOQ should you question a person's religious practices and you should question a person's group membership only if such group membership is job-related and not connected to a protected classification. What do you think would happen if, without a clear business reason, you asked, "Do you go to church on Sunday?" Or, "Do you belong to the Knights of Columbus?" or "Do you belong to the B'nai B'rith?" "Do you have a religious objection to working on Saturday?"

You may not think it, but questions such as, "Do you belong to the NRA (National Rifle Association)?" or "Do you belong to the NAACP (National

Association for Advancement of Colored People)?" are risky. They ask about affiliations that are totally irrelevant to the question, "Are you capable of doing this job and are you willing to do it?"

Health or Disabilities. Under the ADA, during a screening interview or any time *before* offering a person a job (for example, on the application for a job), it's illegal to ask for his or her:

- Medical history
- Prescription-drug use
- Prior workers'-compensation or health-insurance claims
- Work absenteeism due to illness
- Past treatment for alcoholism, drug use, or mental illness

Questions About Drug Use. Except for positions that are safety-sensitive and governed by regulations from the Department of Transportation, Nuclear Regulatory Commission, or Department of Defense, drug testing is not mandatory. Likewise, it's best not to ask an applicant during a selection interview if he or she has ever experimented with or used any kinds of drugs (prescription or illegal). However, universal testing for drugs for *all* new hires is acceptable as a condition of employment. Furthermore, it is permissible under the ADA to ask about an applicant's *current* illegal use of drugs.

Under the ADA drug testing is not considered a medical examination. Compliance with the Drug-Free Workplace Act of 1988 generally requires employers under certain government contracts or grants to forbid employees to manufacture, distribute, or use drugs illegally in the workplace; many employers outside the scope of the law voluntarily adopt the policies of this law. If public safety is at stake, as in the cases of school-bus drivers, train engineers, truck drivers, and other safety-sensitive jobs, then the Department of Transportation (DOT) mandates preemployment testing, periodic and random testing, as well as regularly scheduled testing of all such employees.

Diversity. To achieve more diversity in management, for market or legal reasons, be sure you select from a diverse *pool* of candidates. As obvious as that may sound, too often diversity goals are not achieved because recruiters did not look in the right "pools."

When employers use a search firm to screen candidates for executive roles, they often ask to see only the "top three" applicants. That could be a mistake. What may appear to be the "top three" to someone outside your company may fall somewhere below your own estimates. Do the "top three" include members of protected groups you are seeking? Chapter 5 recommends that you initially screen résumés and Career History Forms with the recruiter, to be sure you are both "singing out of the same hymnal." Further, weekly updates by the recruiter should involve discussing specific candidates—why they are included or excluded. Screen the papers and take recommendations from the search firm, but *you* decide which top three or more you want to see. This is one way you can achieve diversity with talent, not underqualified tokens.

Multiple Interviews. It makes good sense, from the management perspective, to have more than one person interview the candidates. A person reporting to you has to work with other people: peers, middle-level managers, and perhaps customers. How other people see the candidates can influence how well they work together with the person you hire. Chapter 5 recommends nine interviews, including two CIDS interviews, for management candidates.

From a legal perspective, you reduce personal subjectivity or bias by adding properly trained interviewers to the process; this protects you from making decisions that could adversely affect members of a protected group. Having members of protected groups conduct interviews encourages fairness and removes the appearance of favoritism if you reject a member of a protected group applying for a position.

THE EDUCATION DATE DILEMMA

Catch-22s exist. The biggest and most serious is whether you should request education dates (such as graduation) in application forms or interviews. Make the request and you risk an age-discrimination suit, but fail to and you can increase your chances of a negligent hiring suit and leave yourself with such incomplete background information you mis-hire more people. This is a complicated issue, but one worth studying because there are powerful forces in society working against your legitimate interests. The CIDS-interview approach is in jeopardy because some groups want to prevent you from pinning down *any* dates—not just for education but for jobs, too. If these forces prevail, you won't be able to effectively study applicants' work histories, rendering the CIDS interview impotent and causing your mis-hires to skyrocket from 10 percent to 50 percent. This would be an enormous burden to you, it would put your company at risk, and it would lessen our nation's economic strength. Why? Because people over 40 are so determined that prospective employers not be able to calculate age from dates and possibly discriminate against them.

Frankly, the whole issue could evaporate because brains and experience are eclipsing brawn. Companies are becoming more desperate for intellectual capital and are happy to hire older people whose jobs are less and less physical, more and more mental. But the issue is hardly dead.

Complainant's attorney:

> Your honor, the company discriminates against people over 40 and we can prove it. They ask for college-entrance and graduation dates, and since most people start college at age 17 or 18,

it takes about three seconds to calculate age. Why would an employer want graduation dates unless there was a conscious effort to discriminate against older, more experienced people?

Why, indeed. Here's why—you believe the CIDS interview is the most valid assessment tool on earth, and that studying the *entire* educational and work histories reveals patterns crucial to understanding the candidate *today*. Knowing the dates of education are important for exactly the same reasons as for jobs. Precise dates (month and year) permit you to:

- Understand how rapidly and deeply competencies have been inculcated by knowing when each life segment occurred; for example, lacking energy and ambition during college and taking seven years to complete a degree are less serious 15 years ago than 5 years ago.

- Grasp if the growth pattern for certain competencies is uninterrupted (and therefore stronger now) or under pressure declines (and therefore a riskier bet now). Education dates can establish both the baseline in time and level from which revealing patterns emerge.

- Minimize "gaps" in chronology. Because education dates are easy to verify, candidates are less apt to hide them in an effort to conceal a failure (for example, flunking out or being fired from early jobs).

As a simple practical matter, if it is considered prudent (legally justifiable) by attorneys to delve into *all* (part-time *and* full-time) jobs, and to establish dates for *all* jobs, it is difficult for interviewers to not learn education dates. In understanding why a person took a particular job, say, 12 years ago, a candidate is apt to blurt out, "because I was graduating college and my campus interview with ACME impressed me."

A second reason for requesting education dates is to be thorough in accounting for data to protect yourself and your company from a charge of negligent hiring.

For example, suppose you don't ask for date of graduation from high school and, unbeknownst to you, there is a gap between high school and the first full-time job "John Jones" lists on his résumé and his application form. Jones bummed around for three years, living off friends, gambling, and borrowing. He got into a lot of bar fights, broke a lot of noses, and was lucky no one pressed charges. Then he worked for ACME three years, was never violent, and applies for a job with your company. His record is "clean," you hire him, and six months later he breaks his supervisor's nose. The supervisor hires a lawyer who figures Jones must have a violent past, digs up previous victims, and files a charge against your company for negligent hiring.

Had you requested *education* dates, you would have spotted that three-year gap. As a skillful CIDS interviewer, you would have discovered the violence and probably not hired Jones. But your cautious company trained you to *not* request education dates, for fear of an age-discrimination suit.

It seems to me that the Legal and HR communities are consistently against pinning down education dates, figuring the risks of negligent hiring are considerably less than the risks of age-discrimination suits. Their prudence does not eliminate the Catch-22, but provides you the lesser of two legal risks. In this book I have deferred to their prudence, suggesting that you use a carefully prepared Career History Form (Appendix B) that does *not* require any education dates but does require the applicant to provide information on *all* full-time jobs held. In this manner, and with accompanying reference checks, you have been diligent in your efforts to cover "gaps" in the applicant's work record while minimizing potential exposure to an age-discrimination claim that might result from requiring education dates. If a violent applicant fails to provide information on a full-time job in which he was violent, then he lied on the Career History Form that certified *complete* information on all full-time jobs. Your legal risk is minimized.

The biggest risk in not requesting dates for education, as you now know well, is in missing information on current competencies. My vision for the future has CEOs who:

- Assure that their firm does not discriminate against those over 40
- Require CIDS interviews, exploring education and all subsequent years
- Request education dates, in order to assure completeness
- Incur minimal court battles over this issue

I have never heard of a company losing a lawsuit or paying a dime for having requested high-school or college-graduation dates in interviews or application forms. Perhaps someone reading this will let me know of such losses. I've asked more than 30 attorneys to "show me the losses, cite the case!" All have said, "I'll bet the cases exist, but I don't know of them." They explain that it would be very hard to track down out-of-court settlements, for example.

A client not in the United States was ordered by the equivalent of their EEOC to eliminate from their application-form requests for high-school and college-graduation dates. They fought back. They explained that the CIDS interview would be hampered without pinning down those dates. "We need to know if there was a gap between high school and college, or if college took six years, because it gives us data to assess present competencies," they pleaded. They won. So, even if you are prudent (too cautious?) in not requesting education dates please be willing to fight to know complete dates of all full-time jobs. That's the absolute minimum, in my opinion. Otherwise, you will be lucky not to hire 50 percent C players.

SAFE FIRING PRACTICES

Naturally, legal protection when firing someone begins with safe hiring practices. When people have been hired the right and legal way, then if they turn out to be a chronic C player (which *Topgrading* seeks to minimize), it is easier to fire them. There are sensible, fair, reasonable ways you can avoid legal land mines when terminating someone.

Almost all states are "at-will" states, meaning that employers can fire people whenever they want, with no reason or any reason whatsoever, with several exceptions:[8]

- Discrimination (age, race, etc.)
- Violation of a union contract
- Violation of state public policy laws (such as "whistle-blower" laws or laws prohibiting firing because an employee has filed a worker's compensation claim, for example)
- Violation of an employment contract

1. PROMISES THAT BIND

A case reported in *The Wall Street Journal* shows what can happen when you make promises you don't keep: A federal jury in Los Angeles found that a former sales executive was fired from his job primarily because he was about to exercise valuable stock options. Courts increasingly are finding that "companies (can't) fire executives to avoid awarding bonuses or other special compensation."[9] Here's the story behind the case that is currently under appeal.

When the company hired "Alex" as marketing manager, management promised him a large bonus if sales increased by 25 percent in each of his first two years, a bonus worth two-thirds the value of the total increase. Most of that would be paid in stock options that would allow him to buy corporate stock at 25 cents a share at a time when it was trading at more than $50 a share on the NASDAQ. He had achieved the first-year goal (25 percent percent increase over the previous year) and was on target to exceed the second-year goal when, 21 months into the contract, the company fired him for "performance deficiencies." The company never clarified his deficiencies.

Alex sued, charging that "the company had breached an obligation to deal with him in good faith" and fired him "primarily because he was about to become eligible to exercise his valuable stock options." The jury agreed

---

[8] Kathleen Furare, "Employment at Will Makes It Surprisingly Easy to Fire Workers," *Chicago Tribune* (April 5, 1998), Section 6, pp. 1, 3.

[9] "Parametric Ex-Sales Executive Wins Damages for 1992 Firing," *The Wall Street Journal* (August 4, 1997), p. B2.

with him, compensating him for the value of stock options he was not yet eligible to exercise. This decision, one of the first of its kind, is under appeal, but the jury sent a message: *Don't make promises, especially don't make them in writing, unless you know you're going to keep them.* The "covenant of good faith," which is implied by law in every contract, is hard to get around.

Most people get into trouble during the hiring interview more for what they say or offer (or don't say or don't offer) rather than what they ask or don't ask. They commit four common errors that could later lead to charges of wrongful discharge:

- They promise more than they're personally authorized to promise.
- They fail to cover the conditions of employment thoroughly in advance, especially with regard to employment-at-will (that is, that the company has the right to fire employees with or without notice, with or without cause).
- They don't give the new employee an employee's handbook (which should always contain the proper disclaimers that it does not create a contract, based on consultation with counsel because state laws vary).
- They lower their guard, getting too comfortable with the candidate, and say things that can be misconstrued as promises or, too often, as attitudes toward minorities, women, legal aliens, and the like.

Five simple steps can prevent getting into such jams.

1. Unless you're the CEO or president of the company, have in writing what the scope of your authority is when extending a job offer.
2. Prepare for the hiring interview by reviewing all the conditions of employment with HR or counsel, and put them in writing.
3. If permitted in your state, make sure your company has an employment-at-will disclaimer that includes specific language that explains the limitations on employment (including that employment is for no specific duration). It should explain that either party can end the relationship at any time, with or without cause, with or without notice. It should then state that no one but the highest management authority in the group can alter the terms described in the organization's documents. Finally, ask all new employees to sign an acknowledgment that they have read *and* understood the disclaimer.
4. If it's available to your company based on state law, consider asking the candidate for employment to sign an arbitration agreement that states that the employee agrees to submit employment-related claims to an arbitration board and waives the right to a jury trial. (Note that an arbitration agreement does not waive an employee's ability to file an EEOC charge, an issue currently being debated in the courts.) For further protection, the decision to sign should be voluntary and not made a condi-

tion of employment. However, in considering having candidates sign arbitration agreements it is imperative to consult with counsel because such agreements need to be carefully prepared so as to preserve the at-will employment status of employees, which varies based on state law.

5. Regardless of your personal attitudes or feelings toward other people, do not create any appearance of negative attitudes toward anyone. If you do harbor such feelings, don't assume that a person coming to work for you harbors them as well. Remember, anyone can be a witness against you if someone sues you for creating a hostile environment or for discrimination, even if he or she is not a target of your behavior.

2. DOCUMENTING NONPERFORMANCE

Integral to fair, effective, legal redeploying of C players outside the company is a well-documented coaching process (see Chapters 8 and 9). As with all human endeavors, the legal community has its day in court, and the results are some confusing signals and a lot of common sense.

Don't even think of creating documentation *after* making the decision to demote or fire someone. Entering trivial things into a file that happens after a charge of discrimination has been brought against you can be seen as retaliation and harassment and could expose you to a retaliatory-discharge claim. The Minnesota Supreme Court has ruled[10] that performance-management systems that criticize an employee's performance do *not* constitute the infliction of emotional distress as long as the criticism meets four legal standards:

1. The criticism is not extreme and outrageous.
2. The criticism is not intentionally reckless.
3. The criticism is not intended to cause emotional stress.
4. The distress the criticized employee feels is not severe due to outrageous conduct by people in the company.

Document constructive discipline steps (consistent with steps listed in a well-prepared employee handbook) and lack of progress on developmental plans to achieve performance. Document not only the performance standards but the consequences of failing to achieve them. Ratings, critical incidents, and narratives all might simultaneously help the person understand what is expected and motivate and guide improvement while also protecting you legally. An extreme incident merits getting the employee's signature, admit-

---

[10] 330 N.W. 2d 670 (Minn. Sup. Ct., 1983), superceded by statute, 392 N.W. 2d 670 (Minn. Ct. of App., 1986).

ting what occurred, and perhaps including a statement that without significant and immediate improvement, termination of employment will occur.

A solid performance-management system is the best bulletproofing available when firing someone becomes necessary. It includes:

- Thorough job analysis, comprehensive job description, and behavioral competencies
- Documented performance standards and accountabilities
- Managers trained in performance evaluation, coaching, and interviewing
- At least annual, and preferably ongoing, performance evaluation and coaching
- An audit system to prevent bias
- Documentation through performance personnel files, job-related testing, rating systems, appraisal forms, signed memoranda, and so forth
- Written policy statements regarding procedures for conducting performance appraisals and progressive discipline (verbal warning, written warning, 90-day probation, termination, for example)

Defamation Watch out for what you put into employees' personnel files to document nonperformance and take care about what you say when you fire someone for cause. You could put yourself in a jam by forcing employees to make defamatory statements about themselves to a prospective employer. In one case, four claims representatives were told to revise their expense accounts and when they refused to do so because they thought it was illegal or at least immoral, they were fired for "gross insubordination."[11] The four were rejected from potential new jobs when they told prospective employers they were terminated for "gross insubordination," and they sued on the grounds that by specifying that particular course, they were forced to make false statements about themselves. They took their case all the way to the Minnesota Supreme Court, which upheld the jury's verdict that the four had *not* engaged in gross insubordination and found the employer liable for defamation. The court awarded the claims representatives $300,000 in compensatory damages (though not $600,000 in punitive damages they sought). Be fair. Don't document with a sledgehammer if a tack hammer will suffice.

The legal climate in the United States has expanded beyond civil rights laws of 1964 into judicial reviews of the at-will defense. Employees often look beyond civil rights laws to the common laws of contract and tort to take legal action. There is virtually no aspect of personnel practice that hasn't been challenged.

---

[11] 389 N.W. 2d 876 (Minn. Sup. Ct. App., 1983).

So, construct employee policy manuals carefully, adhere to them with precise legal rigor, and don't get "creative" in ways that either hurt employees or will be perceived as hurtful. Your Human Resources professionals should keep a close eye on whether any personnel action (hiring, firing, even reprimands) has a disparate impact on a protected group. Also, depending on your particular state's laws regarding employee handbooks, you may be guilty of breach of contract if you violate the provisions of your employee handbook. For example, if you have a four-step progressive disciplinary procedure,[12] you might be legally required to document all four steps or avoid jumping from step one to step four—unless you specify in your employee manual a list of specific actions that could lead to immediate dismissal (for example, crimes against the company).

Of course, if you want to fire someone, you can "buy" immunity in a severance arrangement. Essentially the employee gives up the right to sue for some sort of payment. This is a common approach at management levels. Use an attorney to construct a severance agreement, because you must carefully follow the law with respect to effectively releasing certain claims. For example, certain statutory periods to review the release document and to revoke their signed release must be provided in order to obtain a valid release of ADEA claims.

Be careful, during a layoff, not to let go a preponderance of members from protected groups. Too many executives remove themselves from the layoff decisions to the point that they don't know until it's too late that in attempting to downsize, their middle managers have laid off a disproportionate number of, for example, African Americans. This becomes painfully apparent if after the downsizing some rehiring takes place and the replacements are all, in this case, white. This type of approach may open up the employer to a charge of "disparate impact." Over the last ten years, a large manufacturer has had to settle several large age-discrimination suits for this reason. The moral: Be as careful in your firing processes as you are in your hiring processes; then the life span of hiring to firing remains safe.

---

[12] For example, a four-step disciplinary procedure might be:
1. Oral reprimand by immediate supervisor; written notice sent to executive vice president
2. Written reprimand for second offense
3. Written reprimand and meeting with EVP, with possible suspension from work without pay for five days
4. Discharge from employment for an employee whose performance or conduct does not improve to acceptable levels

SUMMARY OF WHAT YOU CAN AND CAN'T DO

You can become an employment lawyer, or walk arm-in-arm with an employment law specialist, but this is hardly practical . . . or necessary. You need a bulletproof vest, not total body armor. Just manage your business sensibly and honorably while remaining cognizant of legal constraints. We have walked you through the basics, and now, here are two different tables of "do's" and "don'ts"—first EEOC guidelines and then general advice on what and how to ask for information that will offer you a quick, handy reference to help you bulletproof your employment practices. EEOC does not make law; it issues guidelines that have the force of law, however. If you do something EEOC regards as impermissible, you risk being investigated. If that investigation concludes there is disparate impact, for example, a lawsuit might follow. In addition, there are similar correlating state laws and agencies in many states. Finally, even without any federal or state investigation, violations could lead to or enhance a private employment-related claim from one of your employees or former employees.

EEOC GUIDELINES

SUBJECT	PERMISSIBLE	IMPERMISSIBLE OR SUSPECT
Race, Color, Religion, National Origin	Employers may lawfully collect such information for lawful affirmative action programs in accordance with Title VII, government record keeping, and reporting requirement, or studies to promote EEO recruiting and testing. Employers must be able to prove these legitimate business purposes and keep this information separate from regular employee records.	All direct or indirect inquiries not serving legitimate business purposes may be evidence of bias. State laws may expressly prohibit.
Height and Weight		If minorities or women more often disqualified and meeting height or weight limits not necessary for safe job performance.
Marital Status, Children, Child Care	If information is needed for tax, insurance, or Social Security purposes, get it *after* employment.	Nonjob-related and illegal if used to discriminate against women may create exposure if only asked of (or have different policies for) women.
English Language Skill		If not necessary for job.
Education Requirements		If not directly job-related or no business necessity is proven and minorities more often disqualified.
Friends or Relatives Working for Employer		Preference for friends or relatives of current workers, if this reduces opportunities for women or minorities. Nepotism policies barring hire of friends or relatives of current workers, if this reduces opportunities for women, men, or minorities. State laws may expressly prohibit.

EEOC GUIDELINES *continued*

SUBJECT	PERMISSIBLE	IMPERMISSIBLE OR SUSPECT
Arrest Records		If no subsequent convictions and no proof of business necessity. Mere request for, without consideration of, arrest record is illegal.
Conviction Records	Only if their number, nature, and recentness are considered in determining applicant's suitability. Inquiries should state that record isn't absolute bar and such factors as age and time of offense, seriousness and nature of violation, and rehabilitation will be (and must be) taken into account.	
Military Service Discharge	If information is used to determine if further background check is necessary. Inquiries should be made only if business necessity can be shown and if made, such inquiries should state that less than honorable discharge isn't absolute bar to employment and other factors will affect final hiring decision.	Honorable discharge requirement, because minorities more often disqualified. Also, some state laws expressly prohibit. EEOC says employers should not, as matter of policy, reject applicants with less than honorable discharges, and inquiry regarding military record should be avoided unless business necessity is shown.
Citizenship	Legal aliens, eligible to work, may be discriminated against only in interest of national security or under federal law or presidential order concerning the particular position or premises.	If has purpose or effect of discriminating on basis of national origin. Note: Questions relating to citizenship must also comply with requirements of the Immigration Reform and Control Act of 1986.

EEOC GUIDELINES *continued*

SUBJECT	PERMISSIBLE	IMPERMISSIBLE OR SUSPECT
Economic Status		Inquiries regarding poor credit rating are unlawful, if no business necessity is shown. Other inquiries regarding financial status—bankruptcy, car or home ownership, garnishments—may likewise be illegal because of disparate impact on minorities.
Availability for Holiday/Weekend Work	Only if employer can show that such availability is essential for the performance of the job and that no alternatives with less exclusionary effect are available.	
Data Required for Legitimate Business Purposes	Information on marital status, number and age of children, etc., necessary for insurance-reporting requirements and other business purposes should be obtained *after* the person is employed. "Tear-off sheets," preferably anonymous, which are separated from application forms before the applications are processed, are also lawful.	

ADDITIONAL GENERAL ADVICE

SUBJECT	ASK	DON'T ASK
Physical Condition, Handicap, Disability	"Can you perform the functions of the job with or without reasonable accommodation?" Note: The ADA permits questions about an applicant's ability to perform marginal, as well as essential job functions; however, an employer cannot refuse to hire an applicant based on his or her inability to perform marginal job functions. Note: Except in cases where undue hardship can be proven, employers must make "reasonable accommodation" for the physical and mental limitations of an employee or applicant, including altering duties, altering work schedules, transferring the employee to a vacant position, altering the physical setting, and providing job aids. "Can you meet the attendance requirements of this job?" "How many days did you take leave last year?" "Do you illegally use drugs?" Employer may tell applicants what is involved in the hiring process and then ask them if they need a reasonable accommodation for the process.	"Do you have any physical disabilities or handicaps which would interfere with your ability to perform the job?" "Do you need a reasonable accommodation to perform the job's functions?" "Have you ever been treated for any of the following diseases?" "How many days were you sick last year?" "Have you ever had a drug or alcohol problem?" "How much alcohol do you drink each week?" "What prescription drugs are you currently taking?" Questions regarding applicant's general medical condition, state of health, or illnesses. Questions regarding receipt of or application for Worker's Compensation benefits. Note: If no affirmative action plan is in place, an employer may not ask for voluntary disclosure of a disability. If an applicant is screened out because of a disability, the employer must show that the exclusionary criterion is job-related and consistent with business necessity.

ADDITIONAL GENERAL ADVICE *continued*

SUBJECT	*ASK*	*DON'T ASK*
Physical Condition, Handicap, Disability *continued*	<u>Prior to making a job offer</u>, an employer may: • Invite applicants to identify themselves as individuals with disabilities for purposes of the employer's affirmative-action program (so long as they inform the applicant that information is requested on a voluntary basis, that it will be used only in accordance with the ADA, will be kept confidential and separate from the rest of the application, is being sought only for affirmative-action efforts, and that refusal to provide such information will not result in adverse treatment). • Ask applicants whether they can perform job-related functions in a safe manner. • Ask applicants to describe how they would perform job tasks. • Obtain information about the types of accommodations needed by an applicant whose disability is obvious or disclosed. <u>After a conditional job offer is made</u>, employers may, provided such information is treated confidentially and kept in separate files: • Ask disability-related questions if these questions are asked of all employees who enter into that job. • Require a medical exam if all applicants for that job category are required to take such an exam.	<u>Prior to making a job offer</u>, an employer may not: • Ask questions about whether the individual is disabled, what kind of disability it is, or the severity of the disability. For example, it may not ask: • Do you need an accommodation? • Have you ever suffered any job-related injuries? • Please list previous worker's compensation claims. • How may days were you absent due to illness?

ADDITIONAL GENERAL ADVICE *continued*

SUBJECT	ASK	DON'T ASK
Education	Inquiry into academic, vocational, or professional education and public and private schools attended and degrees received, but only where demonstrably related to the job. Inquiry into language skills, such as reading, speaking and writing foreign languages, but only where relevant to job applied for.	Any inquiry asking specifically about the nationality, racial, or religious affiliation of a school. Inquiries concerning the dates of graduation or receipt of degrees may be legal but are risky (see discussion in this chapter). Inquiry as to how a foreign-language ability was acquired.
Citizenship	"Do you have the legal right to work for any employer in the United States?" "Are you authorized to work in the United States?" The Immigration Reform and Control Act of 1986 (IRCA) prohibits employers from knowingly hiring aliens not authorized to work in the United States. After being hired, an employee must provide the employer with proof (a driver's license and Social Security card) to establish identity and eligibility to work in the United States.	"Of what country are you a citizen?" "Are you (or your parents or spouse) naturalized or native-born citizens?" "When did you (or your parents or spouse) acquire citizenship?" Requirement that applicant produce naturalization papers. It is unlawful under IRCA to discriminate on the basis of a person's citizenship status. This protection extends only to U.S. citizens and "intending citizens"—those granted permanent resident status, refugees, residents granted asylum, and those who have begun the application process for temporary resident status. However, the law provides that if a U.S. citizen and a noncitizen are equally qualified, an employer may give preference in hiring to the citizen.

ADDITIONAL GENERAL ADVICE *continued*

SUBJECT	ASK	DON'T ASK
References	Names of persons willing to provide professional and/or character references for the applicants. "Who referred you for a position here?"	Requiring submission of a religious reference.
Arrest, Criminal Record	Inquiry into actual convictions that reasonably relate to fitness to perform a particular job. (A conviction is a court ruling in which the party is found guilty as charged. An arrest merely is the apprehension or detention of the person to answer a criminal charge.) But inquiries about convictions should be accompanied by a statement that such convictions will not absolutely prohibit employment but will be considered only in relation to the job requirements.	Arrest record. Have you ever been arrested? Any inquiry relating to an arrest. Any inquiry into or request for a person's arrest, court, or conviction record if not substantially related to functions and responsibilities of the particular job in question.
Religion	Statement of regular days, hours, or shifts to be worked. "Are you able to work weekends?" An applicant may be advised by job announcements and advertisements concerning normal hours and days of work required by the job to avoid possible conflict with religious or other personal convictions. However, except in cases where undue hardship can be proven, employers and unions must make "reasonable accommodations" for religious practices of an employee or prospective employee.	Questions regarding applicant's religion, religious affiliations, religious holidays observed. Applicant may not be told "This is a Catholic, Protestant, or Jewish organization." "Does your religion prevent you from working weekends and holidays?" An applicant's religious denomination or affiliation, church, parish, pastor, or religious holidays observed. Any inquiry to indicate or identify religious denomination or customs.

ADDITIONAL GENERAL ADVICE *continued*

SUBJECT	ASK	DON'T ASK
Religion *continued*	Reasonable accommodation may include voluntary substitutes, flexible scheduling, lateral transfer, change of job assignments, or the use of an alternative to payment of union dues.	Applicants may not be told that any particular religious groups are required to work on their religious holidays. The use of such preselection inquiries as "What days and hours are you available for work?" that determine an applicant's availability may be considered by the EEOC to be unlawful unless the employer can show that it: 1. did not have an exclusionary effect on the applicant; or 2. was otherwise justified by business necessity. Generally, this ban on discrimination does not apply to religious institutions.
Race or Color, Physical Description	Statement that photograph may be required after hire. General distinguishing physical (such as scars, etc.) to be used for identification purposes. Race may be requested (preferably not on the employment application) for affirmative-action purposes but may not be used as an employment criterion. Height/weight may be requested if necessary *after* person is hired.	Requiring applicant to submit a photograph at any time prior to hire, or requesting that the applicant, at his or her option, submit a photograph. Race or color of applicant. Inquiries regarding applicant's complexion or color of skin. Question about an applicant's height or weight, unless demonstrably necessary as requirements for the job.

ADDITIONAL GENERAL ADVICE *continued*

SUBJECT	ASK	DON'T ASK
Foreign Language Skills, Ancestry, or National Origin	Foreign languages applicant reads, speaks, or writes, if job related.	"What is your mother (or native) tongue?" Inquiry into how applicant acquired ability to read, write, or speak a foreign language. Inquiries into applicant's lineage, ancestry, national origin, descent, birthplace, or native language. National origin of the applicant's parents or spouse.
Organizations	Inquiry into any job-related organizations of which an applicant is a member provided that the applicant is warned not to name any organization if the name or character of the organization reveals the race, religion, color, age, disability, or ancestry of the membership. "List all job-related professional organizations to which you belong. What offices do you hold?"	"Are you a member of any union?" The names of organizations to which the applicant belongs if such information would indicate through type or name the race, religion, color, or ancestry of the membership.
Prior Military Service	Questions about service in the U.S. armed forces or in a state militia or in a particular branch of the U.S. Army, Navy, etc. Type of education and experience in service as it relates to a particular job.	"Did you receive other than an honorable discharge from the military?" (Note: Questions about discharge are problematic in many jurisdictions.)
Personal Finances	If car travel is required by the job, it is appropriate to ask whether the applicant has use of a reliable car.	Questions about wage garnishments, personal bankruptcy. Questions about home or car ownership. Future child-bearing plans.

ADDITIONAL GENERAL ADVICE *continued*

SUBJECT	ASK	DON'T ASK
Name	"State your name." "Have you ever worked for this company under another name?" "Is any additional information relative to change of name, use of an assumed name, or nickname necessary to enable a check on your work records? If yes, explain."	"State your maiden name." "Have you ever used another name?" Inquiries about the name that would indicate the applicant's lineage, ancestry, national origin, or descent. Inquiry into the original name of an applicant whose name has been changed by court order or otherwise. "Mr., Mrs., Miss, or Ms.?"
Residence	The applicant's address. Inquiry into length of stay at current and previous addresses. "How long have you been a resident of this state?"	"Do you own or rent your own home?" Specific inquiry into foreign residence. Specific inquiry into foreign address that would indicate national origin. Names and relationship of people with whom the applicant resides.
Age	Statement that employment is subject to verification that applicant meets legal age requirements. Requiring proof of age in the form of a work permit or a certificate of age—if a minor. Requiring proof of age by birth certificate *after* being hired.	"State your age." (Questions regarding an applicant's age may be asked after hire.) "State your date of birth." "What are the ages of your children, if any?" Requirements that applicant submit birth certificate, naturalization or baptismal record.

ADDITIONAL GENERAL ADVICE *continued*

SUBJECT	ASK	DON'T ASK
Age *continued*	Inquiry as to whether or not the applicant meets the minimum age requirements as set by law and requirement that upon hire proof of age must be submitted in the form of a birth certificate or other form of proof of age. If age is a legal requirement: "If hired, can you furnish proof of age?" or a statement that hire is subject to verification of age.	Questions concerning the dates of graduation may be legal but risky (see discussion in this chapter). The Age Discrimination in Employment Act of 1967 forbids discrimination against persons who are age 40 or older. Avoid any advertising or age-based language that expresses limitations. The EEOC and the courts will determine if the advertisement has the effect of discouraging people aged 40 or older from applying, or if it limits or discriminates on the basis of age in any way.
Marital Status and Family Responsibility	Whether an applicant can meet specified work schedules or has activities, commitments or responsibilities that may hinder meeting attendance requirements. Inquiries concerning duration of stay on job or anticipated absences that are made to both males and females alike.	"Do you have children?" "Who will care for your children while you are working?" "Are you married, single, divorced, or separated?" "Do you plan to marry?" "Do you wish to be addressed as Miss? Mrs.? Ms.?" Name or other information about spouse. (After hire this is permissible to obtain a contact in case of an emergency.)
Names		"What are the names and ages of your children?"

ADDITIONAL GENERAL ADVICE *continued*

SUBJECT	ASK	DON'T ASK
Relatives	Statement of company policy regarding work assignment of employees who are related. Names of an applicant's relatives already employed by the company. This inquiry, however, could increase the chances of a successful discrimination claim if it results in a preference to friends or relatives of employees and if minority groups are underrepresented in the employer's work force. Names and address of parents or guardian (if the applicant is a minor), but only after hire.	Name, address, or age of any adult relative of applicant not employed by the company.
Gender	Sex of the applicant may be requested (preferably not on the employment application) for affirmative-action purposes under a lawful affirmative-action program under Title VII, but may not be used as an employment-selection criterion unless gender is a BFOQ. Inquiry or restriction of employment is permissible only where a bona fide occupational qualification (BFOQ) exists. (This BFOQ exception is interpreted very narrowly by the courts and the EEOC.) The burden of proof rests on the employer to prove that the BFOQ does exist and that all members of the affected class (e.g., females) are incapable of performing the job.	Inquiry as to gender. "Are you expecting?" or "Are you pregnant?" Inquiry into future child-bearing plans. Any inquiry that would indicate gender of the applicant. For example, a statement that says "indicate Miss, Mrs., or Mr." Gender is not a BFOQ because a job involves physical labor (such as heavy lifting) beyond the capacity of some women, nor can employment be restricted just because the job is traditionally labeled "men's work" or "women's work."

ADDITIONAL GENERAL ADVICE *continued*

SUBJECT	*ASK*	*DON'T ASK*
Gender *continued*		The applicant's gender cannot be used as a factor for determining whether or not an applicant will be satisfied in a particular job.
		Employers may not request information from female applicants that is not requested from males (such as marital or family status).
		Sexual harassment is prohibited by Title VII. Unwelcome sexual advances, requests for sexual favors, and other verbal or physical conduct of a sexual nature constitute sexual harassment when: 1. submission to such conduct is made either implicitly or explicitly a term of employment; 2. submission to or rejection of such conduct is used as the basis of employment decisions affecting that person; or 3. such conduct substantially interferes with a person's work performance or creates an intimidating, hostile or offensive work environment.
Birth Control		Inquiry as to the capacity to reproduce or advocacy of any form of birth control or family planning.
Driver's License	"Do you possess a valid driver's license?"	Requirement that applicant produce a driver's license.

ADDITIONAL GENERAL ADVICE *continued*

SUBJECT	*ASK*	*DON'T ASK*
Notice in Case of Emergency		Name and address of person to be notified in case of an emergency. (This inquiry should be asked only after a person has been hired.)
Place of Birth	"Can you, after employment, submit a birth certificate or other proof of U.S. citizenship?"	Birthplace of an applicant. Birthplace of an applicant's parents, spouse, or other relatives. Requirement that an applicant submit a birth certificate before employment. Any other inquiry into national origin.
Experience	Applicant's work experience, including names and addresses of previous employers, dates of employment, reasons for leaving, and salary history. Other countries visited.	
Miscellaneous	Notice to applicants that any misstatements or omissions of material facts in the application may be cause for dismissal.	

HERE IS EDWARD BEAR, COMING DOWNSTAIRS
NOW, BUMP, BUMP, BUMP, ON THE BACK OF HIS
HEAD, BEHIND CHRISTOPHER ROBIN. IT IS, AS
FAR AS HE KNOWS, THE ONLY WAY OF COMING
DOWNSTAIRS, BUT SOMETIMES HE FEELS THERE
REALLY IS ANOTHER WAY, IF ONLY HE COULD
STOP BUMPING FOR A MOMENT AND THINK OF IT.

FROM WINNIE-THE-POOH

Epilogue: Topgrading in the Future

It's hard to imagine an organization that cannot benefit from topgrading. From a social club to the United Nations, A players get results, C players don't. From burger stands to *Fortune* 50 companies, what organization cannot benefit from a 90-percent success in hiring versus 50 percent?

During the 1900s the world zoomed through the Agricultural Age, Industrial Age, and Information Age. What's next? Futurist Jim Taylor suggests the Age of Chaos. If authors get a vote, I vote for:

▶ The Age of Talent

Industries formerly built on unskilled labor are fast evolving into talent machines. The most valuable parts of jobs are less and less performing mechanical tasks, and more and more using the brain—sensing, judging, creating, building relationships. Under Jack Welch, General Electric has become the most valuable corporation in the world by attracting, retaining, and fully utilizing exceptional talent. Welch has created an organizational power vac, sucking good ideas up to the decision makers. GE's Work-Out program is a perpetual series of town meetings in which workers propose process changes and bosses listen and react. Welch doesn't look to workers for physical brawn, but for intellectual acumen. He says, "The only ideas that count are A ideas.

310

There is no second place. That means we have to get everybody involved. If you do that right, the best ideas will rise to the top."

Accountants are still trying to figure out the value of having the best ideas "rise to the top." While businesses try to distinguish between labor as a cost versus labor as an investment, terms such as "human capital" help. At the managerial level, the focus of *Topgrading*, maximizing the return on investments in people is a long-overdue concept. In the entertainment business careful calculations are made—Michael Jordan gets $30 million, so what is our ROI? Name any realm of human organization in which that concept is not important. Consider just a few new venues for topgrading:

1. COMMUNITY SERVICE

The increase in multi-millionaires has resulted in a new form of philanthropy, results-oriented giving. Instead of throwing money at problems, as old foundations sometimes appear to do, the new millionaires want to see results. They worked damned hard to get the dough, and increasingly I hear, "It's almost as hard giving it away." They don't want to write a check for $1 million to an organization run by C players.

Community-service organizations can attract more money in the future by topgrading them and advertising, "We have a dream team of A players who will spend your donations for maximum results." Rich givers will increasingly require, perhaps even *fund*, topgrading in order that their money be donated wisely.

2. GOVERNMENT

United States presidents, governors, mayors—politicians all promise dream teams, and too often C players are elected or appointed. The national political parties are exercising more authority these days. Why not screen political candidates for financial support by submitting them to CIDS interviews?

In office, politicians perform political favors, but why not use CIDS interviews to staff key positions with A players? Any politician could benefit from reading a ten-page CIDS interview report on every finalist, to choose the best and to know how to work most effectively with each. I know of sporadic topgrading efforts by political leaders. Why not more?

3. FINANCE

Half of mergers and organizations fail because of the human element. Many financial wizards just can't get the people thing right. Some do—Dr. Geoff

Smart's research[1] showed that the most successful venture capitalists (VCs) are very rigorous in assessing management in organizations in which they invest; they qualify as topgraders. The least successful VCs are cursory in their assessment of talent; they aren't even upgraders, for they consider only the deal, the financials, the products, and *not* the management talent. In 86 deals analyzed, the topgraders achieved a spectacular 80-percent return versus a 30-percent return for the VCs who were cursory in assessing management talent.

John Teets, former Chairman of Dial Corp., said the acquisition of Giltspur was the "smoothest, most successful acquisition in Dial's history." CIDS interviews and 360-degree discussions were used to assess Giltspur's top 40 managers; A players were neatly blended into Dial's ExhibitGroup, which under President Charles Corsentino had already topgraded. Giltspur's C players were nudged into smaller jobs where they could be A players, or removed from the company. Contrast this approach with the usual ways acquiring companies assess talent—word of mouth, short interviews, political infighting.

Topgrading offers the world of finance accurate insight into that unfathomable black box—people.

4. LEGALLY MANDATED TOPGRADING

A billion-dollar legal industry thrives on invalid selection and promotion. "We didn't discriminate against him because of race, we just felt the white person was more qualified." "No he wasn't." "Yes, he was." Variations on that scenario produce expensive, embarrassing lawsuits.

Selection systems have been mandated by courts because they promise validity with minimized illegal discrimination. A major metropolitan police department, for example, was required to select officers through assessment centers (case studies, interviews, tests, exercises that replicate the job).

Having devised a dozen assessment centers, one five days and nights long, I have concluded that one component is the most valuable: the CIDS interview. It is the one assessment-center module that draws *all* the information together in a consistent package. Multiple assessors help make assessment centers nondiscriminatory; tandem interviews in centers can achieve the same.

With research *finally* showing structured interviews to be valid predictors of job performance, the CIDS interview is bound to be tested against its shorter, less comprehensive counterparts, as well as long and expensive assessment centers. It will outshine them.

---

[1] Geoffrey H. Smart, "Management Assessment Methods in Venture Capital: Towards a Theory of Human Capital Valuation," Ph.D. dissertation, Claremont Graduate University, 1998.

If I were a judge looking at discrimination that emerged "innocently" from sloppy, shallow selection procedures, I would require:

- CIDS interviews
- Thorough training in CIDS interviewing for all interviewers

With race norming and quotas illegal, and yet the pressure for affirmative action continuing, valid approaches for hiring truly talented protected groups is the solution.

5. EDUCATION

The business of education is crying out for topgrading. C-player administrators hire C-player teachers and professors. French high schools kill U.S. students on standardized tests, yet our per-pupil cost is six times what French students are allocated. The Chicago public schools were so bad, emergency legislation permitted Mayor Daley to fire everyone—administrators, teachers, staff. That was an opportunity for topgrading. Must our educational system be flat on its face in order to topgrade?

Many school systems use a panel of ten interviewers to screen teacher candidates, all of whom are asked exactly the same 12 questions, no more, no less. Imagine if those teachers were CIDS interviewed! Are 90 percent of the teachers in your school system A players?

Perhaps an argument in favor of school choice (e.g., vouchers and charter schools) is that topgrading is more apt to take place in these private institutions than in public schools. When administrators and teachers work in topgraded organizations, the quality of education can soar, overnight.

6. CAREER PLANNING

High schools, trade schools, colleges, universities, and all types of organizations offer some sort of career planning, but it is usually weak. Counselors look at test profiles and say, "You're good in math, so how about a career in engineering?" A few organizations such as General Electric use CIDS interviews to get "missile lock" on people's talent—accurate appraisals of managers on dozens of competencies. GE rarely promotes people over their head, even more rarely leaves a super talent languishing and underutilized. Educational institutions could assess students' career talents a lot better if they would incorporate a CIDS interview.

The Internet already provides job information, even ways to apply for jobs. Someone is going to offer, perhaps on the Internet, a library of more extensive career information. An interactive software package will no doubt be created to help a newly graduated accountant explore all the relevant career paths. Salary data are already available, but how about videotaped interviews with CPAs, vice presidents of finance, analysts? Then a CIDS interview can help that graduate determine if being an individual contributor or a leader makes more sense.

A client professional association experienced extremely high turnover in its field-consultant ranks. Many candidates applied for the job, thinking the high pay and freedom would be terrific. The 18-hour work days were killers for many, however. A 30-minute video was created that accurately portrayed the good and bad elements of the job. Candidates participated in CIDS interviews to better understand their talents. The combination of CIDS interviews and the descriptive video dramatically cut turnover in the field-consultant job and greatly increased job satisfaction and performance.

Just think, what if students and job candidates all had the benefit of both CIDS-interview insights and descriptive videos of various jobs? What if interactive media were also available to answer all their questions about careers? I think talent utilization and human fulfillment would both skyrocket, and the world would be a little better for it.

7. YOUR PERSONAL GROWTH

These are just some ideas for how topgrading can help organizations of all types in the future. I'd like to conclude with a focus on one more topgrading idea that might make your future a little brighter.

I hope you are a committed topgrader, more willing and able than ever to attract, assess, select A players, coach all your people, and redeploy chronic C players. In addition to using CIDS interviews to assess candidates for selection and promotion, use it to assess talent you inherit. This concept has been alluded to in this book, but here is a specific suggestion: When you take a job and inherit a team, announce:

> In order to get to know you and your thoughts about our (company, division, function), I'd like to schedule three hours with each of you individually. This is an opportunity to tell me what you want me to know about your background, accomplishments, skills, and career interests. I also want to hear your impressions of the challenges and opportunities we face and how you feel we can best meet them.

The CIDS-interview approach is inevitably popular with the new team, A, B, and C players alike. All love an opportunity to talk about their favorite subject—themselves. To be afforded a three-hour block of quality time is an unambiguous affirmation of the value of each person. This is quality time, a relaxed meeting in which each team member can feel the warm glow of being fully understood.

FUTURE RESEARCH ON TOPGRADING

Talent as an issue, or opportunity, is as old as the human race. Publications about it began with the advent of printing in China and later in Europe, when Gutenberg's printing presses began cranking out bibles. Business books and articles on how to maximize human capital abound. Yet research lags. My impression is that economic research deals with numbers (pay, turnover) but not with individual human beings. The psychological literature is scientific, but too narrowly focused and too short on economic factors.

I fervently hope this book stimulates more research, a *lot* more research. I hope economists and behavioral scientists link up. Solidly scientific narrowly focused research should continue, because eventually the "trivia" are connected into constructs and then into real-life applications. But I would hope even more for an explosion of field research—sloppy science but "real life" that eventually becomes solidly scientific and more beneficial to society. Every company could contribute to the body of scientific literature, and 1,000 master's theses and Ph.D. dissertations could refine and connect individual corporate studies. A few topics might be:

- *Definition of A, B, C player*. Perhaps "top 1 percent" is a more useful definition of A player than "top 10 percent" in your company or industry. Would the addition of D-player and F-player categories be useful designations?

- *Cost of mis-hires*. Let's move beyond guestimates and anecdoted evidence and really nail down the costs.

- *Hiring success rates*. I performed a mini study for this book, but you, we, and the world need to have more precise definitions of success and more objective measurements of it.

- *Screening approaches*. I obviously consider CIDS the most accurate selection interview for managers. It's high time to see research on management hires, not just on entry-level employees.

- *Impact of topgrading*. This book cites a few case studies. How about research on 100 case studies, or 1,000, to elucidate the benefits and risks of topgrading for various companies, industries, geographic regions? Research should slice and dice data, to continuously refine patterns that will show best practices for small versus large companies, failing companies versus successful companies striving to become ever more successful, different industries, various nationalities, you name it!

- *Relationship of happiness to topgrading*. I think A players are happier than C players, but there are a lot of "it depends" conditions. This book presents my conclusions based on my "sample" of several thousand senior managers, but it's hardly definitive. Longitudinal studies of happiness as it relates to the career myths and advice presented in Chapter 8 offer the prospect of increased happiness and well-being for those embarking on careers in management.

In the meantime, you are conducting your own research on talent maximization every day. You know topgrading is not easy. There are lessons to be learned, by you and by me, about what topgrading approaches work best. Your personal "case study" is an art form, a work in progress. I sincerely hope this book helps you in your daily laboratory to become the best topgrader you can, for your company, your career, and your personal happiness.

Appendices

Applicant_____

Interviewer_____

Date_____

APPENDIX A
Chronological In-Depth Structured [CIDS]
INTERVIEW GUIDE

BRADFORD D. SMART, PH.D.

THERE'S SOMETHING RARE, SOMETHING FINER
FAR, SOMETHING MUCH MORE SCARCE THAN
ABILITY. IT'S THE ABILITY TO RECOGNIZE ABILI-
TY.

ELBERT HUBBARD

This Guide seeks to provide you with the most accurate, most valid, insights into candidates for selection or promotion.

Maximum benefits in using this Chronological In-Depth Structured (CIDS) Interview Guide can be achieved through applying the principles stated in:

Topgrading: How Leading Companies Win by Hiring, Coaching, and Keeping the Best People by Dr. Bradford D. Smart (Prentice Hall Press, 1999).

This Guide is intended to make the interviewer's job easier. It is a comprehensive, chronological guide, providing plenty of space to record responses. It is appropriately used for internal as well as external candidates, or simply to better understand the strengths, areas for improvement, and potentials of employees "inherited."

Thousands of hiring managers have felt that following this Guide has permitted them to gain the deepest insights ever into an interviewee. Experience has shown the following guidelines to be helpful:

1. Review the candidate's Career History Form and résumé.
2. Be sure that the Job Description and Competencies are clear. Both require a solid job analysis that describes essential requirements of the job.
3. Review this Guide prior to the interview, in order to:
   - Refresh your memory regarding the sequence and wording of questions, for a smoother interview.

- Add or delete questions based upon what previous information (résumé, Career History Form, preliminary interviews, record checks) have disclosed about the individual.
- Scratch on this Guide your estimated time to spend on each section.

4. After a couple of minutes building rapport, give the interviewee an idea of the time frame (2½ hours?) and then sell the person on being open and honest. For an external candidate for selection, you might state purposes such as to:

- "Review your background, interests, and goals to see if there is a good match with the position and opportunities here . . ."
- "Determine some ways to assure your smooth assimilation into your new position, should we offer a job and you accept it . . ."
- "Get some ideas regarding what you and we can do to maximize your long-range fulfillment and contributions," and
- "Tell you more about the career opportunities we have to offer and answer any questions you have."

5. Following the Chronological In-Depth Structured Interview:

- Review the completed Guide three times.
- Conduct in-depth reference checks and accumulate opinions from coworkers who conducted interviews with the person.
- Write comments about each Competency on the last three pages of this Guide.
- Make final ratings on the Competencies.

6. Write a brief report . . . an Executive Summary, followed by a list of Strengths and Weaker Points.

7. Make the decision to hire, promote, or transfer . . . or not.

COLLEGE

So that I can get a good feel for your background, first your education and then work experience, let's briefly go back to your college days and come forward chronologically, up to the present. Then we'll talk about your plans and goals for the future.

Note to Interviewer: Start with college or first full-time job, whichever came first.

1. I see from the Career History Form that you attended _____ (college). Would you please expand on the Career History Form information and give me a brief rundown on your college years, particularly events that might have affected later career decisions. I'd be interested in knowing about work experiences, what the school was like, what you were like back then, the curriculum, activities, how you did in school, high and low points, and so forth. (Ask the following questions to obtain complete information not included in responses to the general "smorgasbord" question.)

2. Give me a feel for what kind of school it was (if necessary, specify large/small, rural/urban, cliquish, etc.), and generally, what your college years were like.

   _____

   _____

   _____

3. What was your major? (change majors?) _____

4. What school activities did you take part in? (Note activities listed on Career History Form, and get elaboration.)

   _____

   _____

   _____

5. What sort of grades did you receive, what was your class standing, and what were your study habits like? (Confirm data on Career History Form.)

   GPA: _____ / _____ (scale)
   Study Habits _____ SAT Scores _____ ACT Score _____

6. What people or events during college might have had an influence on your career? _____

_____

_____

_____

7. Were there any class offices, awards, honors, or special achievements during your college years? (Note Career History Form responses, and get elaboration.) _____

_____

_____

_____

8. What were high points during your college years? (Look for leadership, initiative, and particularly what competencies the interviewee exhibits now while discussing those years.) _____

_____

_____

_____

9. What were low points, or least enjoyable occurrences, during your college years? (Again, what happened back then is only important in relation to what is revealed about the interviewee now.) _____

_____

_____

_____

10. Give me a feel for any jobs you held during college—the types of jobs, whether they were during the school year or summer, hours worked, and any high or low points associated with them. (Don't spend much time on these jobs, but look for indications of extraordinary initiative, motivation, etc.; if the person did not work during the summer, ask how the summer months were spent.) _____

_____

_____

_____

11. (TRANSITION QUESTION) What were your career thoughts toward the end of college? _____

_____

_____

_____

_____

GRADUATE SCHOOL

Note: If graduate school occurred later in the interviewee's life, complete this section later. Stay in chronological order.

1. _____ 2. _____

                       School   Degree

3. Why this school and degree _____

_____

4. High Points _____

_____

_____

5. Low Points _____

_____

_____

6. Work Experiences:

    a. _____

_____

    b. _____

_____

    c. _____

_____

7. Career Thoughts/Opportunities_____

_____

_____

_____

_____

_____

WORK HISTORY

Now I would like you to tell me about your work history. There are a lot of things I would like to know about each position. Let me tell you what these things are now, so I won't have to interrupt you so often. We already have some of this information from your Career History Form and previous discussions. Of course, I need to know the employer, location, dates of employment, your titles, and salary history. I would also be interested in knowing what your expectations were for each job, your responsibilities/accountabilities, what you found upon entering the job, what major challenges you faced and how they were handled. What were your most significant accomplishments as well as mistakes, and what were the most enjoyable and least enjoyable aspects of each job? What was each supervisor like and what would you guess each really felt were your strengths and weaker points? Finally, I would like to know the circumstances under which you left each position.

Note: If the person recently worked for a single employer and had, say, three jobs two years each with that employer, consider each one of those a *separate* position and complete a Work History Form on it. Following is suggested wording for information requested on the Work History Form:

1. What was the name of the employer, location, dates of employment? (Get a "feel" for the organization by asking about revenues, products/services, number of employees, etc.)
2. What was your job title?
3. What were the starting and final levels of compensation?
4. What were your expectations for the job?
5. What were your responsibilities and accountabilities?
6. What did you find when you arrived? What shape was the job in—talent, performance, resources, problems? What major challenges did you face?

7. What results were achieved in terms of successes and accomplishments? (As time permits, get specifics, such as individual versus shared accomplishments, barriers overcome, "bottom-line" results, and impact on career—bonus, promotability, performance review.)

8. We all make mistakes—what would you say were mistakes or failures experienced in this job? If you could wind the clock back, what would you do differently? (As time permits, get specifics.)

9. All jobs seem to have their pluses and minuses; what were the most enjoyable or rewarding aspects of this job?

10. What were the least enjoyable aspects of the job?

11. (For management jobs) What sort of talent did you inherit and what changes did you make? (For most recent two jobs, get A, B, C ratings and strengths/weaker points of each subordinate.)

12. What circumstances contributed to your leaving? (Always probe for other reasons.)

13. What was your supervisor's name and title? Where is that person now? May I contact him/her? (Ask permission to contact supervisors in the past ten years, in order to understand the candidate's developmental patterns.)

14. What is/was it like working for (him/her) and what were (his/her) strengths and shortcomings as a supervisor, from your point of view?

15. What is your best guess as to what (supervisor's name) honestly felt were/are your strengths, weaker points, and overall performance?

NOTE: An easy transition to the next job can occur by simply determining employer/title/dates, and then asking WHAT DID YOU DO, HOW DID YOU LIKE IT, and HOW DID YOU DO?

WORK HISTORY FORM 1

1. _____
   Employer   Starting date (mo./yr.)   Final (mo./yr.)

   _____
   Location   Type of business

   Description _____

2. Title _____

3. Salary (Starting) _____ (Final) _____

4. Expectations _____

5. Responsibilities/Accountabilities _____

6. "Found" (Major Challenges) _____

7. Successes/Accomplishments _____

8. Failures/Mistakes _____

9. Most Enjoyable _____

10. Least Enjoyable _____

11. Talent _____

12. Reasons for Leaving _____

SUPERVISOR

13. _____
    Supervisor's Name   Title

    _____
    Where Now   Permission to Contact?

14. Appraisal of Supervisor
    His/Her Strengths _____
    His/Her Shortcomings _____

15. Best guess as to what he/she really felt at that time were your:
    STRENGTHS   **WEAKER POINTS**

    Overall Performance Rating _____

WORK HISTORY FORM 2

1. _____
   Employer   Starting date (mo./yr.)   Final (mo./yr.)

   _____
   Location   Type of business

   Description _____

2. Title _____

3. Salary (Starting) _____ (Final) _____

4. Expectations _____

5. Responsibilities/Accountabilities _____

6. "Found" (Major Challenges) _____

7. Successes/Accomplishments _____

8. Failures/Mistakes _____

9. Most Enjoyable _____

10. Least Enjoyable _____

11. Talent _____

12. Reasons for Leaving _____

SUPERVISOR

13. _____
    Supervisor's Name   Title

    _____
    Where Now   Permission to Contact?

14. Appraisal of Supervisor
    His/Her Strengths _____
    His/Her Shortcomings _____

15. Best guess as to what he/she really felt at that time were your:

    STRENGTHS   **WEAKER POINTS**

    Overall Performance Rating _____

WORK HISTORY FORM 3

1. _____

   Employer   Starting date (mo./yr.)   Final (mo./yr.)

   _____

   Location   Type of business

   Description _____

2. Title _____

3. Salary (Starting) _____ (Final) _____

4. Expectations _____

5. Responsibilities/Accountabilities _____

6. "Found" (Major Challenges) _____

7. Successes/Accomplishments _____

8. Failures/Mistakes _____

9. Most Enjoyable _____

10. Least Enjoyable _____

11. Talent _____

12. Reasons for Leaving _____

SUPERVISOR

13. _____

    Supervisor's Name   Title

    _____

    Where Now   Permission to Contact?

14. Appraisal of Supervisor
    His/Her Strengths _____
    His/Her Shortcomings _____

15. Best guess as to what he/she really felt at that time were your:
    STRENGTHS   **WEAKER POINTS**

    Overall Performance Rating _____

WORK HISTORY FORM 4

1. _____
   Employer   Starting date (mo./yr.)   Final (mo./yr.)

   _____
   Location   Type of business

   Description _____

2. Title _____

3. Salary (Starting) _____ (Final) _____

4. Expectations _____

5. Responsibilities/Accountabilities _____

6. "Found" (Major Challenges) _____

7. Successes/Accomplishments _____

8. Failures/Mistakes _____

9. Most Enjoyable _____

10. Least Enjoyable _____

11. Talent _____

12. Reasons for Leaving _____

SUPERVISOR

13. _____
    Supervisor's Name   Title

    _____
    Where Now   Permission to Contact?

14. Appraisal of Supervisor
    His/Her Strengths _____
    His/Her Shortcomings _____

15. Best guess as to what he/she really felt at that time were your:
    STRENGTHS   **WEAKER POINTS**

    Overall Performance Rating _____

WORK HISTORY FORM 5

1. _____

   Employer   Starting date (mo./yr.)   Final (mo./yr.)

   _____

   Location   Type of business

   Description _____

2. Title _____

3. Salary (Starting) _____ (Final) _____

4. Expectations _____

5. Responsibilities/Accountabilities _____

6. "Found" (Major Challenges) _____

7. Successes/Accomplishments _____

8. Failures/Mistakes _____

9. Most Enjoyable _____

10. Least Enjoyable _____

11. Talent _____

12. Reasons for Leaving _____

SUPERVISOR

13. _____

   Supervisor's Name   Title

   _____

   Where Now   Permission to Contact?

14. Appraisal of Supervisor
   His/Her Strengths _____
   His/Her Shortcomings _____

15. Best guess as to what he/she really felt at that time were your:

   STRENGTHS   **WEAKER POINTS**

   Overall Performance Rating _____

WORK HISTORY FORM 6

1. _____
   Employer   Starting date (mo./yr.)   Final (mo./yr.)

   _____
   Location   Type of business

   Description _____

2. Title _____

3. Salary (Starting) _____ (Final) _____

4. Expectations _____

5. Responsibilities/Accountabilities _____

6. "Found" (Major Challenges) _____

7. Successes/Accomplishments _____

8. Failures/Mistakes _____

9. Most Enjoyable _____

10. Least Enjoyable _____

11. Talent _____

12. Reasons for Leaving _____

SUPERVISOR

13. _____
    Supervisor's Name   Title

    _____
    Where Now   Permission to Contact?

14. Appraisal of Supervisor
    His/Her Strengths _____
    His/Her Shortcomings _____

15. Best guess as to what he/she really felt at that time were your:
    STRENGTHS   **WEAKER POINTS**

    Overall Performance Rating _____

PLANS AND GOALS FOR THE FUTURE

1. Let's discuss what you are looking for in your next job. (Note "Career Needs" section of Career History Form.)

   _____

   _____

   _____

   _____

2. What are other job possibilities, and how do you feel about each one?

   _____

   _____

   _____

   _____

3. Describe your ideal position, and what makes it ideal.

   _____

   _____

   _____

   _____

4. How does this opportunity square with your ideal position? What do you view as opportunities and advantages as well as risks and disadvantages in joining us?

   Advantages

   _____

   _____

   _____

   _____

   Disadvantages

   _____

   _____

   _____

   _____

SELF-APPRAISAL

1. I would like you to give me a thorough self-appraisal, beginning with what you consider your strengths, assets, things you like about yourself, and things you do well.

   (Ask follow-up questions, and urge the person to continue. For example, you might say such things as "good," "keep going," "oh," nod and ask questions such as: "What other strengths come to mind?" "What are some other things you do well?"

   Obtain a list of strengths and then go back and ask the person to elaborate on what was meant by each strength listed—"conscientious," "hard working," or whatever.)

2. OK, let's look at the other side of the ledger for a moment. What would you say are your shortcomings, weaker points, or areas for improvement?

   Be generous in your use of the pregnant pause here. Urge the person to list more shortcomings by saying such things as, "What else comes to mind?" "Keep going, you are doing fine," or just smile, nod your head and wait. When the person has run out of shortcomings, you might ask questions such as: "What three things could you do that would most improve your overall effectiveness in the future?"

   Obtain as long a list of negatives as you can with minimal interruptions on your part, and then go back and request clarification. (If you interrupt the individual for clarification on one, there might be so much time spent on that one negative that the individual will be very hesitant to acknowledge another one.)

SELF-APPRAISAL

STRENGTHS	WEAKER POINTS
_____	_____
_____	_____
_____	_____
_____	_____
_____	_____
_____	_____

LEADERSHIP/MANAGEMENT

1. How would you describe your leadership philosophy and style? _____

   _____

   _____

   _____

2. What would you suppose your subordinates feel are your strengths and shortcomings, from their points of view?

   STRENGTHS   WEAKER POINTS

3. In what ways might you want to modify your approach to dealing with subordinates? _____

   _____

TOPGRADING

Question 11 in each Work History Form addresses topgrading. If questions about talent were not previously asked, do it now, for the most recent two jobs.

4. Would you please give me a paragraph about each subordinate, indicating title, length of employment, strengths, shortcomings, and overall performance?

   Ask how many people were recruited and selected, what approaches were used, how the people were trained and developed, how each worked out in the job, and for those who did not work out well, what happened with them (transferred to a job where successful, fired, simply tolerated). Determine the hiring "batting average" (how many good hires versus mis-hires). Also look for indications of diversity, positive versus negative feedback given, empowerment, fostering teamwork, and how people were/are held accountable. Most of all, look for success in packing the team with A players and redeploying chronic C players.

   _____

   _____

   _____

FOCUSED QUESTIONS

The following questions are optional. Those with an asterisk (*) are asked of all candidates, unless they have been answered in the chronological portion of the CIDS interview. Get specific examples, not general responses.

A general-item format, applicable to all the Focused Questions, is: "Please describe _____ and what specific examples can you cite?" Or, "If a 360°-survey included an item on _____, how were you rated?"

INTELLECTUAL COMPETENCIES

1. INTELLIGENCE

a. Please describe your learning ability._____

_____

_____

b. Describe a complex situation in which you had to learn a lot, quickly. How did you go about learning, and how successful were the outcomes?

_____

_____

2. ANALYSIS SKILLS

a. Please describe your problem analysis skills. _____

_____

_____

b. Do people generally regard you as one who diligently pursues every detail or do you tend to be more broad brush? Why? _____

_____

_____

c. What will references indicate are your style and overall effectiveness in "sorting" the wheat from the chaff? _____

_____

_____

d. What analytic approaches and tools do you use? _____

_____

_____

e. Please give me an example of digging more deeply for facts than what was asked of you. _____

_____

_____

3. JUDGMENT/DECISION MAKING

*a. Please describe your decision-making approach when you are faced with difficult situations, in comparison with others, at about your level in the organization. Are you decisive and quick, but sometimes too quick, or are you more thorough but sometimes too slow? Are you intuitive or go purely with the facts? Do you involve many or few people in decisions? _____

_____

_____

b. What are a couple of the most difficult or challenging decisions you have made recently? _____

_____

_____

c. What are a couple of the best and worst decisions you have made in the past year? _____

_____

_____

d. What maxims do you live by? _____

_____

_____

4. CONCEPTUAL ABILITY

Are you more comfortable dealing with concrete, tangible, short-term, or more abstract, conceptual long-term issues? Please explain. _____

_____

_____

5. CREATIVITY

*a. How creative are you? What are the best examples of your creativity in processes, systems, methods, products, structure, or services? _____

_____

_____

b. Do you consider yourself a better visionary or implementer, and why?

_____

6. STRATEGIC SKILLS

*a. In the past year, what specifically have you done in order to remain knowledgeable about the competitive environment, market and trade dynamics, products/services and technology trends, innovations, and patterns of customer behavior? _____

_____

_____

b. Please describe your experience in strategic planning, including successful and unsuccessful approaches. (Determine the individual's contribution in team strategic efforts.) _____

_____

_____

c. Where do you predict that your (industry/competitors/function) is going in the next three years? What is the "conventional wisdom," and what are your own thoughts? _____

_____

_____

7. PRAGMATISM

Do you consider yourself a more visionary or more pragmatic thinker, and why? _____

_____

_____

8. RISK TAKING

* What are the biggest risks you have taken in recent years? Include ones that have worked out well and not so well. _____

_____

_____

9. LEADING EDGE

*a. How have you copied, created, or applied best practices? _____

_____

_____

b. Describe projects in which your best-practice solutions did and did not fully address customer/client needs. _____

_____

_____

c. How will references rate and describe your technical expertise? Are you truly leading edge, or do you fall a bit short in some areas? _____

_____

_____

d. How computer literate are you? _____

_____

_____

e. Please describe your professional network. _____

_____

_____

10. EDUCATION

a. What seminars or formal education have you participated in (and when)? _____

_____

_____

b. Describe your reading habits (books and articles—global factors, general business, function, industry). _____

_____

_____

11. EXPERIENCE

a. Compose a series of open-ended questions—"How would you rate yourself in _____, and what specifics can you cite?" For Finance, learn expertise in Treasury, Controller, Risk Management, etc., areas. For Human Resources, learn expertise in Selection, Training, Compensation, etc.

- Question: _____? _____

_____

- Question: _____? _____

_____

- Question: _____? _____

_____

- Question: _____? _____

_____

- Question: _____? _____

_____

- Question: _____? _____

_____

b. What are the most important lessons you have learned in your career? (Get specifics with respect to when, where, what, etc.) _____

_____

_____

12. "TRACK RECORD"

Looking back in your career, what were your most and least successful jobs? _____

_____

PERSONAL COMPETENCIES

13. INTEGRITY

*a. Describe a situation or two in which the pressures to compromise your integrity were the strongest you have ever felt. _____

_____

_____

b. What are a couple of the most courageous actions or unpopular stands you have ever taken? _____

_____

_____

c. When have you confronted unethical behavior or chosen to not say anything, in order to not rock the boat? _____

_____

_____

d. Under what circumstances have you found it justifiable to break a confidence? _____

_____

_____

14. INITIATIVE

*a. What actions would you take in the first weeks, should you join our organization? _____

_____

_____

*b. What sorts of obstacles have you faced in your present/most recent job, and what did you do? _____

_____

_____

c. What are examples of circumstances in which you were expected to do a certain thing and, on your own, went beyond the call of duty? _____

_____

_____

d. Who have been your major career influences, and why? _____

_____

_____

e. Are you better at initiating a lot of things or hammering out results for fewer things? (Get specifics.) _____

_____

_____

15. ORGANIZATION/PLANNING

*a. How well organized are you? What do you do to be organized and what, if anything, do you feel you ought to do to be better organized? _____

_____

_____

b. When was the last time you missed a significant deadline? _____

_____

_____

c. Describe a complex challenge you have had coordinating a project.

_____

_____

d. Are you better at juggling a number of priorities or projects simultaneously, or attacking few projects, one at a time? _____

_____

e. Everyone procrastinates at times. What are the kinds of things that you procrastinate on? _____

_____

_____

f. How would you describe your work habits? _____

_____

_____

g. If I were to talk with administrative assistants you have had during the past several years, how would they describe your strengths and weaker points with respect to personal organization, communications, attention to detail, and planning? _____

_____

h. Describe a situation that did not go as well as planned. What would you have done differently? _____

_____

_____

16. EXCELLENCE

Have you significantly "raised the bar" for yourself or others? Explain how you did it—your approach, the problems encountered, the outcomes. _____

_____

_____

17. INDEPENDENCE

a. Do you believe in asking for forgiveness rather than permission, or are you inclined to be sure your bosses are in full agreement before you act?

_____

_____

b. How much supervision do you want or need? _____

18. STRESS MANAGEMENT

*a. What sort of mood swings do you experience—how high are the highs, how low are the lows, and why? _____

_____

_____

*b. What do you do to alleviate stress? (Look for exercise, quiet periods, etc.) _____

_____

_____

c. How do you handle yourself under stress and pressure? _____

_____

_____

d. Describe yourself in terms of emotional control. What sorts of things irritate you the most or get you down? _____

_____

_____

e. How many times have you "lost your cool" in the past couple of months? (Get specifics). _____

_____

_____

f. Describe a situation in which you were the most angry you have been in years. _____

_____

_____

19. SELF-AWARENESS

*a. Have you gotten any sort of systematic or regular feedback (360-degree or otherwise) from direct reports, clients, peers, supervisors, etc., and if so, what did you learn? _____

_____

_____

b. How much feedback do you like to get from people you report to, and in what form (written, face to face)? _____

_____

_____

c. What are the biggest mistakes you've made in the past (10) years, and what have you learned from them? _____

_____

_____

d. What are your principal developmental needs and what are your plans to deal with them? _____

_____

_____

e. What have been the most difficult criticisms for you to accept? _____

_____

_____

20. ADAPTABILITY

*a. How have you changed during recent years? _____

_____

b. What sorts of organization changes have you found easiest and most difficult to accept? _____

_____

c. When have you been so firm people considered you stubborn or inflexible? _____

_____

INTERPERSONAL COMPETENCIES

21. FIRST IMPRESSION

(Judge directly in interview).
What sort of first impression do you think you make at different levels in an organization? _____

_____

_____

22. LIKABILITY

*a. When were you so frustrated you did not treat someone with respect?

_____

_____

b. How would you describe your sense of humor? _____

_____

_____

c. Tell me about a situation in which you were expected to work with a person you disliked. _____

_____

_____

23. LISTENING

Are you familiar with the term "active listening"? How would you define it? What would coworkers say regarding how often and how effectively you use active listening? _____

_____

_____

24. CUSTOMER FOCUS

a. If you were to arrange confidential reference calls with some of your major clients/customers, what is your best guess as to what they would generally agree are your strengths and areas for improvement? _____

_____

_____

b. Relate an example of your partnering with a client/customer—helping the client/customer to achieve its goals and financial results? _____

_____

_____

c. Give examples of your going beyond what was normally expected to enhance your company's reputation or image.

_____

_____

d. Describe your methods of diagnosing client/customer needs. _____

_____

_____

e. What is your "track record" in both acquiring and retaining clients/customers? _____

_____

_____

f. Tell me about the most frustrated or disappointed client/customer you have had in recent years. _____

_____

_____

25. TEAM PLAYER

a. What will reference checks disclose to be the common perception among peers regarding how much of a team player you are (working cooperatively, building others' confidence and self-esteem)? _____

_____

_____

b. Describe the most difficult person with whom you have had to work.

_____

_____

c. When have you stood up to a boss? _____

_____

_____

d. Tell me about a situation in which you felt others were wrong and you were right. _____

_____

_____

26. ASSERTIVENESS

a. How would you describe your level of assertiveness? _____

_____

_____

b. When there is a difference of opinion, do you tend to confront people directly, indirectly, or tend to let the situation resolve itself? (Get specifics.) _____

_____

_____

c. Please give a couple of recent specific examples in which you were highly assertive, one in which the outcome was favorable, and one where it wasn't. _____

_____

_____

27. COMMUNICATIONS—ORAL

*a. How would you rate yourself in public speaking? If we had a videotape of your most recent presentation, what would we see? _____

_____

_____

b. Describe the last time you put your "foot in your mouth." _____

_____

_____

c. How do you communicate with your organization? _____

_____

_____

28. COMMUNICATIONS—WRITTEN

How would you describe your writing style in comparison with others' styles? _____

_____

29. POLITICAL SAVVY

*a. Describe a couple of the most difficult, challenging, or frustrating company political situations you have faced. _____

_____

_____

b. How aware are you of company political forces that may affect your performance? Please give a couple of examples of the most difficult political situations in which you have been involved, internally and with clients. _____

_____

_____

30. NEGOTIATION

Describe situations in which your negotiation skills proved effective and ineffective. _____

_____

_____

31. PERSUASION

a. Describe a situation in which you were most effective selling an idea or yourself. _____

_____

_____

b. Describe situations in which your persuasion skills proved ineffective.

_____

_____

MANAGEMENT COMPETENCIES

32. SELECTING A PLAYERS

*a. What have your most recent two teams looked like (how many A, B, C players) and what changes were made? _____

_____

_____

b. Explain your selection process in terms of job analysis, job description, behavioral competencies, amount of structure to interviews, if there is an in-depth chronological interview, and how reference checks are done. _____

_____

_____

33. COACHING/TRAINING

How would subordinates you have had in recent years describe your approaches to training and developing them? (Look for coaching, challenging assignments.) _____

_____

_____

34. GOAL SETTING

a. How do you go about establishing goals for performance (bottom up, top down, or what . . . and are they easy or "stretch")? _____

_____

_____

b. How are your expectations communicated? _____

_____

_____

35. EMPOWERMENT

How "hands-on" a manager are you? (Get specifics.) _____

_____

_____

36. PERFORMANCE MANAGEMENT

*a. Tell me about the performance management system you now use.

_____

_____

b. How effective have been your methods for following up on delegated assignments? _____

_____

_____

c. Tell me about accountability. What happens when people fail to perform? _____

_____

_____

d. What do you say or do when someone reporting to you has made a significant (serious, costly) mistake? _____

_____

_____

e. Cite examples of your giving negative feedback to someone. _____

_____

_____

37. REMOVING C PLAYERS

* How many nonperformers have you removed in recent years? What approaches were used? (Look for regular, honest feedback, sincere training/development/coaching efforts, C players more apt to ask for a different job or quit than to be fired, and redeployment in months, not years.)

_____

_____

38. TEAM BUILDER

a. How have you tried to build teamwork? _____

_____

_____

b. Which of your teams has been the biggest disappointment in terms of cohesiveness or effectiveness?_____

_____

_____

39. DIVERSITY

*a. When have you actively confronted indications of discrimination or prejudicial behavior? _____

_____

_____

b. How have you added to diversity (ethnic, cultural, racial, gender) in a workplace? _____

_____

_____

c. Have there been any successful employment charges against you (EEOC, sexual harassment, etc.)? _____

_____

_____

40. RUNNING MEETINGS

*a. How productive are meetings you run? How could they become more productive? _____

_____

_____

b. How would you describe your role in meetings—ones which you have called and those in which you have been a participant? _____

_____

_____

LEADERSHIP [ADDITIONAL COMPETENCIES]

41. VISION

What is (was) your vision for your present (most recent) job? How was the vision developed? _____

_____

_____

42. CHANGE LEADERSHIP

a. In what specific ways have you changed an organization the most (in terms of direction, results, policies)? _____

_____

_____

b. What has been your approach to communications in changes? (Look for communicating like mad!) _____

_____

_____

43. INSPIRING "FOLLOWERSHIP"

a. Are you a "natural leader"? If so, cite indications. _____

_____

_____

b. Give examples of when people might have readily followed your lead and when they did not. _____

_____

_____

44. CONFLICT MANAGEMENT

a. Describe a situation in which you actively tore down walls or barriers to teamwork. _____

_____

_____

b. Describe situations in which you prevented or resolved conflicts.

_____

_____

c. If two subordinates are fighting, what do you do? (Look for bringing them together now to resolve it.) _____

_____

_____

MOTIVATIONAL COMPETENCIES

45. ENERGY

*a. How many hours per week have you worked, on the average, during the past year? _____

_____

_____

b. What motivates you? _____

_____

_____

46. ENTHUSIASM

a. How would you rate yourself (and why) in enthusiasm and charisma?

_____

_____

b. Describe the pace at which you work—fast, slow, or moderate—and the circumstances under which it varies. _____

_____

_____

47. AMBITION (see Plans and Goals for the Future)

Who have been recent career influences, and why? _____

_____

_____

48. COMPATIBILITY OF NEEDS

Is there anything we and I can do to help you if there is a job change (relocation, housing, etc.)? _____

_____

_____

49. BALANCE IN LIFE

How satisfied are you with your balance in life—the balance among work, wellness, community involvement, professional associations, hobbies, etc.? _____

_____

_____

50. TENACITY

a. What are examples of the biggest challenges you have faced and overcome? _____

_____

_____

b. What will references say is your general level of urgency? _____

_____

_____

OTHER

51. a. Question:_____? _____

_____

b. Question:_____? _____

_____

c. Question:_____? _____

_____

d. Question:_____? _____

_____

e. Question:_____? _____

_____

f. Question:_____? _____

_____

g. Question:_____? _____

_____

SUMMARY

RATING SCALE:
6 = Excellent; 5 = Very Good; 4 = Good; 3 = Only Fair; 2 = Poor; 1 = Very Poor

Competencies	Minimum Acceptable Rating	Your Rating	Comments
INTELLECTUAL			
1. Intelligence			
2. Analysis Skills			
3. Judgment/Decision Making			
4. Conceptual Ability			
5. Creativity			
6. Strategic Skills			
7. Pragmatism			
8. Risk Taking			
9. Leading Edge			
10. Education			
11. Experience			
12. "Track Record"			
PERSONAL			
13. Integrity			
14. Initiative			
15. Organization/Planning			
16. Excellence			
17. Independence			
18. Stress Management			
19. Self-Awareness			
20. Adaptability			

Competencies	Minimum Acceptable Rating	Your Rating	Comments
INTERPERSONAL			
21. First Impression			
22. Likability			
23. Listening			
24. Customer Focus			
25. Team Player			
26. Assertiveness			
27. Communications—Oral			
28. Communications—Written			
29. Political Savvy			
30. Negotiation			
31. Persuasion			
MANAGEMENT			
32. Selecting A Players			
33. Coaching/Training			
34. Goal Setting			
35. Empowerment			
36. Performance Management			
37. Removing C Players			
38. Team Builder			
39. Diversity			
40. Running Meetings			
LEADERSHIP (Additional Competencies)			
41. Vision			
42. Change Leadership			
43. Inspiring "Followership"			
44. Conflict Management			

Competencies	Minimum Acceptable Rating	Your Rating	Comments
MOTIVATIONAL			
45. Energy			
46. Enthusiasm			
47. Ambition			
48. Compatibility of Needs			
49. Balance in Life			
50. Tenacity			
OTHER			

APPENDIX B
Career History Form

This information will not be the only basis for hiring decisions. You are not required to furnish any information that is prohibited by federal, state, or local law.

Last Name	First	Middle	

Home Address	City	State	Zip Code

Business Address	City	State	Zip Code

Social Security Number
(   )
Area Code   Telephone Number (Home)
(   )
Area Code   Telephone Number (Business)

Position applied for: _____ Earnings expected $ _____

I. BUSINESS EXPERIENCE: (Please start with your present or most recent position and include *all* full-time jobs, using supplemental sheets if necessary)

A. Firm _____ Address_____

City _____ State _____ Zip _____Phone (   ) _____

Kind of Business_____ Employed From _____ to _____
                                        (show months as well as years)
Title _____ Base _____
Initial   Final Total   Bonus _____
Compensation_____ Compensation_____ Other _____

Nature of Work _____

Supervisory Responsibility_____

Name and Title of Immediate Supervisor _____

What (do) (did) you like most about your job?_____

What (do) (did) you least enjoy? _____

Reasons for leaving or desiring to change _____

B. Firm _____ Address_____

City _____ State _____ Zip _____Phone ( ) _____

Kind of Business_____ Employed From _____ to _____
                                            (show months as well as years)

Title _____ Base _____
Initial   Final Total   Bonus _____
Compensation_____ Compensation_____ Other _____

Nature of Work _____

Supervisory Responsibility_____

Name and Title of Immediate Supervisor _____

What (do) (did) you like most about your job?_____

What (do) (did) you least enjoy? _____

Reasons for leaving or desiring to change _____

C. Firm _____ Address_____

City _____ State _____ Zip _____Phone ( ) _____

Kind of Business_____ Employed From _____ to _____
                                            (show months as well as years)

Title _____ Base _____
Initial   Final Total   Bonus _____
Compensation_____ Compensation_____ Other _____

Nature of Work _____

Supervisory Responsibility_____

Name and Title of Immediate Supervisor _____

What (do) (did) you like most about your job?_____

What (do) (did) you least enjoy? _____

Reasons for leaving or desiring to change _____

Other Positions held:

	a. Company b. City	a. Your Title b. Name of Supervisor	Date (mo/yr) a. Began b. Left	Compensation a. Initial b. Final	a. Type of Work b. Reason for Leaving
D.	a. _____	_____	_____	_____	_____
	b. _____	_____	_____	_____	_____
E.	a. _____	_____	_____	_____	_____
	b. _____	_____	_____	_____	_____
F.	a. _____	_____	_____	_____	_____
	b. _____	_____	_____	_____	_____
G.	a. _____	_____	_____	_____	_____
	b. _____				

Indicate by letter _____ any of the above employers you do not wish contacted.

II. MILITARY EXPERIENCE:

If in service, indicate: Branch _____

Date (mo/yr) entered _____

Date (mo/yr) discharged _____

Nature of duties _____

Highest rank or grade _____

Terminal rank or grade _____

III. EDUCATION High School 1 2 3 4   College/Graduate School 1 2 3 4 5 6 7 8
(circle highest grade completed)

A. High School Name of High School _____

Location _____

Approximate number in graduating class _____ Rank from top _____

Final grade-point average _____ (A = _____) Scores on SAT/ACT _____

Extracurricular activities _____

_____

Offices, honors/awards _____

Part-time and summer work _____

_____

B. College/Graduate School

Name & Location	Degree	Major	Grade-Point Average	Total Credit Hours	Extracurricular Activities, Honors, and Awards
			(A =____)		
			(A=____)		
			(A =____)		

What undergraduate course did you like most? Why? _____

What undergraduate course did you like least? Why?_____

How was your education financed?_____

Part-time and summer work _____

_____

Other courses, seminars, or studies _____

IV. ACTIVITIES:

Membership in professional or job-relevant organizations. (You may exclude groups that indicate race, color, religion, national origin, disability, or other protected status.)_____

_____

_____

Publications, patents, inventions, professional licenses, or additional special honors or awards_____

_____

_____

What qualifications, abilities, and strong points will help you succeed in this job?

_____

_____

_____

What are your weaker points and areas for improvement? _____

_____

_____

_____

V. CAREER NEEDS:

Willing to relocate? Yes _____ No_____ If no, explain. _____

Amount of overnight travel acceptable _____

What are your career objectives? _____

_____

_____

VI. OTHER:

Do you have the legal right to work for any employer in the United States?
Yes _____ No_____

Have you ever been convicted of a crime (other than a minor traffic violation)?
Yes _____ No_____

If so, explain _____

_____

_____

I certify that answers given in this Career History Form are true and complete to the best of my knowledge. I have provided requested information about all my full-time jobs. I authorize investigation into all statements I have made on this Form as may be necessary for reaching an employment decision.

In the event I am employed, I understand that any false or misleading information I knowingly provided in my Career History Form or interview(s) may result in discharge and/or legal action. I understand also that if employed, I am required to abide by all rules and regulations of the employer and any special agreements reached between the employer and me.

Signature _____

Date _____

APPENDIX C
In-Depth
Reference-Check
Guide

Reference Check Conducted by _____

Name of Applicant (A) _____

Home Phone _____

Office Phone _____

Individual Contacted _____ Title _____

Company Name _____

General Principles

- In-depth reference checks should be conducted by the hiring manager.
- Checks should be performed after the chronological, in-depth structured (CIDS) interview.
- Contact supervisors, particularly those the applicant (A) has reported to during the past five years. Peers, subordinates, and customers may also be contacted.
- Obtain written permission from (A) to conduct reference checks.
- During the CIDS interview ask the applicant the name, title, and location of each supervisor or other reference you wish to contact. Then ask (A) "Would you please contact (reference) at home, and ask if it would be OK to accept a telephone call at home sometime soon?"
- Contact the person at home, preferably on the weekend.
- Promise those contacted total confidentiality, and honor that promise.
- Create the tone in which you are a trusted colleague . . . a fellow professional who knows (A) very well, who just might hire (A) and who is apt to better manage (A) if (reference) will be kind enough to share some insights.
- Contact the current supervisor. If this is not acceptable to (A) until a written offer is formally accepted, make it clear that a job offer will be contingent upon "no surprises" in reference checks that will be performed at a mutually agreed-upon time. In the meantime, perhaps you could contact someone who has left (A)'s present employer.
- Take notes, and keep them six months.

Introductory Comments

"Hello, (name of person contacted), thank you very much for accepting my call. As (A) indicated, we are considering hiring her and I would very much appreciate your comments on her strengths, areas for improvement, and how I might best manage her. Anything you tell me will be held in the strictest confidence." (Assuming concurrence . . .) "Great, thank you very much. (A) and I have spent _____ hours together. I have thoroughly reviewed her career history and plans for the future and I was particularly interested in her experiences when she reported to you. If you don't mind, why don't we start with a very general question . . ."

Comprehensive Appraisal

"What would you consider (A)'s:

Strengths, Assets, Things You Like and Respect About (A)?"	Shortcomings, Weaker Points, and Areas for Improvement?"

Notes:

- It is OK to interrupt strengths to get clarification, but do not do so for shortcomings. Get the longest list of shortcomings possible and then go back for clarification. If you interrupt the negatives and get elaboration, the tone might seem too negative, thus closing off discussion of further negatives.
- If you are getting a "whitewash," inquire about negatives directly. For example: "Pat said that she missed the software project due date by three months and guesses that that hurt her overall performance rating. Could you elaborate?"

Responsibilities/Accountabilities

"Would you please clarify what (A)'s responsibilities and accountabilities were in that position?"

Overall Performance Rating

"On a scale of excellent, very good, good, fair, poor, or very poor, how would you rate (A)'s overall performance?"

"Why?" _____

Confirmation of Dates/Compensation

"Just to clean up a couple of details:
What were (A)'s starting _____ and final _____ employment dates?
What were (A)'s initial _____ and final _____ compensation levels?"

Description of Position Applied For

"Let me tell you more about the job (A) is applying for." (Describe the job.)

Good/Bad Fit

"Now, how do you think (A) might fit in that job?" (Probe for specifics.)

Good-Fit Indicators	Bad-Fit Indicators

Comprehensive Ratings

"Now that I've described the job that (A) is applying for and you've told me quite a bit about (A)'s strengths and shortcomings, would you please rate (A) on nine categories? An excellent, very good, good, fair, poor, or very poor scale would be fine."

	Rating	Comments*
1. **Thinking Skills** intelligence, judgment, decision making, creativity, strategic skills, pragmatism, risk taking, leading-edge perspective		
2. **Communications** one-one, in meetings, speeches, and written communications		
3. **Experience** education, "track record"		
4. **Initiative** perseverance, independence, excellence standards, adaptability		
5. **Stress Management** integrity, self-awareness, willingness to admit mistakes		
6. **Work Habits** time management, organization/ planning		
7. **People Skills** first impression made, listening, the ability to win the liking and respect of people, assertiveness, political savvy, willingness to take direction, negotiation and persuasion skills		
8. **Motivation** drive, ambition, customer focus, enthusiasm, tenacity, balance in life		

9. **Managerial Abilities** leadership, ability to hire the best people, ability to train and coach people, willingness to remove those who are hopelessly incompetent, goal setting, change management, empowerment, promoting diversity, monitoring performance, building team efforts		

*Note: Probe for specifics. Don't accept vague generalities ("[A] sometimes procrastinates") but ask for concrete examples, dates, consequences, etc.

Questions for Me as Hiring Manager

"What would be your best advice to me for how I could best manage (A)?"

_____

_____

_____

Final Comments

"Have you any final comments or suggestions about (A)?"

_____

_____

_____

Thanks!

"I would like to thank you very much for your insightful and useful comments and suggestions. Before we close, please let me know which of your comments I can share with others and which should be just between the two of us."

_____

_____

APPENDIX D
Interviewer
Feedback Form

Interviewer _____ Interviewee _____

Observer _____ Date _____

Number of Minutes Observed _____

Rating Scale: 6 = Excellent, 5 = Very Good, 4 = Good, 3 = Only Fair, 2 = Needs a Lot of Improvement, 1 = Good Grief, N/A = Not observed or would not have been appropriate or useful in interview.

INITIAL RAPPORT BUILDING   RATING

1. Greeting (warm, friendly, smile, handshake)   _____

   Comments: _____

2. Offered something to drink   _____

   Comments: _____

3. "Idle chit-chat" (couple of minutes—enough to get
   interviewee talking comfortably)   _____

   Comments: _____

4. Stated purposes and expected timing   _____

   Comments: _____

5. Mechanics (appropriate seating, all forms handy, notebook
   used, private location)   _____

   Comments: _____

THROUGHOUT THE INTERVIEW   RATING

1. All appropriate questions in Interview Guide asked
   without harmfully altering the wording.
   Open-ended (not yes/no) questions favored   _____

   Comments: _____

2. Interviewer "connecting" with interviewee on human level   _____

   Comments: _____

3. Eye contact (minimum of 20%, but no staring)   _____

   Comments: _____

4. Friendliness, warmth   _____

   Comments: _____

5. Enthusiasm   _____

   Comments: _____

6. Control maintained   _____

   Comments:_____

7. Humor   _____

   Comments:_____

8. Appears sincere   _____

   Comments: _____

9. Thorough note taking on content and context   _____

   Comments: _____

10. Unobtrusive note taking   _____

    Comments: _____

THROUGHOUT THE INTERVIEW   RATING

11. Follow-up questions asked, with appropriate wording and
    style, and specific meanings determined for vague responses _____

    Comments:_____

12. Absence of (unintended) biasing of question responses   _____

    Comments: _____

13. Interviewee talks: 90% (6), 80% (5), 70% (4), 60% (3),
    50% (2), less than 50% (1)   _____

    Comments: _____

14. Appropriate vocabulary level   _____

    Comments: _____

15. Voice clarity   _____

    Comments: _____

16. Vocal range (not monotone)   _____

    Comments: _____

17. Expressiveness (interested, friendly, half-smile; not blank,
    not excessive frowning)   _____

    Comments: _____

18. Interview pace (neither too fast nor too slow)   _____

    Comments: _____

19. Use of applicant's name (once every 5–10 minutes)   _____

    Comments: _____

20. Show of approval of openness or when interviewee is
    obviously proud of an unambiguous accomplishment   _____

    Comments: _____

THROUGHOUT THE INTERVIEW   RATING

21. Protection of interviewee's ego (use of "weasel words"
   rather than unintended bluntness)   _____

   Comments: _____

22. Control of shock, dismay, surprise, anger   _____

   Comments: _____

23. Breaks (every 45 minutes)   _____

   Comments: _____

24. Consistently shows respect for interviewee   _____

   Comments: _____

INTERVIEW PROBES   RATING

   Note: Not all probes are necessary.

1. Thorough summary (at least one every 10–15 minutes)   _____

   Comments: _____

2. Pregnant pause   _____

   Comments: _____

3. Affirmation of understanding ("I see," "uh huh," a nod, etc.)   _____

   Comments: _____

4. Echo (repeating all or part of a response)   _____

   Comments: _____

5. Active listening (reflecting interviewee's content
   and unstated feelings)   _____

   Comments: _____

INTERVIEW PROBES   RATING

6. Direct questions (usually used when softer approaches
   have failed)   _____

   Comments: _____

7. TORC Methods   _____

   Comments: _____

SUMMARY

Overall level of rapport achieved:

_____   6   Excellent

_____   5   Very Good

_____   4   Good

_____   3   Only Fair

_____   2   Needs a Lot of Improvement

_____   1   Good Grief

APPENDIX E
Sample Competencies —Management

The Management Competencies are generic, derived from job analyses and job descriptions from several companies. A Minimum Acceptable Rating will vary according to specific circumstances. For example, Strategic Skills (#6) might require a Minimum Acceptable Rating of 6 for president of a turnaround company, but only a 2 for store manager of a fast-food chain. When the Minimum Acceptable Rating is 1 or 2, the competency can be omitted.

SCALE: 6 = Excellent, 5 = Very Good, 4 = Good, 3 = Only Fair, 2 = Poor, 1 = Very Poor

INTELLECTUAL COMPETENCIES	Minimum Acceptable Rating	Your Rating
1. **Intelligence:** Demonstrates ability to acquire understanding and absorb new information rapidly. A "quick study." This competency reflects neither motivation to learn nor willingness to accept change; rather, it reflects the intellectual capacity that, when combined with motivation, results in learning. 6 = genius, 4 = average for college graduates.		

	Minimum Acceptable Rating	Your Rating

2. **Analysis Skills:** Identifies significant problems and opportunities. Analyzes problems in depth. Relates and compares data from different sources. Sorts the "wheat from the chaff," determining root causes and subtle relationships among data from various sources. Exhibits a probing mind. Achieves penetrating insights.

3. **Judgment/Decision Making:** Demonstrates consistent logic, rationality, and objectivity in decision making. Achieves balance between quick decisiveness and slower, more thorough approaches, i.e., is neither indecisive nor a hipshooter. Shows common sense. Anticipates consequences of decisions.

4. **Conceptual Ability:** Deals effectively not just with concrete, tangible issues, but with abstract, conceptual matters.

5. **Creativity:** Generates new (creative) approaches to problems or original modifications (innovations) to established approaches. Shows imagination.

6. **Strategic Skills:** Determines opportunities and threats through comprehensive analysis of current and future trends. Accurately assesses own organization's competitive strengths and vulnerabilities. Makes tactical and strategic adjustments, incorporating new data. Comprehends the "big picture." Reads latest books and articles on strategy.

7. **Pragmatism:** Generates sensible, realistic, practical solutions to problems.

8. **Risk Taking:** Shows evidence of having taken calculated risks, with generally favorable outcomes. Does not "bet the farm."

9. **Leading Edge:** Constantly benchmarks "best practices" and expects subordinates to do the same. Strives to be as leading edge as appropriate in light of costs.

Minimum
Acceptable   Your
Rating   Rating

10. **Education:** Meets educational requirements, formal and informal. Exhibits continuous learning through reading, seminars, networks, professional organizations. 6 = MBA from top ten school, or equivalent knowledge, 4 = undergraduate degree from respected, above-average school, or equivalent knowledge.

11. **Experience:** (Written specifically for job).

12. **"Track Record":** Has successful career history. Meets commitments. Repeated failures with "good excuses" probably not acceptable. Recent track record weighed heavily.

PERSONAL COMPETENCIES

13. **Integrity:** "Ironclad." Does not cut corners, ethically. Remains consistent in terms of what one says and does and in terms of behavior toward others. Earns trust of coworkers. Maintains confidences. Puts organization's interests above self. Does what is right, not what is politically expedient. "Fights fair." Intellectually honest; does not "play games" with facts to win a point.

14. **Initiative:** Seeks out and seizes opportunities, goes beyond the "call of duty," finds ways to surmount barriers. Resourceful. Action-oriented "doer," achieving results despite lack of resources. Restimulates languishing projects. Shows bias for action ("do it *now*").

15. **Organization/Planning:** Plans, organizes, schedules, and budgets in an efficient, productive manner. Focuses on key priorities. Effectively juggles multiple projects. Anticipates reasonable contingencies. Pays appropriate attention to detail. Manages personal time well.

16. **Excellence:** Sets high, "stretch" standards of performance for self and all coworkers. Demonstrates low tolerance for mediocrity. Requires high-quality results. Exhibits conscientiousness and high sense of responsibility.

	Minimum Acceptable Rating	Your Rating

17. **Independence:** While committed to team efforts, exhibits a willingness to take an independent stand. At times will "call the big plays." Is not swayed excessively by the last person talked with.

☐ ☐

18. **Stress Management:** Maintains stable performance and poise under heavy pressure from Corporate ("must make your numbers"), time (too little), unions (threat of strike), customers (dissatisfied).

☐ ☐

19. **Self-Awareness:** Recognizes not just one's own strengths but also weaker points and areas for improvement. Demonstrates the courage not to be defensive, rationalize mistakes, or blame others for one's own failures. Learns from mistakes. Builds feedback mechanisms to minimize "blind spots." Institutes 360° feedback for self and subordinates.

☐ ☐

20. **Adaptability:** Flexes to new pressures from competition, loss of talent, new priorities. Converts high self-objectivity into self-correction and personal improvement. Not rigid—intellectually, emotionally, interpersonally. Adjusts quickly to changing priorities. Copes effectively with complexity.

☐ ☐

INTERPERSONAL COMPETENCIES

21. **First Impression:** Professional in demeanor. Creates favorable first impressions through appropriate body language, eye contact, posture, voice qualities, bearing, attire.

☐ ☐

22. **Likability:** Puts people at ease. Warm, sensitive, and compassionate. Builds and maintains trusting relationships with all constituencies (associates, customers, community, professional organizations). Does not "turn people off." Not arrogant. Exhibits friendliness, sense of humor, genuineness, caring. Even when frustrated, treats people with respect.

☐ ☐

Minimum
Acceptable | Your
Rating | Rating

23. **Listening:** "Tunes in" accurately to the opinions, feelings, needs of people. Understands impact of one's behavior on others. Empathetic. Patient. Lets others speak; listens actively, "playing back" a person's point of view.

24. **Customer Focus:** Regularly monitors customer satisfaction. Meets internal and external customer needs in ways that provide satisfaction and excellent results for the customer. Establishes "partner" relationships with customers. Regarded as visible and accessible by customers.

25. **Team Player:** Reaches out to peers to tear down walls. Overcomes "we–they" relationships. Approachable. Earns a reputation for leading peers toward support of what is best for total company. Cooperates with supervisors (but not "yes person") and establishes collaborative relationships with peers (without being a "pushover").

26. **Assertiveness:** Takes forceful stands on issues, without being excessively abrasive. 6 = optimally assertive, 1 = either insufficiently or excessively assertive.

27. **Communications—Oral:** Communicates effectively one to one, in small groups and in public-speaking contexts. Demonstrates fluency, "quickness on one's feet," clarify organization of thought processes, and command of the language. Easily articulates vision and standards. Keeps people informed.

28. **Communications—Written:** Writes clear, precise, well-organized e-mails, memos, letters and proposals while using appropriate vocabulary, grammar, and word usage, and creating the appropriate "flavor."

29. **Political Savvy:** Shows awareness of political factors and "hidden agendas" and behaves shrewdly without being a self-seeking "backstabber." Recognizes where to go to get things done and builds informal network to "wire" information sources and influence.

	Minimum Acceptable Rating	Your Rating

30. **Negotiation:** History of winning as an essential ingredient in win/win negotiations. Demonstrates effectiveness in salvaging tense negotiations (with customers, union, etc.).

31. **Persuasion:** Exhibits persuasiveness in change efforts, selling a "vision." "Charisma" desirable, though soft sell and quiet credibility are acceptable alternatives.

MANAGEMENT COMPETENCIES

32. **Selecting A Players:** Topgrades through effectively recruiting and selecting not less than 90% "A players" (not more than 10% mis-hires).

33. **Coaching/Training:** Actively and successfully trains and coaches people for current assignments, and develops them for promotion into positions in which they succeed. Provides challenging assignments. A people builder.

34. **Goal Setting:** Sets clear, fair, "stretch" goals for self and others, encouraging individual initiative (preference for bottom up as opposed to top down).

35. **Empowerment:** Pushes decision making down to lowest (optimal) level; provides authority and resources. Is "hands on" when appropriate.

36. **Performance Management:** Fosters high levels of accountability through fair, hard-hitting performance-management system. Measures performance thoroughly. Reinforces integrity in the system by personally monitoring performance of subordinates (without "oversupervising"), and rating/ranking people honestly (no "gifts," no taking the easy way out). Ties in reward systems (pay, promotion, removal). Free with deserved praise and recognition. Constructive in criticism. Provides frequent feedback.

37. **Removing C Players:** History of redeploying chronic C players through transfer, demotion, termination or quietly helping person understand it is best to leave.

Minimum
Acceptable   Your
Rating   Rating

38. **Team Builder:** Achieves cohesive, effective (positive, mutually supportive) "team spirit" with subordinates. Team "climate" characterized by open, honest relationships in which differences are constructively resolved rather than ignored, suppressed, or denied. Treats subordinates fairly. Shares credit.

39. **Diversity:** Achieves diverse work force at all levels, for global effectiveness and legal compliance. Decries tokenism; topgrades with diversity. Actively breaks down barriers to diversity; visibly fights discrimination.

40. **Running Meetings:** Demonstrates ability to organize and run effective meetings.

ADDITIONAL LEADERSHIP COMPETENCIES

41. **Vision:** Provides clear, credible vision for the future (what the company will be like internally and in the marketplace) when strategy successfully implemented.

42. **Change Leadership:** Actively intervenes to create and energize positive change. Can cite specific examples of moving organizations through major change. Leads by example.

43. **Inspiring "Followership":** Through whatever combination of competencies, inspires people to follow the lead. Minimizes intimidation and threat. Takes charge. Motivates by pushing appropriate "hot buttons" for individuals.

44. **Conflict Management:** Exhibits understanding of natural sources of conflict and acts to prevent or soften them. When conflicts emerge, effectively works them through to optimum outcome. Does not suppress, ignore, deny conflict.

	Minimum Acceptable Rating	Your Rating
MOTIVATIONAL COMPETENCIES		

45. **Energy:** Exhibits energy, strong desire to achieve, appropriately high dedication level. Although hours per se are less important than results, 60 hours or more per week are probably necessary for results expected. ☐ ☐

46. **Enthusiasm:** Exhibits dynamism, charisma, excitement, positive "can-do" attitude. ☐ ☐

47. **Ambition:** Desires to grow in responsibility and authority. Acknowledging slow growth in company or self not acceptable. ☐ ☐

48. **Compatibility of Needs:** Demonstrates needs (for money, recognition, affiliation, achievement, prestige, promotion, power, location, amount and type of travel, or whatever) consistent with the opportunities available in the foreseeable future. ☐ ☐

49. **Balance in Life:** Achieves sufficient balance among work, wellness, relationships, community involvement, professional associations, friendships, hobbies, and interests. "Sufficient" may be defined variously, reflecting the necessity of meeting current work challenges, the possibility of "burnout," or the consequences of sacrificing so much currently that later in life there are severe regrets. ☐ ☐

50. **Tenacity:** Demonstrates consistent reward of passionately striving to achieve results. Conveys strong need to win. Reputation for not giving up. ☐ ☐

CAREER DERAILERS

- *Selecting A Players* and *Removing C Players*—"mis-hires too many," "has team of B and C players," "afraid to hire someone better than he is," "just won't topgrade"

- *Integrity*—"lies," "can't be trusted to keep promises," "breaks confidences," "gossips," "pushes legal boundaries too far"

- *Likability*—"arrogant," "condescending," "egotistical," "doesn't treat people with respect," "makes a mockery of our people values," "know-it-all," "sarcastic," "demeaning," "acts superior"

- *Ambition*—"too ambitious," "always trying to get the promotion rather than serve the company"
- *Political Savvy*—"a dirty politician," "backstabber"
- *Adaptability*—"over her head," "can't adjust to our reorganization," "job is too complex for her"
- *Team Builder*—"can't empower anyone," "control freak," "old-fashioned autocrat"
- *Team Player*—"builds silos," "thinks his department is the only one," "won't coordinate across departments, causing major production waste"
- *Track Record*—"missed his numbers again," "sandbagger," "more excuses than reasons"
- *Intelligence*—"lacks the brainpower to adapt," "slow learner," "just doesn't get it"
- *Initiative*—"too passive," "doesn't take advantage of opportunities," "always trying to delegate upward"

APPENDIX F
Sample Competencies —Wm. M. Mercer

William M. Mercer, Incorporated, is one of the nation's leading Human Resources consulting firms. Headquartered in New York, and with offices in 39 other U.S. cities, the firm is the U.S. operating company of William M. Mercer Companies, LLC, a worldwide consulting organization serving clients from 105 offices in 27 countries.

William M. Mercer, Incorporated, has a 175-page internal document, spelling out behavioral competencies for various levels (pay grades) and specific functions. This document is used for internal career development, although the competencies are also used for selection. From it I have included Mercer's two-page "Overview" and then two pages of competencies for their level 5 position. It's refreshing to see that a consultancy not only helps its clients create leading-edge Human Resources practices, but they use them internally.

An Overview of Career Development at Mercer

OUR CLIENTS' NEEDS PROVIDE THE BLUEPRINT FOR OUR OWN human resources needs. To effectively address both, Mercer is adopting an integrated approach to our human resources activities. By identifying the values and competencies all employees should possess and demonstrate and by defining the knowledge and skills required by each practice or specialty area, we provide the foundation for:

- staffing plans
- recruitment and selection
- **career development**
- performance management
- compensation
- training
- succession planning.

Since employees have repeatedly asked for help in career development, we are addressing this element first but expect to introduce the remaining modules of this integrated system soon.

This *Sourcebook* is a tool to help you develop at Mercer. It outlines the career development process and its components and contains the Knowledge and Skills required in your practice or specialty area. It also includes comprehensive information about professional development.

Note: Information in this *Sourcebook* will be updated from time to time as our career development system evolves and matures, and as priorities and other directives change.

Mercer believes that helping you develop your career is critical to your success and to the overall success of the company. Every employee, regardless of role or position, must always be in a "growth and development" mode if Mercer is to flourish and prosper.

Your questions of "Where can I go at Mercer?" and "What must I do to get there?" are answered through the career development process. Based on assessments of three sets of criteria — *Mercer Core Values, Competencies* and practice specific or specialty area *Knowledge and Skills* — you can identify your status in one of seven levels. Through scheduled, formal discussions, you and your supervisor (referred to as your Career Advisor) will review your status annually and formulate plans for development consistent with your goals and Mercer's needs.

Mercer believes that your career concerns should be addressed and is committed to providing an environment in which issues can be discussed regularly. However, Mercer views career development as a *shared* responsibility among employees, Career Advisors, and the company itself.

Your Responsibility

You must take charge of your own career development. You must assume responsibility for continuing to grow and develop during your career with Mercer. This means that you must seek opportunities to "stretch" and grow in ways that fulfill personal, company and role-specific success criteria. And you should speak to your Career Advisor when you believe those opportunities are not being provided to you.

Career Advisor's Responsibility

A key component of your supervisor's job is to be your Career Advisor. In this role, supervisors (Career Advisors) will have very specific responsibilities. They will serve as counselors and facilitators in the career development process. They will help you to understand Mercer's goals, assess your individual strengths and development needs and guide you to the right resources to help foster continuous growth and development. Your Career Advisor will meet with you during the annual career development review cycle and will be available during the year to address issues and questions as they arise.

The Career Advisor role in career development is an *ongoing* one. It doesn't end when the career discussion is over or when development needs have been identified. Through the most important elements in career development — on-the-job training and ongoing feedback (including both praise and constructive criticism) — your Career Advisor must consistently challenge you and provide opportunities for you to grow and develop.

Mercer's Responsibility

Mercer provides the training, tools and human resources systems necessary to encourage and support your ongoing development. As a company committed to the continuous growth of our people, we put a high priority on helping you (and your Career Advisor) create an action plan for career development and on providing the resources to help you accomplish it.

Your Office Head is responsible for the implementation of the career development process in your office. He or she will be assisted by the local Human Resources Representative and by a Career Development Coordinator.

Level 5 Profile

Client/Customer Value Creation

Demonstrates concern for meeting internal and external customers' needs in a manner that provides satisfaction and excellent results for the customer.

- Selectively matches products/services in own specialty to client/customer key needs.
- Surfaces potential client/customer satisfaction concerns and takes action to ensure resolution.

Planning and Organizing

Establishes a systematic course of action for self and/or others to assure accomplishment of a specific objective, determining priorities and allocating time and resources effectively.

- Systematically gathers and analyzes pertinent information to plan a course of action.
- Maintains focus on critical path activities and modifies planned actions as needed.
- Optimizes use of time and resources to achieve desired results.

Process Management

Initiates, manages or participates in the change process and energizes it on an ongoing basis, taking steps to remove barriers or accelerate its pace.

- Selects appropriate tools and data to diagnose problems and develop solutions.
- Develops and applies objective criteria for measuring important processes.

Communication and Influence

Effectively transfers thoughts and expresses ideas using speech, listening skills and writing skills to influence others or gain their support.

- Develops written and oral communications that clearly explain technical concepts, using easy-to-understand language that is free of jargon.

People Development

Strives to improve the skills of self and others by identifying areas of performance strengths and development opportunities, by seeking or providing coaching, mentoring or development opportunities and by providing clear, behaviorally specific feedback to team members and subordinates.

- Creates or seeks opportunities to develop new skills or broaden knowledge.
- Provides active mentorship and serves as a training resource to junior employees.
- Supports a team environment of continuous feedback and idea sharing.

Level 5 Profile

Teamwork
Willingly cooperates and works collaboratively toward solutions that generally benefit all involved parties to accomplish overall organizational objectives.

- Participates in team planning and implementation activities in a reliable and enthusiastic manner.
- Openly shares information and own expertise with others to enable them to accomplish group goals.

Strategic Business Perspective
Has a broadly based understanding of key business fundamentals, understands the drivers of the financial health and viability of the organization, and takes responsibility for maintaining its ongoing fiscal soundness.

- Makes work contributions that enhances office's or practice's ability to contribute to overall Mercer strategies.
- Matches best practices and resources in a specialty area with client/customer identified business needs.

Business Development
Uses appropriate interpersonal styles and methods to influence clients, enhancing Mercer's financial success.

- Provides suggestions to team for improving/enhancing business development activities.

Subject Matter Expertise
Acquires and uses professional/technical knowledge, skills, experience and judgment to accomplish a result, serve one's customers effectively and contribute to Mercer's organizational intellectual capital.

- Analyzes client/customer needs or project outline and recommends suitable approaches or options to consider. Implements result.

Corporate Partnership
Identifies oneself as a "citizen" of the larger Mercer organization and works to enhance its image and overall market presence.

- Represents Mercer/unit positively in internal and external situations.

Index

389